the capital budgeting decision

Harold Bierman, Jr.

The Nicholas H. Noyes Professor of
Business Administration,
Graduate School of Business and
Public Administration,
Cornell University

Seymour Smidt

Professor of Managerial Economics,
Graduate School of Business and
Public Administration,
Cornell University

economic analysis and financing

the capital budgeting decision

fourth edition

of investment projects

macmillan publishing co., inc.

New York

collier macmillan publishers

London

Macmillan Publishing Co., Inc.
866 Third Avenue, New York, New York 10022

Collier-Macmillan Canada, Ltd.

Library of Congress Cataloging in Publication Data

Bierman, Harold.
    The capital budgeting decision.

    Bibliography: p.
    1. Capital investments. 2. Capital budget.
I. Smidt, Seymour, joint author. II. Title.
HD52.B5   1975   658.1'527   74–3797
ISBN 0–02–309690–X

Printing: 2345678   Year: 567890

preface to the fourth edition

This edition follows the direction set by the two last revisions. When the first edition was published in 1960, we were convinced that the present-value method was superior to other methods of making investment decisions. We still believe this. In the important area of uncertainty, however, our attitudes have undergone some changes that were first incorporated in the second edition. The greatest change from the first edition will be found in the choice of the rate of discount and general method of incorporating uncertainty in the investment decision process.

We continue to advocate the present-value method, using a default-free discount rate to compute the present value. A dollar risk adjustment is added or subtracted from the present value of the expected cash flows. Thus investments with yields less than the cost of capital may be considered to be acceptable. The procedure is more desirable than evaluating investments on the basis of the cost of capital implicitly including a risk discount and a measure of time-value preference.

This edition differs from the third edition because at the time that book was written we did not yet know how to quantify the adjustment for risk. Now we think there are meaningful things that can be said. Also, although the third edition advocated the use of a default-free rate of interest to take the time value of money into consideration, it did not make entirely clear that the cost of capital could not be used for that purpose. The cost of capital is a useful concept in handling the capital mix question, but it is not useful in evaluating investment alternatives.

The book is divided into four parts, enabling us to establish those conditions in which the suggested decision rules are relatively effective and those in which their effectiveness is limited. In Part I we treat decisions under certainty in a perfect capital market. Although these assumptions are not descriptive of the world, they do enable us to suggest solutions for some types of problems and to introduce the basic concepts of time discounting. In Part II we introduce imperfect capital markets and uncertainty, under which conditions the suggested solutions of Part I must be adjusted. We find under uncertainty that it is necessary to consider many attributes of the investment rather than only one. The more nearly unique the investment, the less reliable are the conventional guides for action that use the cost of capital as a hurdle rate. Part III is a collection of miscellaneous topics that facilitate the application of capital budgeting techniques. Part IV is an extension of Part II, and is somewhat more mathematical than the first three sections.

The suggested approaches to making investment decisions have important implications to corporation managers and to the economy, for investments previously rejected may now become eligible for consideration.

We wish to thank the many persons in government, academic, and business areas, as well as our colleagues Jerry Hass, Vithala Rao, and John McClain, who have raised questions and made suggestions that have advanced our thinking. We thank Don Panton of the University of Kansas for calling our attention to errors in the third edition, so that they could be corrected in the fourth. We especially thank Marge Snedden and the typists of the typing pool for their ever cheerful and intelligent assistance.

HAROLD BIERMAN, JR.

SEYMOUR SMIDT

Ithaca, New York

preface to the first edition

Businessmen and economists have been concerned with the problem of how financial resources available to a firm should be allocated to the many possible investment projects. Should a new plant be built? Equipment replaced? Bonds refunded? A new product introduced? These are all to some extent capital budgeting decisions to which there are theoretically sound solutions. The purpose of this book is to express the solution of the economist in the language of the business manager.

Decades ago, economists such as Böhm-Bawerk, Wicksell, and Irving Fisher laid the theoretical foundation for a sound economic approach to capital budgeting. In recent years the technical literature has contained articles (such as those by Dean, Solomon, Lorie, Savage, and Hirshleifer) that have significantly increased our understanding of what is required for sound capital budgeting decisions. However, these works have not been directed toward business managers and, until recently, the work of these men has had no perceptible influence on the way businessmen actually made capital investment decisions. Businessmen have tended to make capital budgeting decisions using their intuition, rules of thumb, or investment criteria with faulty theoretical foundations and thus have been likely to give incorrect answers in a large percentage of the decisions.

The purpose of this book is to present for an audience that may be completely unfamiliar with the technical literature on economic theory or capital budgeting a clear conception of how to evaluate investment proposals.

The authors are convinced that the "present-value" method is superior to other methods of evaluating the economic worth of investments that have been discussed in the business literature. They recognize that considerations other than that of economic worth are also important in making investment decisions. The early pages of the book show that "cash payback" and "return on investment" may give incorrect results. The "yield" or "investor's method" is shown to be inferior to the present-value method, especially where there are several alternative investments available. The explanation of the reasons for the inferiority of yield to present value is particularly timely, since popular business magazines have carried many articles praising the yield method without mentioning its important drawbacks. In Chapter 4, a positive explanation of the meaning of present value is presented.

The first four chapters present an over-all picture of the method of analysis advocated in this book that would be a suitable introduction for management at any level who need to be informed about the ideas involved in evaluating capital investments, but who are not directly involved in preparing investment evaluations. The remainder of the book elaborates on the basic description of the first four chapters and gives material that will assist a person in actually preparing the analysis of investments.

H. B.

S. S.

Ithaca, N. Y.

contents

part I

part II

part III

part IV

variance of portfolio returns. Sharpe's single index model.
Conclusions.
Appendix 1: The expected return of a portfolio. Appendix 2:
covariance between investment rates of return.

part I

Sirs:
The Indian who sold Manhattan for $24.00 was
a sharp salesman. If he had put his $24 away
at 6% compounded semiannually, it would
now be $9.5 billion and could buy most of the
now-improved land back.

S. Branch Walker.
Stamford, Conn.,
Life, Aug. 31, 1959

In the first seven chapters of this book we present a theoretically correct and easily applied approach to decisions involving benefits and outlays through time, that is, capital budgeting decisions. Essentially, the procedure consists of a choice of a rate of discount representing the time value of money, and the application of this rate of discount to future cash flows to compute their net present values. The sum of all the present values associated with an investment (including immediate outlays) is the net present value of the investment.

In the first seven chapters it is assumed that the cash flows associated with an investment are known with certainty, that there are markets to borrow or lend funds at the rate of interest used in the time discounting, and that there are no constraints preventing the firm from using these markets. The objective of the discounting process is to take the time value of money into consideration, but it includes no adjustment for risk.

chapter 1

the problem of
capital budgeting

The controller points to the ancient, gray, six-story structure and says with pride, "This is one reason we can keep our costs down. Our plant is fully depreciated, so we don't have the large depreciation charges our competitors have."

Another company in the same industry sells a relatively new plant because it is not large enough for a three-shift operation. Rather than operate what is considered to be an inefficient production line (the production line had been completely overhauled within the last twelve months), a new plant is being constructed in another state.

The investment philosophies of the two companies making these decisions were vastly different. One was reluctant to invest money in plant and equipment. The other wanted to operate only the latest in plant and equipment. Which of the two companies was right? Maybe each company was following a policy that was correct for it, or perhaps they were both making faulty decisions. We cannot decide here because the necessary facts are not available to us. But the facts should be available to the responsible executives in both these companies, and these facts should be arranged in a useful manner and then interpreted correctly.

Investment decisions may be tactical or strategic. A tactical investment decision generally involves a relatively small amount of funds and does not constitute a major departure from what the firm has been doing in the past. The consideration of a new machine tool by Ford Motor Company

3

is a tactical decision, as is a buy or lease decision made by Mobil Oil Company.

Strategic investment decisions involve large sums of money and may also result in a major departure from what the company has been doing in the past. Acceptance of a strategic investment will involve a significant change in the company's expected profits and in the risks to which these profits will be subject. These changes are likely to lead stockholders and creditors to revise their evaluation of the company. If a private corporation undertook the development of a supersonic commercial transport (costing over $4 billion). this would be a strategic decision. If the company failed in its attempt to develop the commercial plane, the very existence of the company would be jeopardized.

The future success of a business depends on the investment decisions made today. That businessmen are generally aware of this is indicated by the requirement that important investment decisions must be approved by the chief operating executive or the board of directors. In spite of this fact, the procedures used to help management make investment decisions are often inadequate and misleading. Few manufacturing concerns would sign a long-term contract for supplies of an important raw material without carefully investigating the various sources of supply and considering the relative advantages of each in terms of price, service, and quality. Yet occasionally management groups approve investments without a careful consideration of available alternatives. Even when there is an investigation of alternatives, the information obtained sometimes does not lead to effective decisions, because managements may not organize the information in a way that will help them make better decisions.

Business organizations are continually faced with the problem of deciding whether the commitments of resources—time or money—are worthwhile in terms of the expected benefits. If the benefits are likely to accrue reasonably soon after the expenditure is made, and if both the expenditure and the benefits can be measured in dollars, the solution to such a problem is relatively simple. If the expected benefits are likely to accrue over several years, the solution is more complex.

We shall use the term *investment* to refer to commitments of resources made in the hope of realizing benefits that are expected to occur over a reasonably long period of time in the future. Capital budgeting is a many-sided activity that includes searching for new and more profitable investment proposals, investigating engineering and marketing considerations to predict the consequences of accepting the investment, and making economic analyses to determine the profit potential of each investment proposal. The primary purpose of this book is to help business management analyze the profit potential of investments in plant and equipment, marketing programs, research projects, and the like.

investments as cash flows

To focus attention on the problems of economic analysis, we begin by assuming that we have investment proposals worthy of preliminary consideration and that for each investment proposal the necessary engineering and marketing research has been completed. We assume that these studies will enable us to measure the dollar value of the resources expended and the benefits received from the investment during each future interval of time. In the early chapters of this book we assume that these dollar values can be estimated in advance with certainty. Later we relax this assumption and consider the additional complications that arise when decision makers are uncertain about the amounts and timing of the cash flows that will result from an investment.

By assuming that the consequences of an investment can be described in terms of the certain (or uncertain) cash flows it will generate in each interval of time, we exclude many investments. Even business organizations, which carry further than most other organizations the attempt to measure all costs and benefits in dollar terms, find that the costs or benefits of many investments cannot be completely described in terms of dollars. Consider an advertising program designed to build up the prestige associated with the name of a corporation. This is an investment, because the expenditures are made in the hope of realizing benefits that will continue long after the advertising expenditures have been made. But it is difficult to estimate in dollar terms the exact value of the benefits that will accrue from the advertising program.

In nonprofit organizations, whether private or public, investments whose costs and benefits cannot be measured reasonably well in dollar terms are made even more frequently than in business. Nevertheless, investment proposals for which both the cost and benefits can be measured in dollar terms do arise in all these organizations, and the quantity of resources involved in such investments is considerable. In designing a building, for example, the architect or engineer is frequently faced with alternative means of accomplishing the same objective. The design of the heating or lighting systems are but two examples. Frequently one alternative will have a high initial cost but low maintenance or operating expenses, whereas another alternative will have low initial costs but high operating or maintenance expenses. A choice between the two alternatives is in essence an investment decision.

Thus, although not all the investment decisions in an organization can be described in terms of the dollar value of the expenditures or benefits, important decisions that can be described in these terms seem to occur in all organizations in modern society. As we increase our ability to forecast the consequences of our decisions, the number of investments that can be described reasonably well in dollar terms will also increase.

In this book we shall be mainly concerned with the economic analysis of investments from the point of view of a profit-seeking enterprise. Nevertheless, many of the methods of analysis described apply to investment decisions arising in private nonprofit organizations or in local or national governments, if the investment can be described in terms of cash flows. In these latter organizations, the appropriate definition of the cash flow may be different. For example in considering whether an investment was worthwhile, a private business would not try to take into account the additional profits that might be earned by other businesses as a result of its investment. A government would normally try to consider such profits. We shall consider these questions briefly in Chapter 18. Also, the costs and methods of finance available to business enterprises are often significantly different from those available to governments or private nonprofit institutions. A government cannot sell common stock; a business firm cannot levy taxes to finance the investments it would like to undertake. In other respects the methods of analysis that apply in business organizations are usually applicable in governments as well.

Frequently, an investment proposal will involve both benefits and expenditures during one or more time periods. When this occurs it will be convenient to combine the dollar estimates of the benefits and expenditures for each period of time. If, during a specific period of time, the benefits exceed the expenditures, we may speak of the net benefits or cash proceeds; if the expenditures exceed the benefits, we may refer to the net expenditures or cash outlays. We shall adopt the convention of referring to cash proceeds or outlays during a given period of time by using positive or negative dollar amounts, respectively. We shall refer to the entire series of net proceeds and net outlays associated with an investment as the cash flow of the investment.

If some of the proceeds are subject to taxation, we shall measure the proceeds after taxes. A business corporation is subject to taxes on its income, and this income in turn depends on the amount of depreciation charges that can be used to offset revenues in computing taxable income. The amount of cash proceeds resulting from an investment in any future year will depend upon the regulations or laws established by the tax authority. These laws or regulations will determine the kinds of expenditures that can be charged immediately to expense and those that must be capitalized and written off in subsequent years by depreciating the asset. Nonprofit organizations and governments are not subject to income taxes, and therefore the proceeds they receive from an investment do not depend upon their depreciation accounting method.

It should be stressed that the definition of net benefits or cash proceeds given above is *not* identical with the income concept used in corporate accounting. The major difference is that, in estimating cash proceeds, depreciation charges and other amortization charges of fixed assets are not subtracted from gross revenues because no cash expenditures are required.[1]

We shall define *conventional* investments as those having one or more periods of outlays followed by one or more periods of cash proceeds. Borrowing money is a kind of "negative investment" in which one or more periods of cash proceeds are followed by one or more periods in which there are cash outlays. *Loan-type* investments have positive cash flows followed by periods of cash outlays. There are also *nonconventional* investments that have one or more periods of outlays (proceeds) interspersed with periods of proceeds (outlays).

The possibilities may be illustrated as follows:

	Sign of Cash Flow for Period:			
	0	1	2	3
Conventional investment	−	+	+	+
Loan type of flows	+	−	−	−
Nonconventional investment	−	+	+	−
Nonconventional investment	+	−	−	+

These examples do not exhaust the possibilities. For example, a conventional investment may have many periods of outlays.

Any decisions involving measurable cash flows over one or more periods may be implemented by using the capital budgeting procedures to be developed in this book.

estimate of cash proceeds

It is frequently stated that refinements in capital budgeting techniques are a waste of effort because the basic information being used is so unreliable. It is claimed that the estimates of cash proceeds are only guesses, and that to use anything except the simplest capital budgeting procedures is as futile as using racing forms to pick winners at the track or complicated formulas to determine which way the stock market is going to move next.

It is true that in many situations reliable estimates of cash proceeds are difficult to make. Fortunately, there are a large number of investment

---

[1] The cash outlays associated with the investment are subtracted and these substitute for the depreciation expenses. Corporate accounting computes the income of each year and thus must allocate the cost of the investment over its life. For decision purposes we are interested in the overall effect of the investment on income and do not have to measure its effect on the income of any one year.

decisions in which cash proceeds can be predicted with a fair degree of certainty.

But even with an accurate, reliable estimate of cash proceeds, the wrong decision is frequently made because crude rules of thumb are used in evaluating this information.

When it is not possible to make a single estimate of cash proceeds that is certain to occur, we do not believe it necessarily follows that crude methods of analysis are justified. If it is difficult to predict the outcome of an investment with certainty, and if the investment is large, the use of a more careful and comprehensive analysis is justified, even if this means that the analysis will be more complicated and costly. With small tactical investments, somewhat less involved methods might be used because a more complex analysis would not be necessary, but again there is no need to use inferior methods that decrease the likelihood of making correct investment decisions.

applications of capital budgeting techniques

It is interesting to note that many decisions may be thought of as investments and hence incorporated into the capital budgeting process. We shall illustrate in this section some of the situations of this nature.

Replacement Decision

A company is currently using three pieces of equipment that cost $10,000 each and are 70 per cent depreciated. They can be replaced with one unit of equipment that would cost $20,000. It is expected that at normal activity the new machine would save $40,000 a year in labor, maintenance, and so on, for a period of five years. Should the machines be replaced?

Size of Plant

A company must choose between a small plant that would cost $1 million and a large plant which would cost $1.5 million. The earnings of both plants are computed, and it is found that the small plant would yield a return of 20 per cent and the large plant a return of 17 per cent. Which plant should be chosen?

Lease or Buy

A company can either buy data-processing equipment or rent it. The cost of the equipment is $300,000 and the rental fee is $10,000 per month. It is estimated that improvements will make this equipment obsolete within five years. Should the company lease or buy?

Refunding of Debt

A company currently has $10 million debt outstanding, bearing a coupon rate of 10 per cent. The debt was issued at a discount, which is still unamortized to the extent of $500,000. The company can currently issue bonds to yield 9 per cent. The costs of issuing the new bonds would be $200,000, and there would be a call premium on the old bonds of $300,000. The old bonds have twenty years remaining until they become due. Should the bonds be refunded?

Although none of the preceding examples contains all the facts that would be necessary for a decision, they illustrate well the kind of problem that will be considered. The analytical methods that will be suggested in this book are applicable to all these examples.

measures of investment worth

In the next chapter we shall introduce some methods of evaluating the worth of investments that are in common use or have been frequently recommended as desirable. If we take a group of investment proposals and rank them by each of these methods, we shall find that each method will frequently give a different ranking to the same set of investment proposals. In fact, it can be said that the different measures will only accidentally give identical rankings to a set of investment proposals. Although we shall not be able to rank individual investments in a useful manner, we shall normally be able to make decisions without such rankings.

Various executives faced with the same set of investment possibilities, but using different measures of investment worth, will tend to make dissimilar investment decisions. Clearly, all the measures that will be described here cannot be equally valid. We shall attempt to determine which of the measures have some legitimate reason for use and to isolate the circumstances under which they will tend to give satisfactory results.

In current business practice, each of the methods selected has its advocates, and frequently one is used in combination with another. Because investment proposals are rarely accepted by top management solely on the basis of such analyses, it may be argued that the choice of method is of little significance because the investment decision is likely to be influenced by many different factors. Insofar as the executives making the final decision are aware of the risks involved and are intimately familiar with the proposals, know the possible technical or operating problems that may be encountered, and realize the potential erosion of earnings resulting from competitive action or changing technology, this criticism may very well be valid. However, in most large organizations it is impossible for the top management officials, who must finally approve or disapprove investment proposals, to be intimately familiar with the details of each and every proposal presented to them. To the extent that this intimate knowledge is impossible or impractical, these executives must rely upon the evaluation of the recommendations from their subordinates. To make reasonable choices in weighing alternative investments, it is increasingly necessary that various proposals be evaluated as nearly as possible on some uniform, comparable basis. In such circumstances, although the measure of economic worth of an investment should never be the sole factor considered in making a final decision, it may play an increasingly important part in the majority of the investments under consideration by the firm.

Accordingly, that various measures give different rankings and indicate different accept or reject decisions to identical sets of investment proposals is a matter of concern. Substantial improvements in efficiency and income may result if a more adequate measure can be discovered and widely adopted. Any such progress requires first a more general agreement about the desirable characteristics to be possessed by a good index of the economic worth of an investment. We therefore turn to consider the various criteria that can be used in evaluating the adequacy of a measure of the economic worth of an investment proposal.

criteria for evaluating measures of investment worth

As anyone who has ever attempted the task will recognize, it is difficult to develop an explicit statement of the goals of an organization. The task becomes even harder if, as in the present instance, the purpose of the statement of goals is to provide a test of the extent to which activities and programs are appropriate for the organization. In the case of business organizations the measures of investment worth that have been proposed and that are developed in this book concentrate on a form of the profit-maximization goal, but attempt to include equally important conditions, such as the risks associated with the investments undertaken and the future structure of assets and liabilities that will be determined in part by the investment decisions currently being made.

To be a reasonable criterion, profit maximization has to consider the size of the investment employed and the alternative uses of the funds invested (including the possibility of returning these funds to the stockholders). One way of stating the objective of the investment decision procedure is to describe it as tending to maximize the current market value of the stockholders' holdings in the firm. Although not an exact criterion (for example, it does not help decide between a decision that elevates the value of a stock now but depresses it later and a decision that depresses the stock now and elevates it later), maximization of the value of the stockholders' holdings is a reasonable description of what we would like our measure of investment worth to accomplish.

It is recognized that a complete statement of the organizational goals of a business enterprise would embrace a much wider range of considerations, including such things as the prestige, income, security, freedom, and power of the management group, and the contribution of the corporation to the overall social environment in which it exists and to the welfare of the labor force it employs. Insofar as the attainment of profits, without unnecessary risks or an unduly awkward financial structure, does not conflict with the other goals mentioned, the assumption that the pecuniary objectives are the proximate goals of a business organization is tenable.

The measure of investment worth that best describes the profit potential of a proposed investment is the net present value of the cash flows associated with the proposed investment. It is more consistent with furthering the stockholders' interests than straight maximization of income, because the accounting measures of income do not take into consideration alternative uses of the funds that would be tied up in investments. However, the present-value method does not necessarily provide a useful measure of the additional risks to which the owners of a business will be exposed as a result of accepting an investment. Methods of incorporating such risks into the analysis are discussed in Parts II, III, and IV.

budget process and planning

Frequently we think of the budget of a firm as being part of the cost-control apparatus and forget that it is an important tool for planning. The capital budget for the coming period will affect the cash budget and will be affected in turn by sales forecasts; thus the capital budget must be incorporated into the budgetary process.

The timing of cash flows resulting from capital expenditures is extremely important to the corporate officer attempting to plan the cash needs of the firm. Information is needed on the specific days the bills will have to be paid and when cash will begin to be generated by the investment. Of course, it will hardly ever be possible to predict these events with certainty, but it should be possible to make reasonable estimates that will be useful.

Some firms will prepare a five-year capital budget. If an attempt is being made to project other financial data over one or more years, the composition of the capital budget will affect the nature of the other planning budgets. For example, if an automobile company is planning to enter the steel industry, this would be disclosed in the capital budget and would certainly affect all other budgets.

The capital budget should be an integral part of the budget and planning process. The officer in charge of the capital budget must be in effective communication with the budget officer of the firm (if the positions are separate), because the decisions they make will result in a considerable amount of interaction.

time value of money

This book is founded on the concept of the "time value of money" and the relevance of the timing of cash flows to making investment decisions. We shall find that we want to compute the present equivalent of future sums of money as a basic part of our investment analysis. To accomplish this transformation of future sums into present equivalents, we shall make use of present-value tables. The following example illustrates the basic computations for discounting cash flows, that is, adjusting future cash flows for the time value of money.

Assume that there is an investment opportunity with the following cash flows:

	Period		
	0	1	2
Cash flow	− $12,337	$10,000	$5,000

We want first to compute the present value of this investment using .05 as the discount rate. Appendix Table A[2] gives the present value of $1 due n periods from now. The present value of

$1 due 0 periods from now discounted at any interest rate is 1.000.
$1 due 1 period from now discounted at .05 is .9524.
$1 due 2 periods from now discounted at .05 is .9070.

The net present value of the investment is the algebraic sum of the three present values.

---

[2] Appendix Tables A through E are found at the end of the text, not in the chapter appendixes.

Period	(1) Cash Flow	(2) Present-Value Factor	(3) Present Value Col. 1 × Col. 2
0	− $12,337	1.0000	− $12,337
1	10,000	.9524	9,524
2	5,000	.9070	4,535
		Net present value	$ 1,722

The net present value is positive, indicating the investment is acceptable. Now we shall compute the rate of return of the investment. We want to find the rate of discount that causes the sum of the present values of the cash flows to be equal to zero. Assume our first choice (an arbitrary guess) is .05. In the preceding situation we found that the present value using .05 is a positive $1,722. We want to change the discount rate so that the present value is zero. Should we increase or decrease the rate of discount for our second estimate? To decrease the present value of the future cash flows, we should increase the rate of discount (thus causing the present value of the future cash flows that are positive to be smaller).

Let us try .20 as the rate of discount:

Period	Cash Flow	Present-Value Factor	Present Value
0	− $12,337	1.0000	− $12,337
1	10,000	.8333	8,333
2	5,000	.6944	3,472
		Net present value	− $ 532

The net present value is negative, indicating that the .20 rate of discount is too large. We shall try a value between .05 and .20 for our next estimate. Assume that we try .16:

Period	Cash Flow	Present-Value Factor	Present Value
0	− $12,337	1.0000	− $12,337
1	10,000	.8621	8,621
2	5,000	.7432	3,716
		Net present value	0

The net present value is zero using .16 as the rate of discount, which indicates that .16 is the rate of return of the investment.

annuities and annual equivalents

We can describe an annuity as a series of equally spaced payments of equal amounts, with the interest rate of each period equal. Appendix Table B gives the present value of $1 a period for n periods discounted at r rate of interest, the first payment being received (or paid) one period from now and the last payment n periods from now.

Example: Finding the Present Value of an Annuity

Assuming an effective interest rate of .05, we want to find the present value of annual interest payments of $100,000 a year. The first payment is one year from now and there will be twenty payments. Using Appendix Table B, we find that the present value of a $1 period for twenty periods is $12.4622. The present value of the interest payments is

$$\$100,000 \times 12.4622 = \$1,246,220.$$

In the previous example, Appendix Table B was used to find the present value of an annuity. The same table can also be used to find a series of annual equivalent cash flows for n periods that has a given present value. Depending on the context, these annual equivalents may represent costs, revenues, or profits.

Example: Finding an Annual Equivalent Cost

Consider an investment that requires an initial outlay of $12,337 and will generate revenues for two years. We wish to represent the initial outlay by a two-period annuity that has the same present value. Let C represent the amount of the annuity that measures the annual cost that is equivalent economically to $12,337. We shall assume an interest rate of .05 and use Appendix Table B to determine that the present value of $1 a year for two years at .05 is $1.8594. Thus C must satisfy the following relationship:

$$C \times \$1.8594 = \$12,337.$$

Therefore,

$$C = \frac{\$12,337}{\$1.8594} = \$6,635$$

is the equivalent annual cost of the investment.

Suppose that the revenues from the investment are $10,000 in year 1 and $5,000 in year 2. The present value of the revenues is $14,059. The annual equivalent revenues are $14,059/1.8594 = $7,561.

Subtracting the annual equivalent costs from the annual equivalent revenues, we find the annual equivalent profits are $926 per year. We previously calculated the net present value of this investment as $1,722. The annual equivalent profits could have been calculated directly as follows:

$$\frac{\$1,722}{1.8594} = \$926.$$

One particularly important application of the annual equivalent concept is in comparing investments with different lives, which will be discussed in Chapter 5.

rate of discount

We shall use the "time value of money" as a discount rate. This is the rate of interest associated with default-free securities and does not include an adjustment for risk. The objective of the discounting process is to take the time value of money into consideration. We want to find the present equivalent of future sums, neglecting risk considerations. Later, we shall introduce a technique to adjust for the risk of the investment.

Although the cost of capital is an important concept that should be understood by all managers and is useful in deciding on the financing mix, we do not advocate its use in evaluating investments.

assumption of certainty

In the first part of this book there is an assumption that the cash flows are known with certainty. This assumption may be somewhat difficult to accept since it is well known that there are few cash flows associated with real investments that are actually known with certainty. There are two reasons for proceeding in this manner. First, we have to "walk through our plays" before starting to run. There are many difficulties in just taking the time value of money into consideration without also incorporating risk factors. Second, when the cash flows are finally allowed to be uncertain, we shall suggest the use of a procedure that is based on the initial recommendations made with the certainty assumption, so nothing is lost by initially making the assumption.

appendix: basic mathematical relationships for time discounting

For these introductory examples the reader should assume either that the cash flows are not subject to income taxes, or that they are measured on an after-tax basis. Tax effects will be considered explicitly later in this volume. Let

A = initial sum of money.
r = time value of money per period.
n = number of time periods.
S_n = future value of a sum of money to be received in the n'th period from now.

If A is invested for one period to earn r, we would have at the end of the one period

$$S_1 = A + Ar = A(1 + r).$$

At the end of two periods, if the initial investment and the accumulated interest continue to earn at the rate r, we would have

$$S_2 = A(1 + r) + [A(1 + r)]r = A(1 + r)^2.$$

At the end of n periods, under the same assumptions, we would have

$$S_n = A(1 + r)^n.$$

The term $(1 + r)^n$ is called an *accumulation factor*. Solving for A by dividing both sides by $(1 + r)^n$,

$$A = \frac{S_n}{(1 + r)^n} = S_n(1 + r)^{-n}.$$

If S_n is equal to $1, we can solve for the present value of $1:

$$A = (1 + r)^{-n} = \frac{1}{(1 + r)^n}.$$

See Appendix Table A for values of $(1 + r)^{-n}$. We will define $A(n, r)$ to be the present value of $1 due in n periods discounted at r time value of money. Thus,

$$A(n, r) = (1 + r)^{-n}.$$

An annuity is a series of equal payments that occur at equally spaced intervals for a predetermined period of time. In this book the symbol $B(n, r)$ is used to represent the present value of an annuity of \$1 per period, for n periods, with the first payment one period from now and with an interest rate of r per cent per period. The present value of such an annuity could be obtained from Appendix Table A by going to the column headed r per cent and adding up the first n entries in the table. However, since the present value of an annuity is used so frequently in present-value calculations, the present values are presented in a separate table, Appendix Table B. If the annuity pays some amount other than \$1 per period, the present value of the annuity can be obtained by multiplying the annuity factor from Table B by the actual amount involved.

Instead of using Table B or adding up the entries from an appropriate column of Table A, the present value of an annuity of \$1 per period can also be obtained by using the following formula:

$$B(n, r) = \frac{1 - (1 + r)^{-n}}{r}.$$

The following paragraph explains how this formula is derived.

In the following table each row in column 1 gives the present value of \$1 received at the end of the period indicated in the column headed *Time*. The sum of the items in this column is $B(n, r)$. Each row in column 2 of this table gives the item in that row of column 1 multiplied by $(1 + r)$. The sum of the items in this column is $(1 + r)B(n, r)$. Note that $(1 + r)^0 = 1$, and that all except two of the amounts are in both columns. Taking the difference between the sum of the two columns and solving for $B(n, r)$ gives the formula we wish to derive.

Time	Col. 1	Col. 2
1	$(1 + r)^{-1}$	$(1 + r)^0$
2	$(1 + r)^{-2}$	$(1 + r)^{-1}$
3	$(1 + r)^{-3}$	$(1 + r)^{-2}$
⋮	⋮	⋮
$n - 1$	$(1 + r)^{-n+1}$	$(1 + r)^{-n+2}$
n	$(1 + r)^{-n}$	$(1 + r)^{-n+1}$
	$B(n, r)$	$(1 + r)B(n, r)$

$$(1 + r)B(n, r) - B(n, r) = 1 - (1 + r)^{-n}$$

Simplifying the left-hand side,

$$rB(n, r) = 1 - (1 + r)^{-n}$$

and, dividing by r,

$$B(n, r) = \frac{1 - (1 + r)^{-n}}{r}.$$

Appendix Table B gives the values of $B(n, r)$ (the present value of an annuity of \$1 per period). If the annuity is for \$R, we multiply the value obtained from the table by R. If n is very large (let n approach infinity), we have the present value for a perpetuity of \$1 per period:

$$B(\infty, r) = \frac{1}{r}.$$

The basic mathematical relationships for the present value and the rate of return (yield) of an investment follow.
    Let

X_t = cash flow of period t.
i = time value of money of the firm.
r = rate of return of the investment.
V = present value of the investment.
n = life of the investment.

Then the net present value of an investment is

$$V = \sum_{t=0}^{n} X_t(1 + i)^{-t}.$$

The yield of an investment is found by solving the following equation for r:

$$\sum_{t=0}^{n} X_t(1 + r)^{-t} = 0$$

or, equivalently,

$$\sum_{t=1}^{n} X_t(1 + r)^{-t} = -X_0.$$

X_0 is the outlay and is negative. The equation is solved by a trial-and-error procedure, as illustrated in the section on the time value of money in this chapter.

questions and problems

1-1. Assume that you are given the choice between $100 now and $100 one year from now and that both payments are certain. Which would you choose? Explain. How large would the amount one year from now have to be for you to be indifferent between the two choices? What does the answer to this question imply as to your rate of interest (time value of money) during this time period?

1-2. What basic types of errors may a manager in charge of investment decisions make? How would you evaluate his performance?

1-3. Assume a .05 per year time value of money. Use the tables in the Appendix to compute the value of $100 (a) received one year from now; (b) received immediately; (c) received at the end of five years; (d) received at the beginning of the sixth year; (e) received at the end of fifty years; (f) received at the end of fifty years, but the interest rate is .10; (g) received at the end of each of ten periods.

1-4. Assume a .05 time value of money. Use the tables in the Appendix to compute the value of the following series of payments of $100 a year received for (a) five years, the first payment received one year from now; (b) five years the first of five payments received immediately; (c) ten years, the first payment received one year from now; (d) ten years, the first of ten payments received immediately.

1-5. Assume a .05 time value of money. The sum of $100 received immediately is equivalent to what quantity received in ten equal annual payments, the first to be received one year from now? What would be the annual amount if the first payment were received immediately?

1-6. Assume a .05 time value of money. We have a debt to pay and are given a choice of paying $1,000 now or some amount X five years from now. What is the maximum amount that X can be for us to be willing to defer payment for five years?

1-7. We can make an immediate payment now of $10,000 or pay equal amounts of R for the next five years (first payment due one year from now). With a time value of money of .05, what is the maximum value of R that we would be willing to accept?

1-8. Assume that you are given a choice between incurring an immediate cost (and outlay) of $10,000 and having to pay $2,310 a year for five years (first payment due one year from now); the time value of money is .05. What would be your choice? Explain.

1-9. Each of the following is sometimes listed as a reasonable objective for a firm: (a) maximize profit (accounting income); (b) maximize sales (or share of the market); (c) maximize the value of a share of common stock t time periods from now; (d) ensure continuity of existence; (e) maximize the rate of growth; (f) maximize future dividends.

Required: Discuss each item and the extent of its relevance to the making of investment decisions.

1-10. Explain what is meant by conventional and nonconventional investments. Why is it important to know whether you are discussing a conventional or nonconventional investment?

1-11. Classify each of the following types of business decisions as conventional investments, loan-type investments, or nonconventional outlay–benefits–outlay investments. Explain the reason for your classification in each case.

    a. To enhance the attractiveness of its cars, an automobile manufacturer is considering giving a guarantee to purchasers that certain parts will be replaced if they become defective within a five-year period.

    b. A young man who has just earned his bachelor's degree is trying to decide whether to accept an attractive job offer or to enroll in a two-year graduate program.

    c. The patent on a highly successful product will expire in three years. The company is considering an immediate and drastic price reduction to discourage competitors from entering the market after the patent protection has expired.

    d. To attract a key executive, a company is planning to offer him a five-year contract guaranteeing a minimum of $80,000 per year. The company is obligated to pay this salary even if the executive is fired before the end of the five-year period.

    e. A city is considering using a recreation field for an exposition. The exposition will last three years and then the fields will be converted back to their original use.

1-12. Compute the present value for a bond that promises to pay interest of $50 a year for thirty years and $1,000 at maturity. The first interest payment is one year from now. Use a rate of discount of .05.

1-13. Estimate the present value of a bond that promises to pay interest of $30 a year for thirty years and $1,000 at maturity. The first interest payment is one year from now. Use a .03 rate of discount. After estimating the present value, compute it using the present value tables.

1-14. A twenty-year $1,000 bond promises to pay .045 interest annually. The current interest rate is .05. How much is the bond worth now? How much is the bond worth if the current interest rate were .04?

1-15. Exactly twenty years from now Mr. Jones will start receiving a pension of $10,000 a year. The payments will continue for thirty years. How much is the pension worth now, assuming money is worth .05 per year?

1-16. Assume a .05 interest rate. How much is a perpetuity of $1,000 per year worth?

1-17. Comment on the following:

a. Company A, after paying taxes and its customary dividends ($1 per share), has $1 million of retained earnings available for reinvestment. If the money is invested it would earn $20,000 per year after taxes for perpetuity. This would raise earnings per share from $3 to $3.08. The directors approve the investment.

b. Company A is considering a large expansion program. If it could raise capital of $20 million, it could earn $1 million more per year after taxes. However, the stockholders have rejected the projects because the earnings are too low to justify the investment.

1-18. Assume a .10 interest rate (you can borrow and lend at that rate). Specify which you would prefer:

a. $10,000 in cash or
   $1,000 per year for perpetuity (first payment received at the end of the first period).

b. $10,000 in cash or
   $1,100 per year for perpetuity (first payment received at the end of the first period).

c. $10,000 in cash or
   $900 per year for perpetuity (first payment received at the beginning of the first period).

1-19. The ABC Company has to make a choice between two strategies:
Strategy 1: Is expected to result in a market price now of $100 per share of common stock and a price of $120 five years from now.
Strategy 2: Is expected to result in a market price now of $80 and a price of $140 five years from now.

What do you recommend? Assume that all other things are unaffected by the decision being considered.

1-20. It has been said that few stockholders would think favorably of a project that promised its first cash flow in 100 years, no matter how large this return.

Required: Comment on this position.

chapter 2

illustrating the measures of investment worth

In this chapter we shall describe and illustrate the applications of four different measures of investment worth chosen either because they are used in current business practice or because logical arguments in favor of their use have been advanced. These measures by no means exhaust the possible investment measures. Others, in many cases variations of those discussed, have been suggested or are known to be used by one or more firms. After studying this chapter, the reader should be able to analyze and evaluate for himself the probable performance of other measures of investment worth with which he may be familiar.

Before proceeding to a discussion of the measures of investment worth, we shall describe a series of four hypothetical investments. The four hypothetical investments have been designed so that for two selected pairs it is possible to decide that one investment is clearly preferable to the other. If a measure of investment worth indicates that one investment is better than a second, when it is obvious that the second investment is actually better, then clearly there is a danger in using that measure. Of the four measures considered, we shall find that two can easily be eliminated because in some situations they give obviously wrong answers and another measure gives the "right" answer.

characteristics of the investments

In Table 2-1 a series of four hypothetical investments is described in terms of the initial cost of each and the net cash proceeds expected during each

22

Table 2-1. Description of Hypothetical
Investments

Investment	Initial Cost	Net Cash Proceeds per Year	
		Year 1	Year 2
A	$10,000	$10,000	
B	10,000	10,000	$1,100
C	10,000	3,762	7,762
D	10,000	5,762	5,762

year of earning life. The salvage value or terminal value of each is assumed to be zero. We shall illustrate the ranking that may be given to these investments by each measure of investment worth under consideration.

Some comments on the interpretation of these hypothetical investments are in order. In the first place, nothing has been said about the risk characteristics of the various investments. An evaluation of the risk or uncertainty associated with an investment is a crucial part of the investment decision process. However, the concepts of risk or uncertainty are complex and need to be clarified before they can be discussed intelligently. It has seemed advisable to take these problems up separately later in the book, and for present purposes the reader may assume that the hypothetical investments described in Table 2-1 are completely riskless; thus there is no basis of choice between them on these grounds. We could also assume that the figures presented are mean values, and it is appropriate to use mean values in computing the worth of an investment.

Second, the question of income taxes needs clarification. It is commonly recognized that investment proposals should be evaluated on an after-tax basis. However, the discussion of income tax adjustments is deferred to Chapter 7. In the present instance, the explicit introduction of income taxes would complicate the task of describing the various hypothetical investments and of illustrating the rankings that would result from the use of each of the various measures. Moreover, an explicit consideration of income taxes would not change, in any of their essentials, the conclusions we reach. For this reason we shall assume in the present chapter that corporate income taxes have already been taken into consideration and that the net cash proceeds used in the computations are proceeds after deducting the income tax of the period.

The outlays are made at the beginning of the first year, and proceeds are earned at the end of each year. Each investment is of a conventional nature— that is, there are one or more periods of outlays followed by one or more periods of positive cash proceeds. If there were nonconventional investments, for example, more than one period of outlays interspersed with periods of positive cash flows, the rate of return method would require additional refinements, because in this type of situation a higher rate of return may indicate a less desirable investment opportunity.

ranking by inspection

It is possible in certain limited cases to determine by inspection which of two or more investments is more desirable. The two situations in which this is true are as follows:

1. Two investments have identical cash flows each year through the final year of the short-lived investment, but one continues to earn cash proceeds in subsequent years. The investment with the longer life would be more desirable. Thus investment B is better than investment A, because all things are equal except that B continues to earn proceeds after A has been retired.

2. Two investments have the same initial outlay and the same earning life and earn the same total proceeds. If at the end of every year (during their earning life) the total net proceeds of one investment are at least as great as, and for at least one year are greater than, the total for the other investment, then the first investment will always be more profitable. Thus investment D is more desirable than investment C, because D earns $2,000 more in year 1 than investment C does; investment C does not earn this $2,000 until year 2. The earning of $2,000 more in the first year leads to the conclusion that investment D is more desirable than investment C.

payback period

The payback period is one of the simplest and apparently one of the most frequently used methods of measuring the economic value of an investment. The payback period is defined as the length of time required for the stream of cash proceeds produced by an investment to equal the original cash outlay required by the investment. If an investment is expected to produce a stream of cash proceeds that is constant from year to year, the payback period can be determined by dividing the total original cash outlay by the amount of the annual cash proceeds expected. Thus if an investment required an original outlay of $300 and was expected to produce a stream of cash proceeds of $100 a year for five years, the payback period would be 300 divided by 100, or three years. If the stream of expected proceeds is not constant from year to year, the payback period must be determined by adding up the proceeds expected in successive years until the total is equal to the original outlay.

Ordinarily, the administrator would set some maximum payback period and reject all investment proposals for which the payback period is greater than this maximum. Investigators have reported that maximum payback periods of two, three, four, or five years are frequently used by industrial concerns. The relatively short periods mentioned suggest that different maximum payback periods are required because some kinds of investments (construction, for example) can seldom be expected to have a payback period as short as five years.

Assume that the payback period is also used to rank investment alternatives with those having the shortest payback periods being given the highest ranking. The investments described in Table 2-1 are ranked by this method in Table 2-2.

Let us check the reasonableness of the ranking given the investments by the cash payback approach. Investments A and B are both ranked as 1, because they both have shorter payback periods than any of the other investments, namely one year. But investment A earns total proceeds of $10,000, and this amount merely equals the cost of the investment. Investment B, which has the same rank as A, will not only earn $10,000 in the first year but also $1,000 in the next year. Obviously, investment B is superior to A. A ranking procedure, such as the payback period, that fails to disclose this fact is deficient.

Consider investments C and D modified so as to cost $11,524. Both would be given identical rankings because both would return their original outlay by the end of the second year. The two investments are in fact identical, with the single exception that, out of identical total returns, more proceeds are received in the first year and less in the second year from investment D than is the case with C. To the extent that earnings can be increased by having $2,000 available for reinvestment one year earlier, D is superior to investment C; but both would be given the same ranking by the payback period measure.

Thus the cash payback period measure has two weaknesses: (1) It fails to give any consideration to cash proceeds earned after the payback date; (2) it fails to take into account the differences in the timing of proceeds earned prior to the payback date. These weaknesses disqualify the cash payback measures as a general method of ranking investments.

Table 2-2. Payback Period

Investment	Payback Period (Years)	Ranking
A	1	1
B	1	1
C	1.8	4
D	1.7	3

return on investment

In attempting to get a measure of efficiency, analysts frequently use the ratio of the firm's income to the book value of its assets. Some companies also use this measure as a means of choosing among various proposed internal investments. When this measure is used, the average income is computed after depreciation. If the denominator in the ratio is the book value of the investment, the value of both the numerator and the denominator will depend upon the depreciation method used. An alternative procedure is to divide the average income by the cost of the investment (the accrued depreciation is not subtracted). The use of both the book value (net of depreciation) and the cost of the investment will be reviewed here.

The ratio of income to book value is a common and useful measure of performance, but it is less useful as a device for ranking investments. Table 2-3 shows that the same rankings are given to investments C and D, although D is preferable to C. This procedure fails to rank these investments correctly, because it does not take into consideration the timing of the proceeds.

An alternative procedure (see Table 2-4) is to divide income by the cost of the investment (accumulated depreciation not being subtracted). For purposes of measuring performance and computing return on investment, the use of undepreciated cost has certain advantages over the use of book value.

Table 2-3.   Average Income on Book Value

Invest- ment	Average Proceeds	Average Depreciation*	Average Income (Proceeds Less Depreciation)	Average Book Value†	Income on Book Value (%)	Ranking
A	$10,000	$10,000	$ 0	$5,000	0	4
B	5,550	5,000	550	5,000	11	3
C	5,762	5,000	762	5,000	15	1
D	5,762	5,000	762	5,000	15	1

* Assuming straight line depreciation.
† Investment divided by 2.

Table 2-4.   Average Income on Cost

Investment	Cost	Average Income	Average Income on Cost (%)	Ranking
A	$10,000	$ 0	0	4
B	10,000	550	5.5	3
C	10,000	762	7.6	1
D	10,000	762	7.6	1

These advantages are not so important in capital budgeting and are relatively unimportant compared to the failure to take into consideration the timing of the cash proceeds. It is this failing that leads to the same incorrect rankings that result from the use of book value.[1]

introduction to discounted cash flow methods

We have considered two proposed methods for measuring the value of an investment. In the case of each proposed measure, we have been able to find at least one pair of investments in which it was obvious that one of the pair was more desirable; yet the proposed measure of investment worth gave either the same ranking to both investments or a higher ranking to the less desirable of the pair. On the basis of such evidence we have been able to reject both of the proposed measures of investment worth because of their undesirable characteristics.

One flaw that eliminated from consideration each of the measures reviewed has been the inability of the measure to take proper account of the timing of cash proceeds from the investments. The payback period represents one extreme in this regard, because all the proceeds received before the payback period are counted and treated as equals, and all the proceeds received after the payback period are ignored completely. With the return on investment, the proceeds were related by simple averaging techniques to such things as the original cost of the investment or its book value. Neither of these methods succeeded in bringing the timing of cash proceeds into the analysis.

We turn in the following sections to two proposed measures of investment worth that employ different methods for evaluating the timing of future cash proceeds. As a group these could be called the *discounted cash flow measures*. Before proceeding to analyze them, it is desirable to explain again the concept of the present value of a future sum, because in one way or another this concept is utilized in both these measures.

The present value of $100 payable in two years can be defined as that quantity of money necessary to invest today at compound interest in order to have $100 in two years. The rate of interest at which the money will grow and the frequency at which it will be compounded will determine the present value. We shall assume that funds are compounded annually. The manner in which a rate of interest will be chosen will be discussed later. For the present, let us assume that we are given a 3 per cent rate of interest. Let us examine how the present value of a future sum can be computed by using that rate of interest.

[1] The methods described in this section are commonly referred to as "rate of return analysis" or "return on investment analysis." Terminology is a problem, because both these terms are also used to describe other procedures.

Suppose that an investment promises to return a total of $100 at the end of two years. Because $1 invested today at 3 per cent compounded annually would grow to $1.0609 in two years, we can find the present value at 3 per cent of $100 in two years by dividing $100 by $1.0609. This gives $94.26. Therefore, a sum of $94.26 that earns 3 per cent interest compounded annually will be worth $100 at the end of two years. By repeated applications of this method, we can convert any series of current or future cash payments (or outlays) into an equivalent present value. Because tables are available that give the appropriate conversion factors for various rates of interest, the calculations involved are relatively simple.

We have seen that the measures of investment worth previously considered may give obviously incorrect results because they fail either to consider the entire life of the investment or to give adequate attention to the timing of future cash proceeds. The discounted cash flow concept provides a method of taking into account the timing of cash proceeds and outlays over the entire life of the investment. We now turn to a consideration of two measures of investment worth that incorporate present-value concepts.

rate of return method

The rate of return method utilizes present-value concepts but seeks to avoid the arbitrary choice of a rate of interest in evaluating an investment proposal.[2] The procedure is to find a rate of interest that will make the present value of the cash proceeds expected from an investment equal to the present value of the cash outlays required by the investment. Such a rate of interest can be found by trial and error. For example, if we know the cash proceeds expected and the cash outlays required by an investment in each future year, we can start with any rate of interest and find for that rate the present value of the cash proceeds and the present value of the cash outlays. If the present value of the cash proceeds exceeds the present value of the outlays, then ordinarily some higher rate of interest would make them equal. By a process of trial and error, the approximately correct rate of interest can be determined. This rate of interest is referred to as the rate of return of the investment, and may be described as the investment's yield.

The method is commonly used in security markets in evaluating the yields of bonds and other debt instruments. The yield on a bond having a coupon rate of 5 per cent will be equal to 5 per cent only if the current price of the bond is $100. If the current price is greater than $100, the yield will be

---

[2] Other terms used to define the same concept are yield, interest rate of return, internal rate of return, return on investment, present-value return on investment, discounted cash flow, investor's method, time-adjusted rate of return, and marginal efficiency of capital. In this book, yield and rate of return are used interchangeably.

something less than the coupon rate; if the current price is less than $100, the yield will be greater than the coupon rate.

The rate of return may also be described as the rate of growth of an investment. This is more easily seen for an investment with one present outlay and one future benefit. For example, assume that an investment with an outlay of $1,000 today will return $1,331 three years from now.

This is a .10 rate of return and it is also a .10 growth rate per year:

Time	Beginning of Period Investment	Growth of Period	Growth Divided by Beginning Investment
0	$1,000	$100	$100/1,000 = .10
1	1,100	110	110/1,100 = .10
2	1,210	121	121/1,210 = .10
3	1,331	—	

The rate of return of a conventional investment has an interesting interpretation that may be referred to at this point. It represents the highest rate of interest an investor could afford to pay, without losing money, if all the funds to finance the investment were borrowed and the loan (principal and accrued interest) was repaid by application of the cash proceeds from the investment as they were earned.[3]

The use of the rate of return method to make investment decisions under conditions of certainty will be discussed in the next chapter.

In Table 2-5 we show the rate of return for each of the investments listed in Table 2-1 and the ranking of investments that would result if this method were used.

It will be instructive to examine the rankings given by this method for each of the pairs of investments in this list for which we were earlier able to determine the more desirable investment of each pair.

Table 2-5. Rate of Return of an Investment

Investment	Rate of Return (%)	Ranking
A	0	4
B	10	1
C	9*	3
D	10	1

* Approximate measure.

[3] It should be remembered that all investments being considered in this chapter are conventional investments, consisting of periods of outlays followed by periods of proceeds. For other patterns of cash flows, the interpretation of rate of return given here may not apply. (See Chapter 3.)

We previously compared two pairs of investments and decided that invest-ment B was preferable to A and D to C. In each case, if preference had been determined by using the rate of return of an investment method, the pairs would be given the correct ranking. This is the first method that we have used which gives the correct rankings of both pairs.

A,   0%   C,   9%
B, 10%   D, 10%

net present value

This measure is a direct application of the present-value concept. Its com-putation requires the following steps: (1) Choose an appropriate rate of interest; (2) compute the present value of the cash proceeds expected from the investment; (3) compute the present value of the cash outlays required by the investment.[4] The present value of the proceeds minus the present value of the outlays is the net present value of the investment. The recom-mended accept or reject criterion is to accept all independent investments whose present value is greater than or equal to zero and to reject all invest-ments whose present value is less than zero.

Because the present value of an investment will depend upon the rate of interest used, there is not one present-value measure but a group of measures, depending upon what rate of interest is chosen. This should not be interpreted as meaning that this approach provided purely arbitrary indications of the worth of an investment.

The present value of an investment may be described as the maximum amount a firm could pay for the opportunity of making the investment without being financially worse off.[5] Because usually no such payment must be made, the expected present value is an unrealized capital gain from the investment, over and above the minimum required return on the company's capital. The capital gain will be realized if the expected cash proceeds materialize. If the rate of interest is 10 per cent, a company could make a maximum immediate outlay of $11,000 in the expectation of receiving $12,100 a year later. If it can receive the $12,100 with an actual outlay of only $10,000, the net present value of the investment would be $1,000. The $1,000 represents the difference between the actual outlay of $10,000 and the $11,000, the most the company would have been willing to spend to receive $12,100 a year later.

---

[4] If all the cash outlays required by the investments are made in the first period, then, of course, the present value of these outlays is equal to the actual amount expended. This is true of all the hypothetical investments described in Table 2-1 and used as ex-amples in this chapter.

[5] With income taxes this statement is not exact because of the tax effects. (See Chapter 7.)

Table 2-6.   Present Value of the Investment
             Rate of Interest: 6 per cent

Investment	Present Value of Proceeds	Present Value of Outlay	Net Present Value	Ranking
A	$ 9,430	$10,000	− $570	4
B	10,413	10,000	+ 413	3
C	10,457	10,000	+ 457	2
D	10,564	10,000	+ 564	1

It will be instructive to note the rankings that will be given to the hypo-thetical investments of Table 2-1 by the present-value method, using two sample rates of interest. In Table 2-6 we present the results of using the present-value method and a 6 per cent rate of interest.

In discussing the measures of investment worth that do not use the dis-counted cash flow method, we pointed out that the relative ranking of certain pairs of these four investments was obvious. That is, it is obvious from examining the cash flows that investment B is preferable to A, and D is preferable to C. The reader may note that in each case the present-value method using a 6 per cent rate of interest ranks these investment pairs in the correct relative order.

In Table 2-7 the same investments are ranked by the present-value method, using a 30 per cent rate of interest instead of 6 per cent. The relative ranking of investments C and D does not change with the change in the rate of interest. Investment C, which was ranked second when a 6 per cent rate of interest was used, is ranked fourth when the 30 per cent interest rate is used. The ranking of investment D is changed from first to second by the change in the rate of interest. The higher rate of interest results in the proceeds of the later years being worth less relative to the proceeds of the early years; thus B's ranking goes from 3 to 1, but D is still ranked ahead of C.

Even with a 30 per cent rate of interest, the present-value method maintains the correct ordering of each of the two pairs of investments for which an

Table 2-7.   Present Value of the Investment
             Rate of Interest : 30 per cent

Investment	Present Value of Proceeds	Present Value of Outlay	Net Present Value	Ranking
A	$7,692	$10,000	− $2,308	3
B	8,343	10,000	− 1,657	1
C	7,487	10,000	− 2,513	4
D	7,842	10,000	− 2,158	2

obvious preference can be determined. Thus we still find investment B preferred to A, and D preferred to C. This result is not an accident resulting from the specific choice of hypothetical investments and interest rates used in our examples. Whenever it is possible to determine obvious preferences between pairs of investments by the methods described earlier, the present-value method will rank these investments in the correct order, no matter what rate of interest is used to compute the present value.[6] Thus we are justified in concluding that, in the sense that it will not make certain kinds of obvious errors, the present-value method even when used with the "wrong" rate of interest will give better results than measures that do not incorporate the discounted cash flow method.

summary of rankings

The rankings given by each measure of investment worth for each of the hypothetical investments described in Table 2-1 are summarized in Table 2-8.

The most striking conclusion to be drawn from Table 2-8 is the tendency for each measure of investment worth to give a different ranking to the identical set of investments. This emphasizes the need to give careful consideration to the choice of measures used to evaluate proposed investments. Obviously, all these measures cannot be equally valid. By considering specific pairs of investments, we have shown that the measures of investment worth that do not involve the use of the discounted cash flow method can give rankings of investments that are obviously incorrect. For this reason these measures will be excluded from further consideration.

The rankings given the investments by the present-value measures are not identical with that given by the rate of return of an investment measure. Neither of these rankings can be eliminated as being obviously incorrect;

Table 2-8.   Summary of Rankings

	Investment			
Measure of Investment Worth	A	B	C	D
Payback period	1*	1*	4	3
Average income on book value or cost	4	3	1*	1*
Rate of return of an investment	4	1*	3	1*
Present value: at 6%	4	3	2	1
at 30%	3	1	4	2

* Indicates a tie between two investments.

[6] This conclusion is true only if the same rate of interest is used to determine the present value of both the investments.

yet, because they are different, they could lead to contradictory conclusions in certain situations. In Chapter 3 we shall continue our investigation in an attempt to determine whether the present value or the yield of an investment measure is more useful to a decision maker.

ranking of investments

In this chapter we discussed the ranking of four investments and showed that given a carefully defined set of investments we can make definite statements about the relative desirability of two or more investments. If the investments are not restricted to this set, we would find our ability to rank investments to be very limited.

For the remainder of this book we shall not be concerned with the "ranking" of investments; instead, we shall be attempting to

1. Make accept or reject decisions for investments that are independent (that is, if we undertake one investment, the cash flows of undertaking the other investments are not affected).

2. Choose the best of a set of mutually exclusive investments (that is, if we undertake one, either we would not want to undertake the other or we would not be able to because of the characteristics of the investments).

Although the objectives we are setting are somewhat more modest than the objective of ranking investments, we shall encounter enough difficulty to occupy us. However, there is nothing in our recommendations that will preclude a manager from applying qualitative criteria to the investments being considered to obtain a ranking. Fortunately, for a wide range of decision situations we can proceed without a ranking of investments.

discounted payback

Instead of computing the length of time required to recover the original investment, some analysts compute the length of time required until the present value turns from being negative to positive. This computation gives a breakeven life of the asset or a discounted payback period. If the life of the asset exceeds this breakeven life, the asset will have a positive present value.

Figure 2-1 shows the cumulative present values (with a discount rate of 10 per cent) for an investment with the discounted payback period indicated, and Table 2-9 shows the calculations, assuming a 10 per cent time discount factor.

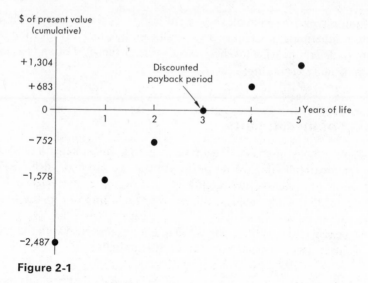

Figure 2-1

relationship between payback period and rate of return

If an investment is expected to earn equal proceeds each year of its life and if the life of the investment is known, it is possible to construct a theoretically correct payback period that will lead to the same accept or reject decisions as the present-value rule. Because of the limiting assumptions, especially equal annual proceeds, this formula has limited usefulness in making decisions, but it does illustrate the weakness of certain payback conventions. In particular, it shows that the longest acceptable payback period depends on the life of the investment and the time value of money.

The payback period is defined as the period of time required to recover the

Table 2-9. Present Values for Different Lives

Period i	Net Present Value for Life of i	Cash Flows and Present Values Period:					
		0	1	2	3	4	5
		− $2,487	$1,000	$1,000	$1,000	$1,000	$1,000
0	− $2,487	− 2,487					
1	− 1,578	− 2,487	909				
2	− 752	− 2,487	909	826			
3	0	− 2,487	909	826	752		
4	683	− 2,487	909	826	752	683	
5	1,304	− 2,487	909	826	752	683	621

initial investment, or as the cost of the investment divided by the proceeds per period. In equation form, with equal proceeds per period,

$$\text{Payback period} = \frac{\text{Cost of investment}}{\text{Proceeds per period}}.$$

The present-value rule is that an investment should be accepted if the sum of the present values of the proceeds from the investment is greater than the cost of the investment. The symbol $B(n, r)$ stands for the present value of an annuity of $1 per period for n periods (the life of the investment) discounted at a rate of r per period. We assume that r is known and is the appropriate discount rate for the firm. With equal annual proceeds we would accept the investment, using the present-value rule, if the following inequality is satisfied:

$$(\text{Proceeds per period}) \times B(n, r) \geq \text{Cost of investment.}$$

As long as proceeds per period are positive, we can divide both sides of the preceding inequality by the proceeds per period without changing the sense of the inequality sign. If we do this, the right-hand side becomes cost of investment divided by proceeds per period, which is the payback period. This leads to the following formulation of the present-value rule:

$$B(n, r) \geq \text{Payback period} \quad \text{or} \quad \text{Payback period} \leq B(n, r).$$

The payback period for an investment with a life of n years must be equal to or less than $B(n, r)$. As the life of the investment increases, so does the maximum acceptable payback period. As the life tends to infinity, the maximum acceptable payback period approaches an upper limit of $1/r$.

Sometimes we may not be sure what life we can expect for an investment. In this case the preceding formula can also be used to find the minimum acceptable life for an investment whose payback period is known. To do this we find the smallest value of n for which $B(n, r)$ is greater than the investment's payback period. The values of $B(n, r)$ are listed in Appendix Table B.

EXAMPLE: The ABC Company requires a two-year payback period or less before accepting equipment. A piece of equipment is being considered that costs $5,000 and is expected to earn cash proceeds per year of $1,000 for a life of ten years. The relevant discount rate is 10 per cent per year. Should the equipment be purchased?

The equipment has a payback period of five years; thus it seems to be undesirable in view of the company's two-year payback criterion. However, because it has a life of ten years, it could have a payback period up to six years ($B(10, .10) = 6.1446$) and would still be acceptable.

Now assume that the equipment has a perpetual life. The reciprocal of the payback period of five years is .2. This is also the rate of return of the investment:

$$\text{Rate of return} = \frac{\text{Income}}{\text{Investment}} = \frac{1,000}{5,000} = .2.$$

If instead of a perpetual life we had assumed a very long life, the reciprocal of the payback period would have approximated the rate of return of the investment.

questions and problems

2-1. Compute the net present value for each of the following cash flows. Assume a cost of money of 10 per cent.

			Period			
Investment	0	1	2	3	4	5
A	($1,000)	$100	$100	$100	$100	$1,100
B	(1,000)	264	264	264	264	264
C	(1,000)					1,611

2-2. Compute the rate of return for each of the cash flows in problem 2-1.

2-3. Compute the payback for each of the cash flows in problem 2-1. Assume a maximum payback period of four years. Which (if any) of the cash flows would be accepted as a desirable investment?

2-4. Assume a cost of money of 5 per cent. Compute the net present value of the cash flows of problem 2-1.

2-5. Assume a cost of money of 15 per cent. Compute the net present value of the cash flows of problem 2-1. Compare with the results obtained from problems 2-1 and 2-4.

2-6. The Arrow Company is considering the purchase of equipment that will return cash proceeds as follows:

End of Period	
1	$5,000
2	3,000
3	2,000
4	1,000
5	500

Assume a cost of money of 10 per cent. What is the maximum amount the company could pay for the machine and still be financially no worse off than if it did not buy the machine?

2-7. The Ithaca Machine Company has a maximum two-year payback period for equipment and a nine-year requirement for buildings. The cost of money for the firm is considered to be 10 per cent. Equipment commonly lasts between ten and twenty years. Buildings are expected to last in excess of twenty years. Do you consider the company's criteria to be useful? Explain.

2-8. Compute the net present value (use a cost of money of .15) and the rate of return for each of the following investments:

	Period		
Investment	0	1	2
A	($1,000)		$1,322
B	(1,000)	$ 615	615
C	(1,000)	1,150	

2-9. Recompute the present values using (a) a cost of money of .20, (b) a cost of money of .05 for each of the investments of problems 2-8.

2-10. Prepare a schedule showing that, with a rate of growth of .15 per year, $1,000 will grow to $1,322 in two years.

2-11. Determine the rate of return of the following investment:

Period	Cash Flow
0	($ 9,120)
1	1,000
2	5,000
3	10,000

2-12. How much could you pay in excess of the indicated cost for the investment of problem 2-11 if you had a cost of money of .10?

2-13. Assume that you can only invest in one of the three investments of problem 2-8.

Required: (a) Using the rates of return of the three investments, which is preferred? (b) Using the present-value method and a cost of money of .05, which is preferred?

2-14. A company uses a 10 per cent discount rate. Assume equal annual cash proceeds. What should be the maximum acceptable payback period for equipment whose life is five years? What are the maximum acceptable paybacks for lives of ten, twenty, and forty years, and infinite life?

2-15. Assume that the discount rate is 5 per cent and answer problem 2-14.

2-16. Assume that $r = .06$. A new machine that costs $7,000 has equal annual cash proceeds and a payback period of 7.0 years. What is the minimum number of full years of life it must have to be acceptable?

2-17. Compute the rate of return of the following investments:

		Period		
Investment	0	1	2	3
A	− $10,000	$4,747	$4,747	$ 4,747
B	− 10,000			17,280

Compare the two investments. Which do you prefer? Are you making any assumption about the reinvestment of the cash flows?

2-18. Determine the rate of return of the following investment:

Period	Cash Flow
0	− $15,094
1	10,000
2	10,000
3	1,000

2-19. *Wellesley Woolen Company*

The Wellesley Woolen Company was an old, established, Massachusetts textile company. It specialized in woolens used in high-style garments.

The controller stated that the company had not made a major investment decision in recent years. Machines were modernized, but were not frequently replaced. In fact, almost all the machines had been purchased over fifteen years ago.

Another member of top management stated, "The woolen industry is intensely competitive. This is illustrated by the fact that mills must work three shifts in order to make a profit. The Wellesley Woolen Company has been able to exist by limiting capital expenditures to modifications of equipment. A large number of the machines now owned were purchased secondhand. The advantages of more modern equipment are that it is somewhat faster, has larger cards, and requires less maintenance. These savings do not justify the purchase of new equipment. Firms that have bought new equipment have run into difficulties. For example, a new Southern mill was recently closed because the owners couldn't pay for the capital equipment they had purchased."

A salesman of textile machinery justified the policy of the Wellesley Woolen Company. The large number of textile firms going out of business created an extensive market in secondhand textile equipment. This machinery was only slightly less efficient than more recent equipment. In fact, much of the used equipment was built after World War II. Prior to 1950 much of the second-hand equipment had been shipped to foreign markets, but in recent years this market had greatly disappeared. For example, the South American textile manufacturers would rather buy new German textile machinery than second-hand American machinery. They considered the German machinery more efficient and less likely to break down.

One problem encountered by textile machinery salesmen was the reluctance of textile manufacturers to accept radical changes in machinery. They preferred small changes because this did not create new problems of maintenance and repair. They also preferred to have all machines of one type to simplify the spare-parts problem.

Required: Does Wellesley Woolen have an investment decision?

2-20. Assume a discount rate of 3 per cent and a machine that generates a constant annual amount of savings. What is the maximum acceptable payback period if the life of the machine is five years? What if the life of the machine is ten years? Fifteen years? Twenty years?

2-21. Assume interest rates of 6 per cent and 12 per cent and answer problem 2-20.

2-22. Assume a discount rate of 3 per cent and a machine that generates a constant annual amount of savings. If the machine has a payback period of five years, what is the minimum acceptable life? What are the minimum acceptable lives for machines with paybacks of eight, twelve, and twenty years?

2-23. Assume a discount rate of 12 per cent and answer problem 2-22.

2-24. Find the net present value at a 5 per cent discount rate for each of the following three investments:

	Period		
Investment	0	1	2
A	− $18,594	$10,000	$10,000
B	− 18,140	0	20,000
C	− 19,080	20,000	0

2-25. Assume an interest rate of 5 per cent from time 0 to time 1 and of 7 per cent from time 1 to time 2. Find the net present value of each of the three investments in problem 2-24.

2-26. Assume an interest rate of 5 per cent from time 0 to time 1 and of 3 per cent from time 1 to time 2. Find the net present value of each of the three investments in problem 2-24.

2-27. Can the rate of return method be used for accept or reject decisions on an investment when the interest rate is not the same in all future time periods?

2-28. An investment costing $31,699 will earn cash flows of $10,000 a year for eight years. The rate of discount is 10 per cent. What is the discounted payback period?

chapter 3

*Long-range investing under rapidly changing
conditions, especially under conditions that
change or may change at any moment under the
impact of new commodities and technologies,
is like shooting at a target that is not only
indistinct but moving and moving jerkily at that.*

—J. A. Schumpeter, *Capitalism, Socialism, and Democracy*
(New York: Harper & Row, Inc., 1947), p. 88.

present value
versus rate of return

In the preceding chapter we saw that neither of the discounted cash flow
procedures for evaluating an investment could be eliminated as being obviously incorrect. In many situations the rate of return procedure will lead
to the same decision as the net present-value procedure. However, there are
also situations where the rate of return method may lead to different decisions
from those obtained by using the present-value procedure. When the two
methods lead to different decisions, the present-value method tends to give
better decisions.

It is possible to use the rate of return method in such a way that it gives
the same results as the present-value method.[1] In this sense the two methods
are identical, and *if* they are used correctly, either one is acceptable. However,
if is the biggest two-letter word in the English language. It is easy to use the
present-value method correctly. It is much more difficult to use the rate of
return method correctly—more difficult to describe what comparisons are appropriate for a given decision, and more difficult to carry out the required calculations. For both these reasons this book will consistently recommend the
use of the present-value method. In the remainder of this chapter we shall
explain why we believe the rate of return method is inferior, and in the

---

[1] This statement is correct only if the rate of discount at which it is appropriate to
discount future cash proceeds is the same for all future years. If the appropriate rate of
interest varies from year to year, even if that pattern of variation is known in advance,
then the two procedures may not give identical answers.

41

process we shall show how that method could be used correctly in arriving at the same answers as the present-value method.

accept or reject decisions

Frequently, the investment decision to be made is whether or not to accept or reject a project. We speak of this type of investment as being an independent investment. With the rate of return procedure the usual recommendation is to accept an independent investment if its rate of return is greater than some minimum acceptable rate of discount. If the cash flow corresponding to the investment consists of one or more periods of cash outlays followed only by periods of cash proceeds, this method will give the same accept or reject decisions as the present-value method, using the same discount rate. Because most independent investments have cash-flow patterns that meet the specifications described, it is fair to say that in practice the rate of return and present-value methods would give the same recommendations for independent investments.

It is sometimes suggested that one of the advantages of the rate of return procedure is that it may be utilized without deciding on a minimum acceptable discount rate, whereas the present-value method requires that this rate be incorporated into the computations. The weakness of this suggestion becomes evident when we consider the accept or reject type of investment decision. The rate of return of an investment must be compared with the minimum acceptable discount rate to reach a decision. The discount rate is no less important to rate of return than to present value, although it enters at an earlier stage in the computations of the present-value method.

In the following pages the terms *cost of money* and *minimum acceptable discount rate* will be used interchangeably.

mutually exclusive investments

If undertaking any one of a set of investments will decrease the profitability of the other investments, the investments are substitutes. An extreme case of substitution exists if undertaking one of the investments completely eliminates the expected proceeds of the other investments. Such investments are said to be *mutually exclusive*.

Frequently, a company will have two or more investments, any one of which would be acceptable, but because the investments are mutually exclusive, only one can be accepted. For example, assume that a company is trying to decide where to build a new plant. It may be that either of two locations would be profitable. But the company will have to decide which one is likely to be the more profitable, because only one new plant is needed. An oil company may need additional transport facilities for its products. Should it build a pipeline or acquire additional tankers and ship by water? Either of these alternatives may result in a net profit to the firm, but the company will wish to choose the one that is more profitable. Suppose that it has decided to build the pipeline. Should a 6- or 10-inch-diameter pipeline be installed? Again the problem is to choose the more profitable of these alternatives. In all these situations, the choice is between mutually exclusive investments.

Mutually exclusive investment alternatives are common. The situation frequently occurs in connection with the engineering design of a new installation. In the process of designing such an installation, the engineers are typically faced at a great many points with alternatives that are mutually exclusive. Thus a measure of investment worth that does not lead to correct mutually exclusive choices will be seriously deficient. In this light, the fact that the two discounted cash flow measures of investment worth may give different rankings to the same set of mutually exclusive investment proposals becomes of considerable importance.

incremental benefits

The rate of return method gives less correct recommendations for mutually exclusive investments than those that result from the application of the present-value method because it reflects the average rather than the incremental cash flows. Let us assume that we must choose one of the following investments for a company whose cost of money is 10 per cent: investment A requires an outlay of $10,000 this year and has cash proceeds of $12,000 next year; investment B requires an outlay of $15,000 this year and has cash proceeds of $17,700 next year. The rate of return of A is 20 per cent and that of B is 18 per cent. A quick answer would be that A is more desirable, on the hypothesis that the higher the rate of return, the better the investment. To see why this answer may be wrong, consider that a rate of return of 1,000 per cent on an investment of a dime is a poor substitute for a rate of return of 15 per cent on $1,000 if only one of the investments can be undertaken.

Clearly, when only the rate of return of the entire investment is considered, something important is left out—and that is the *size* of the investments. The important difference between investments B and A is that B requires an additional outlay of $5,000 and provides additional cash proceeds of $5,700. The rate of return of the incremental investment is 14 per cent, which is clearly worthwhile for a company that can obtain additional funds at 10 per cent.

We can identify the difficulty just described as the "scale" or "size" problem that arises when the rate of return method is used. Because the rate of return is a percentage, the process of computation eliminates size.

The scale problem is sometimes more difficult to identify than in the preceding example. Assume that there are two mutually exclusive investments having different rates of return, but both requiring the same initial outlay. This case seems to be different from the one we have just discussed because there is no incremental investment. Actually, the difference is superficial. Consider investments Y and Z described in Table 3-1. Suppose that they are mutually exclusive investments for a company whose cost of money was 5 per cent. The rate of return of Y is 20 per cent, whereas that of Z is 25 per cent. However, if we take the present value of each investment at 5 per cent, we find that the ranking is in the opposite order. The present value of Z is less than the present value of Y. Neither investment can be said to be obviously superior to the other, and both require the same cash outlays in the first year. Which is preferable for a company with a 2 per cent cost of money?

Suppose that we attempt to make an incremental comparison, as follows:

Period 0	0	Cash flows identical
Period 1	$80.00	Cash flow of Z exceeds that of Y
Period 2	$88.75	Cash flow of Y exceeds that of Z

We see that the cash flow of Y is $80 less in year 1, and $88.75 more than Z in year 2. As before, we can compute the rate of return on the incremental cash flow. An outlay of $80 that returns $88.75 one year later has a rate of return of 10.9 per cent. An investment such as this would be desirable for a company whose cost of money is only 5 per cent. Again we are really dealing with a problem of the scale of the investment, but in this case the opportunity for the additional investment occurs one year later.

The same result can be reached by a somewhat different route if we ask how much cash the company would have on hand at the end of the second year if it accepted investment Y or if it accepted investment Z. Both investments give some cash proceeds at the end of the first year. The value of the investment at the end of the second year will depend upon what is done with the cash proceeds of the first year. Because the cost of money is 5 per cent, we can assume that the cash proceeds of the first year could be

Table 3-1

Investment	Cash Flows for Period			Rate of Return (%)	Net Present Value at 5%
	0	1	2		
Y	− $100.00	$ 20.00	$120.00	20	$27.89
Z	− 100.00	100.00	31.25	25	23.58

reinvested to yield 5 per cent.[2] Then investment Y would result in a total cash accumulation by the end of the year of $141 (105 per cent of $20 plus $120). Investment Z would result in a cash accumulation of only $136.25 (105 per cent of $100 plus $31.25).

One disadvantage associated with the use of the rate of return method is the necessity of computing the rate of return on the incremental cash proceeds in order to determine which of a pair of mutually exclusive investments is preferable. If there are more than two mutually exclusive investments, we shall have to conduct an elimination tournament among the mutually exclusive investments. Taking any pair, we compute the rate of return on the incremental cash flow and attempt to decide which of the two investments is preferable. The winner of this round would then be compared in the same manner with one of the remaining investments until the grand-champion investment was discovered. If there were 151 investments being considered, there would have to be 150 computations, because 150 investments would have to be eliminated.

It is sometimes stated that the rate of return method implicitly assumes reinvestment at a rate of interest equal to the rate of return of the investment. Assume the following investment:

0	1	2	3
− $1,000	$80	$80	$1,080

which has a rate of return of .08. This rate of return is not dependent on any assumption about reinvestment opportunities. For example, the $80 of periods 1 and 2 could be consumed or reinvested at .05 and the rate of return of the investment would still be .08. Although we do not need to know the reinvestment rate to compute the rate of return of an investment, if we are comparing two mutually exclusive investments, we do need to know the opportunity cost of funds to decide between the alternatives. For example, the following investment also has a rate of return of .08.

0	1	2	3
− $1,000	$388	$388	$388

[2] The term *cost of money* as used in the initial chapters of this book refers to a rate of interest that measures both the lending rate (the rate of return on comparable investments outside the firm) and the cost of borrowing (obtaining capital from sources outside the firm). The *lending rate* is assumed to be equal to the *borrowing rate*; thus funds have a minimum cost to the firm equal to this cost. (The firm can lend the funds and obtain a return equal to that yield.) It would *not* be appropriate to assume that funds have a cost *higher* than the cost of obtaining new capital. In Chapter 8 we relax the assumption that the lending rate and the borrowing rate are equal. With uncertainty we will recommend a default free rate to take time value into consideration.

To decide between the two investments we would have to know the uses of the extra $308 in periods 1 and 2 (or equivalently the cost of obtaining $308). The incremental analysis would be as follows:

	Period				Rate of Return
	0	1	2	3	
I	− $1,000	$ 80	$ 80	$1,080	.08
II	− 1,000	388	388	388	.08
I − II		− 308	− 308	692	.08

The term *internal rate of return* is sometimes used to describe the rate of return to emphasize that the value of this measure depends only on the cash flows from the investment and not on any assumptions about reinvestment rates.

graph of present values

The graph of present values is one of the more useful devices for summarizing the profitability characteristics of an investment. On the horizontal axis we measure different discount rates and on the vertical axis the net present value of the investment. The net present value of the investment is plotted for all discount rates from zero to some reasonably large rate. The plot of present values will cross the horizontal axis (have zero present value) at that rate of discount that is also the rate of return of the investment.

Consider an investment with an immediate outlay of $100 and benefits of $115 one year from now. Its graph of present values is shown in Figure 3-1. With discount rates less than 15 per cent the present value is positive; with rates larger than 15 per cent the present value is negative. At 15 per cent the present value is zero; the investment has a rate of return of 15 per cent.

multiple rates of return

When the rate of return method is used, the ability to choose the best of two investments depends on whether a given series of incremental cash flows is like a conventional investment—in which case the higher the rate of return, the better, or whether it is like a loan—in which case the lower rate of return or interest cost, the better. The following example illustrates a case where the choice is not obvious. The cash flows represented by two mutually exclusive

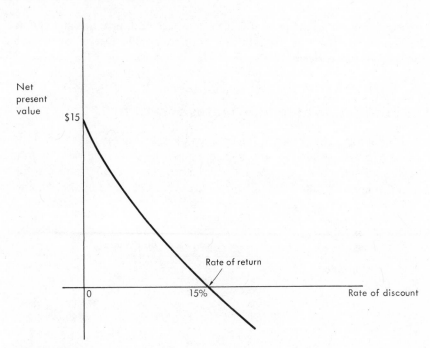

Figure 3-1

investments, R and S, are given in Table 3-2. The last line, labeled I, shows the incremental cash flows (that is, R − S). The cash flows, R and S, are conventional investments because they have outlays *followed by proceeds*. But for investment I, the outlays of period zero are followed by proceeds in period 1 and then by further outlays in period 2. With this kind of cash flow we cannot say, "The higher the rate of return, the better," or "The lower the rate of return the better."

Suppose that the mutually exclusive investments R and S are available to a company whose cost of money is 15 per cent. If the rate of return of the incremental cash flows I is 10 per cent, should the company accept R or S? If the rate of return of the incremental cash flows I is 25 per cent, should the company accept R or S? It turns out that the present value of the cash

Table 3-2

| Investment | Cash Flows for Period | | |
	0	1	2
R	− $162,727	+ $190,909	+ $ 60,000
S	− 90,000	+ 20,000	+ 160,000
I	− 72,727	+ 170,909	− 100,000

proceeds is equal to the present value of the cash outlays at a 10 per cent rate of discount and at a 25 per cent rate of discount. The rate of return of I is *both* 10 and 25 per cent.

interpretation of multiple rates of return

To help illustrate the relationship between the rate of return of an investment and the present-value measure and to explain why multiple rates of return occur and how they should be interpreted, it is helpful to introduce a graph at this point. In Table 3-3 we describe three series of cash flows, T, U, and I.

Table 3-3

	Cash Flows for Period		
Investment	0	1	2
T	− $ 100	+ $ 115	
U	+ 100	− 115	
I	− 72,727	+ 170,909	− $100,000

T can be thought of as a simple one-year loan at 15 per cent interest as seen from the point of view of the lender. U is the same loan as seen from the point of view of the borrower, who first receives funds and later repays them with interest. I is the multiple rate of return incremental cash flow described previously. For T, U, and I in Figure 3-2, the vertical axis represents the net present value of the corresponding cash flow for various possible rates of interest, which are measured along the horizontal axis. By net present value we mean the algebraic sum of the present value of the proceeds and the present value of the outlays.

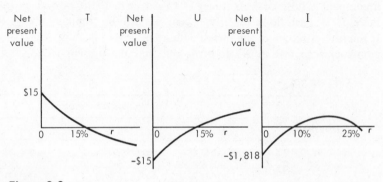

Figure 3-2

Because the rate of return of a cash flow is defined as the rate of discount that makes the net present value zero, the rate of return is the point at which the net present-value line crosses the horizontal axis (which measures the rate of discount).

For T the net present-value line drops as the rate of discount increases. At discount rates lower than 15 per cent, the net present value is positive; at discount rates greater than 15 per cent, it is negative. This general configuration typifies those conventional investments in which a series of cash outlays is followed by a series of cash proceeds. For such cash flows the rate of return represents the highest rate of discount at which the net present value would be positive and the investment desirable.

The results for U are similar to T, but inverted. From the point of view of the borrower, the loan is worthwhile only if the rate at which he finds it appropriate to discount future funds (which represents how much these funds are worth to him) is greater than the rate of interest he pays on the loan. Thus, for the borrower, the net present value of the transaction is negative for rates of discount less than 15 per cent and positive for higher rates of discount. For the loan type of cash flows, the rate of return represents the lowest rate of discount at which the net present value would be positive and the borrowing desirable.

The first part of the graph for I is typical of that of a loan; the second has the downward slope typical of the ordinary investment. This series of cash flows would be worthwhile at rates of discount between 10 and 25 per cent; outside this range it is not advisable. There is a corresponding inverted cash flow that could be obtained by converting the proceeds to outlays and the outlays to proceeds. The resulting cash flows would be desirable only at interest rates that were less than 10 per cent or greater than 25 per cent. Thus we can compare the cash flows that would result from undertaking investment R instead of investment S and obtain a decision that R is more desirable than S at discount rates greater than 10 per cent and less than 25 per cent. Or we can compare the cash flows that result from undertaking S instead of R and obtain a decision that S is more desirable than R at discount rates less than 10 per cent and greater than 25 per cent. These are equivalent ways of saying the same thing.

In each case a simple calculation of the net present value of the investment at the correct rate of discount would have provided the correct answer and would have by-passed the problem of multiple rates of return and the loan type of investments. Figure 3-3 shows that investment R has a higher present value at rates of discount of 10 to 25 per cent.

The cash flows of the unconventional investment I can be broken down into two components, a one-period investment and a one-period loan. To do this we assign part of the cash proceeds of period 1 to the investment and the remainder to the loan. To test whether the investment is desirable if the

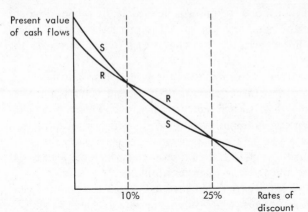

Figure 3-3

cost of money is 15 per cent, we divide the cash flows so that the rate of return on the investment is exactly 15 per cent.

	Cash Flows of Period		
	0	1	2
Investment I	− $72,727	+ $170,909	− $100,000
"Investment"	− 72,727	+ 83,636	
"Loan"		+ 87,273	− 100,000

The investment is marginally desirable since its rate of return is equal to the firm's cost of money. The loan has a cost of .146, which is less than the .15 cost of money; thus the entire package, I, is acceptable.

If R had been subtracted from S, we would have obtained the cash flows of investment V which can be broken down into a loan costing 15 per cent and an investment.

	Cash Flows of Period		
	0	1	2
Investment V	+ $72,727	− $170,909	+ $100,000
"Loan"	+ 72,727	− 83,636	
"Investment"		− 87,273	+ 100,000

The loan costs 15 per cent and is marginally desirable. However, the investment has a rate of return of .146 and is not acceptable with a .15 cost of money. Since the entire package (loan plus investment) must be accepted or rejected, we would reject the package, thus rejecting investment V.

The procedure we used was to set an initial investment or loan at the cost of money and then determine the rate of return of the remaining cash flows after the change in sign.

significance of nonconventional cash flows

In Chapter 1 we defined conventional investments (or loans) as those in which there were one or more periods of net cash outlays (or net proceeds) followed by one or more periods of net cash proceeds (or net outlays). It is important to determine whether a series of cash flows is conventional because *a conventional investment will have one and only one positive rate of return*.

If an investment is not conventional, we consider it to be a nonconventional investment. With a nonconventional investment, any of the following is possible:

1. The investment has *no* rate of return.
2. The investment has *one* rate of return.
3. The investment has *more than one* rate of return.

An example of a nonconventional investment with two rates of return was given in the preceding section. An example of a nonconventional investment with no rate of return would be an investment having cash proceeds of $100 and $150 in periods 1 and 3, respectively, and cash outlays of $200 in period 2. This "investment" does not have a rate of return, but it has a positive present value for all rates of discount.[3]

index of present value

Some authors suggest dividing the present value of the cash proceeds by the present value of the investment type of outlays to obtain an index of present value (proceeds per dollar of outlay, both expressed in terms of present value).

The index-of-present-value method is a variant of the present-value

---

[3] Mathematically, finding a rate of return for this series of cash flows is equivalent to finding a real number x that would satisfy the equation

$$0 = 100 - 200x + 150x^2.$$

But this equation has no solution in the domain of real numbers.

method; its appeal lies in the fact that seemingly it can be used to rank investments. We shall attempt to show that the ranking is frequently spurious. If our objective is limited to accept or reject decisions, the index of present value (accept all investments with an index greater than 1) will give results identical to those of the present-value method.

EXAMPLE: The cost of money is 10 per cent. Assume that an investment has the following cash flows:

0	1	2
− $1,500	$1,000	$1,000

The present value of the $1,000-a-period cash proceeds is $1,736. The index is 1.16.

$$\text{Present-value index} = \frac{1,736}{1,500} = 1.16.$$

One rule to use with an independent investment is the following: If the index is larger than 1, accept the investment.

This rule is sound. However, if the index is greater than 1, the net present value is also positive, and the computation of the present-value index is unnecessary.

A second rule is this: Evaluate mutually exclusive investments by their indexes; choose the investment with the highest index.

This rule may lead to correct decisions, but it may just as well lead to incorrect decisions because of two factors: scale of the investment and classification of cash flows.

EXAMPLE (SCALE): Assume two mutually exclusive investments with the cash flows indicated. Which is the more desirable?

| | Period | | | Present-Value |
Investment	0	1	2	Index
X	− $1,500	$1,000	$1,000	1.16
Y	− 3,100	2,000	2,000	1.12

The index measure indicates that X is preferred to Y. However, a computation of present values will show that Y is better (a net present value of $372 for Y compared to $236 for X). The present-value index is a ratio of benefits to outlay. However, it fails to consider the scale of the investment in the same manner as other ratio measures, such as return on investment and rate of return. This point can be seen more clearly if we look at the incremental investment consequent on moving from X to Y. We shall label that investment Y-X.

| | | Period | | Present-Value |
Investment	0	1	2	Index
Y-X	− $1,600	$1,000	$1,000	1.08

The index is greater than 1; thus the incremental investment is desirable. The problem of scale can be solved by comparing pairs of investments, but this is unnecessary because the problem can be solved more easily by using present value. Also the problem of the classification of cash flows still exists.

EXAMPLE (CLASSIFICATION OF CASH FLOWS): The second difficulty with the present-value index is that it requires a distinction between deductions from cash proceeds and investment-type outlays. Assume the following two mutually exclusive investments:

| | | Period | | Present-Value |
Investment	0	1	2	Index
A Net flows	− $1,500	$1,000	$1,000	1.16
B Proceeds		2,000	2,000	1.08
Outlays	− 1,500	− 1,000	− 1,000	

The index measure chooses A over B. Close inspection of the cash flows of the investments shows that the investment net cash flows are identical for both investments. The difference may be only a matter of classifying the $1,000 outlays of B as investments or as deductions from cash proceeds as with A. Any procedure that depends on arbitrary classifications rests on quicksand. For example, are advertising expenditures an expense or an investment?

A misconception about the present-value index is that it will rank independent investments. This ranking is not reliable. If the company does not intend to accept all independent investments with a positive present value (or an index greater than 1), the cost of money used will not be the appropriate rate of discount and the index ranking will not be reliable. It is not claimed here that the present-value method may be used to rank independent investments. It is claimed only that the present-value method will lead to more easily obtained decisions involving choices between mutually exclusive investments and will give equally correct accept or reject decisions when applied to independent investments.

present value and ranking investments

We can use the present-value method to choose the best of a set of mutually exclusive investments because in this situation the cost of money is an appropriate opportunity cost. As soon as we use the present-value method to rank independent investments for the purpose of choosing a cutoff rate above zero present value (some investments with positive present values will be rejected), the rate of discount that was used in computing the present values is not the appropriate rate to use, because the true opportunity cost is higher than the rate chosen.

EXAMPLE: The time value of money of the firm has been computed to be .10 There are two independent investments, C and D, with the following characteristics:

| | Cash Flows for Period | | | |
Investment	0	1	Rate of Return	Present Value (using .10)
C	− $ 5,000	$10,000	1.00	$ 9,091 − 5,000 = $4,091
D	− 20,000	30,000	.50	$27,273 − 20,000 = $7,273

Using the present values, we would rank D over C and reject C. Using as the opportunity cost the yield of the rejected investment C (1.00), we find the present values to be

$$\text{Present value of C} = \$5,000 - 5,000 = 0,$$
$$\text{Present value of D} = \$15,000 - 20,000 = -\$5,000.$$

If we used the rate of return of the last investment accepted, D (.50), we would have as present values

$$\text{Present value of C} = \$6,667 - 5,000 = \$1,667,$$
$$\text{Present value of D} = \$20,000 - 20,000 = 0.$$

With both of these rates of interest we find that C is preferred to D, but with an interest rate of .10, D is preferred to C. Figure 3-4 shows that as long as the appropriate time value factor is less than 33 per cent the investor pre-

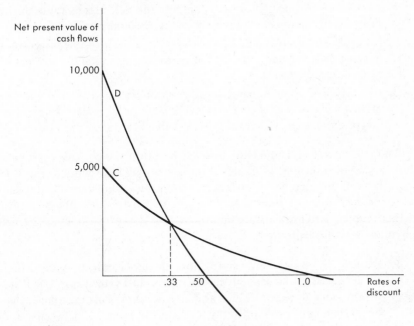

Figure 3-4

fers investment D, but that if the discount factor is greater than 33 per cent, investment C is preferred.

The problem becomes even more complex when we consider the opportunity costs of money for many time periods, and where we have many sets of mutually exclusive investments. The choice of the best of each set will depend on the opportunity cost that is chosen.

Thus we make no claim that the present-value method can be used to rank independent investments where that ranking will be used to eliminate some independent investments with positive present values. This problem will be taken up again in Chapter 8 when we discuss capital rationing.

summary

If a corporation knows its cost of money (at least approximately) and can either obtain additional funds from the market at that cost of money if desirable internal investments are available, or invest any excess funds externally at that cost of money, then either of the two discounted cash flow procedures can be used to make correct investment decisions.

If the present-value method is used, the rules for making correct investment decisions are quite simple in principle. They are

1. For each investment proposal, compute the net present value of the proposal, using the cost of money as the discount rate.
2. If the choice is between accepting or rejecting the investment, accept it if its net present value is greater than zero, and reject it if the net present value is less than zero.
3. If a series of comparable investment proposals is available and the present value of each is greater than zero, but only one can be accepted, accept the one for which the present value is the greatest.[4]

The rate of return method can also be used to make correct investment choices, provided the cost of money is the same in all future time periods. If properly used, this method will in fact lead to the same choices as the present-value method. But the rules that must be followed if the rate of return method is to be used properly are quite complex. The complexities arise from the following considerations:

1. A single investment may have more than one rate of return. The present value of the cash proceeds from an investment may equal the present value of the costs at x and at y per cent. This may mean that the investment is profitable only if the cost of money is between x and y per cent, or it may mean that the investment is profitable only if the cost of money is either less than x per cent or greater than y per cent.
2. If a group of two or more mutually exclusive investments is available, a direct comparison of their rates of return will not necessarily lead to the correct choice of the best alternative. It is necessary to analyze the investment proposals two at a time, decide which one of each pair is more desirable, and then compare the more desirable investment with one of the others to decide which of those two is more desirable, continuing until by a process of elimination the best one can be determined. By contrast, the present-value method indicates immediately which one of a group of mutually exclusive proposals is more desirable.
3. In interpreting the rate of return of a single investment, it is necessary first to determine whether the cash flows correspond to an ordinary conventional investment or to a loan from the point of view of the borrower.
4. It may not be possible to define the rate of return for a cash-flow series. In this case the easiest procedure is to interpret the cash-flow series using the present-value method.

[4] The problem of comparability complicates this analysis. See Chapter 5 for an explanation of the procedure to be followed when two mutually exclusive investments are not comparable because their lives are not equal.

5. If the cost of money is not expected to be the same in all future time periods, the rate of return method as defined in this book cannot be used to give the same decisions as the present-value method.

For most of us the present-value method is simpler, safer, easier, and more direct. The remainder of this book will proceed in terms of this approach.

The "conflict" between present value and rate of return disappears if the graph of present values is used for comparing investments. The rate of return is the intersection of the graph and the X axis, and the present value is the vertical height from the X axis to the graph. Using the rate of return as the rate of discount, the net present value is zero.

appendix: continuous cash flows and continuous discounting

The assumption is made throughout this book that all cash flows occur instantaneously, usually at the end or beginning of a period, and that interest is compounded annually. Either or both of these assumptions may be varied. Interest may be compounded monthly, weekly, daily, or continuously. Instead of assuming that the cash flows occur at the end of a period, they may also be presumed to occur monthly, weekly, daily, or continuously.

If there is a finite number of compounds and payments, the following formula may be used to compute the present value of an annuity.

$$\frac{R}{p} \frac{1 - \left(1 + \frac{j}{m}\right)^{-mn}}{\left[\left(1 + \frac{j}{m}\right)^{m/p} - 1\right]},$$

where R = annual payment,
  j = nominal rate of interest,
  m = number of compoundings per year,
  n = number of years,
  p = number of payments per year, $m \geq p$,
  m/p is an integer.

If we allow m and p to increase beyond bound, that is, to approach infinity, we have the situation in which interest is being compounded continuously and cash flows are occurring continuously. If $p = m = 1$, we have

$$B(n, j) = R \frac{1 - (1 + j)^{-n}}{(1 + j) - 1} = R \frac{1 - (1 + j)^{-n}}{j}.$$

Continuous Compounding

To convert a nominal rate of interest j, which is compounded m times annually, to an effective rate of interest r, compounded annually, we make use of the fact that

$$(1 + r)^{-n} = \left(1 + \frac{j}{m}\right)^{-mn}.$$

Because the present value of a dollar may be computed by using $(1 + r)^{-n}$, we can substitute the right-hand side of the equation and compute the present value of a \$1 by using $[1 + (j/m)]^{-mn}$. If m is allowed to increase beyond bound (approach infinity), we have

$$\lim_{m \to \infty} \left(1 + \frac{j}{m}\right)^{-mn} = e^{-jn}.$$

e is equal to 2.71828 and is the base of the natural or Naperian system of logarithms.

Thus the present value of \$1 for n periods with interest compounded continuously may be computed by using the nominal interest rate.

EXAMPLE:
Let

$$j = .02,$$

$$n = 1.$$

To compute the present value of a dollar, assuming that interest is compounded continuously,

$$e^{-jn} = e^{-.02},$$

$$e^{-.02} = (2.71828)^{-.02}.$$

We can make use of Appendix Table E for finding values of e^{-x}.

$$e^{-.02} = .9802.$$

The .9802 resulting from continuous compounding should be compared with .9804, which is the present value of a dollar, using 2 per cent compounded annually.

Continuous Payments

Instead of $1 being received at the end of each year, there may be k payments per year, each payment being an amount of $1/k$ dollars. The total received during each year is $1. The present value of a series of such payments extending over n years, with interest compounded continuously at a rate j, will be

$$\sum_{t=0}^{n \times k} \frac{1}{k} e^{-jt}.$$

As we let k become very large (so that we receive the $1 per year in a large number of small installments) the summation approaches a limit, which can be written as follows:

$$\lim_{k \to \infty} \sum_{t=0}^{n \times k} \frac{1}{k} e^{-jt} = \int_0^n e^{-jt}\, dt = \frac{1 - e^{-jn}}{j}.$$

EXAMPLE: Compute the present value of $1 per period, assuming that interest is compounded continuously and the cash flows occur continuously.

$$j = .02$$
$$n = 1$$
$$e^{-jn} = e^{-.02} = .9802 \quad \text{(see preceding example)}$$
$$\frac{1 - e^{-jn}}{j} = \frac{1 - .9802}{.02}$$
$$= \frac{.0198}{.02} = .99.$$

The .99 should be compared with the .9802, obtained in the preceding example with continuous compounding but one instantaneous payment, and the .9804 of annual compounding and one payment.

We can convert from interest rates assuming annual compounding to equivalent interest rates assuming continuous compounding, and vice versa.

Table 3-4. Continuous Interest Rates
Equivalent to Various Annually
Compounded Interest Rates

Annual Rate	Equivalent Continuous Rate
r	j
.01	.00995
.02	.01980
.03	.02956
.04	.03922
.05	.04879
.10	.09531
.15	.13103
.20	.18232
.25	.22314
.30	.26236
.40	.33647
.50	.40547
1.00	.69315

Suppose that r is the rate assuming annual compounding and j is the equivalent continuous rate. Then the following relation must hold:

$$(1 + r) = e^j \quad \text{or} \quad r = e^j - 1.$$

To convert from a continuous rate j to the corresponding annual compounding rate, we use $r = e^j - 1$. Alternatively, taking the log of the first relation, we have $j = \ln(1 + r)$. Table 3-4 shows the continuous equivalents of some representative annual rates. For interest rates below 10 per cent, the differences between continuous compounding and annual compounding are not of practical significance for most capital budgeting applications.

Using the preceding analysis combined with Appendix Table E, we can obtain approximations to the entries in the longer Appendix Tables A or B.

To use Table E, we need the value of x, where x is equal to j times n.

EXAMPLE:

j (continuous interest rate)	n (number of periods)	x	Present Value (from Table E)
.05	1	.05	.951229
.05	2	.10	.904837
.05	3	.15	.860708
.15	1	.15	.860708
.075	2	.15	.860708

questions and problems

3-1. Accept or reject the following independent investment proposals, using rate of return and present-value procedures. Assume a cost of money of 10 per cent.

	Period		
Investment	0	1	2
A	($10,000)	$2,000	$12,000
B	(10,000)	10,500	
C	10,000	(12,000)	

3-2. (a) Assume that there are three mutually exclusive investments. Which of the three investments should be chosen? Assume a cost of money of 10 per cent.

	Period				Rate of Return
Investment	0	1	2	3	(%)
A	($ 1,000)	$ 505	$ 505	$ 505	24
B	(10,000)	2,000	2,000	12,000	20
C	(11,000)	5,304	5,304	5,304	21

(b) Compute the corresponding incremental cash flow for investments B and C in problem 3-2(a). Compute the rate or rates of return of this incremental cash flow. Is investment B or C more desirable?

3-3. The Apple Company is attempting to choose between two different machines that accomplish essentially the same task (the machines are mutually exclusive). A comparison of the cash flows of the two machines shows that if the less expensive of the two machines is chosen, there will be a saving of $1,000 at the time of purchase, but there will be additional outlays of $333 per year over the five-year life of the machines. The cost of money of the Apple Company is 10 per cent.

Required: Compute the rate of return of the incremental cash flows and determine whether or not the cheaper of the two machines should be purchased. Make the same decision using the present-value procedure.

3-4. There are two mutually exclusive investments. Assume a cost of money of 10 per cent. Choose the better of the two investments.

Investment	Period			Rate of Return (%)
	0	1	2	
A	($ 16,050)	$10,000	$10,000	16
B	(100,000)	60,000	60,000	13

3-5. There are two mutually exclusive investments. Assume an interest cost of 5 per cent. Choose the better of the two investments.

Investment	Period			Rate of Return (%)
	0	1	2	
A	($10,000)	0	$12,100	10
B	(10,000)	$5,762	5,762	10

3-6. Assume an interest rate of 15 per cent. Choose the better of the two investments of problem 3-5.

3-7. There are two mutually exclusive investments. Assume an interest rate of 5 per cent. Choose the better of the two investments.

Investment	Period		
	0	1	2
A	− $600	$500	$600
B	− 700	800	400

3-8. Compute the relative cash flows of investment (B-A) of problem 3-7. Comment on the computation of the rate of return of this investment.

3-9. There is an investment with the following cash flows:

Period		
0	1	2
− $50	$150	− $100

Assume an interest rate of .05. Is the investment acceptable? What are the rates of return of the investment?

3-10. Use continuous discounting to compute the present value of $1,000 for the following situations:

	Annual Discount Rate r	Number of Years Until Receipt of the Cash n
1	.01	100
2	.10	10
3	.20	5
4	.25	4
5	.05	20
6	.05	40
7	.05	100

3-11. Use continuous discounting to compute the rate of return of the following investment:

Period	Cash Flow
0	-- $15,094
1	10,000
2	10,000
3	1,000

3-12. The ABC Company is considering undertaking an investment that promises to have the following cash flows:

0	1
-- $50	$90

If the firm waits a year it can invest in an alternative (that is, mutually exclusive) investment that promises to pay

1	2
-- $60	$100

Assume a time value of money of .05. Which investment should the firm undertake? Use the present-value and the rate of return methods.

3-13. The IBC Company is considering undertaking an investment that promises to have the following cash flows:

0	1	2	3
-- $100	$150	$50	$50

If it waits a year it can invest in an alternative (that is, mutually exclusive) investment that promises to pay

1	2	3
– $150	$250	$50

Assume a time value of money of .05. Which investment should the firm undertake? Use the present-value method and the rate of return approaches. With the rate of return approach, use the incremental cash flows.

3-14. The Arabian Oil Company is considering an investment that can be undertaken this year or postponed one year. The investment cash flows if undertaken now would be as follows:

Period	
0	1
– $100	$200

The cash flows if delayed one period would be as follows:

Period	
1	2
– $100	$200

Required: Assume a time value of money of .05. Should the company invest now or delay one year? First use the rate of return method and then use the present-value method.

3-15. *Norwalk Screw Company*

The Norwalk Screw Company was located in Norwalk, Connecticut. It was a privately held corporation and capital expenditures were financed entirely out of funds generated by operations.

In choosing among different investment possibilities, management relied heavily on its experience. Because management generally had between fifteen and forty years' experience, the capital budgeting computations frequently were not made for specific decisions, although a capital budget was prepared.

An example of an investment decision that was decided affirmatively was the purchase of a zinc plater. The plater was purchased for $20,000. It increased capacity, eliminated expensive subcontracting, and reduced direct labor on this particular plating process from two workers to one. Management was very satisfied with the purchase. Equipment used in the manufacture of screws generally had a long life. It rarely became obsolete, although it was modified and improved.

A decision to be made was whether or not to operate a truck instead of using common carriers in the states of Connecticut and Rhode Island. The traffic manager prepared an analysis of costs and pounds of product transported during December (see Exhibits 1 and 2). The product transported included raw material, finished goods, and product requiring outside work.

Exhibit 1. Norwalk Screw Company. Inter-Works Communication

To   Controller

Subject   Truck Operation in Rhode Island & Connecticut

The New England Motor Rate Bureau is increasing the trucking rates 6% effective March 10th. In an effort to avoid this increase and other future increases we are planning to operate our own truck on a limited scale in the states of Rhode Island and Connecticut.

At the present time we are planning to use our two and one-half ton truck to start this operation. Connecticut has been selected as the major point due to the fact that we have a round-trip movement to Shelton, Connecticut. Each day we have considerable tonnage going to Shelton and coming back to our plant from there. In addition, we have good accounts at New Haven, New Britain, and Hartford which would enable us to load approximately 5,000 pounds each day. Coming to our plant we also have freight from Bridgeport, Hartford, Torrington, and Providence. The freight from Providence is ideal in that it consists of set-up boxes, a class 1 commodity which would ride perfectly over a load of screws or coils of brass.

Figures based on actual shipping and receiving during the month of December show that we paid $1,761.81 for both shipping and receiving charges covering nineteen shipping and receiving days, an average of $92.72 per day or $463.60 per week.

Based on an average round trip of 280 miles per day at $.06 a mile for gas, oil, depreciation, etc., it would cost us $16.80 per day or $84 a week. The driver's wages would be approximately $100 per week based on forty hours at $1.82 per hour and ten hours overtime at $2.73 per hour. Our cost weekly would be $184 against $463.60 via common carrier or a saving of $279.60 per week and $14,259.60 per year.

The service would by no means be limited to the points mentioned above and would be a very flexible operation to satisfy our customers' and our needs. Eventually it could develop into our using our own larger trucks over a greater area. This operation is scheduled to start March 1.

Your comments will be appreciated.

Very truly yours,

R. Smith

Traffic Manager

Exhibit 2. Norwalk Screw Company. Analysis of Shipments in Rhode Island and Connecticut. (Pounds of Freight)

Month of December	Shelton Out	Shelton In	New Britain Out	Hartford Out	Hartford In	Paw-tucket Out	New Haven Out	Bridge-port In	Middle-ton In	Torring-ton In	Water-ville In	Provi-dence In
1	3,000	5,000	2,552					1,628					
2	2,662	5,475		783								
5	5,000	4,494										
6	3,791	4,412	459		2,935					306			600
7	624	940	519				57			1,010			
8	5,673	2,977			831				2,954	128			
9	1,530	1,075	3,701										2,000
12	4,123	5,297						522					
13	704	3,288	430	319	1,360	443							
14	2,279	2,206			1,057					22			
15	1,928	2,180	2,870	47	374				2,730	608			
16	2,773	2,935		1,035	365								2,000
19	5,000	1,090			217					145	3,500		1,700
20	4,052	1,900		1,002	210						3 000		
21	5,000	815			50								
27	4,953	4,825			48					247		4,000	
28	3,400	5,000				1,584							
29	2,112	1,532	2,015									3,500	
30		1,161	4,951		384							3,500	

The analysis of the traffic manager indicated large savings, but the controller rejected the plan.

The cost of a new two and one-half ton truck was $5,000. The company already owned one truck of this type and a pickup truck. Both of these vehicles were used for odd trips and were driven by one man.

The controller stated: "We generally reject if payback is more than two years." This is the usual approach to investments when the decision can be based on payback or return. Obviously, many investment decisions are made on other bases.

Required: What action should the controller take, based on Mr. Smith's letter?

3-16. Assume that there are two mutually exclusive investments. Which of the two investments would be chosen using the index of present value? Assume a cost of money of 10 per cent. Evaluate the procedure.

	Period	
Investment	0	1
A	− $ 4,000	$11,000
B	− 20,000	33,000

3-17. Assume that there are two mutually exclusive investments. Which of the two investments would be chosen using the index of present value? Assume a cost of money of 10 per cent.

	Period	
Investment	0	1
A	− $4,000	$11,000
B	− 4,000	− 10,000
		21,000

3-18. Assume that an investment has the following cash flows:

0	1	2
− $10,000	$21,600	− $11,600

This investment has rates of return of 0 and .16. Assume that the firm has a time value of money of .10 (it can borrow at .10). Divide the investment into two components, a fictitious investment of $10,000 at time zero and borrowing of $10,600 at time 1. Determine whether the basic investment is desirable.

3-19. Assume that an investment has the following cash flows:

0	1	2
$10,000	− $21,600	$11,600

The investment has rates of return of 0 and .16. Assume that the firm has a time value of .10 (it can borrow at .10). Divide the investment into two components, a fictitious borrowing of $10,000 at time zero and an investment of $10,600 at time 1. Determine whether the basic investment is desirable.

3-20. Assume that an investment has the following cash flows:

0	1	2	3
$10,000	$10,000	$10,000	− $29,000

The firm uses the rate of return method of evaluating investments and has a hurdle rate of .10. Is the investment desirable?

3-21. There are two mutually exclusive investments with the following cash flows:

	Cash Flows for Period		
Investment	0	1	2
R	− $162,727	$190,909	$60,000
S	− 90,000	20,000	160,000

Required: Which of the two investments do you prefer if the firm's time value of money is (a) .05; (b) .20; (c) .30?

chapter 4

The theory is one of investment opportunity *and human impatience* as well as *exchange.*
—Irving Fisher, *The Theory of Interest, As Determined by Impatience to Spend Income and Opportunity to Invest It* (New York: Kelley & Millman, Inc., 1954), p. 149.

the meaning of present value

In the preceding chapters we have argued that measures of investment worth that do not utilize discounted cash flow concepts can frequently give incorrect evaluations of investment alternatives. But the fact that a measure of investment worth incorporates discounted cash flow concepts is no guarantee that it will give correct results in all cases.

The thoughtful reader will have noticed that the argument up to this point has been largely negative. We have emphasized the shortcomings of the methods in common use. But we have not yet developed the arguments for preferring the discounted cash flow approach for measuring the value of an investment. In this chapter we shall attempt to present in a systematic and positive way our reasons for recommending the use of the present-value measure. We hope to make clear the advantages as well as the limitations of this method. It is by no means a cure-all for the problem of the businessman harassed by the difficult problems of developing, evaluating, and choosing long-run investments.

We believe that the present-value method can make a definite and important contribution to the solution of the problems of making investment decisions. But it is vitally important that the user understand what it is he is accomplishing by discounting the cash flow of an investment, and what he is not accomplishing. Unfortunately some of those who have advocated use of this procedure have done so for the wrong reasons or have made claims for it that cannot be fulfilled. All of us recognize that the simple screwdriver is a useful tool when properly used. There is no need to revise that opinion because an inexperienced do-it-yourself enthusiast reports disastrous

69

consequences from his attempt to use a screwdriver in a situation where a chisel was required.

a bird in the hand

Most businessmen will agree that a dollar in hand today is more valuable to them than a dollar to be received a year from now. If we pursue the matter, we would very likely find a variety of reasons for this preference. A survey may reveal the following answers to the inquiry, "Why is a dollar in hand today worth more to you than a dollar to be received in one year?"

1. As a businessman I live in an uncertain world. A dollar in the bank is something I can count on. A promise to pay me a dollar in one year is only a promise until I actually get the money. The promise may be made in perfectly good faith, but any number of things may occur between now and next year to prevent the fulfillment of the promise.

2. Human nature naturally attaches more weight to present pleasures than to the more distant joys. Offer a young man the choice between a trip to Europe during the coming summer, or a trip five summers from now, and he will nearly always choose the earlier trip. Because future income is meaningful in terms of the pleasant things it makes possible, we would always prefer to receive a given total amount of income as nearly as possible in the immediate future, unless considerations of tax effects dictate another choice.

3. A dollar received now is more valuable than a dollar to be received five years from now because of the investment possibilities that are available for today's dollar. By investing or lending the dollar received today, I can have considerably more than a dollar in five years. If the dollar received is used now for consumption, I am giving up more than a dollar's worth of consumption in year five. For that reason future receipts should always be discounted.

Our three hypothetical respondents have suggested three separate reasons for attaching more weight to dollars on hand than to dollars that may be received in the future. Each reason is a correct one in important respects. But only the last one of them is sufficient justification for using discounted cash flow procedures in evaluating investment proposals. The other two reasons, insofar as they are appropriate in any situation, need to be taken into account in other ways. Let us consider each of the three reasons in turn.

uncertainty

Our first hypothetical respondent stressed the fact that one can never be certain about the receipt of future cash. We would not disagree. In fact, we would generalize and say that one can never be certain, even about the future value of present cash held. It can be lost or stolen, the bank in which it is deposited might fail, or our ability to benefit from it may be impaired by death or injury.

It is not the need to allow for uncertainty that is in question, but the suitability of using the present-value approach to make this allowance. The inappropriateness of using high discount rates as a general method of allowing for uncertainty may be illustrated by cases in which there is great uncertainty about the cash flows in the near future, but relatively little uncertainty about the more distant cash flows. Suppose that we are considering investing in a building which, once it is built, could be rented on the basis of a long-term lease. The prospective lessee is willing to sign a contract now, and his credit standing is excellent, so that there is minimum uncertainty about his ability to meet the rental payments. However, there may be considerable uncertainty about how much it will cost to construct the building. In a situation such as this, it is difficult to justify using a high rate of discount applied to the relatively certain future cash receipts. There is considerable uncertainty about the magnitude of the cash outlays required to build the building, but varying the discount rate will have little effect on the present value of these outlays, because they will occur in the near future.

Some suggestions for handling data to improve the judgments of the risks involved in investments will be discussed later. However, no completely satisfactory and universally applicable method is known.

subjective time preference

The second reason suggested as a justification for discounting future income is the time preference of the individuals involved. Undoubtedly there are individuals who, if given the choice, would prefer an additional $100 of consumption immediately to the opportunity of obtaining an additional $110 of disposable income available a year from now. Such an individual might be acting rationally if he rejected a riskless opportunity to invest $100 today in such a way that it would return $110 in one year. The investment should be rejected if acceptance of the investment requires a corresponding reduction in the investor's immediate consumption.

But acceptance of the investment will not require a reduction in immediate consumption if opportunities to borrow money at less than 10 per cent are also available now. Suppose the individual in question accepts the investment and at the same time borrows $100 at 5 per cent to maintain his immediate consumption. At the end of a year the proceeds from the investment will enable him to pay off the loan, plus its accrued interest, and still retain an additional $5.

In general, the subjective time preferences of the owners of a corporation do not need to be consulted in making investment decisions for that corporation, provided the corporation can obtain additional funds in the capital market and invest its excess funds, if any, on the capital market. It is only the rates at which the corporation can obtain or lend funds that are relevant. Accordingly, the purpose of a business enterprise in discounting expected future cash proceeds is not to take account of the subjective time preferences of the owners (unless the owners do not for one reason or another have access to the capital market).

The manager of a business owned by a small group of individuals may, and sometimes should, adjust the investment policy of the company to take into consideration the cash requirements of the owners. But the shareholders of a large corporation are usually a diverse group. They may pay marginal tax rates on dividends of anywhere from zero (for certain individuals and non-profit institutions) to significantly over 60 per cent. At any given time, some shareholders will be reinvesting a part of their dividend receipts, while others will be reducing their portfolios. The large corporation cannot easily adjust its investment policy to the needs of individual shareholders.

alternative uses of money

The purpose of discounting the cash flows expected from an investment is to determine whether the investment yields more cash than alternative uses of the same amount of money. In the case of an independent investment proposal in a firm not subject to capital rationing,[1] whose current dividend has been determined, the consequences of accepting the investment are to borrow more funds or to lend less outside the firm. If the costs of borrowing are the same as the rate that could be earned by lending elsewhere, the alternatives are equivalent. It should be mentioned that the term *borrowing* is used here in a very broad sense to include raising additional equity capital as well as the more conventional forms of debt.

investment financed by borrowing

To illustrate the meaning of the present-value computation when the investment must be financed by borrowing, we may use an investment that requires an initial outlay of $10,000 and offers proceeds of $5,000 per year for three years. At a 6 per cent rate of interest, compounded annually, the present

---

[1] For a discussion of capital rationing, see Chapter 8.

value of the proceeds is $13,365, so the net present value of the investment is $3,365. The value of the proceeds expected from the $10,000 investment is sufficient to pay off the principal and accrued interest on a loan of $13,365 at 6 per cent payable in three instalments of $5,000 each. One way of interpreting the meaning of the present-value calculation is to realize that a firm could borrow a total of $13,365 at 6 per cent, apply $10,000 of the loan proceeds to the investment, and immediately distribute the remaining $3,365 as a divident to the owners. The proceeds of $5,000 per year from the $10,000 investment would be sufficient to repay the loan and interest by the end of the third year. The calculations in Table 4-1 illustrate this arrangement.

We mentioned earlier that making allowances for the subjective time preferences with respect to receipt of income is not the purpose of the discounting process as long as the income recipient has access to the capital market. In the case of the preceding example we assumed that the owners of the firm chose to receive the profit resulting from the investment in the year it was made. Actually, any pattern of cash receipts, such that their present value was equal to $3,365, could have been selected. If some or all of the income withdrawals were deferred past the year in which the investment was made, the actual withdrawals that could be made would exceed $3,365. Suppose the owners elected to borrow $10,000, the amount required to undertake the investment, and to withdraw their proceeds only after the initial loan had been repaid. Under these circumstances the owners would be enabled to withdraw $4,008 at the end of the third year, because this amount has a present value of $3,365 with an interest rate of 6 per cent. Table 4-2 illustrates the loan balances outstanding at various times under this arrangement.

If the owners preferred to withdraw the same amount each year over the life of the investment, annual payments of $1,259 could be withdrawn. The reader may wish to test his understanding of the meaning of present-value calculations by working out an example to prove to himself that annual payments of this amount could be made to the owners, the remainder of the cash proceeds applied to repayment of the loan, and the loan completely paid off by the end of the third year.

Table 4-1. Loan Values Outstanding at the End of Each Period When a Loan Equal to the Present Value of the Proceeds of an Investment Is Made and Proceeds Are Used to Repay Loan

Period	Loan Outstanding at Beginning	Accrued Interest (6%)	Total Amount Owed Before Payment	Investment Proceeds Applied to Loan	Loan Outstanding at End
1	$13,365	$802	$14,167	$5,000	$9,167
2	9,167	550	9,717	5,000	4,717
3	4,717	283	5,000	5,000	0

Table 4-2. Loan Balances Outstanding at the End of Each Period When a
Loan Equal to the Initial Investment Outlay Is Made and Proceeds
Are Used to Repay Loan Before Any Withdrawals

Period	Loan Outstanding at Beginning	Accrued Interest (6%)	Total Amount Owed Before Payment	Investment Proceeds Applied to Loan	Loan Outstanding at End
1	$10,000	$600	$10,600	$5,000	$5,600
2	5,600	336	5,936	5,000	936
3	936	56	992	992	0

Proceeds available for distribution to owners = $4,008 at time 3.

investment financed internally

So far we have considered the case where the investment within the firm was
to be financed by obtaining additional capital from outside the firm. This
may seem to be an artificial comparison to a company whose past operations
are generating enough cash to undertake all the worthwhile investments that
seem to be available within the company. This situation is not uncommon.
However, it is a mistake to assume that such funds are "free," because there
is the possibility of lending funds outside the firm. For example, if a riskless
possibility of earning 6 per cent from loans outside is available, then risk-
free internal investments ought to be compared with these external profit
opportunities; otherwise, the company may undertake internal investments
that are not so profitable as those outside uses of its funds.

Consider the previous example. In the situation in which the funds to
finance the investment were obtained from outside the firm, we said that we
could interpret the fact that the investment had a present value of $3,365 as
meaning that a loan equal to the amount required to finance the investment,
plus $3,365, could be negotiated, the excess over immediate needs ($3,365)
withdrawn, and the proceeds from the investment then would be sufficient
to repay the entire loan.

Assume that the firm has funds available from internal sources. The
owner has estimated that by applying $10,000 of those funds to the internal
investment the company could generate cash proceeds of $5,000 per year for
three years. We could ask how much money the firm would have to lend
outside at 6 per cent per year in order to generate cash proceeds of $5,000
per year for three years. Because the present value of $5,000 per year for three
years at 6 per cent is $13,365, it would require an external loan of that
amount to generate the same cash proceeds that would be generated internally
from an investment of only $10,000. This is illustrated in Table 4-3. The
reader will note that the figures used in Table 4-3 are precisely the same for

Table 4-3. External Loan Earning 6 Per Cent Required to Produce Cash Proceeds Identical to Those Produced by an Internal Investment

Period	Initial External Loan	Accrued Earnings (6%)	Total External Loan Before Withdrawal	Equivalent Proceeds Withdrawn	Remaining External Loan
1	$13,365	$802	$14,167	$5,000	$9,167
2	9,167	550	9,717	5,000	4,717
3	4,717	283	5,000	5,000	0

each period as those in Table 4-1. The only difference is that a different set of labels for the column headings is appropriate in this instance.

In the case where funds are available from internal sources, and external lending opportunities to earn 6 per cent per year are available, the fact that an internal investment with a present value of $3,365 is available means that $13,365 would have to be lent externally to generate the same cash proceeds as the internal investment of $10,000.

As in the previous case, the subjective time preferences of the owners should not affect the choice between the internal or external investment loan. The reader may verify for himself by working out examples that any pattern of cash generated by lending $13,365 externally could also be generated with a commitment of $10,000 in the investment of the example and an appropriate decision in regard to the application of the proceeds of that investment.

One further interpretation of the net present value of $3,365 of the investment is possible. The $3,365 is like an unrealized capital gain. For an expenditure of $10,000 we obtain the right to proceeds whose present value totals $13,365 and whose net present value is $3,365. Before investing, we have $10,000 in cash; after investing, we have prospects of cash proceeds whose present value is $13,365. Thus our asset position can be improved in terms of present values (by $3,365) by making the investment.

present-value factors as prices

Suppose that a businessman is considering an investment that requires an immediate outlay of $100 that would generate proceeds of $60 at the end of each of the next two years. If the businessman understood that dollars received at different times have different value, he would request more information to make the investment decision. The additional data needed are today's prices (or values) for dollars to be received one and two years from now. Today's price for a dollar to be received today is $1.00. If the price of a dollar to be received one year from now is $.9091, and the price of a dollar two years from now is $.8264 (reflecting a 10 per cent time-value factor), the businessman is in a position to evaluate the future cash flows. He can multiply the price of each of the three kinds of dollars involved by their quantities and find the net benefit in terms of today's dollars. Thus:

Value of second period's benefits	$.8264 × 60 =	$ 49.58
Value of first period's benefits	$.9091 × 60 =	54.55
Total value of proceeds in terms of today's dollars		104.13
Less required outlay in today's dollars		100.00
Equals net benefit from the investment in terms of present value		$ 4.13

The example illustrates that the process of making investment decisions involves using market prices (when possible) to put otherwise noncomparable quantities (dollars of different time periods) on a comparable basis in terms of today's dollars. Second, calculating the net present value of an investment is equivalent to the net benefit from an investment in terms of today's dollars. The net present value of an investment simply measures the benefits (in terms of today's dollars) that can be earned by accepting the investment.

intuitive explanations of present value

Consider an investment that will generate cash flows of $10,000 one year from today and will cost $8,000. With a discount rate of 5 per cent the investment has a net present value of $1,524 [that is, ($10,000 × .9524) − 8,000]. The $1,524 is the present value of the unrealized profit that the firm will earn if the expectations are realized by operations immediately after the expenditure of the $8,000. The present value of the investment will be $9,524 and the cost is only $8,000, so there will be $1,524 of unrealized profit associated with the investment. An accountant would report $2,000 of income in period 1, but if 5 per cent of $8,000 is subtracted, we obtain a net earnings after interest of $1,600. The present value of $1,600 is $1,524.

Another useful interpretation of the net present value of the investment is that the firm could afford to pay $1,524 more than the cost of the investment and still break even (on a present-value basis) on the investment. For example, if the firm paid $9,524 for the investment, 5 per cent interest on $9,524 would be $476. Since the investment will earn $10,000, there will be enough cash to pay the original investment of $9,524 plus the $476 interest cost on the investment.

Describing the net present value of an investment as the amount you could afford to pay in excess of the scheduled cost is helpful in giving management an estimate of the amount of room for error that is in the estimation of the cost of the investment. It is a useful intuitive definition of net present value.

logical basis for the net present-value method

In our discussions of the net present-value method we have consciously chosen to present our explanation in terms that we hope have a maximum intuitive appeal. If the desirability of the net present-value method depended only on its intuitive appeal, there would be the possibility that somebody might discover or invent another method that had even stronger intuitive appeal. Our confidence in the net present-value method is derived from the fact that it is at least as good as any other solution to the problem of measuring the economic worth of an investment under certain well-defined circumstances.

First, we assume that a decision maker wants investment choices that give him the greatest satisfaction. The decision maker can be thought of as a single individual, a family unit, a business firm, or some other organizational entity. The satisfaction that the decision maker derives from the investment decisions depends upon the amount and timing of the cash flows that he is able to withdraw from his business operations. It may be helpful to think of these cash flows as consumption. In a business organization the analogue to consumption on the part of an individual is dividends paid to stockholders.

The decision maker faces two sets of decisions that together determine the pattern of consumption he will be able to enjoy. One set of decisions concerns his investment choices; the second determines how these investment choices will be financed.

Each possible investment alternative may be described by a series of cash flows representing the amount that would be paid out in each period or the amount that would be received in each period. The size and timing of the cash flows associated with each investment choice are assumed to be known in advance and with certainty. The number of separate investment choices open to the decision maker may be small or extremely large.

The cash flow of a period will be positive if the decision maker receives money in a given period and negative if he is required on balance to pay out money in that period. The cash flow received on a day can be used either for consumption on that day or for lending, in which case it will become available for consumption at some future date. Similarly, if outlays in excess of the current period's cash flows are required in the investment process for a particular period, these outlays may be obtained either by borrowing against future cash flows or by using proceeds from loans made in previous periods.

It is assumed that there is a known market rate of interest at which the individual can lend as much as he wants or borrow as much as he wants. The only restriction on borrowing is that loans must be repayable out of future cash flows.

How should the decision maker select from among the investment options open to him in such a way that it will be possible for him to achieve the maximum attainable level of satisfaction? All the investment opportunities should be arranged into groups of mutually exclusive investments. Some of these groups may contain only one option; others may contain a large number of mutually exclusive options. From each mutually exclusive group select the investment whose net present value is algebraically the largest when the net present value is computed at the market rates of interest. If this investment has a positive net present value, accept it; otherwise, reject all the investments in that mutually exclusive group.

Now imagine that the decision maker has selected from among all the investment options open to him the ones that have a positive net present value and that do not violate the restriction that no more than one of a set of mutually exclusive investments can be accepted. These investments will determine the amount of money he will receive or must pay out in each time period as a result of his investments.

Assume that the decision maker has two independent investment opportunities with the following cash flows projected:

	Period		
Investment	0	1	2
A	− $ 900	$1,000	
B	− 1,500		$2,000

The rate of interest (this is both the borrowing and lending rate) is assumed to be .05. All we need to know to make the investment decisions is the present value of these two investments ($52.40 for A and $314 for B). Because the two present values are positive, the investments should be undertaken, and no further information or computations are required. The investor can borrow the funds at a cost of .05 and repay the debt using the cash flows from the investments. There is no question that the funds should be obtained to finance the investments. The conclusion not only holds for the two investments illustrated, but is valid for any investment with a positive present value using the .05 borrowing rate. (Remember that there is no uncertainty; thus the cash flows of the investments are known.)

So far we have not taken consumption preferences into consideration. It is not necessary to make restrictive assumptions about the nature of these preferences. We are assuming that the decision maker knows whether he prefers one of several alternatives or whether he is indifferent. Assume also that, other things being equal, he prefers more consumption to less. Specifically, if two patterns of consumption are identical in all time periods except one, and if the first pattern of consumption results in more consumption in a given time period than the second pattern of consumption, the decision maker will prefer the first to the second.

Accepting investments A and B will enable the investor to finance any pattern of consumption he may desire, provided the present value of the amounts consumed does not exceed the sum of the net present values of the investments accepted, in this case $366.40. If the investor is presented with a third independent investment option whose net present value is positive, he should accept it. By doing so he will be able to increase the amount he consumes in one or more periods without having to decrease consumption in any period. On the other hand, if the investor is presented with another investment option whose net present value is negative, he should reject it. Accepting it would require him to reduce, in one or more periods, the amounts he consumed. The details of the investor's consumption preferences do not need to be known in order to advise him about which investments to accept. One would need to know something about these consumption preferences in order to advise him about how to finance the investment—that is, what loans he should make and when they should be repaid.

Assume that a decision maker selects his investments using the present-value procedure and then makes the appropriate financial decisions—that is, he does not borrow more than he can eventually repay. The appropriate financial decisions are those that enable him to reach as high a level of satisfaction as is possible given his opportunities. No other method of selecting investments can, in these circumstances, lead to a different selection of investments that will enable the decision maker to reach a higher level of satisfaction than that reached using present value. It is possible that a different method of selecting investments may lead to the same level of satisfaction.

qualifications

The problem we have just described is not exactly the problem faced in practice by businessmen. There are two important ways in which businessmen might feel that the problems they face are different from the problem just described.

The businessman may feel that the financial alternatives open to him are not considered in the preceding problem. He may feel that he is not able to obtain any additional funds, or if he borrows, the lender may impose undesirable restrictions on his actions, or he may not know for future dates what the cost of borrowing or the return from lending will be. In any of these circumstances the present-value method, as we have described it, is not strictly applicable. Second, the businessman may not feel he is able to predict with perfect certainty the cash-flow consequences of his investment alternatives. Thus he cannot describe the outcome of making an investment in terms of a single set of cash flows. Rather, there may be a large number of possible cash flows, any of which could be the outcome of selecting the particular investment, and the businessman does not know in advance which one of the possible outcomes will occur.

Later we shall consider what modifications should be made to the net present-value method to make it more useful as a method of selecting investments in these more general circumstances.

questions and problems

4-1. Assume a cost of money of 10 per cent. How much could you afford to pay now for $1,000 per year (payable at the end of each year, with the first payment a year from now) for (a) five years; (b) ten years; (c) twenty years; (d) thirty years; (e) perpetuity?

4-2. It costs $20,000 to make a new machine that promises to return cash flows of $10,000 per year for five years. Assume a cost of money of 10 per cent. How much could you pay the owner for the patent rights to this machine and still be no worse off than if the new machine were not made?

4-3. If the patent rights for the machine described in problem 4-2 could be purchased for $10,000, what is the largest extra dividend the company could declare immediately on the basis of the net cash flows expected from these transactions?

4-4. Assume the transactions described in problem 4-3 were financed by a "loan" costing 10 per cent. How large a loan would be required? Set up a payment schedule for this loan so that the machine is self-financing.

4-5. If the "loan" described in problem 4-4 were to be repaid in a single payment (including "interest"), what financial arrangements would be required at the end of five years?

4-6. There are two investments that have different degrees of risk associated with them. With the first investment it is thought that a dollar to be received one period from now is worth $.9524 today (implying a 5 per cent rate of discount). With the second investment it is thought that a dollar to be received one period from now is worth $.9091 (implying a 10 per cent rate of discount). Use the implied rates of discount to determine the value today of $1 to be received fifty years from now, for each of the two investments.

4-7. Mr. Jones can borrow $1,000 or more at a cost of 6 per cent. He has an investment opportunity costing $1,000 that will earn 10 per cent. Should his consumption preferences affect the amount he invests or borrows?

4-8. The ABC Company has an investment opportunity that costs $6,000, has a life of one year, and will return $10,000 one period from the time of the investment. Money can be borrowed at a cost of 5 per cent.

Required: (a) What is the net present value of the investment? (b) Assume the company borrows $9,524 from the bank and purchases the investment. How much can it pay as immediate dividend and still repay the loan? (c) If the investment cost $9,524, what would be the yield of the investment?

4-9. The ABC Company has an investment opportunity that requires an immediate outlay of $10,000 and will have a payoff of $12,155 four years from now. It can borrow short-term funds now for the investment at a cost of .04, and then at the end of the first year it will be able to issue a long-term debt at a cost of .06.

Required: Should the investment be undertaken?

4-10. *The N Manufacturing Company*
A product is currently being manufactured with an old machine, and the costs of the product are as follows:

	Unit Costs
Labor, direct	$ 4.00
Labor, variable indirect	2.00
Other variable overhead	1.50
Fixed overhead	2.50
	$10.00

In the past year 10,000 units were produced and sold for $8 per unit. It is expected that with suitable repairs the old machine can be used indefinitely in the future, but it has no salvage or trade-in value. A new machine would cost $60,000 and the project costs associated with new machine are as follows:

Labor, direct	$2.00
Labor, variable indirect	3.00
Other variable overhead	1.00
Fixed overhead	2.25
	$8.25

The fixed overhead costs are allocations from other departments plus the depreciation of the equipment. It is not expected that the costs of these departments will be changed by the acquisition of the new equipment.

The new machine has an expected life of ten years.

The appropriate time discount rate for this company is .05.

It is expected that future demand of the product will remain at 10,000 units per year for the next ten years. After ten years the product will be obsolete.

Required: (a) Should the new equipment be acquired? (b) If the product can be purchased at a cost of $7 per unit from a reliable supplier, should it be purchased or made?

chapter 5

What is usually called a reasonable wage, or a reasonable profit, proves on investigation to be not so much "reasonable" as "usual," to be in fact the wage or profit determined by free competition under the prevailing conditions of time and place.

—Knut Wicksell, *Lecture on Political Economy, Vol. I* (London: George Routledge and Sons, Ltd., 1946), p. 51.

classifying investments

Investments tend to involve large expenditures that benefit many time periods, and to have lives longer or shorter than the time period for which the decision is being made. In these situations we find it useful to compute the annual equivalent cost of utilizing a long-lived asset. This concept has a large number of potential uses, including computing the cost of making a product and solving the decision problem when different alternatives or components have different lives.

Before proceeding with the annual equivalent cost computation, we shall discuss the classification of investments. For many purposes it is helpful to be able to use one or two words to describe a class of investments or investment decisions. We shall suggest a wide range of classification schemes.

methods of classifying investments

Any useful scheme of controlling investments must be based on a classification of types of investments. Different kinds of investments raise different problems, are of different relative importance to the firm, and will require different persons to evaluate their significance. By classifying types of investments, each investment proposal will receive attention from persons qualified to analyze it.

Investments may be classified according to the following categories:

1. The kinds of scarce resources used by the investment. For example, whether or not the investment requires important amounts of cash, of floor space, of the time of key personnel (and personnel may also be

classified: sales, production, research, top management, legal staff, and so on).

2. The amount of each of the resources that is required. For example, with respect to the amount of immediate cash outlays required, we could classify investments as requiring less than $500, between $500 and $5,000, and over $5,000.

3. The way benefits from the investment are affected by other possible investments. Some investments stand on their own feet. Others will be improved if supplementary investments are made; still others will be useless if competing investments are accepted. For example, the worth of another fork-lift truck may depend on whether or not the plan for adding an automatic conveyor system is accepted.

4. The form in which the benefits are received. Thus investments may generate greater cash flows, reduce the risks associated with poor business conditions, reduce the accident rate, improve employee morale, or eliminate a community nuisance such as excessive smoke or noise.

5. Whether the incremental benefits are the result of lower cost or increased sales, or whether they merely prevent a decline in sales or market share.

6. The functional activity to which the investments are most closely related. Thus an oil company may classify investments according to the following activities: exploration, production, transportation, refining, or marketing.

7. The industry classification of the investment. Thus the manager of a conglomerate may want to know if the investment being considered has to do with its professional football team, producing steel, or space activities.

8. The degree of necessity. Some investments are necessary in the sense that if they are not undertaken the entire operation stops (the stoppage may be desirable, thus the *necessity* may not be absolute). Other investments are highly optional and move the firm in directions it does not have to go in order to keep operating.

Many other methods of classification could be suggested.[1] Clearly no single scheme of classification will be equally valid for all uses or for all companies. The essential task is to develop a classification system for investments that is appropriate to the activity of the business and the organizational structure of the particular company.

In this book we are first concerned with investments for which both the resources used and the benefits to be received can be measured to an im-

---

[1] An interesting discussion of possible methods of classifying investments can be found in Joel Dean, *Capital Budgeting* (New York: Columbia University Press, 1951), pp. 82–88.

portant degree in terms of cash flows. Second, the analytical methods developed in this book will be most useful for investments that are important enough to the firm to warrant a relatively careful study of their potential profitability. Next we shall consider a classification of investments that is based on the way the benefits from a given investment are affected by other possible investments.

dependent and independent investments

In evaluating the investment proposals presented to management, it is important to be aware of the possible interrelationships between pairs of investment proposals. A given investment proposal may be economically independent of, or dependent on, another investment proposal. The first investment proposal will be said to be *economically independent* of the second if the cash flows (or more generally the costs and benefits) expected from the first investment would be the same regardless of whether the second investment were accepted or rejected. If the cash flows associated with the first investment are affected by the decision to accept or reject the second investment, the first investment is said to be economically dependent on the second. It should be clear that, when one investment is dependent on another, some attention must be given to the question of whether decisions about the first investment can or should be made separately from decisions about the second.

economically independent investments

In order for investment A to be economically independent of investment B, two conditions must be satisfied. First, it must be technically possible to undertake investment A whether or not investment B is accepted. Thus it is *not* possible to build a school and shopping center on the same site, and therefore the proposal to build the one is not independent of a proposal to build the other. Second, the net benefits to be expected from the first investment must not be affected by the acceptance or rejection of the second. If the estimates of the cash outlays and the cash inflows for investment A are not the same when B is either accepted or rejected, the two investments are not independent. Thus it is technically possible to build a toll bridge and operate a ferry across adjacent points on a river, but the two investments are not independent because the proceeds from one will be affected by the existence of the other. The two investments would not be economically independent in the sense in which we are using the term, even if the traffic across the river at this point were sufficient to operate profitably both the bridge and the ferry.

Sometimes two investments cannot both be accepted because the firm does not have enough cash to finance both. This situation could occur if the amount of cash available for investments were strictly limited by management rather than by the capital market, or if increments of funds obtained from the capital market cost more than previous increments. In such a situation the acceptance of one investment may cause the rejection of the other. But we shall not then say that the two investments are economically dependent. To do so would make all investments for such a firm dependent, and this is not a useful definition for our purposes.

economically dependent investments

The dependency relationship can be further classified. If a decision to undertake the second investment will increase the benefits expected from the first (or decrease the costs of undertaking the first without changing the benefits), the second investment is said to be a *complement* of the first. If the decision to undertake the second investment will decrease the benefits expected from the first (or increase the costs of undertaking the first without changing the benefits), the second is said to be a *substitute* for the first. In the extreme case where the potential benefits to be derived from the first investment will completely disappear if the second investment is accepted, or where it is technically impossible to undertake the first when the second has been accepted, the two investments are said to be *mutually exclusive*. It is also possible to define an extreme case for investments that are complements. Suppose that the second investment is impossible (technologically) or would result in no benefits whatsoever if the first investment were not accepted. Then the first investment can be said to be a *prerequisite* of the second.

It may be helpful to think of the possible relationships between investments as being arrayed along a line segment. At the extreme left we have the situation where investment A is a prerequisite to investment B. In the center of the line we have a situation where investment A is independent of investment B. At the extreme right-hand end of the line we have the situation where investment A is mutually exclusive with respect to investment B. As we move to the right from the left-hand side of the line, we have varying degrees of complementariness, decreasing as we proceed to the right. Similarly, on the right-hand side of the line we represent varying degrees of substitutability, increasing as we proceed outward to the right. The following is a graphic representation.

Prerequisite		*Independent*		*Mutually exclusive*
Strong complement	Weak complement		Weak substitute	Strong substitute

One additional complication in connection with complementary investments should be mentioned here. The complementary relationship need not be symmetrical. Suppose that we consider the building of a new factory as one investment and the purchase of an air-conditioning unit for the factory as the second investment. The two investments are clearly complementary. But the relationship need not be symmetrical, because the new factory may be profitable without air conditioning. With air conditioning, worker efficiency may go up, so that the factory is even more profitable. The additional efficiency resulting from the addition of air conditioning may properly be called the return or benefits resulting from the expenditure on air-conditioning equipment. But the air-conditioning equipment by itself is useless unless there is a factory in which it can be used. The factory is a prerequisite to the investment for the air-conditioning equipment, but the air conditioning is not a prerequisite to the investment in the factory building.

statistical dependence

It is possible for two or more investments to be economically independent but statistically dependent. Statistical dependence is said to be present if the cash flows from two or more investments would be affected by some external event or happening whose occurrence is uncertain. For example, a firm could produce high-priced yachts and expensive cars. The investment decisions affecting these two product lines are economically independent. However, the fortunes of both activities are closely associated with high business activity and a large amount of discretionary income for the "rich" people. This statistical dependence may affect the risk of investments in these product lines, because the swings of profitability of these two product lines will be wider than those of two product lines having less statistical dependence. Statistical dependence is defined and its importance for investment decisions discussed in Part II.

administrative implications

The number of possible relationships that may exist between pairs of complementary investments is very large. In dealing with investments that are complementarily related, the most effective technique is to combine sets of investment proposals in such a way that the new proposal is either an independent proposal or one of a set of mutually exclusive proposals. In the preceding example, instead of considering two complementary investment proposals, a factory and the air-conditioning equipment for the factory, we can reformulate the problem as one involving a choice between mutually exclusive investment alternatives—a factory with air conditioning or a factory without air conditioning.

In most large organizations, operating procedures require that proposals for capital investment which exceed specified limits must be submitted by the sponsor to higher executive levels for review and approval before actual expenditures can be authorized. Except in unusual circumstances such proposals should consist of independent investment proposals for which an accept or reject decision is appropriate; or they should comprise a set of mutually exclusive proposals, such that either the whole set must be rejected or only one of the mutually exclusive alternatives can be accepted.

No system of controlling capital expenditures can operate effectively if management finds that, after having approved a seemingly highly profitable investment, additional investments that do not generate any profits on their own account are presented as being absolutely necessary to implement the profit potential of the initial investment proposals.

Example:

The research and development section of a large chemical manufacturing firm submitted technical data on a new product to one of the firm's operating divisions. After investigation of the product by the engineering, production, and sales staffs, the operating division management decided that the product should be added to their line. Because existing facilities were not adequate for the production of the new product, a capital appropriation request for the new plant and equipment was submitted for review and approval to the firm's executive committee. On review by the executive committee the following deficiencies were uncovered: (1) The appropriation request did not include an estimate of the working capital requirements that would be required to operate the new plant and market the resulting product; (2) one of the raw materials required in the new process would be purchased from another operating division of the company, and the increased output of that division would have required additional plant and equipment expenditures by the supplier division; (3) the new product was partially competitive with one of the company's existing products, and the decline in the profit potential from this existing product had not been taken into consideration; (4) distribution of the new product would require acquisition of additional storage facilities, because demand for the product was seasonal, but efficient production would require a steady rate of production. The proposal was returned to the operating division for further study. After additional investigation it was determined that the company could most effectively utilize the new product by licensing other manufacturers to produce and market it.

In developing an investment proposal to be submitted to higher levels for review and approval, the sponsor and his staff should normally include as a part of the single package whatever complementary investments seem necessary or desirable. Similarly, if the proposed investment will serve as a partial substitute for any investments to which the firm is already committed or which are under consideration, this fact should be noted in submitting the proposals.

If some of the choices involved in planning the investment are considered sufficiently important that the final decision must be made by top management, the investment proposals should be submitted in the form of a set of mutually exclusive alternatives. Examples would be the decision on the location of a new plant or the possibility of including an important piece of auxiliary equipment. This procedure has the advantage of enabling top management to examine in an orderly fashion the major alternatives involved. It also enables management to make decisions at a stage in the planning of the expenditure when the special knowledge, experience, and insight of the senior executives can be effectively brought to bear on the proposal. Too often such choices are not presented to management until previous commitments have largely foreclosed the opportunity to exercise choice, and management is presented in effect with a *fait accompli.*

Ordinarily, the cost figures contained in an investment proposal submitted to top management will be based on a careful but necessarily preliminary estimate of the final cost of the proposed project. On major projects the expensive step of preparing detailed specifications and working drawings should be deferred until the project has actually been approved. Once approval has been obtained, management will proceed with the detailed planning of the project. At this stage a great many decisions will have to be made on such questions as the type of materials to be used in construction, the choice of equipment, and even the location of a plant if no definite decision on this point was made in the preliminary plans. Given the general approval for the project as a whole, these choices are mainly among different ways of accomplishing the same objective—that is, the alternatives are mutually exclusive. Although the most important of these choices, such as plant location, may be submitted to higher management levels, many of the less important decisions will necessarily be made by lower levels of management or by staff personnel.

To ensure coordination when decision making is decentralized, it is necessary to set up means of communicating information about the policies and objectives of the organization so that decisions made independently in various parts of the organization will contribute to the goals of the organization. When the decentralized decision-making powers grant authority to make investment-type decisions, the procedures recommended in this book can provide an important means of assuring that uniform standards of choice consistent with overall organizational goals are available to the many separate decision-making centers.

As could be expected, these problems occur not only in business organizations but also in nonprofit organizations, both public and private. The following example is based on a situation that occurred in a university.

Example:

The head of the buildings and grounds department of a large university obtained approval to replace and modernize the lighting system in one of the university gymnasiums. The old lighting system had been installed thirty years earlier, when the building was built. It was expensive to maintain, and the quality of the lighting was definitely low by modern standards. The detailed job of designing the new lighting system was turned over to a lighting engineer in the Office of the University Architect. Three types of lighting equipment were initially considered. Of these, one was eliminated on the basis of having excessive glare for this application. The two remaining possibilities were both capable of producing satisfactory light conditions, and therefore an attempt was made to choose between the two on the basis of cost. The cost analysis disclosed that system A would require a high initial outlay but would have low maintenance and operating costs. System B would require lower initial outlays but higher maintenance and operating costs than system A. As a result, the lighting engineer felt that no clear choice could be made on the basis of cost; therefore, the final decision was made on the basis of admittedly unimportant differences in the quality of the light produced by the two systems. If the engineer had applied the discounted cash flow approach, taking into account the fact that the university was able to earn a 4.5 per cent return on its funds, it would have been clear that system A had a very decided cost advantage.

comparability

The problem of comparability arises if the profitability of future investment proposals will be affected by decisions made currently. A group of investments will be said to be comparable (and mutually exclusive) if the profitability of subsequent investment possibilities will be the same, regardless of which investment is accepted or if all are rejected. Investment alternatives should be combined into groups that are both mutually exclusive and comparable before a final decision is made.

For example, a new plant could be heated by using forced hot air or steam. These are mutually exclusive alternatives. However, they are not comparable if it seems likely that the installation of an air-conditioning system will become necessary at some time in the future. The air-conditioning system would cost less to install in a building already equipped with air vents, and the present value of this difference in expected costs should be taken into account when choosing the heating system.

This simple example brings out two points. First, it may not be practical to make a group of mutually exclusive investment alternatives exactly comparable. In designing a new plant, the number of possible changes that may be desirable at some future date (such as remodeling, installation of new machinery, and additions or extensions) is very large, and the cost of each such possible change will depend upon the basic plant design originally adopted. In such circumstances, to make an analysis of truly comparable investments would require consideration of an unduly large number of alternatives.

Second, the importance of having mutually exclusive investments comparable is a matter of degree. In choosing a heating system for a new plant, the importance of the fact that future installation of air conditioning would be more expensive with steam heating will depend on the likelihood that air conditioning will eventually be required, the lapse of time until it may be required, the extent of the extra installation costs, and so on. In deciding whether a group of mutually exclusive alternatives is sufficiently comparable for practical purposes, one must apply a reasonable approach.

comparable alternatives with different lives

In practice, the question frequently arises, "Must mutually exclusive investment alternatives have the same lives in order to be comparable?" The answer is no. In some instances investment alternatives with different lives will be comparable; in other instances equal future time periods are necessary to achieve comparability.

An example of comparable mutually exclusive alternatives not having the same life occurs in connection with deciding how to exploit a new patented product. One alternative is to sell the patent rights to another firm. This results in a single, lump-sum payment. The patent may also be exploited by manufacturing and selling the product.

In this example the two choices are comparable, although the expected cash proceeds from one would extend only one year, and from the second for a longer period of time. When this is the case, the two alternatives should be compared using the net present value of each over its own life. For example, if selling the patent rights would generate immediate cash proceeds of $2 million and manufacturing and selling the product would produce cash flows having a net present value of $1.5 million over a twelve-year period, the immediate sale is more desirable.

It is possible to compare these two alternatives using equivalent annual returns, but to do this we must divide the comparable net present values by an annuity factor for a common period. For example, suppose that the appropriate discount rate is 8 per cent and we wish to find the equivalent annual return from each alternative for a twelve-year period. The annuity factor B(12, .08) is approximately 7.5. The equivalent annual return from selling the patent rights is $2,000,000/7.5 = $266,667. The comparable equivalent annual return from producing and manufacturing the product is $1,500,000/7.5 = $200,000. Dividing by 7.5 in both cases cannot change the decision.

comparability and mutually exclusive investments

When mutually exclusive investments have unequal lives, we have essentially three choices of assumptions that we can make.

1. We can assume that at the expiration of life of each asset the firm will invest in assets that earn the time value of money.[2] In this case the alternatives are comparable even though their lives are unequal.
2. We can assume that the firm will reinvest in assets of exactly the same characteristics as those currently being used.
3. We can make specific assumptions about the reinvestment opportunities that will become available in the future.

The present-value method will lead to a correct decision with all three assumptions as long as the facts of the decision are consistent with the method chosen.

The third alternative is the best of the three and does not require elaboration. It is easy in theory, but is the most difficult to implement in practice because it requires a great deal of forecasting about the future. The first alternative is the simplest of the three in practice, because it merely requires the computation of the present value of the first round of equipment with no further forecasts about the future (other than the implicit forecast that the time value of money will be earned). We shall consider in more detail the implementation of the assumption that the firm will reinvest in assets of exactly the same characteristics as those currently being used.

As an example, suppose that there are two mutually exclusive investments, A and B, with the following characteristics:

	Cash Flows for Period			
Investment	0	1	2	3
A	− $10,000	$12,000		
B	− 10,000	5,000	$5,000	$5,000

[2] Under uncertainty the assumption required is that at the expiration of the life of each asset the firm will invest in other assets whose expected rate of return is the minimum required for the risk involved.

A and B may be different types of equipment that perform the same task, with A having a life of one year and B a life of three years. With a cost of money of 10 per cent, the present values of the cash flows of A and B with assumption 1 are as follows:

Investment	Present Value of Cash Flows
A	$ 909
B	2,434

Investment B would seem to be the more desirable investment; however, this analysis is incomplete if we assume (assumption 2) that after one year the equipment of type A (or similar equipment) will again be purchased. Where it is likely that investment A will be repeated at the beginning of periods 2 and 3, the following cash flows would occur for investment A:

Investment	Period			
	0	1	2	3
A	− $10,000	− $10,000	− $10,000	
		12,000	12,000	$12,000

The present value of the cash flows as now presented is $2,488 for investment A; thus A is more desirable than B. When the mutually exclusive investments have unequal lives, we may want to take into consideration the possibility of reinvesting in a similar type of equipment.

If we choose assumption 3, we have to forecast the nature of the equipment available after one period and after two periods for investment A.

In most situations the lowest common multiple of the lives of the two investments results in a length of time longer than the life of the longest-lived alternative. For example, if there are two types of equipment, one of which has a life of three years and the other of eight years, the lowest common multiple of lives is twenty-four years. In a situation of this nature the equivalent cost per year, the cost for perpetuity, or the present value of the costs for twenty-four years could be computed. The equipment with the lowest cost would be the most desirable alternative. The three methods of computation being discussed will all lead to the same decision. Each method implicitly adopts assumption 2.

Example:

Assume that two pieces of equipment have the following characteristics:

Equipment	Expected Life (Years)	Initial Cost	Operating Cost per Year
X	3	$10,000	$2,000
Y	8	30,000	1,500

This problem can be solved by taking the lowest common multiple of 8 and 3, twenty-four years, and by computing the costs for a twenty-four-year period.

Annual Equivalent Cost

An alternative procedure is to compute the equivalent cost per year of an outlay of $10,000 every three years, and the equivalent cost per year of an outlay of $30,000 every eight years.

$RB(3, .10)$

$10,000   R   R   R

| | | |
0   1   2   3

$$RB(3, .10) = \$10,000$$
$$R \times 2.4869 = \$10,000$$
$$R = \$\ 4,021 \quad \text{Annual equivalent of}$$
$$\$10,000 \text{ every three years}$$

$$RB(8, .10) = \$30,000$$
$$R \times 5.3349 = \$30,000$$
$$R = \$5,623 \quad \text{Annual equivalent of}$$
$$\$30,000 \text{ every eight years}$$

The equivalent cost per year of using equipment X is $6,021 (that is, 2,000 + 4,021), and the equivalent cost per year of using equipment Y is $7,123 (that is, 1,500 + 5,623). On the basis of annual equivalent costs, X is the more desirable equipment.

To find the cost of using the equipment forever, we multiply the equivalent cost per year by the present value of a perpetuity. The general formula for the present value of a perpetuity of $1 a period is

$$\text{Present value of a perpetuity} = \frac{1}{r}$$

where r is the appropriate rate of interest.

Since r is equal to .10, the factor in this example is 10. The present value of using X forever is 10 × $6,021, or $60,210. The present value of using Y is

$71,230. Because the equivalent annual costs of both alternatives are being multiplied by a constant factor of 10, the relative merits of the alternatives are not changed. X remains more desirable than Y.

replacement chains

Suppose that a real estate company is considering whether to remodel a motel and to continue operating it for an additional ten years, or to raze the old motel and build a new one that would have an economic life of twenty years.

If the alternatives were comparable, we would compare the present value of expected cash outlays and proceeds from the two unequal-lived streams. However, in this instance the two investments are not comparable. If the company chooses to remodel the existing motel now and scrap it after ten years, it will then have the options of selling the land, building a new motel, or using the land in some other way. These possibilities must be taken into account in making the present decision.

One possibility is to convert the two investments into equivalent average annual cash flows. Suppose that the company has a cost of money of 10 per cent and that remodeling the old motel would yield a net present value at 10 per cent of $100,000 during the next ten years. To convert this into equivalent annual cash flows, we would find the annual amount for ten years, which has a present value of $100,000. Similarly, if the expected net present value from building a new motel were $125,000, we would find the twenty-year annuity which has a present value of $125,000. At 10 per cent the equivalent annual payments are $16,274 and $14,682. With this system the alternative having the largest equivalent annual cash flow is most favorable. Note that, by using net present value, building a new motel is favored; by using equivalent annual returns, remodeling the present motel is better. Using net present value, we ignore the profits that could result from using the land during years 11 through 20, when the present motel will be torn down if it is remodeled now. This creates a bias towards the alternative of building a new motel now. On the other hand, by converting to equivalent annual returns, we assume that an investment as profitable as remodeling the current motel will reappear ten years from now. Another possible assumption would be that ten years from now it will be possible to build a new motel that would be as profitable and long-lived as the new motel to be built now. Although it may turn out upon investigation in a particular case that this assumption is reasonable, we cannot assume that this will be the case.

If we considered ourselves sufficiently clairvoyant, we might attempt to estimate the cost of building a new motel ten years from now and also the cash proceeds that would be generated by operating this new motel. Even this would be of little avail if it turned out that this new motel would last for more than an additional ten years, because the two alternatives would not then be comparable.

Sometimes a practical solution is found by putting an upper or lower limit on the value of potential future opportunities. For example, in the motel problem one can safely estimate that, if the motel is remodeled now, in ten years there will be a potential cash flow of at least equal to the value of the land at that time. It may turn out that even an optimistic estimate of the value of the land will not be sufficient to make the alternative of remodeling the old motel more attractive than the prospect of constructing a new motel.

components of unequal lives

An investment alternative (possibly one of several mutually exclusive investments) may be made up of several components of unequal lives. For example, we may have a building with a life of fifty years costing $5 million, a furnace with a life of twenty-five years costing $4 million (exclusive of lining), and a furnace lining costing $1 million with a life of four years. With a time value of money of .05, the annual equivalent cost for the first four years of operations is

$$\frac{5,000,000}{B(50, .05)} = \frac{5,000,000}{18.25593} = \$273,884 \quad \text{Cost of building}$$

$$\frac{4,000,000}{B(25, .05)} = \frac{4,000,000}{14.09394} = \ 283,810 \quad \text{Cost of furnace}$$

$$\frac{1,000,000}{B(4, .05)} = \frac{1,000,000}{3.54595} = \ 282,012 \quad \text{Cost of furnace lining}$$

Total annual equivalent cost = $839,705

cost of excess capacity

It is easy to conclude incorrectly that excess capacity has no costs—that is, sunk costs are not relevant to incremental decisions. Assume that the ABC Chemical Corporation has extra boiler capacity and is considering the addition of a new product which will take one half of the extra capacity. How is the cost of the boiler brought into the analysis? The quick, easy answer is to say there is no boiler cost. Unfortunately, this conclusion may not be correct. Add the information that undertaking the new product and using one half of the excess capacity moves up the expected date of purchase of a new utility system from five to three years in the future. This acceleration of purchase has costs, and these costs are part of the new-product decision.

The means of incorporating the cost of accelerating the acquisition are not obvious. Assume that the expected cost of the boiler acquisition is $2.595 million and it has an estimated life of fifteen years. With a cost of money of .05, the annual equivalent cost per year of use is

$$CB(15, .05) = \$2,595,000$$
$$10.38C = \$2,595,000$$
$$C = \$250,000.$$

Without the new product, years 4 and 5 will not have the cost of a new boiler. With the new product there is an additional equivalent cost of $250,000 for years 4 and 5.

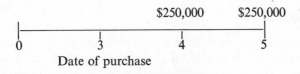

Date of purchase

The present value of the additional costs is $401,550.

$$.8227 \times 250,000 = \$205,675$$
$$.7835 \times 250,000 = 195,875$$
$$\overline{\$401,550}$$

An advocate of the new product might argue that the cost should be less because the degree of utilization of the boiler during the first two years will be very low, and there will not be much wear and tear. If we assume no wear and tear (also no obsolescence), there would only be the interest cost of $129,750 (.05 of $2,595,000) occurring four and five years in the future. Just taking interest into account gives a cost of approximately $208,404 present value.

$$.8227 \times 129,750 = \$106,745$$
$$.7835 \times 129,750 = 101,659$$
$$\overline{\$208,404}$$

However, some amortization of cost for tax purposes and some decrease in value (that is, depreciation) should be recognized. Thus the exact present value of the cost of adding the product has not been determined. One estimate is $401,550, but it could be $208,404 if we assume the life of the new equipment is not shortened by the early purchase. Including either of these estimates is better than assuming that there is no cost associated with using the excess capacity.

We may want to include an analysis in which we did not include the capacity cost but rather dropped the product when capacity was reached and it was time to add new facilities. This possibility should be checked out, but generally it is appropriate to assume that once the product is added it will be produced in the future. This will tend to occur because of the momentum principle (it is difficult for a firm to change directions), and because after the costs of getting a product under way have been incurred, there is a good chance that an economic analysis would indicate the desirability of continuing the sale of the product and taking advantage of the goodwill that was created.

conclusions

Although techniques such as those we are recommending force one to make difficult estimates in the face of imperfect and incomplete information, they have the advantage of focusing attention on the important unknowns. Simpler techniques achieve their simplicity by using general assumptions about the nature of future opportunities rather than conjectures tailor-made to a particular situation. They save time and effort at the expense of a less precise analysis of the decision-making situation.

questions and problems

5-1. The Roger Company has the choice between two different types of dies. One type costs less, but also has a shorter life expectancy. The expected cash flows after taxes for the two different dies are as follows:

		Period			
Die	*0*	*1*	*2*	*3*	*4*
A	($10,000)	$8,000	$8,000		
B	(12,000)	5,000	5,000	$5,000	$5,000

The cost of money of the firm is 10 per cent.
Required: Choose the more desirable die. Explain.

5-2. Assume that there are two mutually exclusive investments that have the following cash flows:

		Period	Rate of Return
Investment	0	1	(%)
A	($10,000)	$12,000	20
B	(5,000)	6,000	20

Assume that either investment will require modification to the basic building structure, which will cost $1,000, and that this amount is not included in the preceding computations. The cost of money is 10 per cent.

Required: (a) Compute the actual yields of the investments. (b) Does the additional $1,000 change the ranking of the two investments? Explain.

5-3. Consider the following two mutually exclusive investments.

		Period	
Investment	0	1	Rate of Return
A	($20,000)	$ 30,000	.50
B	(100,000)	130,000	.30

Required: Assuming a cost of money of .10, which investment is to be preferred?

5-4. An existing machine must be replaced. Two new models are under consideration. Both cost $15,000. Model X will generate savings of $10,000 per year and has a life of two years. Model Y will generate savings of $18,000 per year; it has a life of one year. The machine will be needed for two years. Which model should be purchased if the cost of money is .05?

5-5. Assume that two pieces of equipment have the following characteristics:

Equipment	Expected Life (Years)	Initial Cost	Operating Cost per Year
A	9	$20,000	$10,000
B	5	25,000	8,000

Required: Assuming a cost of money of .10, which equipment is the more desirable?

5-6. The A Corporation's computer currently has excess capacity. The controller would like to prepare and distribute a report that would take approximately one hour a day of the computer's time. The computer could do this task and still have excess capacity. The annual cost of this type of computer is $1 million a year. The discount rate is .05. The long-range planning group estimates that without the report the corporation would be shifting to a more powerful computer five years from now. With the report, they estimate the shift four years from now. The new computer will cost $1.5 million per year. Assume that the computer payments take place at the end of each year.

Required: What is your estimate of the cost of adding the report?

5-7. The New York State Utility Company is considering the construction of a new utility plant. It has accumulated the following cost information:

	Fossil Plant (Oil and Gas)	Nuclear Energy Plant
Initial outlay	$60,000,000	$100,000,000
Annual operating cost	15,000,000	20,000,000*

* This is the projected cost for year 1. It is expected that the operating costs will decrease by $2,000,000 per year and level off at $10,000,000. The expected decrease is a result of decreased fuel costs. Both plants have an expected useful life of fifty years.

Assume a time value of money of .05 per year.

Required: (a) Which plant should be built? (b) Assume that the only question is the year of construction of the nuclear plant. Should it be built now, assuming that the needed electricity for the first five years can be purchased at a cost of $16 million per year? Should it be built in year 6? (c) If the fossil plant were built, would you replace it at the end of six years with a nuclear plant? Assume that the preceding cost projections are valid and that the nuclear plant would still cost $100 million.

5-8. Continuing part b of problem 5-7. Assume that the cost of the needed electricity is $17 million: (a) Should the nuclear plant be built now? (b) Compute the present value today of building (that is, completing) the nuclear plant six years from now when the operating costs would be $10 million per year, compared to buying electricity.

5-9. The A Corporation is considering the construction of a new plant to build a component part that it is currently purchasing. It has the following information:

	Cost	Expected Life
Plant	$20,000,000	Forty years
Utilities	10,000,000	Twenty years
Equipment	15,000,000	Ten years

The operating costs are estimated at $5 million per year, assuming an output of 1 million units of product per year.

The corporation uses a discount rate of .05. It can purchase the product at a cost of $10 per unit. Should the new plant be built (on a straight economic basis)?

5-10. A company is considering two alternative marketing strategies for a new product. Introducing the product will require an outlay of $15,000. With a low price the product will generate cash proceeds of $10,000 per year and will have a life of two years. With a high price the product will generate cash proceeds of $18,000, but will have a life of only one year. The cost of money for the company is .05. Which marketing strategy should be accepted?

5-11. Compare your answers to problems 5-4 and 5-10. Are the relevant cash flows the same in both problems? If not, why?

5-12. State Electric wants to decide whether to repair or replace electric meters when they break down. A new meter costs $30 and on the average will go twelve years without repair. It costs $18 to repair a meter, and a repaired meter will, on the average, go eight years before it again needs a repair. Repairs can be made repeatedly to meters because they are essentially rebuilt each time they are repaired. It costs $6 to take out and reinstall a meter. The time value of money is .05.

Required: Should the company repair old meters or buy new meters?

5-13. *Fall River Lumber Company*

In considering the purchase of equipment for debarking logs, the Financial Analysis Department of the Fall River Lumber Company prepared the following report.

Proposed Debarking Installation for Flakeboard Plant

Introduction

The flakeboard plant is using peeled aspen so that our finished board will have a light-colored appearance. This lighter appearance is felt to be necessary by the Sales Department if we wish to continue to point our product toward a higher-quality market.

Moreover, as the plant's operating efficiency is a direct function of the life of its flaker knives, the peeled wood will contribute somewhat to increasing this life by eliminating the abrasive action caused by the sand and dirt that is often found within the bark.

However, the primary consideration in maintaining an adequate knife life is that the moisture content in the aspen be sufficient (above 35 per cent air dry) to act as a cooling agent on the flaker knives.

If the aspen supplied to the plant is too dry, the flaker knives heat up, thereby becoming dull, and the plant's operations are impaired. Past experience has demonstrated to us that the difference in flaker knife life is almost insignificant between using *freshly peeled aspen* and *freshly unpeeled aspen*, but quite significant between using *dry peeled aspen* and *freshly peeled aspen*.

In the initial stages of operations, the plant used fresh "hand-peeled" aspen direct from the wood dealers. However, because the hand peeling (commonly known as sap peeling) season lasts only during the trees' annual growth period (a six-week period from spring to early summer), it is only during this time that a sufficient volume (2 cords per man per day) can be maintained. Out of season this type of production drops to $\frac{1}{2}$ cord per man per day, thus becoming uneconomical. Although a sufficient year's supply of aspen could possibly be bought during the six-week sap-peeling season, the wood would dry out in storage and the problem of flaker knife life again becomes the critical factor.

Chemical debarking must be ruled out as a possibility because the wood becomes too dry in the one-year period that is required for the tree to die and the bark to fall off.

Thus the use of some kind of mechanical debarking equipment that would ensure a year-round supply of peeled wood with the correct moisture characteristics becomes necessary if we wish to continue producing our lighter-colored flakeboard plant:

Alternative Solutions

The following proposals exist as a possible means of supplying peeled aspen to the flakeboard plant:

1. Installing permanent debarking facilities at Fall River employing King or Elmo equipment.

2. Utilizing portable debarkers at Fall River, such as the Leswork.

Recommendations

This study recommends installing a King debarker out in the woodyard. In addition, it recommends the use of mechanical feeding accessories and a bark burner. The estimated savings would be $40,000 per year compared to our present portable Leswork installation. The total estimated investment would be $70,000. The return on this investment would be at the rate of 57 per cent, or payback in one and three-quarters years.

Summary of Findings

The problem as outlined in the introduction of this study of determining the most economical and sound engineering method of debarking aspen for the flakeboard plant is complicated.

Basically, it boils down to balancing our rate of production required to supply the flakeboard operations against a capital investment and estimated debarking cost per cord that we are willing to pay for.

Certain assumptions were made. The main ones, subject to the most variability, are

1. The estimated useful life of the debarkers.
2. The estimated repair and maintenance costs.
3. The machine production per hour.

The alternative of *buying peeled wood* is not recommended and such rejection is based mainly on the following considerations:

1. The wide diversity in the location of the aspen stands, creating a difficult peeling set-up in the field.
2. The uncertain supply in the winter season.
3. The higher operating costs for the wood dealer necessitated by his increased handling and depreciation expenses.
4. The possible legal problems arising from buying and renting debarkers to the wood dealers.
5. The reluctance of the wood dealers to debark in the field.
6. The uncertainty of getting clean wood.

Rejection of *portable debarkers at Fall River* is primarily based on a pure cost consideration. To maintain our estimated production requirements of 1 million square feet per month in the flakeboard plant would necessitate reinvesting in portable debarkers at a rate that would more than offset the initial low investment cost. The low production inherent in these debarkers means running them at their capacity practically around the clock and thereby quickly reaching their estimated life of 5,000 cords.

The choice lies between buying a King debarker, either new or used, or an Elmo. A used King is rejected because its return on investment is less than that of a new King. Both the Elmo and King are substantially the same machine as far as the efficiency in debarking the wood goes. However, the rugged design of the Elmo has kept its repair and maintenance charges well under that of the King. While there are over 100 King installations in operation, certain companies, such as the United States Paper Company of Flint, Michigan, are replacing their King with Elmos, as the latter seemed to hold up better. Nevertheless, the economic advantage evidence by the higher rate of return of the new King as compared to the Elmo, 57 per cent versus 49 per cent (see Table 5-4), takes into consideration this more rugged design of the Elmo; yet this report still concludes that the King investment is the more advantageous for our requirements.

It is well to mention that the inherent savings of using an Elmo or a King debarker lie not only with the increased production (both over twice the hourly capacity of a Leswork), which lowers the total unit cost per cord of wood debarked, but also with the longer estimated life of the machines. The savings are not a result of an overall reduction in manpower.

Although the debarkers themselves do not require operating labor, the machine's higher productive capacities require that such men be utilized as spotters on the infeed and outfeed conveying equipment.

The economics of the study are summarized in Tables 5-1 to 5-4. The first three compare the operating costs and investments of a King, an Elmo, and

Table 5-1.   Cost Estimates for Flakeboard Plant Debarkers

	King (New)	King (Used)	Elmo	Leswork*
Debarker cost (with power)	$23,200	$16,000	$ 44,000	$4,000
Accessories (conveyors and deck, etc.)	37,425	27,700	52,000	—
Installation	9.650	14,600	9,800	300
Total investment	$70,275	$58,300	$105,800	$4,300
Fixed costs per cord	$0.82	$1.08	$0.74	$0.95
Variable costs per cord	1.16	1.32	0.72	2.87
Total estimated cost per cord	$1.98	$2.40	$1.46	$3.82

* Present Fall River operations (estimated three Lesworks required to meet production demands).

a Leswork debarking installation. Table 5-4 summarizes the return-on-investment data of the King and Elmo installations as compared to our present Leswork operations.

Location

The location of a debarker installation is an important factor in determining the efficiency of its operation. The installation could be placed in one of two places:

1. Adjacent to the flakeboard plant, or
2. Out in the woodyard.

Wood handling is a major consideration to this location decision, in particular supplying the infeed side of the debarker. On the outfeed side, stacking the slick debarked logs is also a job. If the sticks are maintained with a minimum end-to-end spacing on the infeed conveyor, full utilization of the debarker is obtained. This requires production equipment. By having the debarker in the woodyard the crane could be utilized in unloading the trucks directly onto the infeed line deck conveyors leading into the debarker, thereby producing at rated capacity. If the volume of trucks is too high at any one period, the crane could stack the wood in ranks adjacent to the infeed table, and in a slack period feed the debarker from these ranks. Whereas, if the crane was brought into the plant site, this would cut down on the yard efficiency for stacking wood when the debarker is not in use. The only other solution would be to use a Cary Lift in place of the crane. However, this means an increased investment of $22,000.

Other advantages of locating the debarker installation in the woodyard are the following:

1. More space, thereby allowing for flexibility of operations.
2. Possible future infeed application utilizing a "hot" pond. This type of wood handling appears to be the most practical way of solving loading

Table 5-2. Analysis of Total Investment Estimate for Flakeboard Plant Debarkers

Type of Debarker	King (New)	King (Used)	Elmo	Leswork
Debarker (with power)	$23,200	$16,000*	$ 44,000	$4,000
Building	$ (7,000)†	$ (4,500)†	$(No	
Infeed and outfeed conveyors	9,000	6,000	exact	
Cross chain conveyor	10,000	10,000	break-	
Bark conveyor	5,000	3,500	down	
Starting equipment	1,425	1,200	given,	
Cary Lift	(21,400)†		similar	
Bark burner	10,000	3,000	to new	
Special roll conveyor and flipper		2,000	King	
Spare parts	2,000	2,000	equip.)	
Total accessories	$37,425	$27,700	$ 52,000	$ —
Dismantling old King equipment and accessories	$ —	$ 5,000	$ —	$ —
Freight—In	250	200	400	50
Power line to woodyard				
2,100-foot wire at $2/foot $4,200				
22 poles on 100-foot intervals at $100/pole 2,200	6,400	6,400	6,400	—
Labor and materials to install equipment (3 men, 3 days)	3,000	3,000	3,000	250
Total installation	$ 9,650	$14,600	$ 9,800	$ 300
Total investment	$70,275	$58,300	$105,800	$4,300

* Estimated.
† Not included in totals for accessories.

Table 5-3. Analysis of Cost Estimates per Cord for Fall River Flakeboard Plant Debarkers

Type of Machine	Elmo	King (New)	King (Used)	Leswork (Fall River)
Estimated life*	20,000 hours	14,000 hours	10,000 hours	2,000 hours
	5 years	$3\frac{1}{4}$ years	$2\frac{1}{4}$ years	$\frac{1}{4}$ year
Rated capacity—rough cords per hour	9	7	6	$2\frac{1}{4}$
Fixed costs per cord		Cost estimate per cord		
Depreciation charges: $\dfrac{\text{total equipment cost}}{\text{tot. est. life} \times \text{rated cap.}}$	$0.59	$0.71	$0.96	$0.90
$\dfrac{\$106,000}{20,000 \text{ hr} \times 9 \text{ cords/hr}}$ (sample calculation)				
Interest, taxes, insurance: avg. annual invest. $\times$ 10%	0.15	0.11	0.12	0.05
$\dfrac{\$106,000 \times .1}{2 \times 4,000 \text{ hr/yr} \times 9 \text{ cd/hr}}$				
Total fixed costs	$0.74	$0.82	$1.08	$0.90

Variable costs per cord

Repairs and upkeep	0.05†	$0.32†	$0.37†	$0.05
Maintenance (½ hr/8-hr shift)				
(routine lubrication and adjust.) $\dfrac{\$.125 \text{ hr}}{\text{rated capacity}}$	0.01	0.02	0.02	0.05
Operating labor: $\dfrac{2 \text{ men} \times \text{hourly wage} \times 113\%‡}{\text{rated capacity}}$	0.05	0.65	0.75	1.67
$\dfrac{2 \text{ men} \times \$2/\text{hr} \times 113\%}{9 \text{ cords/hr}}$				
Operating supplies and power: 50% hr./rated capacity	0.06	0.07	0.08	0.10
Bark hauling: $\dfrac{\$4/\text{truck/hr} \times 1 \text{ hr/load}}{4 \text{ cords/truck load}}$	—	—	—	1.00
Bark burning	0.10	0.10	0.10	—
Total variable costs	$0.72	$1.16	$1.32	$2.87
Total estimated cost per rough cord	$1.46	$1.98	$2.40	$3.82

* Estimated life based on 16 hr/day × 5 days/wk × 50 wk/yr = 4,000 hr/yr × 5 yr = 20,000 hr.
† Estimated from actual operations at Great Falls Paper Company (Elmo) and Paper Products (King installation).
‡ Thirteen per cent increased for Social Security, workmen's compensation, retirement benefits.

into King-type debarkers. The wood is simply dumped into the pond, which has impellers submerged in the water. If the sticks are not in contact with the water for more than half an hour, the moisture content of the wood is not affected.

3. Ease of installation, because there would be no interference with the existing supply of wood to the plant.

The principal advantage to locating near the flakeboard plant site is the reduced material handling on the outfeed end. Instead of stacking the wood on trailers for hauling to the plant or in ranks for inventory, it could be fed directly to the flakers. However, this means that the debarking operation is dependent *directly* on the flakeboard plant's operations, for if the plant shuts down so must the debarker. Otherwise, if the debarker would run when the plant was down, the material handling would increase, since the peeled wood would have to be set off. Out in the woodyard this would not be the case. Wood racks mounted on rails or the present trailers could be placed under the outfeed end conveyor and easily removed sideways away from the flow of materials when each rack has been filled.

Bark Disposal
Another important aspect in a debarking operation is the problem of bark disposal. The bark could possibly be

1. Burned in a regular "bark burner."
2. Utilized as fuel at our boiler house, provided the necessary adapting equipment was installed.
3. Possibly pressed into logs and sold as fireplace wood.
4. Hauled away and dumped as refuse.

This study compares returns with and without a bark burner. (See Table 5-4.)
If the efficiency of burning is high enough to prevent excessive smoke, the investment in such a piece of equipment would pay for itself by the savings ($1 per rough cord × 22,000 cords per year = $22,000) resulting from eliminating hauling to the dump.

Discussion of Alternative Solutions
1. *Portable Debarkers at Fall River.* It is possible to utilize *a series* of Leswork portable debarkers for the flakeboard plant's wood requirements. At the present time we are barking approximately 45 rough cords per day ($2\frac{1}{4}$ rough cords per hour × 20 hours per day). This appears to be maximum capacity for these debarkers. Assuming a 15 per cent bark loss and a 2 per cent wood loss, this results in a production of 37 finished cords per day (45 × .83). This is enough capacity for 750,000 square feet of board per month (assuming 1.5 finished cords per 1,000 square feet). Basing our wood requirements at a minimum of 1 million square feet per month, we would need a production of about 50 finished cords per day. Thus it would be necessary to invest in a minimum of two more debarkers (one for reserve) to fulfil our minimum

Table 5-4.   Estimated Return on Investment Comparing Proposed Debarkers
with Present Leswork Debarker

	With Bark Burner*		
	Elmo	King (New)	King (Used)
Estimated savings per rough cord	$ 2.63	$ 1.84	$ 1.42
Estimated required rough cords/year† (59 cords/day × 360 days)	22,000	22,000	22,000
Estimated total savings per year	$ 52,000	$40,000	$31,000
Estimated total investment	$106,000	$70,000	$58,000
Estimated return on investment	49%	57%	54%
Payback period	2 years	$1\frac{3}{4}$ years	$1\frac{4}{5}$ years

	Without Bark Burner		
	Elmo	King (New)	King (Used)
Estimated savings per rough cord	$ 1.55	$ 1.05	$ 0.68
Estimated required rough cords/year† (59 cords/day × 360 days)	22,000	22,000	22,000
Estimated total savings per year	$ 34,000	$23,000	$15,000
Estimated total investment	$ 96,000	$60,000	$48,000
Estimated return on investment	35%	38%	31%
Payback period	3 years	$2\frac{1}{2}$ years	$3\frac{1}{4}$ years

* Cost of bark burner including installation is $10,000.
‡ Based on production requirements of 50 finished cords per day, which provides for 1 million square feet of board per month and a 15 per cent bark loss.

production requirements. This would be an investment of $12,000 (3 ×
$4,000), excluding the necessary conveying accessories. However, based on
an estimated life of 2,000 hours or 5,000 cords, two thirds of this investment
would theoretically be replaced approximately every 4 months or one third
year $\left(\dfrac{5,000 \text{ cords}}{45 \text{ cd/day} \times 30 \text{ days/mo}} = 3.7 \text{ mo} \right)$. Thus a $12,000 initial investment
becomes a $28,000 yearly investment.

Expanding this investment to a comparable figure with the King and Elmo
debarkers, the following result is seen:

Type	Elmo	King (New)	Portable Leswork
Estimated life	5 years	$3\frac{1}{2}$ years	4 years
Total investment	$106,000	$70,000	$112,000

2. *Permanent Debarking Facilities.* In considering permanent debarking
facilities for the Fall River flakeboard operations, the first question that must

be answered is what type of bark-removal operation is feasible. Some principal methods of bark removal apart from manual labor with a spud or draw knife are the following:

a. By means of friction by tumbling or rotating action, such as the rotating cylindrical drum at Williamsburg.
b. By hydraulic pressure.
c. By shear principle.
d. By the rosser head, or cutter head, principle, such as the present Leswork debarker.

An attempt to debark some aspen in the Williamsburg drum was not successful because the wood was not dry enough to experience sufficient friction for effective bark removal. Since the flakeboard operations demand this higher moisture content in the wood, this generally recognized quick, cheap bark-removal system cannot be utilized.

A hydraulic pressure debarker is ruled out chiefly on the grounds of the water pollution problem it would create.

The basic feature of a King-type debarker consists of a blunt-edge pressure elastically against the log, which then penetrates the bark down into the cell-forming cambium layer between the bark and wood. Tangential pressure against the bark produces shear stresses between bark and wood sufficient to overcome the strength of the cambium layer. The principal feature of such a machine is the removal of bark at a substantially low wood loss. The trade names of debarkers of this type are the King and the Elmo. Both of these debarkers could be used for our flakeboard operations.

The rosser, or cutter head, principle is employed on the Leswork machine we now are using. While these machines remove the bark sufficiently, the wood loss appears to be higher than with the King type. In addition, as these machines are portable, production is not as great as on the King machines. As an example, the Leswork debarks between 2 to 2½ rough cords per hour as compared to 5 to 10 rough cords per hour on the King. Nevertheless, the Leswork is a proven debarker that could be utilized in our operations.

Both the King and the Elmo have been utilized in flakeboard operations. It is generally felt that the King does an excellent job in debarking, but the maintenance requirements are high. Moreover, there seems to be more of a problem debarking wood with varying diameters with the King than with the Elmo. (Our operations use wood ranging from 4 to 15 inches in diameter.)

Because the Elmo has been designed for more rugged operations, its weight is approximately 2½ times the King (22,000 pounds versus 9,000 pounds). Simultaneously, its cost is $20,000 more ($44,000 versus $24,000).

The rating of a debarker is dependent on the number of sticks per cord, the percentage of bark removal required, and the infeed system to the debarker. In addition, under wintertime conditions it is necessary to slow down the debarker in order to maintain the same percentage of bark removal. For this study, the average rated capacity of the King and Elmo debarkers was based on automatic conveying accessories. It should be kept in mind that manual feeding to either of these debarkers would tend to reduce their rated capacity.

Required: Assume a zero tax rate and a time value of money of .05. What decision should the firm make?

5-14. The following facts apply to an investment the ABC Company is considering:

Plant costing $10,000,000 with a life of 50 years.
Equipment costing $2,000,000 with a life of 20 years.
Annual fixed costs are $180,000, of which $100,000 are incremental with the decision (but excluding depreciation) and $80,000 are allocations from other departments and projects.
The net revenue contribution per unit sold is $2.
The cost of money of the firm is .10.
It is expected that 1,000,000 units of product will be used per year.

Required: How many units have to be produced and sold per year to break even? If 1,000,000 units are produced, what will be the per unit cost?

5-15. Continuing problem 5-14. Assume that the plant and equipment described have been purchased. One million units of the product are needed in the coming year. These units can be purchased at a cost of $1.20 per unit from a reliable supplier. The variable manufacturing costs per unit are $.20. If the units are purchased, the plant and equipment will be shut down (this can be done with little additional cost).

Should the units be made or bought? Assume that the probability of the product being supplied on time and the quality of the product are the same whether made or bought.

chapter 6

*The chances of success of a given investment
(whether of capital or labour) depend on the
efficiency with which all those who work in the
same firm cooperate with the factor in question.*

—J. R. Hicks, "The Theory of Uncertainty and Profit,"
Economica (London, May 1931), p. 185.

the use of cash flows in evaluating investments

In Chapter 1 an investment was defined as a commitment "of resources made in the hope of realizing benefits that are expected to occur over a reasonably long period of time in the future." According to this definition, neither the resources nor the benefits need be in the form of explicit cash flows. A decision to have an accounting executive spend a month studying the capabilities of various types of electronic data-processing equipment would be an investment in the sense of this definition. The executive's time is a scarce resource, because he would have spent the month in other activities that are valuable to the firm. In the first instance, at least, the expected benefits will be increased knowledge by management of a relatively new technology. Thus there is no explicit cash outlay or cash inflow, but there is an investment.

We have argued that investments ought to be evaluated in terms of the present value of the cash flows expected from them, in preference to any other measures of investment worth that have been suggested. However, we have not given a complete or careful definition of the term *cash flows*. In the present chapter we shall attempt to do this and also to explain some of the difficulties that arise in applying a cash-flow analysis to investment proposals. In Chapter 7, the influence of income taxes on the timing of cash flows will be discussed.

cash flows and profits

Cash flows are not identical with profits or income. Changes in income can occur without any corresponding changes in cash flows. During a period of

112

investment in plant and inventories, a corporation can even experience a decrease in cash at the same time that income is increasing.

The popular conception of an investment is typified by a one-period outlay of funds, followed by a series of periods in which incomes are earned. The incomes are then related to the investment, and some type of return on investment is computed. One main advantage of the cash-flow procedure is that it avoids difficult problems underlying the measurement of corporate income, which necessarily accompanies the accrual method of accounting. These problems include the following:

1. In what time period should revenue be recognized?
2. What expenses should be treated as investments and therefore capitalized and depreciated over several time periods?
3. What method of depreciation should be used in measuring income as reported to management and stockholders (as distinct from income measurement for tax purposes)?
4. Should LIFO (last in, first out), FIFO, (first in, first out), or some other method be used to measure inventory flow?
5. What costs are inventoriable? Should fixed, variable, direct, indirect, out-of-pocket, unavoidable, administrative, or selling costs be included in evaluating inventory?

There are disagreements as to the answers in each of these questions. Different approaches may lead to different measures of income. If income is used to evaluate investment worth, investments may look good or bad, depending on how income is measured. The utilization of cash flows minimizes many of these complications.

why cash flows

In evaluating an investment we suggest that the cash flows of the investment be used in the analysis. We are not interested in the conventional "cost" of the investment, but rather in the cash outlays required and the timing of these cash flows. We are not using the earnings of period 1, but rather the cash flows of period 1. These distinctions can be important. A builder may tell us that a construction project will cost $1 million, but this is not sufficient information. We want to know when the outlays will be required. For example, if the outlays are made on completion of the building, the cost is truly $1 million. If the payment is required one year prior to completion, the true cost is $1 million plus the interest on the $1 million for one year. The use of expected earnings to measure the benefits of an investment would require a much more sophisticated theoretical accounting system than is currently being used by any corporation. The earnings figures resulting from current accounting practices are not usable. Also, even with improved measures of income, there would remain the question of whether the use of cash flows or earnings is more appropriate. If earnings are measured correctly, both measures should give identical results. The advantage of the use of the cash flow is that the receipt of cash is an objective, clearly defined event that leads to a significantly different situation than before the receipt of cash.

A sale on account is an economic event recorded by the accountant and affecting accounting income. However, the firm has not yet received the cash, it cannot spend the cash, and the ultimate collection of the cash is uncertain. For purposes of investment analysis we are more interested in the moment when the cash is to be received. At that moment the firm reaches a new decision point. The cash may be returned to the stockholders by the payment of a dividend. It may be used to retire debt, increase the working capital, or be reinvested in new long-lived assets.

It might be suggested that to be correct the dollar of cash received in period 1 should be followed to its disposition at the end of the firm's life. However, we find it more convenient to take the receipt of cash associated with a specific asset to be a self-contained event, and we do not normally concern ourselves with the final disposition of the dollar. The assumption that the funds can be borrowed and lent at a given discount rate allows us to make this simplifying assumption.

Thus for purposes of investment analysis, unlike conventional accounting, we choose the receipt or disbursement of cash to be the crucial event. It should not be thought that a sale on account or other accruals are ignored. A sale on account in period 1 will affect the expected cash collection in period 2; hence it is brought into the analysis in the period in which the firm has the cash in hand and has reached a decision point.

absolute and relative cash flows

Every investment analysis involves a comparison of alternatives. If there are not at least two possibilities, there is no problem of choice. Usually the number of alternatives is large. The question may be whether the company is better off with investment A or without it, or whether investment A is better than investment B, or whether both A and B should be accepted or both should be rejected. In any case, because the investment analysis involves a comparison of two or more alternatives, it is not surprising to find that any estimate of cash flows must also be on a comparative basis.

Suppose that the question is whether to start a new business. After a careful analysis we arrive at an estimate of the net cash flows that we expect to occur in each future period after we start the business. Our estimate will tell us how much money we would have to invest during each period as the business got started and how much more money would be available after necessary expenses and additional investments in each period after it began to operate successfully. Perhaps we would plan to sell the business after five years if it were successful, and we would include as a cash flow the amount we would expect to receive for the business five years hence. The present value of the net cash flows might then be calculated, using a rate of discount of 10 per cent. What comparisons are we making in analyzing the investment? What comparisons are we making in estimating the net cash flows?

If we say that the cash outlays in the first year are $100,000 (because that amount of money would have to be expended during that period, over and above any cash receipts), we are implicitly comparing the cash flows from operating the business with a cash flow of zero. When cash flows are being compared with zero cash flows, we shall speak of *absolute* cash flows. In evaluating the present value of these cash flows, using a 10 per cent rate of interest, we are implicitly comparing this investment with an investment that would return 10 per cent per year indefinitely for each net outlay.

Suppose now that the question is whether to start one kind of business or another, for example, a retail store or a wholesale distributorship. One possible analysis would be to estimate the absolute cash flows from each business and compute the present value of the corresponding cash flows. Again, in this case, we are comparing each business separately against a hypothetical investment that could earn 10 per cent. Because the hypothetical standard of comparison is the same for both businesses, the two can be readily compared with each other by noticing which business would probably give a higher present value of cash flows. In practice, the final decision would depend on many other factors as well, such as the degree of risk involved in each business, the degree of confidence we feel in our estimates, and so on. A further discussion of some of these factors is given in Chapter 9.

An alternative analysis would be to compare directly one business with the other. In looking at the cash flow estimates, for example, we can subtract (algebraically) the cash flows of the retail store from the cash flows in corresponding periods of the wholesale distributorship. If the difference is positive in a particular period, it will tell us how much better the cash flows from the wholesale business are than those from the retail business during that period. The cash flows, in this case, can be called *relative* cash flows; the wholesale business is being measured relative to the retail business. Again we can compute the present value of this series of relative cash flows. It can be shown that the present value of this series of relative cash flows will be the same as the present value of the absolute cash flows from the wholesale distributorship minus the present value of the absolute cash flows from the retail business. Thus the present-value method will lead to the same conclusion, whichever approach is used.

There is an important difference between the two series of cash flows, however. With the series of absolute cash flows, if the corresponding investment (the retail or wholesale businesses) were accepted and actually began to operate, we could compare, period by period, the actual cash flows with our previous forecasts. There is not, however, any similarly identifiable series of cash flows that could be compared with the relative cash flow estimates. If we decided to operate the wholesale business on the basis of a comparison of relative cash flows, and wished after a few periods to compare our actual results with those we had forecast earlier, we would need to know what assumptions had been made about the retail business in order to make this comparison.

Frequently, when we are considering investments to be made in a going business, it may be difficult to define the absolute cash flows that would result from the investment. It may be easier to use a relative cash flow concept in computing flows. Suppose, for example, that an automobile manufacturer is trying to decide whether to invest in the tools and dies necessary to make a particular modification in the body style of his product. He might compare what sales would be if he made the investment and what they would be if he did not make the investment. This may still be a very difficult estimate to make, because all sorts of other changes are taking place at the same time, both in his product and marketing strategy, and in those of his competitors.

importance of considering all alternatives

Apart from those difficulties in making estimates of relative cash flows that are a by-product of the difficulties of estimating the incremental effects of various actions of the firm, there is an important conceptual danger that must be avoided in estimating relative cash flows. As explained, an estimate of relative cash flows always involves an implicit or explicit comparison of two alternatives. The size of the estimated relative cash flows from making a particular investment will depend upon the alternative that is used as a basis of comparison. *This means that almost any estimate can be made to seem worthwhile if it is compared with a sufficiently bad alternative.* Consider a problem that was once faced by many railroads. Should the old coal-burning locomotive used on a particular passenger run be replaced with a modern and more efficient diesel? Assuming that the change would not affect passenger revenues, the natural basis of comparison would appear to be to take the present value of the extra outlays required to purchase the new engine (minus the scrap value of the old coal burner) and the cash savings resulting from the difference between the operating costs of the old and the new engines. On this basis it may seem that the investment in a new diesel engine would be quite profitable. But suppose, using the old coal-burner, that the revenues from the passenger run are insufficient to cover the incremental out-of-pocket costs of operating the train. In such circumstances the purchase of a diesel may serve to decrease the loss, but it may not convert the passenger run into a profitable operation. If there is no possibility of eliminating the passenger run, the decision to purchase the diesel may be wise. But if the passenger train could be eliminated, purchase of the diesel would not be justified. This situation could be handled by examining the absolute cash flows generated by the diesel—that is, by comparing the cash flows resulting from the passenger train with a diesel locomotive and the cash flows resulting from no train at all. When using relative cash flows, we must remember to consider all alternatives, including the alternative of continuing as we are now or abandoning the operation entirely, if these alternatives are both possible.

In general, an investment should not be accepted unless the relative cash flows generated by it are positive when compared with the next best alternative. Frequently, the analyst will be faced with a situation in which there are quite a number of possible alternatives whose relative advantages are not yet known. In such cases any one of the investments can be used as the standard of comparison, and the relative advantage of each estimate can be compared to this standard. If all the other alternatives have a negative present value when compared with the standard, the standard is the most advantageous insofar as explicit cost and revenue considerations are the determinants. In the railroad locomotive example, if continuing to operate the coal-burning locomotive were taken as the standard, it could turn out that discontinuing the passenger train altogether would give a higher present value than buying a diesel, although the latter is better than continuing to operate the coal-burning locomotive. As long as all feasible alternatives are considered, it makes no difference which alternative is tentatively accepted as the standard of comparison. The final answer will be the same in any case. The choice of a standard of comparison may lead to mistaken conclusions only if some advantageous alternatives (such as ceasing production entirely) are excluded from the analysis.

opportunity costs

Usually, the cash outlays included in the computation of net cash flows are the outlays incurred because of the investment that would not be incurred otherwise. Outlays that would be incurred by the firm whether or not the investment is accepted should not be charged to a particular investment project. Thus the practice of allocating a share of general overhead to a new project on the basis of some arbitrary measure, such as direct labor hours or a fraction of net sales, is not recommended *unless* it is expected that general overhead will actually increase if the project is accepted.

On the other hand, in some instances an investment project may require the use of some scarce resource available to the firm, although the explicit cash outlays associated with using that resource may be nonexistent or may not adequately reflect the value of the resource to the firm. Examples are projects that require a heavy drain on the time of key executive personnel or that use valuable floor space in a plant or store already owned by the business. The costs of using such resources are called *opportunity costs*, and they are measured by estimating how much the resource (the executives' time or the floor space) would earn for the company if the investments under consideration were rejected.

It may appear that the practice of charging opportunity costs against an investment project when no corresponding cash outlay can be identified is a violation of, or exception to, the procedure of evaluating investments in terms of actual cash flows. Actually, including opportunity costs is not so much an exception to the cash-flow procedure as an extension of it. The opportunity cost charged should measure net cash flows that could have been earned if the project under discussion had been rejected. Suppose that one floor of a factory building owned by a business could either be rented out at $1,200 per month or used to produce a new product. After an initial outlay for equipment the new product could produce an absolute net cash inflow of $2,000 per month after taxes but before an allowance has been made for use of the factory space. The figure of $2,000 per month overstates the benefits to be derived from the new product, because the space required could otherwise be used to earn $1,200 per month. By charging a rental opportunity cost of $1,200 per month against the new product, a more meaningful measure of its actual value to the company is obtained. An alternative procedure would be to estimate the relative cash flow from the new product compared with that produced by renting the extra space and not producing the new product.

In some instances it will be extremely difficult to estimate opportunity costs. The temptation then is to use some other, more easily identifiable basis of charging for the use of such things as floor space or the time of key executives. This temptation must be viewed with some skepticism. The pro rata share of the costs of owning a building may be much higher or much lower than the true opportunity costs of using that space. When there is really no basis for estimating the opportunity costs associated with the use of a factor, such as the time of certain key executives, it may be preferable to note merely that the proposed project is likely to require considerably more or considerably less than the usual amount of attention from such key executives.

The only valid justification for the prorating of the actual costs to the proposed project would be if the actual costs are a reasonable basis for estimating the opportunity cost. For example, if an additional executive can be hired for the same cost as a present executive, the opportunity cost of using some of the time of the present executive should not be greater than this current salary (a new man could be hired). If it is felt that the manager is currently earning his salary when he is doing his least profitable task, the cost should not be less. Thus we can correctly say that the opportunity cost of this executive's time is equal to his actual salary.

acquiring assets without cash disbursements

The term *cash outlay* is also applied to a transaction in which an asset is acquired by incurring a long-term debt or by issuing stock. Even though there may be no explicit borrowing of cash, receipt of cash, and disbursement of cash, these transactions are assumed to occur when an asset is acquired via a promise to pay in some distant time period, and the transaction is treated as if there has been a cash outlay as well as a source of new capital.

When an asset is acquired by the incurrence of a non-interest-bearing current liability, the convention is adopted in this book that it is the timing of the actual cash disbursement that is important. Thus, if the investment results in an increase in inventories of $100 and the source of capital is an increase in current liabilities of $100, the net cash outlay that is required in the period of inventory acquisition is zero. If the $100 increase in inventories required cash outlays of $20 and current liabilities increased by $80, then the net cash outlay in the period of inventory acquisition is $20.

excluding interest payments

Cash disbursed for interest is normally excluded from the cash-flow computation used in analyzing investments. The interest factor is taken into consideration by the use of the present-value procedures. To include also the cash disbursement for interest would result in double counting. Assume that the discount factor being used to take into consideration the time value of money is 6 per cent. There is an investment that requires an outlay of $1,000 and promises to return $1,080 at the end of one period. This investment would seem to be desirable. Assume that we can raise money for this investment at a cost of 6 per cent—that is, obtain $1,000 now and pay $1,060 a year from now. The incorrect analysis would show the $60 interest as a deduction from the cash flows of period 1:

	Year	
	0	1
Investment	− $1,000	$1,080
Interest	−	60
Net cash flows	− $1,000	$1,020

This series of cash flows would lead to a reject decision, using higher than a 2 per cent rate of interest because of a double counting of interest.

including all debt flows

As stated previously, it is incorrect to include the interest payments in the cash flows. However, we can choose for certain purposes to include all cash flows of the debt financing associated with an investment.

Continuing the preceding example, the cash flows of the investment and the cash flows of the debt would be as follows:

	Year	
	0	1
Investment	− $1,000	$1,080
Debt financing	1,000	1,060
Net cash flows	0	20

An inspection of the table shows that the present value of the cash flows is positive for any choice of interest rate greater than zero. Whenever we allow the inclusion of the debt financing cash flows in the investment analysis with no limit on the amount of debt, by a suitable usage of debt we can make any conventional investment with a rate of return greater than the cost of debt have a positive present value (or equivalently have an acceptable rate of return). If we were using the rate of return method we would say that the rate of return resulting after the subtraction of the debt cash flows would be the rate of return on the stockholders' investment. In like manner, using the present-value method, we are computing the present value of the cash flows associated with the stockholders' investment. Because by combining suitable amounts of debt with the investment cash flows we can make investments with rates of return only slightly greater than the cost of debt have acceptable present values and acceptable rates of return, the method of analysis being illustrated should never be used arbitrarily for some investments and not for others.

The computation of the rate of return and present value of the cash flows associated with the stockholders' investment are interesting calculations. They follow naturally from the assumption that the stockholder is interested in the expected return (and risk) of his investment.

salvage and removal costs

The salvage and removal costs introduce no real problem if we keep in mind that we are interested in the periods when cash outlays are made or when cash flows into the firm. In the following descriptive material, the term *salvage* refers to "net salvage"; removal costs have been subtracted.

Let us first consider the salvage value of the new investment. Any funds obtained from selling the new investment when it is retired will increase the flow of cash in the last period. Thus the salvage value of the new investment will increase the cash flow of the last period of use.

When the investment is being made to replace an item of equipment currently being used, there are two additional salvage values to be considered: (1) the salvage value now of the old equipment, and (2) the salvage value that the old equipment would have had at the end of its physical or useful life (whichever comes first) if it were not replaced now. If the asset is replaced now, the present salvage will have the effect of increasing the cash flow of this period (or decreasing the required cash outlay). However, if the old equipment is being retired now, the salvage that would have been obtained at the end of its life will not be obtained. Thus there is a decrease in the relative cash flows of that last period because of the salvage which will not be obtained at that time. To summarize:

Salvage value of the new equipment: Increase the cash flow of the last year of use.

Present salvage value of the old equipment: Increase the cash flow for this year (decrease the cash outlay).

Salvage value of the old equipment at time of normal retirement: Decrease the cash flow of that year (because the salvage value would be obtained if the replacement did not take place and would not be obtained if the replacement did take place).

The cash flows arising from salvage of the old equipment would be treated in a somewhat different manner if the present values of the alternatives were computed individually. It would only increase the cash flows at the time of retirement.

The analysis of the cash flows arising from salvage is complicated by the fact that the cash-flow analysis may be made in terms of relative or absolute cash flows. The preceding description assumes that the cash flows are relative, that is, the cash flows from buying the new equipment minus the cash flows which would occur if the old equipment were retained. It is frequently reasonable to analyze the absolute cash flows of the several alternatives. Thus the cash flows of retaining the old would be computed, as would the cash flows of purchasing the new equipment. The present salvage value of the old equipment and the future salvage value of the new equipment would affect the cash flow of the alternative of purchasing the new equipment. The salvage value on retirement of the old would affect the cash flow of retaining the old equipment.

EXAMPLE: Assume the present equipment has a salvage value now of $1,000 and an expected salvage value in five years of $400 (at which time the equipment would be physically unusable). The new equipment will have a salvage value at the time of its expected retirement of $650. All figures are on an after-tax basis. The cash flows arising from the salvage values would be as follows:

	Year		
	0	5	10
Absolute flows of			
Retaining the old		$ 400	
Purchasing the new	$1,000		$650
Relative flows of			
replacing now	$1,000	$(400)	$650

terminal value

Salvage value is one form of terminal value. Another form of terminal value is the release of cash necessary to operate the investment. Other examples of items that may result in released cash at cessation of operations are collections of accounts receivable and reduction in required inventories. All these items gave rise to outlays of cash when they were purchased and then lagged in their generation of cash. When the outlays of cash cease, because the production is being phased out, the coming periods will have increases in cash flows resulting from the conversion of these non-cash current assets into cash; similarly, reductions of current liabilities reduce cash.

income taxes and cash flows

The question of income taxes and cash flows is reviewed in detail in Chapter 7. It should be remembered that *the term* cash flows *in this chapter refers to flows after the deduction of income taxes.* The income taxes are computed by applying the expected tax rate for each period to the taxable income (excluding interest charges) of that period. The taxable income will not be equal to the cash flow of the period, and frequently the taxable income will not equal the income computed in accordance with generally accepted accounting principles. Thus no matter what method is being used to accept or reject investments, it will be necessary to compute the income for tax purposes.

cash flows and uncertainty

Each computation of cash flows makes specific assumptions about the level of business activity, actions of competitors, future availability of improved models of machines, costs of factors of production, future sales, and the like. Because there is a large amount of uncertainty connected with each of these factors, it should be appreciated that computations using the present-value method are indications rather than numbers with 100 per cent certainty and accuracy. A more detailed discussion of the consequences of uncertain estimates and some suggestions for making analyses when basic assumptions are subject to uncertainty are presented in later chapters. It should be stressed that any decision about investments must be based on as complete a consideration of all the relevant factors as it is possible to provide, and that the probable present value of an investment proposal is only one factor, although a very significant one, to be considered in arriving at a final decision.

questions and problems

6-1. The Bright Machine Tool Shop is considering replacement of the equipment in a section of its shop. The equipment performs a function that could be completely eliminated. A comparison of the present equipment being used with new equipment indicates that the following relative cash flows would result if the new machine were purchased instead of continuing with the old:

Period	
0	*1*
($10,000)	$12,000

The yield of the investment is 20 per cent, and the cost of money is 15 per cent. The net present value of the investment is $435. Based on the positive net present value, the decision was made to replace the present equipment.

In the period of operation the machine performed exactly as predicted, and all costs were as predicted. The absolute cash flows were as follows:

Period	
0	*1*
($10,000)	$11,000

Required: Comment on the investment decision made by the Bright Machine Tool Shop.

6-2. The Dotted Airline Company is considering replacement of its fleet of ten two-engined planes with five new-model jets. One jet can replace two of the present planes. The airplane company has prepared an analysis showing that each new plane will cost $343,000 and will earn cash proceeds of $100,000 per year for five years. Assume that after five years the salvage value will be zero for both the new and old planes. The analysis was based on the load and operating characteristics of the new plane and the past experience of the airline, as well as the number of passengers and the routes traveled, adjusted in a reasonable manner for additional passengers who will be attracted by the new planes.

The planes currently being used are considered to be safe workhorses, but are not as glamorous as the new planes. In competition with jets, they are expected to earn net cash proceeds of only $10,000 per year per plane. There is no discernible trend of earnings. The present planes now have a zero salvage value.

The cost of money of the Dotted Airline is 10 per cent. Assume that the company has access to the necessary funds.

Required: Should the Dotted Airline purchase the new jets? Explain. What would be your recommendation if the salvage value is now $40,000 on an old plane?

6-3. The following facts relate to an investment that costs $10,000 being considered by the ABC Company:

	Period	
	1	*2*
Cash revenues	$12,000	$12,000
Depreciation	5,000	5,000
Net income	7,000	7,000

The company intends to declare dividends of $12,000 in period 1 and $12,000 in period 2 as a result of the investment. The company is not subject to income taxes.

Required: What are the cash flows of the two years for purposes of the analysis of the investment?

6-4. For problem 6-3, assume that all the sales were made on account, and collection lagged the sale by one period. The company will distribute dividends equal to the cash generation.
Required: What are the cash flows of each year?

6-5. An investment will require an increase in the following working capital items:

Cash	$1,000,000
Accounts receivable	3,000,000
Inventories	6,000,000

It is also expected that current liabilities will increase by $4 million.
Required: How will the preceding items affect the cash flows of the investment?

6-6. In computing the cash flows of a period, should interest payments be included or excluded? Explain.

6-7. The ABC Company is considering an investment in a new product. The information for one year is as follows:

Sales	$200,000
Manufacturing costs of sales	80,000
(includes $20,000 of depreciation)	
Selling and administrative expenses	40,000
(directly associated with the product)	
Equipment purchases	10,000
Decrease in contribution of other products	5,000
Increase in accounts receivable	15,000
Increase in inventories	20,000
Increase in current liabilities	30,000
Income taxes associated with product income	12,000
Interest on bonds expected to be used in financing	18,000

Required: Compute the cash flow that can be used in the present-value computations of this investment.

6-8. A product is currently being manufactured on a machine that has a book value of $10,000 (it was purchased for $50,000 twenty years ago). The costs of the product are as follows:

	Unit Costs
Labor, direct	$ 4.00
Labor, variable indirect	5.00
Other variable overhead	2.50
Fixed overhead	2.50
	$14.00

In the past year 10,000 units were produced and sold for $10 per unit. It is expected that the old machine can be used indefinitely in the future.

An equipment manufacturer has offered to accept the old machine as a trade-in for a new version. The new machine would cost $80,000 after allowing $15,000 for the old equipment. The projected costs associated with the new machine are as follows:

Labor, direct	$ 2.00
Labor, variable indirect	3.50
Other variable overhead	4.00
Fixed overhead	3.25
	$12.75

The fixed overhead costs are allocations from other departments plus the depreciation of the equipment. Repair costs are the same for both machines.

The old machine could be sold on the open market now for $6,000. Ten years from now it is expected to have a salvage value of $1,000. The new machine has an expected life of ten years and an expected salvage of $10,000.

There are no corporate income taxes. The appropriate time discount rate for this company is .05. It is expected that future demand of the product will remain at 10,000 units per year.

Required: (a) Should the new equipment be acquired? (b) If the product can be purchased at a cost of $8 per unit from a reliable supplier, should it be purchased or made?

6-9. The ABC Company is considering an investment in a new product. The information for one year is as follows:

Sales (all on account)	$200,000
Manufacturing costs of sales	90,000
(include $20,000 of depreciation and $6,000 of fixed cost allocations from service departments)	
Selling and administrative expenses	40,000
(directly associated with the product)	
Equipment purchases	10,000
(purchased on account and not yet paid)	
Decrease in contribution of other products	5,000
Increase in accounts receivable	15,000
Increase in inventories	20,000
(includes $4,000 depreciation)	
Increase in current liabilities	30,000
Income taxes associated with product income	12,000
Interest on bonds expected to be used in financing	18,000
Uncollected accounts receivable expected to be written off	2,000
Increase in accumulated depreciation	19,000

Required: Compute the cash flow that can be used in the present-value computations of this investment.

6-10. Assume that the investment of problem 6-9 is financed partially by sinking fund bonds and there is a requirement to place $50,000 per year into a sinking fund. Does this additional information change the computation of the cash flows?

chapter 7

Ben Franklin:
A penny saved is a penny earned.
Accountant:
*Wrong. An after-tax penny saved is equal to two
pennies before tax.*

corporate income taxes
and investment decisions

Accounting theory suggests three basically different methods of recording a cash outlay for an asset or cost factor; these in turn affect the measurement of income. The outlay may be considered to be an expense of the period in which it is incurred, or to represent the acquisition of a wasting asset that will be charged to expense over a number of future periods, or to represent the acquisition of a nonwasting asset, in which case it is never charged to expense. The first is typified by outlays for salesmen's salaries, the second by outlays for plant and equipment, and the third by outlays for land. For some outlays a reasonable case can be made for one or another accounting treatment. Thus outlays for research, certain types of advertising, and some kinds of maintenance may be treated as current expenses or capitalized and depreciated over a longer period; outlays for land may be treated as wasting assets if the important characteristics of the land are its possession of certain minerals or soil fertility, or as partially nonwasting if its site value is considered.

The accounting treatment accorded a particular outlay will influence the amount and timing of income measurement. But in the absence of income taxes, the choice of investments should not be influenced by the method of accounting for a particular outlay. The amount and timing of the cash outlays and the amount and timing of future cash proceeds are what is relevant to the choice of investments.

In the case of corporations subject to income taxes, the accounting treatment adopted for income tax purposes must be considered in evaluating a potential investment, because the choice will affect the amount and timing of income tax payments. Because income taxes do not affect all investments in the same manner, it is necessary to place cash flows associated with each

128

investment on an after-tax basis before evaluating the investments. In this chapter we shall be concerned with the mechanics of computing the after-tax cash flows associated with investments. We shall consider separately the problems associated with depreciable assets, nondepreciable assets, and outlays chargeable to current expense.

measuring the effects of depreciation charges on cash flows

Suppose that we are considering the purchase of a new piece of equipment that is expected to have no salvage value on retirement. If there were no income taxes, the cash proceeds resulting from the use of the equipment could be estimated by subtracting the additional cash outlays required to operate the equipment from the additional revenues that result from acquiring it. That is,

$$\text{Before-tax cash proceeds} = \text{revenues} - \text{cash outlays}. \qquad (1)$$

The term *cash proceeds* is used here to refer to the proceeds generated by operating the investment. It assumes that all revenues are accompanied by an immediate generation of cash equal to the revenues. It also assumes that all cash outlays, except the initial investment, are charged to expense—that is, none is charged to inventory—and that inventory is not reduced. Thus cash outlays are equal to the expenses (excluding depreciation) in this simple example.

For a nonprofit hospital or government bureau this is the only calculation that would be necessary. For a business it is necessary to subtract the additional income tax liability that occurs because of the investment:

$$\text{After-tax proceeds} = \text{revenues} - \text{cash outlays} - \text{income tax} \qquad (2)$$

or

$$\text{After-tax proceeds} = \text{revenues} - \text{expenses other than}$$
$$\text{depreciation} - \text{income tax} \qquad (3)$$

The income tax liability is computed by applying the income tax rate to the additional taxable income. One allowable deduction for tax purposes is the depreciation of the investment. It is possible to express the determination of the income tax in the following way:

$$\text{Income tax} = (\text{tax rate}) \times (\text{taxable income})$$

and

$$\text{Income tax} = (\text{tax rate})$$
$$\times (\text{revenues} - \text{expenses other than depreciation} - \text{depreciation}). \quad (5)$$

From equation 5 it can be seen that the higher the depreciation taken for income tax purposes, the lower the income tax will be and the greater the after-tax cash proceeds. Substituting equation 5 in equation 3 and simplifying gives equations 6 and 7.

$$\text{After-tax proceeds} = (1 - \text{tax rate})$$
$$\times (\text{revenues} - \text{expenses other than depreciation} - \text{depreciation})$$
$$+ \text{depreciation} \quad (6)$$

or

$$\text{After-tax proceeds} = (1 - \text{tax rate})$$
$$\times (\text{revenues} - \text{expenses other than depreciation})$$
$$+ (\text{tax rate} \times \text{depreciation}) \quad (7)$$

Equations 6 and 7 are mathematically equivalent, and therefore give identical answers, although one or the other formula may be easier to use in a particular instance. Equation 7 is particularly useful, because it highlights the fact that the cash proceeds of the period are increased by the allowable depreciation times the tax rate. Thus we can compute the present value of the "tax savings" by multiplying the depreciation by the expected tax rate of each period and discounting that amount back to the present.

EXAMPLE: A piece of new equipment costs $10,000. It can be depreciated for tax purposes in four years, and it has been decided to use the sum-of-the-years'-digits method. It is expected to have no salvage value on retirement. The company uses straight-line depreciation in its accounting. The equipment is expected to result in an increase in annual revenues (sales are all for cash) of $8,000 and additional annual costs requiring cash outlays of $4,000 (not including depreciation of the equipment). The income tax rate is 52 per cent. The cost of money is 10 per cent.

The first step is to compute the taxable income and income tax of each year. This is accomplished in Table 7-1.

It should be noted that the use of a tax rate of 52 per cent for all years carries an assumption that the tax rate will not be changed. If a change is expected, the tax rates of the future years should be used.

The second step is to compute the cash proceeds of each year (Table 7-2.) It is important to note that the book depreciation does not enter into this

Table 7-1. Computation of Income Tax

Year	Revenues	Other Costs	Depreciation for Tax Purposes	Taxable Income	Tax Rate (%)	Income Tax
1	$8,000	$4,000	$4,000	$ 0	52	$ 0
2	8,000	4,000	3,000	1,000	52	520
3	8,000	4,000	2,000	2,000	52	1,040
4	8,000	4,000	1,000	3,000	52	1,560

computation at all, but the depreciation for tax purposes influences the income tax and thus does indirectly affect the proceeds.

Using equation 6 to compute the cash flows of year 2, we would have

$$\text{After-tax proceeds} = (1 - .52)(8,000 - 4,000 - 3,000) + 3,000$$
$$= 480 + 3,000$$
$$= 3,480.$$

Using equation 7, we have

$$\text{After-tax proceeds} = (1 - .52)(8,000 - 4,000) + (.52 \times 3,000)$$
$$= 1,920 + 1,560$$
$$= 3,480.$$

The next step is to compute the present value of the cash flows, using 10 per cent as the rate of discount (see Table 7-3).

The present value of the proceeds, $10,403, is greater than the cash outflows of $10,000; thus the investment is apparently desirable.

In the preceding example the "other costs" allowed for tax purposes were equal to the "other costs" for which cash outlays were made. It is possible for these two amounts to differ. For example, costs may be incurred that are not allowable for tax purposes because the cost factors are in inventory. The cash outlays are required, but they do not give rise to decreases in the income tax of the period.

Table 7-2. Computation of Cash Proceeds

Year	Revenue	Other Costs	Income Tax	Cash Proceeds
1	$8,000	$4,000	$ 0	$4,000
2	8,000	4,000	520	3,480
3	8,000	4,000	1,040	2,960
4	8,000	4,000	1,560	2,440

Table 7-3.   Computation of the Present Value of Proceeds

Year	Cash Proceeds	Discount Factor (Using 10 Per Cent)	Present Value of the Proceeds
1	$4,000	.9091	$ 3,636
2	3,480	.8264	2,876
3	2,960	.7513	2,224
4	2,440	.6830	1,667
			$10,403

A different schedule of depreciation deductions for tax purposes is obtained if the twice-straight-line, declining-balance method is used (Table 7-4). The company using this procedure for tax purposes has the option to switch to the straight-line procedure. When the depreciation charge following twice straight line becomes less than it would be following straight line, the company should switch to the latter procedure. This will result in $1,250 of depreciation for year 4. The next step would be to compute the taxable income, income tax, and cash proceeds for each year of the life of the investment so that the present value of the cash flows may be computed, just as was done when using the sum-of-the-years'-digits depreciation.

Table 7-4.   Computation of Twice-Straight-Line Depreciation

Year	Decreasing Balance	Depreciation Rate (%)	Depreciation of the Period	Accumulated Depreciation
1	$10,000	50	$5,000	$ 5,000
2	5,000	50	2,500	7,500
3	2,500	50	1,250	8,750
4	1,250	100*	1,250	10,000

* Assuming the asset is to be retired at end of the fourth year.

choosing the most advantageous depreciation procedure

Under the internal revenue code, a company has a choice (among other methods) of depreciating a new asset by using straight-line depreciation, sum-of-the-years' digits, or twice straight line on the declining balance. In the often discussed problem of what depreciation method to use, it has frequently been noted that the choice of depreciation method will affect the profitability of the investment. It has not usually been realized that the best depreciation method for a company may depend upon the appropriate discount rate as well as upon the life of the investment and its expected salvage value. The present-value method can be put to use in making this

Table 7-5.   Present Value of After-Tax Cash Proceeds Excluding Depreciation

Year	(1) Revenues Less Current Expenses	(2) After-Tax Equivalent (Col. 1 × .48)	(3) Discount Factor	(4) Present Value (Col. 2 × Col. 3)
1	$ 4,000	$1.920	.9091	$1,745
2	4,000	1,920	.8264	1,587
3	4,000	1,920	.7513	1,443
4	4,000	1,920	.6830	1,311
	$16,000	$7,680	3.1698	$6,086

decision. For this purpose equation 7 for computing the after-tax cash proceeds is most advantageous, because it divides the after-tax cash proceeds into two parts. The first part is independent of the depreciation method, and the second part depends only on the depreciation method. The depreciation method giving the highest present value should be chosen.

As is indicated in Table 7-5, the present value of the after-tax equivalent of $4,000 a year for four years is $6,086 when the tax rate is 52 per cent and the discount rate is 10 per cent. This part of the calculation is independent of the depreciation method used.

To determine the best depreciation method, we need to compute the present value of the tax saving resulting from the use of each possible depreciation method. These computations are shown in Table 7-6, assuming a 52 per cent tax rate and a 10 per cent rate of discount. We assume the firm has other taxable income to absorb the tax loss of year 1. It is clear from this table that the investment would be most advantageous if it could be used with the twice straight-line method of depreciation, because in that case the present value of the cash proceeds would be $10,457 ($6,086 + $4,371). The present value of the proceeds, when the sum-of-the-years'-digits method of depreciation is used, would be $6,086 plus $4,317, or $10,403, which is less than the $10,457 obtained previously.

In this example the present value of the savings from the most advantageous method of depreciation as compared with the next best method amounts to about .5 per cent of the initial outlay of $10,000, or $54. In the case of a similar investment whose initial cost was $10 million, the present value of the difference between the two depreciation methods would be $54,000. With a longer-lived asset the difference would be larger.

use of tables to choose optimum depreciation method

Appendix Tables C and D have been prepared to assist in the choice of method of depreciation and in the computation of the tax saving that will result from

Table 7-6. Present Value of Tax Savings from Different Methods of Depreciation, Assuming a 10 Per Cent Rate of Discount

Year	Straight Line			Twice Straight Line			Sum-of-the-Years' Digits		
	Allowable Expense	Saving (52%)	Present Value	Allowable Expense	Saving (52%)	Present Value	Allowable Expense	Saving (52%)	Present Value
1	$ 2,500	$1,300	$1,182	$ 5,000	$2,600	$2,364	$ 4,000	$2,080	$1,891
2	2,500	1,300	1,074	2,500	1,300	1,074	3,000	1,560	1,289
3	2,500	1,300	977	1,250	650	488	2,000	1,040	781
4	2,500	1,300	888	1,250	650	445	1,000	520	356
	$10,000	$5,200	$4,121	$10,000	$5,200	$4,371	$10,000	$5,200	$4,317

making the investment. Two tables have been prepared. Table C shows the present value, following the sum-of-the-years'-digits method, using different discount rates and assuming assets of different lives. Table D shows comparable data for the declining-balance method of depreciation (twice straight line). If an asset has a nonzero salvage value, the tables cannot be used to determine the present value of the depreciation charges for the declining-balance method.

To use the tables, it is first necessary to enter the sum-of-the-years'-digits table, using the column that represents the discount rate chosen and going down it until the life of the asset is found. The amount obtained is the present value of the depreciation per dollar of depreciable base. This amount should be multiplied by the depreciable base (cost less salvage of the investment). The next step is to enter the proper table for the declining-balance method (assuming zero expected salvage). The column that represents the interest rate should be entered, and the number opposite the proper life of the asset should be determined. This number represents the present value per dollar of cost of the depreciation of the investment and must be multiplied by the cost of the investment to obtain the present value of the depreciation.

The choice of the method of depreciation will be dependent on which of the two present values is the greater. The present value of the tax savings can be found by multiplying the present value of the depreciation times the tax rate.

When a positive salvage value is expected, the present value of the depreciation deductions using the declining-balance method must be computed by following the same detailed procedures given earlier in this chapter. If the removal costs are expected to exceed the salvage (the salvage value is negative), the tables may be used. For the purposes of computing income taxes, the salvage is zero.

A change in the tax law has liberalized the treatment of expected salvage. The taxpayer may reduce the amount of salvage by 10 per cent of the cost of the depreciable property. Thus, if $1 million is spent on equipment with an expected salvage of $120,000, only $20,000 would be subtracted from the cost of the asset to compute the depreciable base.

It may be possible under some conditions to use double-declining-balance, then switch to sum-of-the-years-digits. When this switch is available it is optimum.

additional complications affecting choice of depreciation methods

The examples presented in the preceding section are intended primarily to illustrate the type of analysis that can be undertaken when it is considered worth the effort to determine the most advantageous method of depreciating a wasting asset. The examples chosen were deliberately oversimplified to bring out the point that the present-value approach can be used to determine the most advantageous method of depreciating an asset. A full treatment of the complications that arise in determining a proper and acceptable method of depreciation under the internal revenue code would require a book in itself and is beyond the scope of this chapter. However, some of the more important complications that may arise in practice will be mentioned briefly.

In the examples presented it was assumed that the assets to be depreciated would have no salvage value at the end of their expected useful life. If a salvage value is expected at the end of the asset's useful life, the amount of depreciation expense will be affected. The salvage value will affect the depreciation of each year, using the sum-of-the-years' digits; but by using the twice-straight-line, declining-balance procedure, it will affect only the changeover point (point at which a shift is made to straight line from twice straight line) and the depreciation after the changeover.

Another complication is that many companies use the group method of depreciation instead of the unit method. Under the group method the rate of depreciation is based on the average life of many units of like items (for example, telegraph poles). This rate of depreciation is then applied to the balance of unretired units. As the units are retired, no loss or gain is recognized at the time of retirement. The depreciation of successive periods is based on the estimate of average life (which is computed by using mortality experience for this type of asset) and the number of units that are retired in each period. Thus the use of the group procedure of depreciation requires a forecast of the number of units in use in each period in order to compute the depreciation of each period as well as a rate of depreciation.

In the examples given in this book it is assumed that the asset is purchased in year 0 and that depreciation expense is not charged until the end of the year. In practice, two alternatives are also available. Depreciation may be taken on a monthly basis, beginning in the month the asset is acquired. If the cost of the asset is not too large, and especially when straight-line depreciation is not being used, the extra expense involved in computing monthly depreciation charges for each asset may be greater than the possible saving. Another alternative is to adopt what is called the half-year convention, in which one half of a year's depreciation is charged in the year the asset is acquired, regardless of when during the year the asset is acquired. When straight-line depreciation is used, the amount to be charged each year under this system is one half the annual depreciation. With the twice-straight-line, declining-balance method, one half the usual rate is applied in the first year, and the usual rate is applied to the remaining book value in subsequent years.

A final complication is the timing of tax payments and of tax savings resulting from depreciation. In the past years tax payments have lagged the earning of corporate income, but at present they have been advanced to such an extent that to assume that the tax payment (or the tax saving) occurs at the end of the period in which income is earned will generally do no great harm.

working capital

In focusing attention on outlays for plant and equipment it is possible to lose sight of the fact that the working capital needed to operate the investment project should also be included in computing the investment outlays. Because residual working capital is recoverable at the termination of operations, this leads to the investment having a net terminal value that should be taken into consideration. The term *working capital* is used here in a net sense, and applicable current liabilities are subtracted from the increase in current assets to compute the use of cash. It is assumed that the additional current liabilities do not change the proportion of current liabilities to other sources of capital.

An investment in plant assets will usually lead to funds being tied up in working capital. This will include the cash necessary to meet payroll and other bills, funds invested in the raw material, work-in-process and finished-goods inventory, and receivables from customers. The size of these items will depend on the exact nature of the capital investment, but all the previously mentioned fund requirements will usually accompany an investment in long-lived assets. The one possible exception would be an investment that would decrease the need for working capital by increasing efficiency. Examples of this nature are accounting machines that expedite the billing to customers or storage facilities and inventory-control devices that reduce the amount of inventory which must be kept on hand.

A working capital increase has the effect of increasing the investment outflow today. Ignoring this factor will lead toward the acceptance of investments that should be rejected. If the investment has a limited life and the working capital is expected to be recovered at the end of the life of the investment, the recovery of the working capital in the last period should be considered as cash proceeds and treated in the same manner as the other cash flows are treated. It should not be thought that ignoring the working capital investment and the recovery of working capital will balance each other out. The factor that must be considered is the required return on the working capital during the period of use.

terminal value and taxes

If taxes are introduced into the analysis of working capital, strange things happen to the conclusions of the investment analysis. The presence of taxes in some situations can actually make terminal value undesirable.

High costs of money, high tax rates, and long-lived assets, combined with accelerated depreciation for tax purposes, can result in the presence of terminal value adversely affecting the desirability of an investment.

EXAMPLE: Assume a discount rate of 5 per cent, a 50 per cent tax rate, a life of twenty years for the asset, and a tax depreciation scheme that allows a company to write off a depreciable asset in five years. In this case $100 of depreciable assets may be worth more than $100 of terminal value.

The present value of $100 of terminal value due in twenty years, assuming a rate of interest of 5 per cent, is

$$\$100 \times .3769 = \$37.69 \quad \text{(present value of salvage).}$$

The $100 of additional depreciable assets (assuming no salvage value) will reduce taxes a total of $50, or $10 per year. The present value of an annuity of $1 per period for five periods, with an interest rate of 5 per cent, is $4.3295.

$$\$10 \times 4.3295 = \$43.30 \quad \text{(present value of the tax deductions)}$$

With the facts as given, tax deduction is worth more than the terminal value. Note that the facts of this situation are reasonable and close to reality: the corporate tax rate in recent years has been close to 50 per cent; depreciable assets do frequently have lives of twenty years; 5 per cent is not excessively high for a discount rate; and assets have frequently been written off for tax purposes over a period of sixty months.

The ideal situation from the point of view of the investor would be to write off the investment for tax purposes as if it had no salvage, and then wait and see if any salvage would develop. The taxpayer is going to be better off with a conservative estimate of salvage. This argument would be even more important if the gain on disposition of the investment were to qualify as a capital gain, thus receiving special tax consideration. There are provisions in the present internal revenue code that tend to result in such gains being taxed as ordinary income if the asset is held for a short period of time.

The preceding analysis leads to several interesting conclusions. In the presence of income taxes, situations can develop when, all other things being equal, it may be more desirable to accept a depreciable investment that has no terminal value than one which has terminal value. This conclusion must be tested by existing facts; it cannot be assumed. The factors that tend to make it valid are high tax rates, high discount rates, long-lived investments, and the privilege of writing off an investment for tax purposes at a faster rate than its actual service potential warrants. Not all these factors have to be present, but the presence of all leads to the conclusion that a depreciable asset that is deductible for tax purposes is more desirable than an asset that is not depreciable for tax purposes. Second, other things being equal, an expenditure that can be expensed immediately for tax purposes is more desirable than an expenditure that must be written off for tax purposes over a period of years. Thus, under the present tax code, inreasing net revenues by research may be more desirable than increasing net revenues by the same amount through increasing plant and equipment, since research may be expensed immediately, but plant and equipment must be depreciated.

changes in inventories and income taxes

The computation of cash flows makes use of the cash expenditures for factors of production in the period of outlay when computing the amount of outlays. Some of the factors of production may be lodged in inventory at the end of the accounting period and thus not charged against the revenues of the period. This would affect the cash flows of the period, because the items would not be expensed for purposes of computing income taxes. The income taxes of this period will be higher than they would be if all cash expenditures were expenses for tax purposes. In some future accounting period, these items will be expensed and will result in taxes for that period being reduced, thus in effect increasing the cash flows (by decreasing taxes) in a period long after the cash expenditure was made. Thus buildups of inventory required by an investment will adversely affect the desirability of the investment by requiring an immediate cash outlay, whereas the cash flows, both by reducing income taxes and by generating revenues upon sale of the item, are delayed for one or more periods. The inventories must generate enough cash flows not only to recover the initial outlay of funds, but also to pay the interest costs of the differences in time of outlay and recovery of cash.

taxes and present value

We have defined the net present value of an investment as the amount a firm could afford to pay for an investment in excess of its cost. This implicitly assumes a zero tax rate. With a corporate tax rate of t_c, the amount that a firm would be willing to pay for a stream of benefits must take into consideration the fact that the benefits will be taxed and that the amount paid for the investment generally will be deductible for tax purposes. If D is the present value of the depreciation deductions using sum-of-the-years'-digits (see Appendix Table C), the cost of an investment (C) net of the tax savings from depreciation is

$$C(1 - t_c D).$$

Setting this equal to the present value of the benefits of the investment, we can then solve for C, the amount we could afford to pay for the investment.

EXAMPLE: An investment will result in cash proceeds of $10,000 per year before tax and $6,000 after tax ($t_c = .4$) for a period of ten years. The time value of money is .05 after taxes. If we use sum-of-the-years'-digits method of depreciation, how much could we pay for the investment?

The present value of the benefits are

$$\$6,000 \times B(10, .05) = \$6,000 \times 7.72173 = \$46,330.$$

The present value of depreciation deductions (from Appendix Table C) per dollar of investment is .82846.

$$C(1 - t_c D) = 46,330$$

$$C = \frac{\$46,330}{(1 - t_c D)} = \frac{\$46,330}{1 - .4 \times .82846} = \$69,292.$$

We could pay $69,292 for the investment that has cash flows with a present value of $46,330, because tax depreciation deduction reduces the cost of the investment from $69,292 to $46,330. With a .07 investment tax credit we could afford to pay

$$C = \frac{\$46,330}{(1 - t_c D - .07)} = \frac{\$46,330}{1 - .331384 - .07} = \frac{\$46,330}{.598616} = \$77,395.$$

timing of tax payments

The timing of income tax payments is relevant to the investment analysis if the payment of the tax occurs in a time period significantly later than the earning of the proceeds. There are two possible methods of incorporating the delayed income tax payments into the analysis.

One possibility is to consider the cash outlay to occur when the actual cash disbursement occurs, not when the obligation to pay is created. The second possibility is to consider the incurrence of the obligation to pay income taxes to consist of two simultaneous transactions. The government acts as a source of capital and supplier of assets; the assets are then expended to "pay" for the income tax expense. This second possibility then leads to the inclusion of "Income Taxes Payable" as a non-interest-bearing source of capital in computing the cost of capital. To be consistent with other recommendations made in this book, the first procedure is recommended. If the second possibility is used, the income taxes payable should equal the present value of the taxes that are owed.

EXAMPLE: Assume that a firm has an opportunity to invest $20,000 today in promoting a sport contest. The promised return to be received one year from today is $24,000. The income tax of $2,080 (assuming a 52 per cent tax rate) is to be paid two years from today. The interest rate is 10 per cent. The schedule of cash flows would be as follows:

Year	Cash Flows	Present-Value Factor	Present Value of Cash Flows
0	($20,000)	1.0000	($20,000)
1	24,000	.9091	21,818
2	(2,080)	.8264	(1,719)
			$ 99

The net present value is positive and therefore the investment should be undertaken.

If the income taxes were collected during period 1, the cash flows of that period would be $21,920, and the net present value of the cash flows, using a 10 per cent rate of discount, would be a negative $73. This would indicate that the investment should not be undertaken.

taxes and investment incentives

Governments have available many devices for encouraging or discouraging firms to undertake investments. Among the variables are the method of depreciation, the allowed life of assets, the treatment of salvage, and investment tax credits or investment allowances.

The investment tax credit that has been used several times in the United States allows most corporations to deduct 7 per cent of the cost of qualified investments from their federal income taxes.

Business managers should be knowledgeable as to the nature of the current tax laws and sensitive to changes in the laws. The tax laws are a powerful tool for governments to influence the level of investments. Businesses must make decisions that are consistent with the tax laws under which they will have to operate.

questions and problems

7-1. Assume that the internal revenue code allows a tax credit of .07 of the cost of eligible investments to be deducted from the amount of federal income taxes payable. It also allows the use of accelerated depreciation.

Assume a marginal income tax rate of .4, and an after-tax discount rate of .03. (a) How much is $1 of tax credit worth today? (b) How much is the "right" to deduct $1 of depreciation today worth today? (c) Assume that we pay $1 million for equipment eligible for the tax credit. The equipment will be depreciated for tax purposes in ten years. What is the cost of the equipment? What is the cash flow of the period of purchase of the equipment? What do we know about the value of the equipment as of the beginning of the period after the taking of tax credit?

7-2. Assume a rate of discount of 5 per cent. Prepare a set of rules for when to choose the straight-line, double-declining-balance, and the sum-of-the-years'-digits methods of depreciation, if the salvage value is zero. How does your rule change if the rate of discount is 10 per cent?

7-3. Assume that a rate of discount is 5 per cent and that a firm is making other income. It is considering an investment eligible for the investment credit that costs $1 million. The investment has an expected life of twenty years. Compute the present value of the cash flows that result because of the income tax and the income tax laws (assume a .40 tax rate).

7-4. Assume a tax rate of .4 and a rate of discount of .05. (a) If the firm is basically a profitable operation, what is the present value of $1 of tax-deductible expense incurred and paid for at the end of period 1? (b) If the firm is a loss operation, what is the present value of $1 of tax-deductible expense incurred and paid for at the end of period 1?

7-5. Compute the present value of the right to deduct $1 million in depreciation immediately compared with the right to deduct the $1 million in twenty years from now. The tax rate is .4 and the after-tax rate of discount is .05.

7-6. *The XYZ Manufacturing Company*
A product is currently being manufactured on a machine that is fully depreciated for tax purposes and that has a book value of $10,000 (it was purchased for $30,000 twenty years ago). The costs of the product are as follows:

	Unit Costs
Labor, direct	$ 4.00
Labor, indirect	2.00
Variable overhead	1.50
Fixed overhead	2.50
	$10.00

In the past year 1,000 units were produced and sold for $18 per unit. It is expected that the old machine can be used indefinitely in the future. An equipment manufacturer has offered to accept the old machine as a trade-in for a new version. The new machine would cost $60,000 after allowing $15,000 for the old equipment. The projected costs associated with the new machine are as follows:

Labor, direct	$2.00
Labor, indirect	3.00
Variable overhead	1.00
Fixed overhead	3.25
	$9.25

The fixed overhead costs are allocations from other departments plus the depreciation of the equipment.

The old machine could be sold on the open market now for $5,000. Ten years from now it is expected to have a salvage value of $1,000. The new machine has an expected life of ten years and an expected salvage of $10,000.

The current corporate income tax rate is .40 and the capital-gain tax rate is .25. Any salvage from sale will result in a capital gain at the time of retirement. (For tax purposes the entire cost may be depreciated in ten years.) The appropriate after-tax time discount rate for this company is .10.

It is expected that future demand of the product will stay steady at 1,000 units per year.

Required: (a) Should the equipment be acquired? (b) If the product can be purchased at a cost of $7.80 per unit from a reliable supplier, should it be purchased or made? Explain.

7-7. Manufacturers of heavy electric generating equipment have been arguing for years over the value of buying in advance of need. The following analysis was presented by one manufacturer in order to persuade utilities to order in advance under a "buy and store" plan.

Cost of boiler if purchased a year early and stored	$1,000,000
(90 per cent of the purchase price would be paid immediately and 10 per cent one year later, when the boiler is completed)	
Storage costs for one year	$ 10,000
(this amount would be paid two years from now)	

It is expected that there will be an 8.5 per cent increase in cost ($85,000) if the purchase is delayed one year (this is based on the experience of the post-World War II period).

Assuming a short-term interest rate of .04, the interest cost of buying early is $36,000, and with a .52 tax rate the after-tax interest cost is $17,200. Comparing the $85,000 of cost saving with the storage cost plus the interest indicates that it is desirable to purchase early.

Assume that the boiler is to be placed into use two years from now. The after-tax cost of money of the company considering the purchase is 7 per cent.

Required: Prepare an estimate of the incremental after-tax cash flows resulting from ordering a boiler immediately. The estimated cash flows should be suitable for determining the value of advance ordering, using a discounted cash flow approach. Assume that the boiler would be depreciated on a straight-line basis over a twenty-year period from the date it is installed and ready to use. The 7 per cent tax credit does not apply.

7-8. While discussing the pros and cons of an automated collator with an executive of a large corporation, the dean of a school in a large university said, "You are lucky; with a tax rate of .40 you pay only $6,000 for a $10,000 machine." Assume that there is a labor saving of $2,500 per year associated with the collator being considered. The expected life is ten years and the before-tax time value of money is .05 to both the university and the corporation.

Required: Who has more incentive to purchase the machine, the university or the corporation?

7-9. Continuing problem 7-8. Assume that a university and a corporation both are considering spending $5 million for an administrative office building. The expected life is fifty years. Take the 7 per cent tax credit and depreciation into consideration; what is the net saving to each? The tax rate is .40 and the time value of money is .05 before taxes (.03 after taxes to the corporation). The alternative for both is to rent at a before-tax cost of $300,000 per year with a cancellable lease.

7-10. *The NSV Manufacturing Company*
A product is currently being manufactured on a machine that is fully depreciated for tax purposes and has a book value of $10,000 (it was purchased for $30,000 twenty years ago). The costs of the product are as follows:

	Unit Costs
Labor, direct	$ 4.00
Labor, variable indirect	2.00
Other variable overhead	1.50
Fixed overhead	2.50
	$10.00

In the past year 10,000 units were produced and sold for $18 per unit. It is expected that with suitable repairs the old machine can be used indefinitely in the future. The repairs are expected to average $25,000 per year.

An equipment manufacturer has offered to accept the old machine as a trade-in for a new version. The new machine would cost $60,000 after allowing $15,000 for the old equipment. The projected costs associated with the new machine are as follows:

Labor, direct	$2.00
Labor, variable indirect	3.00
Other variable overhead	1.00
Fixed overhead	3.25
	$9.25

The fixed overhead costs are allocations from other departments plus the depreciation of the equipment.

The old machine could not be sold on the open market. The new machine has an expected life of ten years and no expected salvage at that time.

The current corporate income tax rate is .40. For tax purposes the cost of the new machine may be depreciated in ten years. The appropriate time discount rate for this company is .10.

It is expected that future demand of the product will stay steady at 10,000 units per year.

Required: (a) Should the new equipment be acquired? (b) If the product can be purchased at a cost of $7.80 per unit from a reliable supplier, should it be purchased or made? Explain.

chapter 8

*In practice we have tacitly agreed, as a rule, to
fall back on what is, in truth, a* convention. *The
essence of this convention—though it does not,
of course, work out quite so simple —lies in
assuming that the existing state of affairs will
continue indefinitely, except insofar as we have
specific reasons to expect a change.*

J. M. Keynes, *The General Theory of Employment, Interest and
Money* (New York: Harcourt, Brace & Company, 1936), p. 152.

capital budgeting under capital rationing

In the preceding chapters we concluded that under conditions of certainty, if a firm could borrow or lend funds at a given market rate of interest, it should accept independent investments when the investments have positive net present values at this market rate of interest. In this chapter we consider situations in which the assumption that a firm can borrow or lend any quantity of funds that it desires at a given market rate of interest is not valid. There are two distinctly different situations in which this assumption may not hold.

One of these situations arises because of a decision by management to limit arbitrarily the total amount invested or the kind of investments the firm undertakes, or to set acceptance criteria that lead it to reject some investments that are advantageous when judged by market criteria. For example, instead of using the market interest rate it might use some higher rate as a cutoff rate.

A second situation that must be considered is when there is a difference between the market rate of interest at which the firm can borrow money and the market rate at which it can lend.

Both situations are frequently labeled *capital rationing*. To distinguish between them, we shall refer to the former situation as *internal capital rationing* and to the latter as *external capital rationing*. External capital rationing is actually the result of market imperfections or transaction costs.

Two observations should be noted. First, capital rationing in both the first and second form is present throughout the economy, but usually to a relatively minor degree, and thus may frequently not be incorporated into the analysis (although it should not be ignored without trying to estimate its impact). Second, when capital rationing is present, there is no simple solution to the internal investment decision. Two possible approaches are offered. The first possibility is to make simplifying assumptions where appropriate and to recognize that the answer obtained is an approximation. The second approach is to use mathematical techniques to develop possible solutions, following different possible investment alternatives (including all possible combinations of investments through the succeeding years). This analytical technique may lead to a sound solution to the capital-budgeting decision under capital rationing, but it is complex and requires detailed knowledge of future investment alternatives that is frequently not available.

external capital rationing

In this chapter the term *borrow* is used when a firm obtains capital from the market by issuing any type of security. The term *lend* is used to mean the use of funds to purchase any type of security. We specifically assume that borrowing takes place in such a way that the borrowing firm's capital structure (the relative proportion of the various kinds of securities it has issued) is not changed. Thus *borrowing* would normally involve issuing both debt and equity securities. Similarly, we assume that *lending* means acquiring a portfolio of securities that has approximately the same average risk characteristics as the assets presently owned by the firm.[1]

If capital markets were such that a firm could lend or borrow as much money as it desired at the going rate of interest, this rate of interest would be the same for both the borrowing and lending transactions. The goal of profit maximization would then require that the firm accept all independent investments whose present values were positive, using this rate of interest. With such capital markets the choice of investments would not be dependent on the amount of funds available to the firm, because by an appropriate combination of borrowing and lending, each firm could finance investments that had positive present values.

---

[1] Under conditions of certainty the term *lending* could be interpreted literally, because there is no problem of risk. Under uncertainty we want to define lending so that the process does not change the risk characteristics of the firm's assets compared to expanding the firm's operations by investing internally. A firm is lending if it purchases the securities of other firms whose assets have the same risk characteristics as its own assets.

A firm may purchase its own securities in amounts proportional to their market value. Suppose that a firm has only equity shares outstanding and it buys some of its own shares. The effect is very nearly the same as if it had used the same amount of cash to pay a cash dividend. It differs from lending in that it is not expected that the funds will be returned to the corporation.

This theoretical situation is an ideal never encountered in practice. There will almost always be some divergence between the rates of interest at which the firm can lend surplus funds and the rates at which it can borrow funds. The size of the gap may vary for many reasons, including the effect of the brokerage costs of raising new money and the fact that there may be hidden costs or risks connected with one or other of the investments. Another reason is that moneylenders may prefer firms having certain characteristics, thus driving up the cost of borrowing by firms that lack these characteristics.

If the borrowing rate and the lending rate are almost equal, little is lost by neglecting the difference and speaking of a market rate of interest. If the difference is large, it cannot be ignored in determining the investment and financial policies of the firm. This gives rise to the situation we describe as external capital rationing.

An approximate solution to the capital-budgeting process with external capital rationing can be described as follows: Assume that a schedule is prepared showing the total current outlays required for investments having a positive present value at various rates of discount.[2] Such a schedule will show greater current outlays at lower rates of interest, because some investments whose present values are negative at high discount rates will have positive present values at low discount rates. The schedules are shown by curves $I–I$ in Figure 8-1(a), (b), and (c). We let the distance OQ_1 represent the quantity of internally generated funds available for investment during the current period. Three situations are possible. In Figure 8-1(a) the vertical line drawn up from point Q_1 intersects curve $I–I$ at a rate of interest higher than r_2, the borrowing rate. This indicates that some investments which would be profitable at a cost equal to the borrowing rate could not be financed from internally generated funds. It would be profitable for the firm to borrow an amount Q_1Q_2 to enable it to accept all investments that would be profitable at the borrowing rate. It would not be profitable to borrow any more than this amount, because all remaining investments have negative present values at the borrowing rate of discount.

In Figure 8-1(b) the internally generated funds currently available are more than sufficient to enable the firm to undertake all the investments that would be profitable when evaluated at the lending rate of interest. Only OQ_2 dollars would be invested internally. The remaining funds, Q_1Q_2, would either be invested externally by buying the securities of other organizations or used to reduce the capitalization of the firm by returning the funds to the suppliers.

A third possibility is that the firm has sufficient funds to accept all independent investments whose present values are positive when evaluated at the borrowing rate, but that the firm does not have enough funds to accept all

---

[2] Current outlays are the net outlays required in period zero.

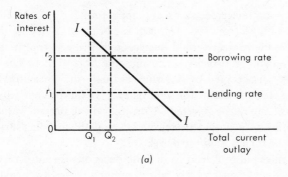

(a)

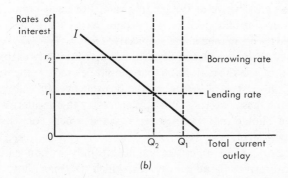

(b)

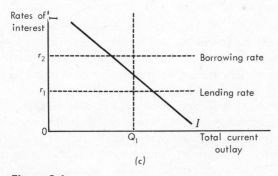

(c)

Figure 8-1

investments whose present values are positive when evaluated at the lending rate. This is illustrated in Figure 8-1(c). Under those circumstances the firm would neither borrow any additional funds nor lend any part of its present funds, and the proper rate of discount for investments would be lower than the borrowing rate, but higher than the lending rate.

Based on this analysis, an incomplete set of rules for dealing with individual investment projects can be derived. Consider independent projects for which accept or reject decisions are appropriate. Evaluate the present value of the cash flows from the project at the borrowing rate. If the present value is positive, the project should be accepted. Projects that meet this test will be worth accepting even if money must be borrowed to finance them. If the project is not accepted by this rule, evaluate the present value of the cash flows from the project at the lending rate. If the present value is negative, the project should be rejected. A project whose present value is negative at the lending rate should be rejected even if the firm has surplus funds that it cannot use for internal purposes.

These two rules will not lead to definite decisions for all projects. There may be some independent projects whose present values are negative at the borrowing rate and positive at the lending rate. For such projects no strict rules can be given. The final decision will depend partly on the firm's financial position and partly on management's objectives.

A similar set of tests can be applied to pairs of mutually exclusive alternatives, but in this case the cash flows that should be used are the incremental cash flows. If the best of a set of mutually exclusive alternatives can be identified utilizing these two tests, it is still necessary to consider whether this best alternative should be accepted or rejected when considered as an independent investment.

Strictly speaking, these rules are applicable only to conventional cash flows. Modifications to handle cases in which the cash-flow sequences alternate between outlays and proceeds are possible but are beyond the scope of this book.[3]

The analysis of this chapter assumes a capital market with a significant difference between the borrowing and lending rates. The solution suggested is only approximate, because we have not indicated what assumption is being made as to the probable lending and borrowing rates in the future, and the firm's position relative to them. The appropriate interest rates in future time periods are relevant to decisions made in the present because they affect the profitability of funds reinvested at those times. Cash flows expected in each future time period should be discounted at the rate of interest which will apply in that period. If we predict future lending and borrowing rates, we can assume that the appropriate rate of discount for each future period will lie somewhere between these upper and lower limits. Occasionally, a firm will have some basis for predicting whether in a given future year it is more likely to be operating somewhere near its borrowing rate or near its lending rate. If a firm, even in a growing industry, is faced with a temporary excess of capacity, it may feel safe in predicting that for the next few years it will have more internally generated funds than it needs for the available profitable

[3] On this point, see Gordon Pye, "Present Values for Imperfect Capital Markets," *Journal of Business*, 39, Jan. 1966, pp. 45–51.

investment alternatives. This can be reflected by using a rate of discount for these years that is relatively close to the lending rate. In other cases the firm may anticipate product improvements that are presently in the research and development state but which are expected to be perfected within a few years. If the introduction of these innovations will require large-scale capital investments, the firm may feel confident in predicting that it will be likely to be operating relatively close to its borrowing-rate point during the years these investments are being made.[4]

Although such predictions of future cutoff rates under external capital rationing are inevitably rather crude, they serve a useful purpose if the predicted rates are in the right general direction. By using a high rate of discount for a future year in which there is likely to be a shortage of internally generated funds relative to the available investment opportunities in that year, the firm is recognizing that the opportunity cost of funds may be higher in some periods than in others. Investment proposals that release funds for use in periods when the demand is greatest will thus be preferred, all other things being equal, over investments that utilize funds in the periods of high demand. Similarly, if excess funds are likely to be available, the use of a lower discount rate will tend to lead toward the choice of investments that do not generate funds during these periods. The opportunity cost of funds during periods of excess funds is low; thus a low rate of discount is appropriate.

If a company is in a situation of external capital rationing, it may be useful for the top management to predict the appropriate cutoff rate that will apply in future years. By this means the investment planning in various parts of the organization can be coordinated in terms of the best available estimates of future cash needs and requirements for the company as a whole. If fluctuating cutoff rates are expected in the future, the company may wish to prepare and use present-value tables that show the appropriate discount factors to be used for each future period.

Example:

Suppose a firm expects that the appropriate cutoff rate for it will be 5 per cent for periods 1, 2, and 3, and 10 per cent for periods 4 and 5. The firm is considering two mutually exclusive investment alternatives. Both require initial outlays of $100 now. Investment G will return $150 in year 3; investment H will return $200 in year 5. The present value of G's proceeds is $150 $(1.05)^{-3}$ = $150(.8638) = $130. The present value of H's proceeds is $200 $(1.05)^{-3}(1.10)^{-2}$ = $200(.8638)(.8264) = $200(.7138) = $413. Investment H with a net present value of $43 is preferred to G with a net present value of only $30.

[4] See Figure 8-1(c) and assume that curve *II* has shifted upward to the right (meaning there are more profitable investments) until the situation is described by Figure 8-1(a). In this situation the borrowing rate is applicable.

internal capital rationing

There are two types of internal capital rationing. In the first, the firm sets a cutoff rate for investments that is higher than the firm's cost of money. In the second type the firm decides to limit the total amount of funds committed to internal investments in a given year to some fixed sum, even though investments having positive present values at the firm's cost of money must be rejected as a result of this decision.

Consider the first kind of internal capital rationing. Suppose a firm requires that investments must have a positive present value at 15 per cent, even though the firm's cost of money is only 10 per cent. In this case, if the same cutoff rate is maintained from year to year, the cutoff rate in future years will be known, and the firm can evaluate all investments *as if* the cost of money were 15 per cent. This will have some advantages compared to many other measures of investment worth. We have shown in Chapter 2 that whatever rate of discount is used, the present-value measures will avoid some errors in making investment decisions that could be committed if the pay-out period or other measures were used.

But although a definite cutoff rate is available, the logic of using that rate to discount cash flows is no longer completely correct. The rate of discount used should measure the alternative uses of funds available to the firm. In the present instance, however, it indicates only that an investment of $1 now yielding less than 15 per cent will not be undertaken. If next year the company has more internally generated funds than it is willing to invest following the 15 per cent cutoff rule, then an extra dollar of funds that becomes available next year will have an opportunity cost that is less than 15 per cent. How much less will depend on what use the firm makes of the "excess" cash that it will not invest. Usually, these excess funds are invested in short-term government securities.

internal capital rationing and dividend policy

In the second type of internal capital rationing, the cutoff rate is not specified, but the maximum amount that will be invested is determined by top management, because it is unwilling to go to the market to obtain additional funds, even though there are desirable investments. This reluctance to go to the market may result from a wish to prevent outsiders from gaining control of the business, or from a feeling that there will be a dilution of earnings if additional equity funds are raised under the given market conditions.

In these circumstances, the correct amount and selection of investments will depend on the firm's dividend policy. One possibility is that the firm will maintain (over the life of the investments) the current level of dividends, regardless of any increases in earnings that may come about because of additional investment. Assume that past investments will support the dividend; then the net cash flows generated in future periods by the investments of the current period will be available for reinvestment in the period in which they are earned. The amounts of cash available for investment will vary from period to period, as will the desirability of investments (the demand schedule for investments may shift). This situation may result in the firm's rejecting internal investments with yields greater than the borrowing rate. For this reason it will be very difficult to make predictions of future cutoff rates (the opportunity costs for future cash flows).

A common dividend policy is that whereby the firm pays a dividend equal to a given fraction of its income (the income is measured by ordinary financial accounting techniques). In this case only a fraction of the future cash proceeds generated by current investments will be available for reinvestment. It is theoretically desirable to divide future cash flows generated by investments into that part which will be used as dividends and that part which will be available for reinvestment. The value of a dollar of reinvestible funds earned in future period t will be greater than the value of a dollar used for dividends in the same future period, if we ignore uncertainty and assume that the dollars will be reinvested in projects with positive net present values. But even if the firm has an overabundance of cash, it should not invest the funds in investments with a negative net present value. Such investment would result in the reinvested dollars having less value than the dollars paid as dividends. It is unnecessary for the firm to accept investments whose yields are less than the yields of alternative opportunities available to the stockholders, because these same investments are generally available to the corporation.

summary—capital rationing and present value

Capital rationing in one form or another exists to some extent in most corporations. We may distinguish among minor and severe cases of capital rationing. In the minor cases the present-value rules suggested in this book may be used with confidence. In the more severe forms of capital rationing, the present-value method may still be used, but it is now less correct to use a constant rate of discount for all future years. The rate of discount used for each future year must reflect the cost of obtaining additional funds, the value of external investments available to the firm, or the desires of the owners for present versus future proceeds. In Chapter 22 we return to capital rationing and offer a mathematical solution to the problem.

questions and problems

8-1. The ABC Company is planning its investment budget. Currently, it can raise money at a cost of .06. It assumes that its stockholders are able to invest funds so as to earn .04. There are also opportunities for the company to lend its funds and earn .04 (a) Assume that the company expected a large amount of investment opportunities. What discount rate should it use in making investment decisions? (b) Assume that the company expected a large amount of cash compared to internal investment opportunities. What rate of discount should it use in making decisions? (c) Assume that the company expected a shortage of cash for the coming twenty-four months, but then expected a surplus amount of cash. What does this imply about the rate of discount to be used?

8-2. The ABC Company has a stable dividend policy ($2 per share a year). It also has a policy of not raising new capital from the market. The policy is to invest the available funds after payment of the dividends (excess cash is invested in marketable securities). What does this imply about the use of the present-value method of making investment decisions?

8-3. The ABC Company has more investment opportunities than it can use (it is unwilling to borrow or issue more common stock). Management estimated that the investment cutoffs for the next two years will be as follows:

Year	Cutoff
0–1	.20
1–2	.30

It is attempting to choose between two mutually exclusive alternatives both of which will require an initial outlay now and payoff at the end of two periods.

What discount rate should be used in evaluating the mutually exclusive investments? What rate would you use if the investments had a life of one year? [*Hint:* $(1 + R_n)^n = (1 + r_1)(1 + r_2)\cdots(1 + r_n)$, where r_i is the value of money of period i and R_n is the equivalent interest rate for the n periods.]

8-4. The president of the ABC Company wants a ranking of three investments. The firm considers its cost of money to be .05. The following three independent investments are ranked.

Investment	Cash Flows of Period: 0	1	2	Present Net Value, Using .05	Ranking
A	− $1,000	$1,120		66.69	3
B	− 1,000		$1,210	97.47	1
C	− 1,000	400	775	83.89	2

The firm has $1,000 of uncommitted funds available (without borrowing) for investment. Based on the preceding ranking, the president decides to accept investment B. It is then brought to his attention that because investment B has a yield of .10 this could be considered to be the investment cutoff rate (other investments already approved having higher yields).

Evaluate the decision process.

8-5. In September 1964 the Commonwealth Edison Company announced it would discontinue its stock dividend policy. The policy of the company had been to issue stock dividends of 1 to 2.4 per cent for the earnings in excess of the cash dividends. The stated purpose of the stock dividends was to help finance expansion without public offerings of common stock. The dividends were stopped because it was feared that a further increase in the common stock equity ratio would increase the company's overall cost of money.

Required: Discuss the company's use of stock dividends.

8-6. An investor can earn .05 (before taxes) in default-free investments. He is considering purchasing stock in a corporation that will pay a dividend of $10 a year for perpetuity (assume this information is known with certainty). The investor is in a marginal .7 tax bracket (a) Compute the value of the stock to the investor. (b) Compute the value of the stock, assuming that an investor has a marginal tax rate of .4. (c) Compute the value of the stock for the investors of parts (a) and (b). Assume that there are tax-exempt securities that can be purchased to yield .03.

8-7. Assume a situation where it is known that the dividend of $10 a year will not begin for eleven years and that the price at the end of ten years will be $200. The capital gains tax rate is .25; the after-tax opportunity cost to high tax investors is .03, and the after-tax opportunity cost to low tax investors is .05. (a) How much would a high-tax investor be willing to pay for the stock now? Assume that he will sell at the end of ten years for $200. Why is this selling assumption reasonable? (b) How much would a low-tax investor (say zero tax) be willing to pay for the stock now? Would he sell at the end of ten years?

8-8. Recompute parts (a) and (b) of problem 8-7. Assume that the expected price at the end of ten years is $100.

8-9. Refer to problem 8-7. (a) How much would the high-tax investor be willing to pay for the stock at the end of year 9? How much would the low-tax investor be willing to pay? (c) How much would the high-tax investor realize in year 9 if he liquidated his investment at a price of $190? Assume that he paid $130 for the investment. (d) Compute the present value of the investment at the end of year 9. Assume that the high-tax investor intends to hold until year 10 and sell at $200.

8-10. Company X's reported net earnings have increased to $3 per share after having remained at the $2 per share level for a number of years. Dividend payments have been $1.20 per share for quite a few years. Its dividend payout has been somewhat more liberal than that of its industry.

Practically all the increase in earnings has resulted from consolidated earnings of new foreign subsidiaries and affiliated domestic companies. The earnings of these companies are available for Company X dividends only to the extent that Company Y receives dividends from them. The foreign companies and affiliates are relatively new and their capitalizations are highly leveraged, so a major portion of their net earnings is currently required to repay debt and provide funds for expansion, leaving only a small portion available for dividend payments to Company X.

The treasurer considers the general financial position of Company X to be quite satisfactory. Although cash is kept at the minimum amount necessary to run the business, long-term debt represents only 15 per cent of total capitalization and could be increased readily to finance major capital expenditures. Depreciation is adequate to support replacement of worn-out and obsolete equipment, but not a significant expansion of plant and equipment. Long-term debt repayments are equivalent to approximately $.60 per share of net earnings.

Required: With the increase in reported earnings, management is receiving inquiries as to why the dividend has not been increased. Based on the information presented, the dividend could be increased by about $.20 per share from parent company earnings plus dividends from foreign subsidiaries and affiliates, which may average $.20 to $.30 per share over the next several years, but this would reduce or eliminate retained earnings for expansion.

The company's dividend policy is to maintain a dividend rate once established. The problem facing management is whether to increase the dividend or not, and, if so, how much and still provide adequately for future expansion.

8-11.

The United Fruit Company

During the annual stockholders' meeting held April 21, 1965, the following exchanges took place:
Question: When capital investment is being considered to reduce costs, what minimum rate of return is considered acceptable by the company?
Mr. Fox: To reduce costs, the minimum rate of return that we would be at all interested in would be about 11 per cent after taxes, which is the target we are setting on our return for investments.

There are other considerations than just straight cost reductions. If they improved the quality of the product or improved the safety of our operations, these would also have to be considered. But by and large, anything that didn't enable us to have 11 per cent after taxes would not get serious consideration.

Question: Is there a chance the company again may offer to buy its stock at $26 a share?

Mr. Fox: I think that what you are really asking here is: Are we contemplating acquiring a large amount of our stock and inviting tenders at whatever the price might be at that particular time?

We have better opportunities to broaden and expand this company by using our cash and our credit if need be to acquire other businesses. And rather than retrenching the company, I would like to see it expand. This, of course, would pretty much preclude a tender in the near future at least.

Question: Would you comment, sir, about our oil leases?

Mr. Fox: There is little to report. We have not made any major strikes and have ceased exploring. We would like to find some way to profitably dispose of these properties to someone who might like to proceed with them. The cost of exploring for oil is too big a gamble for this company to take.

Question: Has there been a tremendous investment of corporate assets in the oil explorations or is it relatively insignificant?

Mr. Fox: No, it has been insignificant.

Required: Discuss the preceding questions and answers.

part II

All hope abandon, ye who enter here.

—Dante Alighieri (1265–1321), *Divine Comedy, Inferno,*
Canto III, Line 9. Translation from *Oxford Dictionary of
Quotations*, 2nd ed. (New York: Oxford University
Press, Inc., 1959).

In Part I we described easily applied decision rules
that use the present-value procedure. With conditions
of certainty and no capital rationing, we are able to
make accept or reject decisions involving independent
investments or to choose the best of a set of mutually
exclusive investments. In Part II we introduce uncertainty. Although the decision rules offered in Part II are
analogous to those of Part I, they are more complex.

A business decision maker could possibly read
Part II and then despair of ever finding an easily
applied rational approach to making investment decisions. We hope that the opposite will occur—that a
knowledge of the complexities will lead to more
reasonable procedures.

We think it is important that the decision maker
understand all aspects of the investment decision and
realize the limitations of the present-value procedure
as well as the advantages of this very useful tool for
business decision making. The purpose of Part II is to
ensure that the reader is able to analyze situations in
which it is appropriate to supplement the simple
decision rules of the present-value procedure with an
analysis of risk.

The chapters in Part II have the general characteristic of requiring the reader to have somewhat more
patience with mathematics than in the first part of this
book. We have attempted to keep the mathematics as
simple as possible.

In any event, if you want a better understanding of
decision making under uncertainty, you are encouraged
to try reading this material.

chapter 9

Business men play a mixed game of skill and chance, the average results of which to the players are not known by those who take a hand. If human nature felt no temptation to take a chance, no satisfaction (profit apart) in constructing a factory, a railway, a mine or a farm, there might not be much investment merely as result of cold calculation.

—J. M. Keynes, *The General Theory of Employment, Interest and Money* (New York: Harcourt, Brace & Company, 1936), p. 150.

an introduction to uncertainty

Up to this point we have assumed that an investment could be described as a unique sequence of cash flows. In the present chapter the complication of uncertainty is introduced. With uncertainty there may be many alternative sequences of cash flows that could occur if an investment were accepted. The decision maker does not know in advance which sequence will actually occur. The objective of the present chapter will be to consider methods of describing these uncertain outcomes. Decision-making procedures will be considered in later chapters.

uncertain events and forecasts of cash flows

The difficulty of specifying unique cash flows derives from the fact that there are future events that will affect the cash flows. but we do not know in advance which of these events will occur. For each possible event, we have to make a somewhat different forecast of the cash flows from the investment. The uncertainty arises because we do not know for certain which of the possible events will occur, and thus cannot be sure which cash flow will actually occur.

We shall use the term *event* to describe a future state of the world. For some purposes it may be useful to combine fundamental occurrences to form a master event. For example, rain or snow may result in the cancellation of a game; hence we may use an event "bad weather" rather than one event "rain" and another event "snow."

To take a simple example, suppose that you have an opportunity to bet on the outcome of the flip of a coin. If the coin lands heads, you win $1; if the coin lands tails, you lose $1. The cash forecast is a plus $1 with one event and a $1 loss with the other event. Before the toss you do not know whether the coin will land heads or tails. Only if you know that the coin is two-headed or two-tailed will the cash flows be known with certainty.

To take a more immediately relevant case, suppose that a firm is contemplating investing in a plant to produce a product whose demand is very sensitive to general business conditions. If general business conditions are good, the demand for the product is likely to be high and the plant profitable. If general business conditions are poor, the demand is low and the plant unprofitable. Again, in this case, uncertainty about the cash flows associated with the investment derives from uncertainty about some other event— general business conditions. If the future state of general business conditions could be perfectly forecast, the outcome of the investment could be predicted.

Table 9-1 illustrates the effect of business conditions and product design on the potential profits from introducing a new product. In this case, the state of business conditions has some effect on the present value of the investment; but product design is more important. If the product design turns out to be unpopular with customers, producing the new product will result in a loss, and only the exact size of the loss depends on general business conditions. However, if the product is popular with customers, it will be profitable; but profits will be somewhat better if business conditions are favorable than if they are unfavorable.

Events could be classified in a large number of ways, and no one classification will be useful for all purposes. We might consider as one category those events that affect the level of business activity generally. The international political situation, the monetary and fiscal policies of the government, and the general state of confidence of the business community might be considered to be factors that help determine the actual level of the business activity which occurs. Another category might be events that tend to affect all companies in an industry. For example, all companies in the steel industry would be affected

Table 9-1. Conditional Forecasts of Net Present
Value of a New Product Investment

Product Design	General Business Conditions	
	Favorable	Unfavorable
Popular design	$1,500,000	$1,400,000
Unpopular design	− 250,000	− 400,000

by the outcome of the labor negotiations that determine the wage rates in the industry, by new important discoveries of iron ore, by changes in the cost of rail or water transportation and by excise taxes affecting steel. A third category would be events directly affecting a particular company, such as a change in its management or a natural disaster such as a flood or fire. Similarly, uncertain events affecting primarily one product category or one particular investment project could be isolated.

The classification of events is the first step in focusing attention on what is most relevant for a particular decision. The desirability of an investment is likely to be affected more by some events than by others.

A new product with a popular design would generate positive new profits even under unfavorable business conditions that would eliminate the profits for most of the other lines of activity. A product that could produce high positive profits under such conditions might be extremely attractive to a company. This has very important consequences in determination of the effect of the decision on the uncertainty of total profits for the company.

The considerations discussed suggest that, in evaluating a specific uncertain investment, we need to consider the outcomes of the investment in relation to the outcomes of the other investments that have been undertaken by the investor. Methods of evaluating the outcomes of a portfolio of investments will be considered in detail in later chapters. In the present chapter we concentrate on methods of describing the likelihood of the different possible events that can occur, and on methods of summarizing the possible investment outcomes associated with those events. These methods, which are applied in this chapter to individual investments, can also be applied to portfolios of investments.

probability: a measure of likelihood

Probability may be described as a measure of someone's opinion about the likelihood that an event will occur. If an event is certain to occur, we say that it has a probability of 1 of occurring. If an event is certain not to occur, we say that its probability of occurring is 0. All events have a probability of occurrence somewhere between 0 and 1. By convention, probabilities follow several rules. Among them are the following: (1) the probability assigned to each possible event must be a positive number between 0 and 1, where 0 represents an impossible event and 1 represents a certain event; (2) if a set of events is mutually exclusive and exhaustive (covers all possible outcomes), the probabilities of the events must total 1.

Suppose that we consider events associated with one flip of a coin. With a new, fairly machined coin that has a head on only one side, most of us would be willing to agree that the probability of landing a head on one fair toss is .5 and the probability of a tail is .5 (these two events are mutually exclusive and exhaustive, if we do not allow the coin to stand on its edge). If we did not know that the coin was fair (for example, if the coin were worn unevenly), there would be some question if the probability of landing a head would be exactly .5. One can easily imagine that different people might have different opinions about the probability in this case. However, if we were to take such a two-sided coin and flip it in a fair manner a very large number of times, say 100,000 times, the ratio of the actual number of heads to the total number of flips would be a reasonable estimate of the probability of the event "heads" for that particular coin. The probability estimate is based on the objective evidence of 100,000 trials and is called an *objective probability*.

If the concept of probability were applicable only to events that could be repeated a large number of times under controlled circumstances, the concept would be of relatively little use in analyzing business investment decisions. Most business decisions are either unique or are made a small number of times. One does not generally make the same decision in essentially the same circumstances a great many times and observe the outcome of each decision. Even when decisions are repetitive, conditions tend to change. If a businessman is considering opening a drugstore, there may be a great deal of evidence that helps him form a judgment about whether a drugstore in a particular location could be profitable. But there is no other location and period of time that is exactly the same in all respects as the location and time he has in mind, and the businessman cannot resort to an objective measure of probability to describe the events associated with the profitability of the drugstore.

Some statisticians have taken the position that it is not very useful to describe a businessman's beliefs in terms of probability (for example, to specify a probability that a drugstore opened at that location could be profitable). We believe that a useful measure of probability can be applied to such situations, provided it is kept in mind that the probability measure describes the state of belief of the decision maker, and that this measure is being used to cause the decision to be consistent with these beliefs. Probability measures that reflect the state of belief of a person rather than the objective evidence of a large number of trials are called *subjective probabilities*. The use of this concept will be illustrated by examples in the remainder of this chapter and in several of the following chapters. After reading these pages and perhaps attempting to apply some of the ideas to his own decisions, each reader can determine whether subjective probability measures are useful.

Let us consider an election and ask ourselves the meaning of a statement such as the following: Mr. A has a .65 probability of winning this election. The election will not be repeated in exactly the same form, nor has it been held before, although there may be all sorts of evidence relevant to a belief about the outcome. If we say that there is a .65 probability that Mr. A will win the election, this statement implies a comparison of the following sort:

Suppose that a jar is filled with 100 beads identical in all respects, except that 65 are blue and 35 are red. We mix the beads thoroughly and randomly draw out one bead. The statement that Mr. A has a .65 probability of winning the election means we believe that we are as likely to draw a blue bead as Mr. A is to win the election. Suppose that we were to be paid $10 if the bead drawn is blue and to pay $10 if it is not blue. If we believe the statement about the election, and are concerned only with how much we win or lose, we should be equally willing to enter a bet in which we would receive $10 if A won the election and lose $10 if A did not win the election. That is, we should be in-different as to whether the outcome of the bet is determined by the actual outcome of the election or by drawing a bead from a jar of the nature described.

In the case of any unique event (like an election) all observers will not exactly agree on the probability that any particular candidate will win. The adjective *subjective* applied to probabilities suggests that the probabilities described are opinions or statements of belief held by individuals. The purpose of expressing an opinion about the likelihood that an event will occur in terms of a numerical subjective probability is to facilitate the development of decision-making procedures that are explicit and consistent with the decision maker's beliefs.

describing and evaluating uncertain investments

The process of making investment decisions under uncertainty can be broken down into three steps: (1) describing the expected return, (2) describing the uncertainty associated with the returns, and (3) evaluating the risk and return characteristics of the investment and if possible quantifying these factors.

1. What is the expected monetary return from the investment? The word *expected* is used in a technical probability sense, and is equal to the sum of possible outcomes weighted by their respective probabilities. Presumably businessmen generally mean expected value when they speak of the estimated cash flows from an uncertain investment. With bonds, however, the cash flows usually referred to are not the expected amounts, but the quantities that would be realized if the bond contracts are fulfilled. In the case of an ordinary bond, this amount is also the maximum amount that would be received. The expected amount will be less than the maximum if there is a possibility of default. This possibility of default is the main reason why bonds issued by private corporations carry higher interest rates than bonds of similar maturities issued by the federal government. The higher yield on industrial bonds is a compensation to the holder for the possible loss if the interest payments are missed or if the bond is not paid at maturity.

2. What is the nature of the dispersion of possible outcomes around the

expected value? When there is uncertainty, the investor would want to know more than just what the expected return would be from his investment. What is the maximum possible loss that may be incurred if the investment is undertaken? How rapidly, for example, do the proceeds fall with a decrease in business activity? What is the relationship between the return on this investment and the return on other investments that have already been accepted or are currently under consideration? If something happens that causes a low return from the other investments, is it likely to cause a low return on this investment also?

3. Do the monetary consequences of the investment accurately measure their importance to the investor? Consider, for example, an investment requiring an outlay of $100,000 for which there was a .5 probability of a return of $0 and a .5 probability of a return of $250,000. The expected return is $125,000. However, most persons whose total wealth was $100,000 would reject this investment.

All the preceding factors must be considered if a reasonable investment decision is to be made. Just looking at profitability for one given set of assumptions, with no statement as to the uncertainty connected with the assumptions, or at the possibility of losses occurring if the assumptions are not realized, is not a sound method of decision making.

As another example of the way the range of possible outcomes could affect the choice of investments, consider investments A and B of Figure 9-1. The possible net cash flows of the two investments, given different assump-

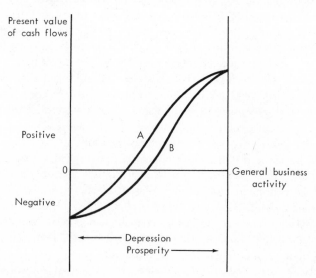

Figure 9-1

tions as to general business activity, are given in Figure 9-1. Note that both investments have the same maximum possible positive flows and the same maximum possible loss (maximum possible negative cash flows). Yet the diagram indicates that investment A is more desirable. At all points the present value of cash flow of investment A is equal to or greater than that of investment B.[1]

Two mutually exclusive investments C and D are shown in Figure 9-2. The maximum present value for investment C, V_4, is less than investment D's maximum, which is V_5. Which of the two would be the better investment? The answer to this question is more complicated. One possible answer is that the investment with the largest area under the curve is the better investment (the negative cash proceeds and the resulting area should be subtracted). The answer might be valid if each possible present value were equally likely to occur. But there is little justification for assuming that each outcome is equally likely. Ordinarily, another set of curves must be drawn (see Figure 9-3) showing the likelihoods of the events.

However, in using Figure 9-3, it is not clear which of the two investments is more desirable. Both investments have the same maximum possible loss (V_1), but the maximum possible gains differ. Investment D has a larger maximum gain (V_5) than investment C (V_4). If we consider only the gain associated with the most likely outcome, we note that the most likely outcome of D (V_3) is greater than the most likely outcome for investment C (V_2).

It should be noted that once we take account of the pleasures and disappointments—that is, how the individuals would be affected psychologically by the profits and losses—then the possibility of large gain may outweigh in importance to the investor the possibility of a very large loss, or just the opposite.

The problem of evaluating uncertain investments will be considered in

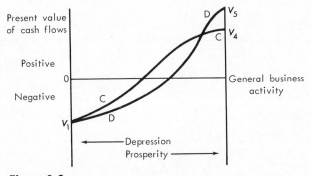

Figure 9-2

[1] We can say that investment A dominates investment B.

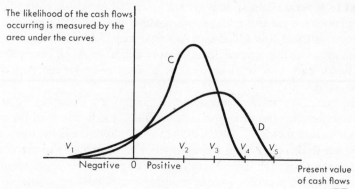

The likelihood of the cash flows occurring is measured by the area under the curves

Negative   0   Positive

Present value of cash flows

Figure 9-3

succeeding chapters, In the next sections of this chapter we shall be concerned mainly with methods of describing the likelihood of various possible outcomes, and of summarizing the set of possible outcomes associated with an uncertain investment.

expected values, variances, and standard deviations

In working with probabilities, the concepts of expected value, variance, and standard deviation are essential. These basic ideas will be introduced with an example.

In Table 9-2, column 1 lists six possible events, column 2 shows the net present value of a particular investment if the event in question occurs, and column 3 lists the probability of each event. We wish to calculate the "expected" net present value. To do this we multiply the probability in each row

Table 9-2. Calculating the Expected Net Present Value of an Uncertain Investment

(1) Possible Events	*(2)* Net Present Value for Each Event	*(3)* Probability of Event	*(4)* Col. 2 × Col. 3
a	− $100	.3	− $30
b	0	.1	0
c	50	.1	5
d	0	.2	0
e	50	.1	5
f	200	.2	40
		1.0	20

by the corresponding net present value. The products are shown in column 4 of the table. The sum of the amounts in column 4 is the expected net present value for this investment, which is a weighted average. Each possible net present value is weighted by the probability that it will occur.

In Table 9-2, two events, b and d, both result in net present values of zero. Although the two events lead to the same net present value, they are not necessarily indistinguishable. For example, assume that the cash flows for events b and d are as follows:

	Period		
	0	1	2
b	− $200	$110	$121
d	− 100	55	60.5

Both sets of flows have a zero net present value with a .10 discount rate.

If the only relevant characteristic of an event is the net present value to which it will lead, events that lead to identical net present values can be combined (by adding their probabilities). However, if the cash flows of specific periods are important, the events can be combined only if the cash flows of each period are identical.

A redescription of the events is shown in Table 9-3. The expected net present value is not changed by this recombination of the data; it is still $20.

Further insight into the meaning of an expected value can be obtained if we examine the differences between the net present values that can occur and their expected value. In Table 9-4, column 1 lists the possible net present values and column 3 the corresponding differences, or deviations, of each from the expected value. That is, each value in column 3 is the corresponding

Table 9-3. Alternative Method for Calculating the Expected Net Present Value of an Uncertain Investment

(1) Possible Values of Net Present Value	(2) Probability of That Value	(3) Expectation (Col. 2 × Col. 3)
− $100	.3	− $30
0	.3	0
50	.2	10
200	.2	40
	1.0	20

Table 9-4. Calculating the Expected Deviation Between Net Present Value
and Expected Net Present Value

(1)	(2)	(3)	(4)
Possible Values of Net Present Value	Probability of That Value	Net Present Value Minus Expected Net Present Value	Expectation (Col. 2 × Col. 3)
− $100	.3	− $120	− $36
0	.3	− 20	− 6
50	.2	30	6
200	.2	180	36
	1.0		0

value in column 1 minus the expected value of 20. The values in column 4 are
these deviations times the corresponding probabilities. The sum of the items
in column 4 is the expected value of the deviations, and the sum of these
deviations is zero. In fact, it could be proved that the expected deviation must
always be zero.

This suggests another interpretation of the expected net present value. It
is a number in the center of the possible values, in the sense that the sum of
positive deviations from the expected net present value equals the sum of the
negative deviations, provided both types of deviations are weighted by their
respective probabilities.

The variance and its square root, the standard deviation, are commonly
used as measures of how concentrated the possible present values are around
their expected value. The variance is calculated by squaring each deviation
and taking the expected value of the squared deviations. The procedure is
illustrated in Table 9-5. The first three columns in that table contain the same

Table 9-5. Calculating the Variance of the Net Present Value of an
Uncertain Investment

(1)	(2)	(3)	(4)	(5)
Possible Values of Net Present Value	Probability of That Value	Net Present Value Minus Expected Net Present Value	Squared Deviation	(Col. 2 × Col. 4)
− $100	.3	− $120	$14,000	$ 4,320
0	.3	− 20	400	120
50	.2	30	900	180
200	.2	180	32,400	6,480
	1.0		Variance =	11,100

Standard deviation = $\sqrt{\$11,100}$ = $105.36

entries as in Table 9-4. Column 4 of Table 9-5 shows the square of the deviation, and column 5 the squared deviation multiplied by its probability. The sum of the items in column 5 is the variance. For some purposes it is more convenient to work with the standard deviation, since its units, dollars in this case, are the same as the units of the expected value. In this example, the variance of the net present value is 11,100 (dollars squared) and the standard deviation is the square root of 11,100 or $105.35.

symbolic notation for random variables and their expected values

In the preceding paragraphs the concepts of expected value variance, and standard deviation have been introduced using the net present value of an uncertain investment as an example. However, these concepts have a much more general applicability. If we can describe all mutually exclusive and exhaustive outcomes by assigning a numerical value to each uncertain event, the expected value and variance of these numerical quantities can be calculated. Whether the numerical quantities represent the number of units sold, the cash flow of the period, the yield of an investment, or the highest temperature for a day, the concepts of expected value, variance, and standard deviation are applicable.

If the specific value of a quantity, such as the net present value, depends on the outcome of an uncertain event, the quantity is called a *random variable*. The net present value of an investment might be denoted by the symbol X, where the specific numerical value of X depends on the outcome of an uncertain event. X is a random variable.

The symbol E is used to denote the process of finding the expected value of a random variable; the specific random variable whose expected value is being taken is placed in parentheses or brackets following the E. Thus in our example

$$E(X) = 20$$

could be used to summarize, in symbolic terms, the results of the calculations shown in Tables 9-2 and 9-3. Although X is a random variable, note that $E(X)$ is just a number whose value depends on all the events that could occur.

Using the notation, the deviation of net present value from its expected value could be denoted as

$$X - E(X).$$

The quantity $X - E(X)$ is itself a random variable and we can calculate its expected value. The equation

$$E[X - E(X)] = 0$$

summarizes the results of the calculation shown in Table 9-4.

In Table 9-5 we illustrated the computation of the variance by squaring each deviation and then calculating the expected value of the squared deviations. In symbols, this process could be described as

$$E[(X - E(X))^2] = 11,110.$$

In using this notation, it is important to distinguish between

$$[E(X)]^2 = 20^2 = 400$$

and

$$E(X^2) = 11,500.$$

The first equation indicates that an expected value was found and then squared. The second equation indicates that each possible value of the random variable is first squared, and the expected value of these squared quantities is then found.[2] We shall find it convenient to represent the expected value using $\bar{X}$ rather than $E(X)$. Thus we could write $\bar{X}^2 = 400$ instead of $[E(X)]^2 = 400$.

We shall have frequent occasion to utilize this notation in the remainder of this book.

summarizing the set of possible outcomes of an uncertain investment

Ordinarily, there are a large number of different possible events that are relevant to any uncertain investment. Corresponding to each distinct event, there is a unique set of cash flows associated with the investment. One way of describing an uncertain investment is to list all the possible events, the probability of each event, and the cash flows that would be associated with each event if the investment were accepted. This method of describing an uncertain investment has the advantage and the disadvantage of being detailed. The disadvantage is that the decision maker may be presented with more infor-

---

[2] It can be shown that $E[(X - E(X)]^2 = E(X^2) - E(X)^2$.

Table 9-6. Alternative Cash Flow Sequences for an Uncertain Investment

Event	Probability of Event	Cash Flows in Period		
		0	1	2
a	.3	− $200	$110	$ 0
b	.1	− 200	110	121
c	.1	− 200	165	121
d	.2	− 100	55	60.5
e	.1	− 100	55	121
f	.2	− 100	110	242

mation than he can readily comprehend or evaluate. A means of summarizing the possible outcomes is often desirable.

In Table 9-6 an uncertain investment is described by listing all the possible events, the probability of each event, and the sequence of cash flows that would occur if the investment was accepted and that event occurred. In this example there are six possible events, and cash flows can occur in only three different periods, so the complete description is manageable. Nevertheless, the need for methods of summarizing the description of the investment should be apparent.

A number of possible strategies for summarizing the kind of information in Table 9-6 are possible and will be described next. In describing these different strategies we shall attempt to indicate some of the advantages and disadvantages of each. However, we shall not attempt to evaluate the different strategies at this point. Except in very special circumstances, any method of summarizing the outcomes of an investment decision will involve some loss of information. We would like to choose methods in which the information lost is relatively unimportant to the decision maker. But this requires a consideration of the objectives of the decision maker and the circumstances in which he operates. These will be considered in a later chapter.

Period-by-Period Summaries

One strategy for summarizing the information in Table 9-6 begins by summarizing the possible outcomes for the cash flows period by period. A straightforward way to do this would be to calculate the expected cash flow in each period. If information on the dispersion of outcomes is desired, the range or the standard deviation of each period's cash flows can be shown.

Table 9-7 presents a period-by-period summary of the cash flows of the uncertain investment described in Table 9-6. Line 1 shows the expected value of each period's cash flows. In practice, most investment decisions are based

Table 9-7. Period-by-Period Summary of the Cash Flows of an Uncertain
            Investment

		Periods		
Line	Item	0	1	2
1	Expected cash flow	− $150	$ 99	$ 96.8
2	Optimistic cash flow for each period	− 100	165	242
3	Pessimistic cash flow for each period	− 200	55	0
4	Standard deviation of cash flows	50	33	86.1

on the kind of information contained in line 1 of this table with no further
formal analysis of uncertainty. The numbers reported will usually represent a
judgment as to the magnitude of the expected cash flows, rather than a listing
of the alternative outcomes.

Lines 2 and 3 in Table 9-7 give a rather crude indication of the range of
dispersion of possible outcomes (since an extreme value may have a very
small probability of occurring). The standard deviation is in some respects a
better measure of dispersion, but it is not widely used in practice.

If a further summary of the worth of the investment is desired, the expected
cash flows from line 1 of Table 9-7 can be used to compute any of the commonly used measures of investment worth, such as those discussed in Chapter
2. A number of these measures are displayed in Table 9-8.

Table 9-8. Summary Measures of the
            Worth of an Uncertain
            Investment, Based on
            Expected Cash Flows

Measure	Value
Net present values at 5%	$32.09
at 10%	20.00
at 15%	9.28
Rate of return	19.9%
Payback	1.5 years
Return on average investment	30.5%

Sequence-by-Sequence Summaries

A useful method for summarizing the information in Table 9-6 is to present
the cash flows for each possible event, and then to select a measure of investment worth (for example, net present value) and calculate the value of this
measure for each event. As an example of this strategy, Table 9-9 presents
the net present values at 10 per cent for each possible event.

Table 9-9. Summary of the Cash Flows of an Uncertain
            Investment

Possible Events	Probability of Event	Value of Summary Measures, Net Present Values at 10%
a	.3	− $100
b	.1	0
c	.1	50
d	.2	0
e	.1	50
f	.2	200
Expected net present value		$ 20
Standard deviation of net present value		105.36

The expected present value and the standard deviations are shown at the bottom of Table 9-9. It should be noted in this connection that the expected present value of the cash flows at 10 per cent is the same as the present value of the expected cash flows in Table 9-8 using 10 per cent.[3]

discount rate

The weighted-average cost of capital is widely used as a discount rate for making investment decisions. However, there are several drawbacks to its use. To compute the cost of capital, it is necessary to know the cost of stock equity funds, and this cost is very difficult (and sometimes impossible) to measure. A second and more important drawback is that the cost of common stock includes a measure of the attitudes toward risk of the investors in common stock. Thus we speak of an .08 return required for a relatively safe stock and a .15 return required for a stock of high risk. The cost of common stock funds measures both the attitudes of the stockholders relative to the time value of money and their attitudes toward risk.

It is sometimes stated that the cost of capital of a firm may be used when returns of the investment being considered are perfectly correlated with the firm's present returns. This is not correct, since the risk may be the same but the cash flows might have different timing; thus the same discount rate cannot be used to take both time value and risk into consideration.

Consider a situation where a gamble is being performed today with payoffs one year from today of $0 or $1,000, both with .5 probability. Assume that an investor is indifferent between this gamble and $400 for cer-

[3] However, for any uncertain investment with cash flows in more than two periods, the rate of return of the expected cash flows will always be less than the expected value of the rates of return from the different cash-flow sequences.

tain (the expected value of the lottery is $500 and a .25 rate of discount would equate the $500 to the $400). The choice of $400 implies a cost of capital of .25. Assume that the results of the lottery will be disclosed now, but the final payoffs will be twenty years from today. If a discount rate of .25 is applied to the expected value of .25, we obtain $5.75 (.0115 × $500). However, if one has a time-value factor of .10, it is not clear that he would be indifferent between $5.75 and the lottery. The present value of $1,000 discounted at .10 is $148.60. Multiplying by the .5 probability, we obtain an expected value of $74.30. The certainty equivalent of this lottery for most people is more than $5.75.

If the benefits from all investments are perpetuities, the use of different discount rates, where the rates increase with increased risk, may give an evaluation of investments using their present values that is consistent with their risks. For example, if all investments have cash flows of $1,000 per year and if there are three investments with different risks (high, medium, and low), we can use a high discount factor (say, .20) with the high risk, a medium discount factor (say, .10) with the medium risk, and a low discount factor (say, .05) with the low risk. The three different present values we obtain are as follows:

	Discount Factor	Perpetual Cash Flow Present-Value Factors	Present Value of $1,000 per Year
High risk	.20	5	$ 5,000
Medium risk	.10	10	10,000
Low risk	.05	20	20,000

If there is another investment in the high-risk classification, its cash flow (also a perpetuity) would be multiplied by the same factor of 5. Instead of being perpetuities the same general approach could be used if all the investments were one-period investments.

There is a $.50 discount per dollar of proceeds for risk as we move from the low- to the medium-risk investment, and a $.75 discount per dollar for risk as we move from the low- to the high-risk investment. These risk adjustments may not be correct, but at least the adjustment for risk is in the correct direction, and they apply in the same manner to all investments in the same risk class.

It is less obvious than with common stock, but the cost of corporate debt also includes an adjustment for risk, because there is generally the possibility of default. A bond yield of .07 is partially a result of time preference (say, .04) and partially a result of the risk of default. It may also include an allowance for the risk and dilution of value resulting from changes in the purchasing power of the dollar.

As normally defined and computed, the cost of common stock equity funds and the yields of most debt instruments include an allowance for risk, but it does not necessarily follow that the use of a higher discount rate applied to future cash flows is a desirable way of determining the present value of an asset that is subject to risk.

The results of any evaluation of debt can be expressed in terms of yield. For example, suppose that a bond contract involves a promise to pay $50 per year for ten years and $1,000 at the end of the ten-year period. If a potential investor decides that he would pay no more than $371 for this bond, we may choose to describe the investor as willing to buy the bond if it is priced to yield 20 per cent. This statement tells us nothing about how the investor actually decided what the bond was worth. Does the investor have a time value of money of 20 per cent per year, or is it that he has an aversion to risk and fears a possible inability to collect interest and principal?

The use of high discount rates to allow for uncertainty makes a very special assumption about the nature of uncertainty. For example, suppose that we consider an investment to build and equip a plant for producing a new product. In some instances the major uncertainty may be related to the cost of constructing the plant, whereas the demand for the resulting output may be easily predictable in advance with very little uncertainty. This could be the case if the product to be made were to be sold in advance through a long-term sales contract, whereas the design, construction, and operation of the plant involved new or unusual engineering problems creating an unpredictable cost. The use of atomic energy to generate electric power is a tangible example of this situation. In such a situation the discounting of future revenues, themselves fairly certain, seems a poor way of allowing for the uncertainty about how much the fixed plant will cost. In another instance the main element of uncertainty may revolve around consumer acceptance of the product. The alternatives may be either a very high or a very low level of consumer acceptance, with a corresponding probability of either a series of years of very high cash proceeds or a series of years of little or no cash proceeds.

We shall use two examples to illustrate the difficulty of predicting the effect of using different discount rates in an attempt to take risk into consideration.

EXAMPLE 1 : Assume that we have two investments, the first more risky than the second. Do not be bothered by the vagueness of the description of the amount of risk. With the first investment we shall use a discount rate of .10, and with the second a discount rate of .20. The two investments have mean cash flows of $10,000 in years 1 and 50.

Year	Cash Flows	Present-Value Factor Using .10	Present Value Using .10	Present-Value Factor Using .20	Present Value Using .20
1	10,000	.9091	$9,091	.8333	$8,333
50	10,000	.0085	85	.0001	1

Note that the present value of the cash flows of year 1 of the less risky investment is 1.09 times as large as the cash flow of the more risky investment. However, the present value of the cash flows of year 50 is approximately 85 times as large. The use of a larger rate of discount for a more risky investment may move the decision in the correct direction (that is, the riskier the investment, the lower the value of the future cash flows). However, it does this in an approximate and somewhat unpredictable manner. We cannot be sure of the impact of the risk discount added to the time value of money without considerable computation, and the effect of the risk discount will not be equal each year.

The use of a risk discount assumes that the risk difference between the two investments is increasing as we move farther into the future. As we have already mentioned, this assumption may not be correct. Even if the assumption is correct, we still need to inquire whether the discount factor appropriately measures the disadvantage of this risk.

This difficulty with the use of a risk discount (that is, a larger interest rate) to take risk into consideration is not limited to situations involving long time periods.

EXAMPLE 2: Assume that we are given the opportunity to bet on a horse race being run today and the information we receive is so good that we consider the probability of obtaining $3 for each dollar invested to be .5. There remains a .5 probability of losing our entire investment, so we want to apply a large interest rate to take the risk into consideration. However, the benefits are zero time periods in the future. When the discount factor $(1 + r)^{-t}$ is computed for t equal to zero, we find the present-value factor is 1 and is independent of the choice of the discount rate, r.[4]

We conclude that, for practical business decision making, varying the rate of discount is not a good way of accomplishing the objective of taking risk into consideration. It is true that most persons would require a higher return for risky investments than for less risky investments; however, determining the exact amount the rate of discount should be increased for different types of risk in different time periods is a difficult task.

---

[4] Suppose that we receive the information about the race (a tip) one hour before the race results will be determined. Then, of course, there will be finite discount rates that make the present value of the proceeds equal to the outlay.

default-free rate of discount

Assume that a reasonable person prefers $1 now rather than $1 in the future, and that there is a positive rate of discount.[5] There are many choices of discount rates that may be suggested for use in making investment decisions. The following are the two possibilities we shall consider in this section: (1) interest rate of government securities, and (2) interest rate of long-term bonds of the firm.

Before proceeding further, however, it is desirable to establish more clearly the characteristics we seek in selecting an interest rate. The term *risk free* might be used to describe the interest rate. This is suggestive, but not strictly accurate. There are certain risks that cannot in practice be eliminated and that affect all interest-bearing securities to a greater or lesser extent. The interest rates we have in mind are those at which the investor could lend money with no significant danger of default or at which he could borrow if his collateral were so good that his creditor would feel that there was negligible chance of default.

Even if the risk of default is practically negligible, there are other risks inherent in fixed money debt instruments as long as there is uncertainty about the future changes that might take place in the economy. We shall describe these risks from the point of view of the lender. The counterparts of these risks also exist for a borrower.

One source of risk arises because of uncertainty about the future price level. Expectations about possible future price levels influence the market determination of interest rates. Lenders will tend to be hurt if the price level rises; hence they require a higher interest return with an expected price-level increase than with an expected price-level decrease, or with constant prices.

Another source of risk arises because of the possibility of changes in the level and structure of interest rates. Normally, the interest rate on bonds will vary with the number of years to maturity even when there is no risk of default. Bonds that mature in a few years may have higher (or lower) yields than bonds that mature in the more distant future. If there is no risk of default, the lender can always be sure of earning the going yield by buying a bond of given maturity and holding it until it matures. However, the possibility exists that some other strategy would result in earning a higher yield. If an investor wants to lend money for a five-year period and expects

---

[5] It is possible to have a situation where the discount rate is negative and we are satisfied to invest $1 now and get back less than $1 in the future just to be sure of getting something. Imagine a family with four children approaching college age. They might invest even with a negative discount rate, if holding cash was impractical.

a decline in interest rates, he may be able to earn a higher yield by buying a fifteen- or twenty-year bond and selling it after five years than by buying a five-year bond and holding it to maturity. However, when this strategy is followed, there is no longer any guarantee that a certain minimum rate of interest will actually be earned.

Even if a lender wishes to avoid the uncertainty that results from the possibility of changes in the term structure of interest rates, he may be unable to do so. This will happen if he is uncertain about the amounts of cash he will require on various future dates. If he invests in short-term debt instruments, such as treasury bills, he will face uncertainty about the rates he will be able to earn when the time for reinvesting these funds arises. If he invests in longer-term securities, he will face uncertainty about the actual return that will be realized if he must liquidate the securities before they mature.

In spite of these limitations the interest rates on government debt constitute a reasonable choice of discount rates representing default-free lending opportunities. These rates represent actual market opportunities at which firms or individuals could lend money with essentially no risk of default.

Unfortunately, neither private corporations nor individuals can actually borrow money at these rates, even with the best available collateral. For various reasons the rates at which one could actually borrow for a given term would be higher than the rates at which the government can borrow for loans of the same maturity.

borrowing rate

Any individual or private business corporation that borrows money will find the interest rate it must pay will be greater than the default-free rate. An analysis of the discounting of debt-type cash flows is an interesting special problem that helps us to understand the discounting process, and it is worthwhile considering this problem even when the difference between the interest rate promised on a debt and the default-free rate is not large enough to be material in relation to investment decision making.

We shall ignore income tax considerations. Suppose that the interest rate on default-free one-year debts is 6 per cent, and a private corporation offers to sell a bond that promises to repay $1,060 one year from now. If such a bond were offered by the federal government it could be sold for $1,000, because the obligations of the government are default-free. With a private corporation there is some possibility of default, although the possibility may be remote. Suppose that the potential buyers judge the probability distribution of future cash payments that would result from purchasing this bond to be as follows:

(1) Possible Cash Proceeds	(2) Probability	(3) Col. 1 × Col. 2
$1,060	.9990	$1,058.94
1,000	.0005	.50
500	.0003	.15
0	.0002	.00
	1.0000	Expected value $1,059.59

The bondholders view the bond contract as nearly default-free because they consider that there are only 2 chances out of 10,000 that they will receive nothing from the bond, and only 1 chance in a 1,000 that they will fail to receive the total amount promised. The bondholders, discounting the expected cash flows of $1,059.59 at the default-free rate of interest, would find the present value of the bond to be $999.62 ($1,059.59/1.06). If the potential purchasers were willing to buy the bond on the basis of the present value of its expected cash flows, they would offer $999.62 for it. It is customary to quote bond yields on the basis of the payments promised, not the expected payments. On this basis it would be said that the bonds were sold to yield 6.04 per cent ($1,060/1.0604 = $999.62).

One might question whether in fact potential buyers would pay $999.62 for the bond. Their expected return on a default-free government obligation would be just as high, although the most probable return on the corporation's bond is higher than on the government's. Suppose that the buyers offered to pay $998 for the bond, and the corporation sold it at that price. The present value of the expected cash flows is $999.62. The difference of $1.62 is a risk premium that serves to induce the bond buyers to buy this slightly risky asset instead of a default-free government bond.

It is interesting and relevant to note that the analysis made by a potential bond buyer is essentially the same as the analysis that the corporation would make in analyzing a risky investment. From the point of view of the buyer, a bond is a risky investment. The future cash flows can be adjusted for timing by discounting at the default-free interest rate, but the expected present value is not the amount that would be paid for the asset. The value depends on the risks involved and the risk attitudes of the purchaser.

Now let us look at the debt transaction from the point of view of the issuing corporation. Say the corporation receives $998. It is legally obligated to pay an amount whose most likely present value is $1,000. The corporation may agree with the bondholder's assessment of the possible cash proceeds of the bond and their probabilities. That is, the corporation recognizes that there is a small probability that it may be unable to meet its legal obligations under the contract. Even so it has received only $998 for entering into an obligation having a present value of expected cash payments of $999.62, for which the most likely consequences (probability .999) is that it will make payments whose present value is $1,000.

In analyzing the consequences of issuing the bond, the corporation should consider the reactions of the stockholders. The issuance of bonds may affect the risk premium stockholders use, and thus the market value of the common stock. Despite the incurrence of a liability that exceeds the cash received, the contract is not necessarily disadvantageous to the borrowing corporation. To balance the debt contract, it has received cash plus an intangible asset that we may call "increased liquidity." Why does the firm want increased liquidity? There may be several reasons, but we shall concentrate on one.

Assume that there is an advantageous investment with a positive expected net present value using the default-free rate. By expending the cash and the intangible asset called increased liquidity, the firm can acquire this investment. If the expected present value of the proceeds of the investment exceeds its cash cost plus its liquidity cost, the investment might be worthwhile. The financial accountant will record only the cash obtained from liability and the cash cost of the investment. The investment analyst should recognize that the asset is worth acquiring if the cash outlay plus intangible liquidity cost given up is less than the expected net present value plus a risk adjustment. Typically, the reason the firm is willing to incur a liability greater than the cash obtained is that it expects to use the cash to acquire an asset whose value is greater than the value of the liability.

If the firm has other assets, the decision about whether an investment is acceptable or not may have to be made on the basis of an analysis of its risk characteristics combined with the risk characteristics of the assets already owned by the firm. With uncertainty there are examples of undesirable investments whose expected net present value is positive, and of desirable investments whose expected net present value is negative. Life insurance is an example of the latter type.

If there is uncertainty, the discounting of future cash flows serves to place cash flows to be received at different points in time on a comparable basis relative to time. This process facilitates the making of investment decisions. But expected net present values cannot be used as a sole decision-making criterion when there is uncertainty. In Chapters 11 and 12 we shall offer an effective decision rule to take the place of net present value when the assumption of certainty is dropped.

summary

In Part I we proceeded on the assumption that an investment could be characterized by the cash flows that would occur if the investment were accepted. Uncertainty was bypassed by assuming that only one set of cash flows was possible. In this chapter the complication of uncertainty is introduced. An investment is uncertain if more than one set of cash flows can result from accepting the investment, and the decision maker does not know at the time he makes his decision which set of cash flows will occur.

The concept of probability was introduced as a means of describing the likelihood of the different possible outcomes. If the outcomes are described in numerical terms, whether as cash flows, net present values, rates of return, or some other numerical measure, the expected value, variance, and standard deviation can be used to help summarize the possible outcomes.

Using these concepts, two main strategies for summarizing the possible outcomes of an uncertain investment were presented. One strategy summarized the cash flows on a period-by-period basis. A second strategy was to find a summary measure for each possible sequence of cash flows.

We have argued that when cash flows are discounted at a default-free interest rate, the resulting net present values adjust the cash flows for differences in timing, but not for risk. If any higher discount rate is used, there is an implicit risk allowance, and the decision maker must ask himself whether the appropriate risk allowance has been made. Some firms may prefer to use the rate at which they can borrow long-term funds as a discount rate. If their credit rating is good, this rate will not be far above the default-free rate, and it may be easier to explain and justify to management. Our preference is to use a default-free interest rate and make risk adjustments separately.

Even more important than the choice of a specific discount rate is the recognition that when cash flows are uncertain some investments may be undesirable, even though their expected cash flows have a positive net present value; whereas other investments may be desirable even with expected cash flows having a negative net present value. Because the risk characteristics of the investment will greatly influence the investment decision and the present-value calculation is viewed as only one information input, it is most important that good investments should not be rejected by the use of a high rate of discount, so that they drop from consideration.

questions and problems

9-1. In 1965 the Boeing Airplane Company was faced with a major decision: to what extent should it independently develop a supersonic air transport? The estimates of the cost of developing such a plane ranged from $1 to $4 billion. During the period of decision the English and the French were acting jointly in the development of such a plane, and the United States government considered undertaking a similar project. The reader is referred to the financial reports of Boeing for the year 1965 for financial information.

Required: If you were advising the president of Boeing, what would you suggest? If you were advising the President of the United States, what would you suggest?

9-2. Assume that $1,000 is to be received 30 years from today. Compare the present values obtained using .05 and .20 as rates of discount.

9-3. Assume that there are two investments of different risk. A return of .05 is required on one investment; on the other a return of .10 is required. Compare the present values obtained for each investment for expected cash flows of $1 billion one year, twenty years, and fifty years from now at the required rates of return.

9-4. The ABC Company issued $1,000 bonds with a coupon interest rate of .05 per year at a price to yield .06 (the price was $885.30 per bond). The life of the bonds is twenty years.

Required: Give three different reasons as to why the bond yield is .06.

9-5. The ABC Company has issued a $1,000, .05 bond with a four-year life. The interest rate for default-free securities is now .05. Assume that the following probabilities of payment apply (the probability of collecting in a given year is statistically independent of whether or not a collection occurred in the previous year; missed collections are not made up):

Principal or Interest of Period	Probability of Collection	Probability of No Collection
1	1.0	.0
2	.9	.1
3	.6	.4
4	.5	.5

(a) Assume that you are willing to pay the expected present value; what amount would you pay for this bond? (b) If the investor pays the amount in (a), what is the approximate cost to the firm issuing the bond? (c) What is the market price of this investment likely to be?

9-6. The ABC Company has been offered a certain investment that yields .05. It can borrow funds at .06, and the interest rate on government securities of a similar maturity is .04. There are no taxes. Should the investment be accepted?

9-7. The capital structure of the ABC Company is .8 stock and .2 long-term debt. Assume that investors have a time value of money of .05, and there is a corporate tax rate of .4. What is the appropriate rate of discount?

9-8. The ABC Company wants to use its cost of capital in evaluating investments. By a secret process it has succeeded in obtaining the forecasts of future dividends used by investors who currently purchase the stock. By equating the present value of these dividends to the price of the stock, it has obtained a number that it considers to be an estimator of the cost of common stock funds.

Required: Comment on the suitability of the measure obtained.

9-9. The IBC Company has the choice between two mutually exclusive investments. One requires an outlay of $10 million and has a net present value of $10,000 The second has an outlay of $500,000 and a net present value of $6,000. Both investments have a life of one year. The time value of money is .05.

Assume certainty; which investment should the firm undertake? With uncertainty, does your answer change?

9-10. The Tin Can Company must choose between two plants. One is large and has sufficient capacity for working efficiently at the higher ranges of possible sales estimates. The other plant is smaller and is more efficient at lower ranges of sales, but is less efficient if sales are high. The net present values of the two plants are shown with different assumed levels of budgeted sales. The probability of reaching that level of sales is also shown.

Level of Expected Sales (as % of budgeted sales)	Probability	Present Value Large Plant	Present Value Small Plant
150	.10	$50,000,000	$40,000,000
100	.70	35,000,000	30,000,000
50	.20	(10,000,000)	20,000,000

Required: Which of the two plants should the company build based on the information presented?

9-11. Assume that you have the choice between the following two investments:

Investment A	
Probability	Immediate Outcome
.5	$ 0
.5	1,000

The outcome of B will be known now, but the payoff is one year from now and consists of the following outcomes:

Investment B	
Probability	Outcome
.5	$ 0
.5	1,100

Required: Which investment do you prefer? What amount does B have to offer with .5 probability for you to be indifferent between the two investments?

9-12. Continuing problem 9-11. Assume that investment B after ten years pays an amount of $2,594 with .5 probability or $0 with .5 probability. Do you prefer A or B?

9-13. Assume that a small firm has enough funds to drill one oil well and the cost of drilling a well is $1 million. A large firm has enough funds to drill fifty wells. (a) What is the maximum loss of the small firm? (b) What is the maximum loss of the large firm? (c) Which of the two firms has more risk?

9-14. Assume that the average oil well returns a present value of benefits of $1.5 million for every well drilled (a well costs $1 million on the average to drill), resulting in a net present value of $500,000 per well. Assume that you are in charge of investing $1 million. You have the choice of investing in one well and owning it completely or investing in a series of ten wells and having .1 ownership. The probability of a successful well is .1. What decision would you make? Explain.

9-15. Assume that you have to predict the number of successful wells for a small firm that will drill one well and for a large firm that will drill 100 wells. Which prediction would you guess will be closer to the actual number of successful wells?

9-16. Continuing problem 9-15. Assume that you are to estimate the proportion of successes for the two firms. Which estimate is likely to be closer?

9-17.

Investing in Oil Land

A lease sale is, from the point of view of the individual oilmen participating, a harrowing, risky poker game for enormous stakes—deuces and one-eyed jacks wild.

First the company must decide which tracts of land it wants to drill on. Once that decision is made, based normally upon the geological evidence

available, company personnel enter a strange world of uncertainty and con-
jecture. How much will they have to bid to get the lease?

The reasoning involved can be infinitely complex. The first and obvious
question is: How much has been bid for comparable tracts in the area? In the
case of the Hopi sale, the closest tracts were dozens of miles away on Navajo
land. The Hopi reservation was a blank page.

Some facts can be learned by watching the competition. It may be known,
for example, as the result of painstaking scouting work, that the seismographic
crew employed by Company A spent considerable time going over a tract. It
may also be known that the company has, in recent lease sales, been willing to
spend large sums of money to obtain a tract.

Armed with these facts, Company B may decide it will require a lot of
money to outbid Company A for this tract in which so much interest has been
shown. Company B makes a very substantial bid, and finds out at the sale that
Company A has not even made a bid on the tract. The results of the seismographic tests had been discouraging.

On the other hand, Company B may decide not to compete for this tract
but rather to bid a much smaller amount for the mineral rights to a tract
immediately beside it. Thus, If Company A does buy the first tract, and if oil
is found, Company B may be able to latch on to some oil production next door.

Sometimes a company will make a bid on a tract primarily to see that a
competitor doesn't "get away with anything" by obtaining a tract too
cheaply. Or a company will put in a bid just to let the other companies know
that it is still around and competing. Or a company that has not been known
to be interested in the sale will suddenly appear from nowhere and succeed in
picking off a tract that everyone else had, for any one of a hundred reasons,
decided to ignore.

No company wants to spend more money than is needed. But as one oilman
commented, "The important thing is to get the tract you want, even if you
have to leave some money on the table."

How does all this work out in practice? At the Keams Canyon sale, as an
example, there was no pattern discernible. In the case of one tract, the top
bid was $95,748.76. There were three other bids made on the tract, the highest
of which was $2,802.12. Thus the high bidder spent approximately $93,000
more than was necessary to get the tract; he left that amount "on the table."
Yet in the case of other tracts, the difference between high and low bids was
sometimes only a few hundred dollars.

And the consideration that gives point to the whole unlikely procedure is
that until actual drilling takes place, no one knows whether there is oil on the
reservation—or if there is, under which tract it is located.

"You play your cards as you see them," one man commented, "and you
don't look back." [6]

Required: Assume that the following payoff table applies:

---

[6] Reprinted from the Winter 1965 issue of *Petroleum Today*.

		Well Characteristics		
Evidence	Probability	Producer	Probability	Dry
Favorable	.10	$4,000,000	.90	$0
Unfavorable	.01	4,000,000	.99	0

The following decision matrix is prepared for Company B.

Profits of Company B
(Expected Net Present Value)

	Company B Bids	
Company A's Evidence Is—	Low, Say $2,000	High Say $100,000
Favorable	$19,000†	— $60,000*
Unfavorable	0	150,000†

* Assumes probability of 1 of Company B getting the bid.

‡ Assumes probability of .5 of Company B getting the bid.

What decision should Company B make?

Now consider Company A's decision. Assume that A has two choices, bidding $3,000 or $200,000. It expects that B will bid $2,000 or $100,000. Assume that the results of the evidence were encouraging. The analyst prepares the following payoff matrix for A's president (A's expected profits are shown):

Company A Bids	Company B Bids	
	Low, Say $2,000	High, Say $100,000
Low, say $3,000	$397,000	$ 0
High, say $200,000	200,000	200,000

What decision should Company A make?

9-18. Assume that you are approached about the possibility of investing in a Broadway play. After conducting some research you find that the expected profits are $800,000 per play and that approximately 25 per cent of the plays that open on Broadway show a profit.

Required: Explain whether you would be willing to invest in a play being prepared for Broadway.

9-19. In 1964 a broker argued that although the Dow-Jones industrial average was high there were still many stocks that were far from their own highs.

Assume that common stocks can be divided into sixteen groups and that each firm in a group reacts identically to events, but that each group is independent of each other's movements (except for certain major events such as war or depression, which we shall assume have not occurred). Assume that the probability of each group hitting a high during a given period is .6. What is the probability that all groups will hit a high during that period?

9-20. Through their subsidiaries, the ABC Company and the XYZ Company are both currently distributing automobiles in the country of Afro. The profits per year of the two subsidiaries are currently as follows:

ABC	$10,000,000
XYZ	20,000,000

The ABC Company is considering establishing a manufacturing plant in Afro. An analyst has projected a profit of $38 million after the plant begins operations (this assumes that the XYZ Company continues to distribute but not manufacture in the country).

An analyst for the XYZ Company has heard of the plans of the ABC Company. If the plant by ABC is built, he projects XYZ's profits to fall to $4 million. If the XYZ Company builds a plant and the ABC Company does not, he anticipates profits of $38 million and a decrease in the profits of ABC to $4 million.

If both companies build plants it is expected that they would both earn $5 million per year.

Required: What course of action would you recommend for the ABC Company?

9-21. Answer the following three questions as you would if *you* were faced with the betting situations. Assume that the bets are legal and moral.

Situation 1: A fair coin will be tossed fairly. If a head appears, you will receive $5. If a tail appears, you will receive nothing. How much would you pay to participate in this game?

Situation 2: A coin whose characteristics you do not know will be tossed. You can call heads or tails. If you call correctly, you receive $5. If you call incorrectly, you will receive nothing. How much would you pay to participate in this game?

Situation 3: Two evenly matched basketball teams (say, U.C.L.A. and N.C. State) are playing this Saturday. You will receive $5 if you pick the winner, $0 otherwise. How much would you pay for this gamble?

9-22. If A is an event, which one or more of the following numbers could not represent the probability of A? Explain.

1.5, .6, .3, −.4.

9-23. Two events are said to be mutually exclusive if, at most, one of them can occur. Suppose A and B are two mutually exclusive events. For each of the following pairs of numbers, if someone told you that "The first number represents the probability of A and the second the probability of B," could you believe him? Explain.

    a. .5, .5
    b. .4, .3
    c. .4, .7
    d. −.2, 1.2
    e. 0, .9
    f. 0, 1.0

9-24. Two events are said to be exhaustive if at least one of them must occur. Suppose C and D are exhaustive events. For each of the following pairs of numbers if someone told you that "The first number is the probability of C and the second number is the probability of D," could you believe him? Explain.

    a. .5, .5
    b. .4, .3
    c. .4, .7
    d. −.2, 1.2
    e. 0, .9
    f. 0, 1.0

9-25. Suppose the events E and F are mutually exclusive and exhaustive. If someone told you, "The first number is the probability of E and the second number is the probability of F," could you believe him? Explain.

    a. .5, .5
    b. .4, .3
    c. .4, .7
    d. −.2, 1.2
    e. 0, .9
    f. 0, 1.0

9-26. "Our research labs have just developed this great new product. We feel it almost has to be profitable. Unless, of course, business conditions are really bad; or if our sales engineers have drastically misjudged customer acceptance. With the stock market behaving the way it has been, we think the probability of really bad business conditions is only two tenths. Our sales engineers make drastic misjudgments of product acceptance only three times out of ten."

Based on the above information, what is the maximum probability you would be willing to assign to the event that the new product will be profitable? What is the minimum probability you would assign to that event?

9-27. A new product has been proposed. In terms of after-tax net present values, introducing the new product will cost $600,000 for specialized production facilities and promotional expenses. Over the lifetime of the product, the after-tax net present value of the proceeds could be any of the following.

Present Value of Proceeds	Probability
$1,000,000	.8
400,000	.1
200,000	.05
100,000	.05
	1.00

Find the expected net present value and its standard deviation.

9-28. A proposed exploratory well for oil will cost $1,000,000 to drill. A large oil deposit would be worth $20,000,000, and a small oil deposit would be worth $2,000,000; the probabilities of these events are .04 and .10 respectively. If no oil is found, the drillers can collect $200,000 in dry hole money from the owners of nearby leases. What is the expected profit from drilling and its standard deviation?

9-29. In the table below, X, Y, and Z are three different investments, each with four different outcomes. The decision maker is free to accept or reject each investment.

Find the expected NPV and the standard deviation of NPV for each of the following:

a. X alone
b. Y alone
c. Z alone
d. $X + Y$
e. $X + Z$

Event	Probability of Event	NPV for Event		
		X	Y	Z
e_1	.25	1000	0	1000
e_2	.25	1000	0	0
e_3	.25	0	1000	1000
e_4	.25	0	1000	0

chapter 10

*If we have a correct theory but merely prate about
it, pigeonhole it and do not put it into practice,
then that theory, however good,
is of no significance.*

—Mao Tse-Tung, On Practice (July, 1937) in *Quotations
from Chairman Mao Tse-Tung* (New York.
Bantam Books, Inc., 1967), p. 176.

introduction to portfolio analysis

In this book the term *investment* refers to commitments of resources made in
the hope of realizing benefits that are expected to occur over several time
periods. These are the kinds of investments or capital expenditures ordinarily
made by business organizations. However, in another context, the term
investment is used to refer to the purchase and holding of marketable securities, particularly stocks and bonds.

There are certain similarities between these two activities that justify
using the same term to refer to both. There are also important differences.
Because the two kinds of "investment" are similar, certain analytical techniques originally developed for use in connection with investments in stocks
and bonds are applicable to some extent to the long-term investments of
business firms.

Normally, an individual does not put all his money into the one best
stock or bond. The disadvantage of concentrating investments is that if some
unfavorable event occurs that affects the one investment he owns, it may have
a drastic effect on his total financial situation.

The stock market investor typically attempts to divide his assets into stocks
of a number of different companies. When this strategy is followed, an unfavorable event affecting the value of any one company will have relatively
less effect on the value of his entire portfolio, because much of his investment
will be unaffected by the occurrence of such an event.

The collection of marketable stocks and bonds held by an individual
investor is referred to as a *portfolio*. The *portfolio problem* might be defined
as the problem of choosing a collection of securities that, taken together, has
desirable characteristics with respect to risk and expected return. The portfolio problem arises in the following way. Suppose that we agree on a reason-

able way of measuring the expected profit and the risk of individual securities. Imagine an investor who begins with a portfolio that consists entirely of one security. Now he considers diversifying by adding to his portfolio a second security. How will this change affect the expected profit and the risk of his portfolio? The portfolio problem is concerned with constructing a portfolio with desirable characteristics with respect to both risk and expected profit, where there is a trade-off with profit and risk.

In much of what follows, the portfolio problem will be developed in a context in which the differences between investments in stocks and bonds, on the one hand, and business capital expenditures, on the other, are assumed to be of negligible importance. Before proceeding, however, it is desirable to mention briefly two of the differences between the two types of investments. One difference is the relevant time horizon and transaction costs. The transaction costs associated with purchasing or selling most stocks and bonds are a relatively small fraction of their value. Thus the holder of these assets can, if he chooses, make decisions within the framework of a relatively short time horizon. By contrast, the transaction costs associated with buying or selling the capital assets to which many business decisions refer may be a large fraction of their value. When acquisition of such assets is under consideration, the relevant time horizon is often the life of the asset.

Another important difference is the nature of the dependency of the profits from the investments. As mentioned earlier, the profit from a portfolio consisting of two securities can be obtained by adding the profits of the two securities. But the profit from a portfolio consisting of a blast furnace and a rolling mill is often greater than the sum of the profits that could be earned from each of the assets by itself.

introduction to the portfolio problem

With an individual investment we must consider risk or, more specifically, our attitudes toward the undesirable events that might occur. As soon as a firm has one asset or is considering the purchase of more than one asset, we must consider the risk not of the individual assets, but of the entire collection of assets.

Consider the following investment. (We shall call this investment A.)

Time			
0	1	Rate of Return	Net Present Value (5%)
− $400	$500	.25	76

Investment A has a rate of return of .25, and assuming a desired time value of money of .05. the investment is apparently acceptable. Now add the information that the $500 is an expectation and that for time 1 the outcomes are either $0 if event a_1 with .5 probability occurs, or $1,000 if event a_2 with .5 probability occurs.

Most of us would reject the investment. If you happen to find this investment acceptable, consider adding one or more zeros to each of the dollar amounts to increase the scale of the investment and then decide whether or not you find the investment acceptable.

Now consider a second investment (investment B) that has the following expected cash flows:

Time			
0	1	Rate of Return	Net Present Value (5%)
− $500	$500	.0	− 24

This investment seems to be unacceptable, but again the $500 is an expectation. Assume that the possible outcomes are $0 if event a_2 with .5 probability occurs, or $1,000 if event a_1 with .5 probability occurs.

Investment B with a rate of return of 0 is clearly undesirable if we consider it as an individual investment. However, when we combine A and B we have an investment that most of us would find acceptable (see Figure 10-1).

The outcomes of the individual investment A and the individual investment B are uncertain. However, when we combine the investments, the uncertainty about the joint outcomes is eliminated. The factor at work to reduce the uncertainty of the sum of the investments is called the *covariance*. Whether event a_1 occurs or event a_2 occurs, the outcome of A + B is equal to $1,000. For example, if a_1 occurs, the outcome of A is 0, the outcome of B is $1,000, and the outcome of A + B is $0 + $1,000 = $1,000.

This additivity also holds if the results of the investment are measured either in period 1 dollars or in present values. In period 1 dollars the expected outcomes are $500 for A, $500 for B, and $1,000 for A + B. In present val-

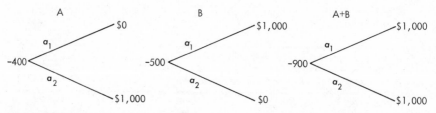

Figure 10-1

ues using .05 as a discount rate the expected net present values are \$76 for A, − \$24 for B, and \$52 forA + B.[1]

variance and covariance

The variance of a random variable X is equal to the expectation of the square of the differences from the mean:

$$\text{Var}(X) = E(X - \bar{X})^2 = E(X^2) - \bar{X}^2.$$

If we have two random variables X and Y, the variance of their sum is

$$\text{Var}(X + Y) = \text{Var}(X) + \text{Var}(Y) + 2\,\text{Cov}(X, Y).$$

The covariance of X, Y may be defined as

$$\begin{aligned}
\text{Cov}(X, Y) &= E[X - \bar{X})(Y - \bar{Y})] \\
&= E(XY - Y\bar{X} - X\bar{Y} + \bar{X}\bar{Y}) \\
&= E(XY) - \bar{X}\bar{Y} - \bar{X}\bar{Y} + \bar{X}\bar{Y} \\
&= E(XY) - \bar{X}\bar{Y}.
\end{aligned}$$

For the preceding example, if we let values of X represent the dollar outcomes of investment A, and values of Y represent the dollar outcomes of B, we would have the following computations:

	A				B			A + B	
	X	$\bar{X}$	$(X-\bar{X})^2$	$P(a_1)$	Y	$\bar{Y}$	$(Y-\bar{Y})^2$	XY	$\bar{X}\bar{Y}$
a_1	− \$400	\$100	\$250,000	.5	\$500	0	\$250,000	− \$200,000	0
a_2	600	100	250,000	.5	− 500	0	250,000	− 300,000	0
			Var (X) = \$250,000		Var (Y) = \$250,000			E(XY) = − \$250,000	

$$\text{Cov}(X, Y) = E(XY) - \bar{X}\bar{Y} = -250,000$$
$$\text{Var}(X + Y) = \text{Var}(X) + \text{Var}(Y) + 2\,\text{Cov}(X, Y)$$
$$= 250,000 + 250,000 - 500,000 = 0$$

[1] Additivity does not in general hold if rates of return are used. Based on expected period 1 dollars the yield of A is .25, of B is .0 and of A + B is .11. In the case of one-period investments, if the rates of return of A and B are weighted by the amounts invested, the expected value will equal the rate of return of the combination. Thus

$$\frac{400\,(.25) + 500\,(.0)}{900} = \frac{100}{900} = .11 = \text{expected rate of return of A + B}.$$

But this relationship between rates of return will not generally hold true if the cash flows extend over more than two periods. However, expected present values are always additive.

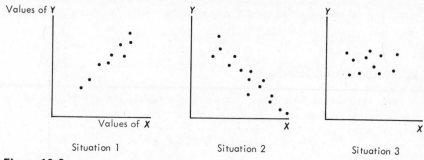

Figure 10-2

The variance of the sum of the two investments is zero because of the large negative covariance. Although the preceding calculations use monetary values (to simplify the arithmetic), similar results would be obtained using net present values.

The covariance is a useful means of measuring how two random variables (say, the net present values of two investments) react to events. When the value of one investment is large, will the other be large or small? Consider the two random variables X and Y.

Three basic relationships are illustrated in Figure 10-2. If we take the product of each pair of values for X and Y in all three situations, we would arrive at a positive amount for the sum or the average of these products. However, in situation 1 the higher the value of X, the higher the value of Y; in situation 2 the higher the value of X, the lower the value of Y; and in situation 3 the value of Y is not affected by the value of X. This difficulty is solved by subtracting the mean of X and the mean of Y from the observed values of X and Y. The result is a shifting of the X and Y axes so that the

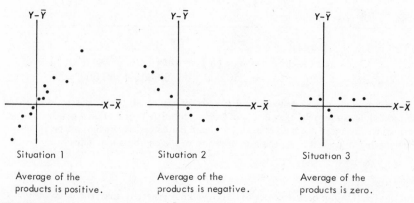

Figure 10-3

average of the products is positive for situation 1, negative for situation 2, and zero for situation 3. This is shown in Figure 10-3.

If X, Y are statistically independent, then $E(XY) = \bar{X}\bar{Y}$ and Cov $(X, Y) = 0$. However, the covariance can also be equal to zero when there is not statistical independence.

The covariance is affected by the scale used to measure the variables. The correlation coefficient is invariant to scale and is defined as

$$\rho_{X,Y} = \frac{\text{Cov}(X, Y)}{\sigma_X \sigma_Y}.$$

The correlation coefficient $\rho_{X,Y}$ can take on values between -1 and 1. (see Figure 10-4).

The covariance may be written in terms of the correlation coefficient:

$$\text{Cov}(X, Y) = \rho_{X,Y}\,\sigma_X\sigma_Y.$$

If we have more than two variables, we have several covariances; for example,

$$\text{Var}(X_1 + X_2 + X_3) = \text{Var}(X_1) + \text{Var}(X_2) + \text{Var}(X_3) + 2\,\text{Cov}(X_1, X_2) + 2\,\text{Cov}(X_1, X_3) + 2\,\text{Cov}(X_2, X_3)$$

or, more generally,

$$\text{Var}\left(\sum_{k=1}^{n} X_k\right) = \sum_{k=1}^{n} \text{Var}(X_k) + 2\sum_{k=1}^{n-1}\sum_{j=k+1}^{n} \text{Cov}(X_k, X_j).$$

We can let

$$\sigma_{ij} = \text{Cov}(X_i, X_j) \quad \text{if} \quad i \neq j,$$
$$\sigma_{ij} = \text{Var}(X_i) \quad \text{if} \quad i = j,$$

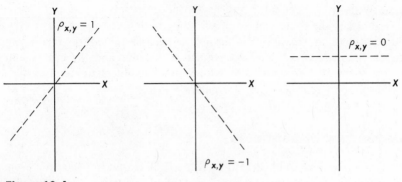

Figure 10-4

Table 10–1.   Subjective Probability Distributions of Returns from Two
              Investments

Triggering Events for A	Triggering Events for B	Cash Flow of Period 1 (Both A and B)	Probability
e_1	e_3	$ 0	.4
e_2	e_4	2,000	.6

and then

$$\text{Var}\left(\sum_{k=1}^{n} X_k\right) = \sum_{i=1}^{n} \sum_{j=1}^{n} \sigma_{ij}.$$

The previous computations illustrate a situation where the covariance is
negative. (The correlation coefficient was equal to -1.) We shall now consider three variations of another basic investment situation. In the first
example the covariance will be 0. The investments are statistically independent. (The correlation coefficient will be equal to zero.) In the second example
the covariance will be negative. (The correlation coefficient will be equal to
-1.) In the third example the covariance will be positive. (The correlation
coefficient will be equal to 1.)

As the first example we present in Table 10-1 data on two investments,
A and B. We assume that each of these investments would require an outlay
of $1,000 and each could return one year later either $0 or $2,000. In each
case the probability of the $0 return is .4, and the probability of the $2,000
return is .6. The investor is assumed to have a choice of either accepting
investment A or investment B or both or rejecting both.

It might appear that the two investments are identical. However, this may
not be the case. Assume that with investment A the cash flow of $0 would
occur if event e_1 occurred. The return of $2,000 would occur if event e_2
occurred. We assume that e_1 and e_2 are mutually exclusive and exhaustive
events. With investment B the returns depend on events e_3 and e_4.

To evaluate the consequences of accepting both investments A and B, we
need additional information that has not yet been presented: the relationship
between the events on which investment A depends and the events upon
which investment B depends. We shall examine possible extreme cases of the
relationship between the series of events.

independent investments

Case 1, the relationship illustrated in Table 10-2, is that in which the events
that investment A depends on are statistically independent of the events upon

Table 10-2. Joint Probability of Two
Independent Investments: Case 1

Investment B Outcomes	Investment A Outcomes		
	$0	$2,000	
	e_1	e_2	
$ 0 e_3	.16	.24	.40
2,000 e_4	.24	.36	.60
	.40	.60	1.00

which investment B depends. In this context the term *statistical independence* means that the probability of any particular outcome for investment A is the same regardless of what the outcome is for investment B. The probabilities listed in the table show the probability that both the event described by the column head and the event described by the row stub will occur. For example, if the outcome of investment B is $0 (that is, if e_3 has occurred), any of the two outcomes for investment A is possible, and each is relatively as likely as if the other outcome for B had occurred.

To help understand the implications of statistical independence more clearly, divide each of the two probabilities in row 1 (.16 and .24) by the row total of (.40). For example, for row 1, column 2, .16 ÷ .40 = .40. This is the conditional probability of event e_1, given that event e_3 has occurred. In symbolic terms, this conditional probability is expressed by $P(e_1|e_3)$. We can also compute the conditional probabilities given that e_4 has occurred[2]:

$$P(e_1|e_4) = \frac{.24}{.60} = .40, \qquad P(e_1|e_3) = \frac{.16}{.40} = .40,$$

$$P(e_2|e_4) = \frac{.36}{.60} = .60, \qquad P(e_2|e_3) = \frac{.24}{.40} = .60.$$

[2] The general mathematical relationship being used is

$$P(X|Y) = \frac{P(X, Y)}{P(Y)}$$

where $P(Y)$ = probability of event Y,
  $P(X|Y)$ = conditional probability of event X, given that event Y has occurred,
  $P(X, Y)$ = joint probability of X and Y; that is, the probability of events X and Y both occurring.
In the context of the example, $e_i = X$ and $e_j = Y$ and

$$P(e_i|e_j) = \frac{P(e_i, e_j)}{P(e_j)}.$$

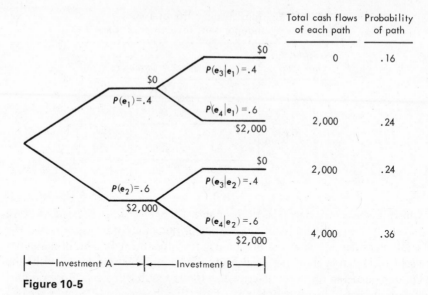

Figure 10-5

It should be noted that the probability of e_1 does not depend on the outcome of investment B. In like manner we could show that the outcomes of investment B are independent of the outcome of investment A (see Figure 10-5). Note that all the paths of investment B are independent of the path followed for investment A.

Let e_i be any event that determines the outcome of one investment, and let e_j be any event that determines the outcome of a second investment. If the events e_i and e_j are statistically independent, then $P(e_i|e_j) = P(e_i)$; that is, the probability of the event e_i given that e_j has occurred is equal to the probability of e_i. The probability of e_i is the same whether or not e_j has occurred. If this relationship holds for every possible pair of events that determines the outcomes of the two investments, the two investments are statistically independent.

We can summarize the results of undertaking both investments by combining the events that have equal monetary outcomes. The expected monetary value is obtained by weighting each cash outcome by its probability and summing.

(1) Cash Flow	(2) Probability of Cash Flow	(3) Col. 1 × Col. 2
$ 0	.16	$ 0
2,000	.48	960
4,000	.36	1,440
	Expected monetary value	$2,400

The expected values for each of the investments are $1,200. The variances of the two investments are also equal. The computation of the variance of X, the outcomes for investment A, follows:

Event	Outcome X	E(X)	X − E(X)	[X − E(X)]²	P(X)	P(X)[X − E(X)]²
e_1	$ 0	$1,200	− $1,200	144×10^4	.4	57.6×10^4
e_2	2,000	1,200	800	64×10^4	.6	38.4×10^4
					Var (X) =	96×10^4

Because the two investments are statistically independent, the covariance of their outcomes, Cov $(X, Y) = 0$. Thus the variance of the sum of their outcomes, $X + Y$, is Var $(X + Y) =$ Var $(X) +$ Var (Y):

$$\text{Var}\,(X + Y) = 96 \times 10^4 + 96 \times 10^4 = 192 \times 10^4.$$

The variance of the joint investment can also be computed using the basic definition of a variance. Let $Z = X + Y$.

Event	Outcome Z	E(Z)	Z − E(Z)	[Z − E(Z)]²	P(Z)	P(Z)[Z − E(Z)]²
$e_1 e_3$	$ 0	$2,400	− $2,400	576×10^4	.16	92.16×10^4
$e_1 e_4$	2,000	2,400	− 400	16×10^4	.24	3.84×10^4
$e_2 e_3$	2,000	2,400	− 400	16×10^4	.24	3.84×10^4
$e_2 e_4$	4,000	2,400	1,600	256×10^4	.36	92.16×10^4
				Var (Z) = Var (X + Y) =		192.00×10^4

negatively correlated investments

We shall use the term *negatively correlated investments* to refer to a situation where events affecting one investment in a desirable fashion will affect the second investment in an undesirable fashion.

In the second case, illustrated in Table 10-3 and Figure 10-6, it is assumed that there is a type of dependence between the returns of investment A and investment B; so if event e_3 occurs (investment B has a return of $0), we can be certain that event e_2 will have occurred (the return from investment A will be $2,000). If event e_1 occurs (investment A's return is $0), we can be certain that e_4 will then occur (investment B's return is $2,000). In this second case, there is uncertainty about which events may occur and about the

Table 10-3. Joint Probability of Two
Investments: Case 2

Investment B Outcomes	Investment A Outcomes		
	$0 e_1	$2,000 e_2	
$ 0 e_3	.00	.40	.40
2,000 e_4	.40	.20	.60
	.40	.60	1.00

returns from either investment taken by itself. But if both investments are accepted, we can be certain that the total return will be at least $2,000.

The tree diagram for case 2 (Figure 10-6) is simplified by leaving off the branch with zero probability.

Event	Outcomes Z	E(Z)	Z − E(Z)	$[Z − E(Z)]^2$	P(Z)	$P(Z)[Z − E(Z)]^2$
e_1e_4	$2,000	$2,400	− $ 400	16 × 10⁴	.4	6.4 × 10⁴
e_2e_3	2,000	2,400	− 400	16 × 10⁴	.4	6.4 × 10⁴
e_2e_4	4,000	2,400	1,600	256 × 10⁴	.2	51.2× 10⁴
						64.0 × 10⁴

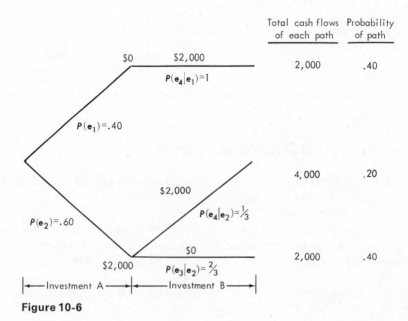

Figure 10-6

The expected value of undertaking both is $2,400 ($2,000 × .8 + $4,000 × .2) and the variance is $640,000. In this case the two investments are negatively correlated. The correlation coefficient, ρ, is $-.75$. In general,

$$\text{Var}(Z) = \text{Var}(X + Y) = \text{Var}(X) + \text{Var}(Y) + 2\rho\sigma_X\sigma_Y.$$

Since in this case $\text{Var}(Z) = 64 \times 10^4$ and $\text{Var}(X) = \text{Var}(Y) = 96 \times 10^4$, we have

$$64 \times 10^4 = 96 \times 10^4 + 96 \times 10^4 + 2\rho 96 \times 10^4,$$
$$-128 \times 10^4 = 2\rho 96 \times 10^4,$$
$$-.75 = \rho.$$

positively correlated investments

The third case, illustrated in Table 10-4, is that in which the returns from the two investments have a type of risk-intensifying dependency. Under these circumstances the occurrence of event e_1 ($0) guarantees that e_3 ($0) will occur. Similarly, if the return from one of the investments is $2,000, the return from the other will also be $2,000. The returns are perfectly correlated.

The tree diagram for case 3 is shown in Figure 10-7.

The expected value of undertaking both investments is $2,400 (that is, $4,000 × .6 + $0 × .4). The variance is

$$\begin{aligned}\text{Var}(X + Y) &= \text{Var}(X) + \text{Var}(Y) + 2\rho\sigma_X\sigma_Y \\ &= 96 \times 10^4 + 96 \times 10^4 + 2 \times 96 \times 10^4 \\ &= 384 = 10^4.\end{aligned}$$

Event	Outcome Z	E(Z)	Z − E(Z)	[Z − E(Z)]²	P(Z)	P(Z)[Z − E(Z)²]
e_1	$ 0	$2,400	− $2,400	576×10^4	.4	230.4×10^4
e_2	4,000	2,400	1,600	256×10^4	.6	153.6×10^4
					Vw (Z) = Var (X+ Y) =	384.0×10^4

Table 10-4. Joint Probability of Two
Dependent Investments: Case 3

Investment B Outcomes	Investment A Outcomes		
	$0	$2,000	
	e_1	e_2	
$ 0 e_3	.40	.00	.40
2,000 e_4	.00	.60	.60
	.40	.60	1.00

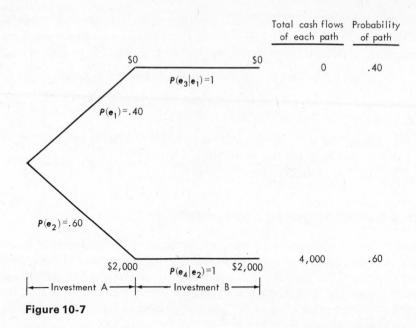

Figure 10-7

Summary of Example. In Table 10-5 all combinations of events that yield the same total cash flows are grouped together and the corresponding probabilities for each of the three cases described are presented in a single table. At the bottom of Table 10-5 several summary measures are presented.

The standard deviation (σ) is a measure of the risk, because it measures the spread of the possible outcomes. The expected outcome $[E(Z)]$ is a measure of the value of the benefits. We can divide the standard deviation by

Table 10-5.   Summary of the Results of the Three Cases

Total Cash Flows	Probabilities		
	Case 1	Case 2	Case 3
$ 0	.16	.00	.40
2,000	.48	.80	.00
4,000	.36	.20	.60
	1.00	1.00	1.00
Expected cash flow	$2,400	$2,400	$2,400
Variance (σ^2)	1,920,000	640,000	3,840,000
σ	1,388	800	1,959
Coefficient of variation $\sigma/E(Z)$	.58	.33	.82

the expected return in order to relate the risk measure to expected benefits. The resulting measure is called the coefficient of variation by statisticians:

$$\text{"Risk" per dollar of expected return} = \frac{\sigma}{E(Z)}.$$

If two different sets of investments require the same outlay and have the same expected return, the variance or standard deviation of the return from each set is a useful measure of the amount of risk. However, it will normally be the case that the standard deviation of investments will vary with the size of the investment, and the size of the standard deviation may not be a very satisfactory measure of the riskiness of an investment set. In Table 10-5, the three cases outlined require the same outlay and also have the same expected return, so one could make comparisons using the standard deviation. Case 2 has the least amount of risk associated with it; case 3 has the greatest amount of risk (using σ as the measure of risk).

We have also computed the coefficient of variation in order to relate the standard deviation to the expected value of the investment. Because the expected values are the same, this additional measure adds little information in this special situation.

In practice, most events that tend to stimulate general business conditions will tend to increase the returns from most investments. Similarly, events that affect an entire industry, or all the operations of a particular company, are likely to increase or decrease the returns of most projects in a particular company. These factors will tend to introduce a situation analogous to case 3 between the returns of individual investment projects within a company.

conclusions

The corporation should take into consideration the nature of the risk associated with the investment and its interaction with the risks of other investments. The process by which risk is incorporated into the decision can be complex. However, there remains the mechanism of the security markets, and this helps simplify the decision process tremendously. Assuming investors who are able and willing to diversify, the only risk components that need be taken into account by the corporation (from the point of view of stockholders) are those that the individual investor cannot eliminate by diversifying his portfolio. This suggests that many investments that have been traditionally considered to be highly risky, such as exploring for new reserves of oil, may turn out to be relatively riskless. Methods of adjusting for risk when a firm is owned by stockholders who have diversified stock portfolios are presented in Chapters 11 and 12.

However, corporate management may wish to apply a significant risk premium to large investments that could jeopardize the existence of the firm. If a manager has special skills and experience that make him more valuable to his present employer than to other firms, and if he derives a large fraction of his income from his employment, he is less able than most stockholders to diversify against events that could threaten the continued existence of the firm.

If we drop the assumption of a large publicly owned firm, we can no longer assume that the investor has attained diversification. Now, the investor may be adversely affected by a decision. The corporation may try to take into consideration the affairs of this investor; but this is very difficult, because the investor may be either seeking risk, in the hope of large gains, or attempting to avoid risk. This problem will be considered in Chapter 13.

questions and problems

10-1. Two investments have the following characteristics for a commitment of an outlay of $800:

	Expected Net Present Value	Variance
Investment A	$1,000	$100
Investment B	2,000	900

Required: For an outlay of $800 in each of the two investments ($1,600 in total),

a. Compute the expected benefits (return).
b. Compute the variance of the returns if the correlation coefficient is .8.
c. Compute the variance of the returns if the correlation coefficient is −.8.
d. Compute the variance of the returns if the investments are independent.

10-2. The outcomes of investment A are as follows:

Event	Outcome	Probability
e_1	$200	.4
e_2	100	.5
e_3	− 100	.1

Required: Compute the expectation and variance of the investment.

10-3. All you are told about an investment is that there is an outlay of $100 and that the returns (net of outlay) have an expectation of $120 and a variance of $7,600.

Required: Would you accept this investment? Explain.

10-4. Two investments have the following net returns for the two events indicated:

Event	Probability	Net Present Value of Investment	
		A	B
e_1	.6	$600	− $100
e_2	.4	− 400	500

Required: (a) Compute the expectation and variance of each investment and the covariance of the two investments. (b) Compute the correlation coefficient of the two investments.

10-5. Continuing problem 10-4. What is the expected return and variance of the net returns of investment in both A and B?

10-6. An investment X has the following net return for the two events indicated:

Event	Probability	Net Present Value
e_1	.6	$500
e_2	.4	100

Required: Compute the expectation and variance of investment in X.

10-7. Two investments whose outcomes are statistically independent have the following net present values with the indicated probabilities:

Event	Probability	Investment	
		R	S
e_1	.4	− $400	$500
e_2	.6	600	− 100

Required: (a) Compute the expected return and variance of each of the two investments. (b) Compute the covariance and correlation coefficient of the two investments. (c) Compute expected return and variance of the returns if investment is made in both R and S.

10-8. An investment has the following outcomes and probabilities;

− $ 500	.24
100	.16
500	.36
1,100	.24

Required: Compute the expectation and variance of this investment.

10-9. The Eatwell Company is considering the purchase of a new machine to replace one currently in use. The new machine would cost $100,000 and be depreciated over a four-year period on a straight-line basis. It would have no salvage value. Ignore the investment tax credit in making your analysis.

Let us suppose that the new equipment whose purchase is proposed is to be used to replace an older machine that is fully depreciated and has no salvage value. The older machine could be continued in use for another four years, if this were economically desirable. Either machine could be used to produce a part that is a component of one of the company's products. The company's engineering department estimates that the use of the proposed new machine would most likely result in a reduction of $.25 per unit in the manufacturing cost of the component. This cost-reduction calculation takes into consideration savings in direct labor, material, and variable overhead, on a before-tax basis; the cost attributed to depreciation on the new machine is not included in this calculation.

There is some chance that the savings may not be as great as anticipated. The engineering department considers that there is .1 probability the machine produces savings of $.15 per unit, and it further believes that there is .9 probability that savings of $.25 per unit will actually be realized.

Because the total savings that will be realized will depend on the number of units produced, the sales department of the company was asked to estimate total sales for the next four years for the product. The product has an established and stable market. The sales department expected that demand would continue at the present rate for the next four years, in which case total sales would amount to 600,000 units, but added an important qualification. It was known that a competitor was about to introduce a product that might be more satisfactory than the company's product to some consumers. If the competitive product is successful, unit sales for the four-year period might be only 400,000. However, the sales department believed the probability is only .3 that the competitor's product would be successful.

Considering both the engineering and technical uncertainties connected

Table 10-6. Joint Probabilities of Possible Outcomes
           Associated with Use of New Equipment

Unit Cost Reduction	Unit Sales		Marginal Probability
	400,000	600,000	
$.25	.27	.63	.90
.15	.03	.07	.10
Marginal probability	.30	.70	1.00

with the proposed new equipment, four possible outcomes (events) need to be considered. These outcomes and their probabilities are given in Table 10-6. The joint probabilities were calculated on the assumption that the unit cost reduction achieved by the machine would be statistically independent of the unit sales of the product. The assumption seems reasonable in this instance.

The financial consequences of these four outcomes are described as follows, assuming a .4 tax rate.

Although the cash inflows that might result from using the new equipment are uncertain, the cash outflows associated with a decision to acquire the new equipment, and the tax savings from depreciation, are not uncertain (see Table 10-7).

The Eatwell Company produces about 100 different food products, which are distributed through retail foodstores. The machine in question would be used to help manufacture one of these products. The product in question accounts for about 3 per cent of sales and of net profits.

Eatwell has a capital structure consisting of 80 per cent equity and 20 per cent debt. It is able to borrow money on a long-term basis at 5 per cent (before taxes). The financial committee estimates that the company's average cost of capital is 10 per cent.

Table 10-7. Annual After-Tax Savings Before Depreciation

Event	Unit Cost Reduction	Unit Sales for Four Years	(1) Prob- ability	(2) Total Before Taxes	(3) Savings After Taxes Col. 2 × .6	(4) Annual After-Tax Savings Col. 3 × ¼	(5) Expectation Col. 1 × Col. 4
e_1	$.25	600,000	.63	$150,000	$90,000	$22,500	$14,175
e_2	.25	400,000	.27	100,000	60,000	15,000	4,050
e_3	.15	600,000	.07	90,000	54,000	13,500	945
e_4	.15	400,000	.03	60,000	36,000	9,000	270
			1.00				19,440

The company has no established policy as to the minimum acceptable level of return. It feels that both profitability and risk need to be considered in deciding whether or not an investment is desirable.

Should Eatwell purchase this new machine? What data would you use to defend your judgment?

10-10. The ABC Book Company is considering investing $3 million in an advanced teaching mechanism. If the advanced mechanism is successful, the company expects the investment to have a net present value of $4 million. If it is unsuccessful, the investment has a negative net present value of $2 million. The probability of success is .7 and failure .3. A loss of $2 million would be very material to this firm.

The company is also considering investing $1 million in a new method of producing books. The method has a .4 probability of being workable. If the method works, the net present value of this investment is computed to be $2 million if the teaching mechanism fails and $0 if the teaching mechanism is successful. If the method of producing books is not successful, there will be a net loss of $1 million resulting from this investment, with a successful teaching mechanism; and the company will break even on this investment if the teaching mechanism is not successful.

Payoffs of $1 Million Investment in Book Production

Successful Book Method	Successful Teaching Mechanism	
	Yes	No
Yes	0	$2,000,000
No	− $1,000,000	0

Required: Should the company undertake either or both of the investments?

10-11. The Rokal Company is a small regional hardware wholesaler. In recent years the company has been earning approximately $500,000 per year after taxes. Approximately half the earnings have been paid out as dividends. The stock is closely held by descendants of the founder, many of whom rely on their dividends for a substantial part of their personal income. The board of directors of the company consists of the principal stockholders or their representatives, including the president. Day-to-day management of the company is concentrated in the hands of the president, Mr. John Chalishan, who, it is generally agreed, is the only family member capable of effectively running the business. The board is consulted on important policy matters. Their main objective is to have the company maintain a stable dividend, with some growth if possible.

Recently, several of the board members have become concerned about the possible dangers to dividend stability arising from the fact that management is so heavily concentrated in the hands of the president. In case of a serious sickness or unexpected death, there would be no one else capable of quickly and effectively taking over the management. The board recognized that, in time, an effective professional manager could be found to replace Mr. Chalishan. It also recognized that the company would suffer some financial impairment if it operated without an experienced and energetic head for the six to twenty-four months that would be required to find a new president. The ability of the company to pay its regular dividend during such an interim period was questionable.

The possibility of hiring a potential replacement now was considered but rejected. A person of the necessary experience and ability would be expensive; he would have no real future with the company if Mr. Chalishan, who was only forty-seven years old, remained in good health; thus he might become a source of friction and factionalism.

The board members finally concluded that the purchase of an insurance policy on Mr. Chalishan's life in the amount of $500,000 would be the best way of handling this risk. Inquiries with an insurance broker indicated that a single payment of $15,000 would provide a five-year term policy on Mr. Chalishan's life, assuming he passed the usual medical examination. The policy provided for renewal if desired with no subsequent medical examination.

When the subject was raised at a board meeting, Mr. Chalishan reacted rather coolly and asked to have the subject tabled until the next meeting.

Exhibit 10-1. Analysis of Life Insurance Policy As an Investment
A. Present-Value Analysis

Year	Cash Flow	Probability*	Expected Cash Flow	Present- Value Factor†	Present Value
0	− $15,000	1.000		1.0000	− $15,000
1	500,000	.005	$2,500	.9524	2,381
2	500,000	.005	2,500	.9070	2,268
3	500,000	.005	2,500	.8638	2,160
4	500,000	.005	2,500	.8227	2,057
5	500,000	.005	2,500	.7835	1,959
				Net present value	− $4,177

B. Rate of Return Analysis
The discounted cash flow rate of return on the expected cash flows associated with this policy is approximately minus 6 per cent.

* Probability based on mortality experience for males of like age and occupation.
‡ Using a 5 per cent discount rate.

This was done. At the subsequent meeting Mr. Chalishan presented an analysis of the proposed life insurance policy as an investment, which he felt it was. He recommended that the proposal should be rejected on the grounds that it was an obviously unprofitable investment. He presented Exhibit 10-1 to justify his opinion.

Required: Can the purchase of a life insurance policy be treated as an investment? Why or why not? Is it reasonable for the Rokal Company to purchase this policy?

chapter 11

the capital asset pricing model

In principle, there is a clear criterion for determining whether the financial community considers an investment worthwhile. Worthwhile investments increase the wealth of the owners of the firm's securities.

For example, suppose that the stock of a particular company is currently quoted at $50 per share. During the next year management will have to make a decision about a major investment opportunity, and the outcome of this decision will become known to the financial community shortly after the decision is made. Management believes that if it rejects this investment opportunity the company will be able to pay a dividend of $5 per share, its stock will sell for $53 per share one year from now, and a stockholder will have a total value of $58 per share. However, if the investment opportunity is accepted, the company will be able to pay a dividend of only $3 per share (because a larger quantity of cash and retained earnings will be required to help finance the investment), but the price per share at the end of the year will be $57, reflecting the market's recognition of the earnings potential from the new investment. This is a total of $60. Ignoring the important complication of personal taxes, stockholder's wealth will be $2 per share greater if the company accepts the investment than if it rejects it.

In practice, it is not easy to implement this criterion. The major difficulty is predicting how an investment decision will affect the price of a company's stock. Given the present state of knowledge, a totally satisfactory procedure for making such predictions cannot be given. However, we believe that procedures can be suggested that will be helpful in practice to businessmen.

The necessary tasks can be broken down into two parts: (1) determine the main factors that influence stock prices, and (2) determine the relationship between investment projects and stock prices.

The present chapter is concerned with the theory of stock prices. Many of the basic ideas underlying the theory are simple, intuitively appealing, and have been known for a long time. What makes the theory important and relevant are the relatively recent developments that make it possible to re-state these old ideas into mathematical terms. As a result, it is now possible to quantify some of the factors that affect stock prices and the value of real investments.

The basic ideas are as follows: first, most investors dislike risk. Other things being equal, most investors would prefer higher returns to lower returns. Whenever it is possible to reduce risk without reducing expected returns, it follows that investors will attempt to do this. It will be assumed that the standard deviation of the rate of return from a portfolio of securities is a reasonable measure of risk. Thus there is an incentive to use diversification to reduce risk. For example, if the rates of return from two securities have the same expected value and are independent, it can be shown that a portfolio consisting of both securities in appropriate proportions will have a lower risk than any portfolio which consists of one of the securities.

To the extent that the rates of return from different securities are not highly correlated, risk-averse investors who diversify their holdings can reduce their total risk. However, to the extent that rates of return from different securities are correlated with one another and thus tend to fluctuate more or less in unison, diversification does not lead to complete risk elimination.

We find it useful to break down risk into two components: (1) risk that can be eliminated by diversification, which we refer to as *unsystematic* risk, and (2) risk that is still present with an efficient portfolio (all unsystematic risk has been eliminated), which we refer to as *systematic* risk. The latter reflects how the investments in the portfolio are correlated with the market.

If the costs of diversification are relatively low, investors will not be willing to pay more for a security simply because it carries a relatively low burden of unsystematic risk (which can be diversified away). Similarly, securities that carry a large amount of unsystematic risk will not suffer a serious price disadvantage.

To anticipate the conclusions of this chapter, to the extent that security prices are determined by the activities of the investors who can diversify their portfolios at low cost, the prices of securities will be set in such a way that differentials in expected rates of return will reflect primarily differences in the amount of systematic risk to which the securities are exposed.

market portfolio

Imagine an investor whose objective is to achieve the maximum amount of diversification. To this end, the investor follows a policy of including in his portfolio every security available. Securities are defined here to include common stock and any other security for which there is a market. Thus warrants, convertible bonds, and preferred stock issues would be included in this portfolio.

In deciding how to allocate his assets, the investor does not attempt to anticipate future changes in the value of each security, but uses the existing market valuations. Thus, if the outstanding common stock of company X represented .035% of the value of the equity of all companies, the stock would represent .035% of the value of the portfolio. We assume that the price per share will always reflect the current market value of the assets held. The investor would literally be buying a share in the capital market; we shall call the resulting investment the *market portfolio.*

We shall assume that, because of the diversification characteristics of the market portfolio and the risk aversion of most investors, the prices of the securities in the market portfolio have adjusted so that an investor could not earn a higher rate of return for the same or a lower level of risk in some other form of investment. However, the level of risk associated with the market portfolio may be too high or too low for a particular investor. We next consider how an investor can vary the level of risk to which he is exposed and still invest in the market portfolio.

capital market line

Suppose that r_f represents the rate of return that could be earned on a government security maturing one period from now. For an investor with a one-period planning horizon, there would be no default risk associated with owning a one-period government security. We shall call such a government security a *default-free asset* since we are considering only the risk of default. Now consider the possible portfolios that could be constructed by taking combinations of the market portfolio and these government securities. Suppose that our hypothetical investor devoted a proportion α of his assets to the market portfolio and a proportion $1 - \alpha$ to this government security. Assume that the fraction α is between 0 and 1. Denote by $\bar{r}_m$ the expected rate of return from $1 investment in the market portfolio. Similarly, let σ_m denote the standard deviation of the rate of return r_m from the market portfolio, and r_f the default-free return. The expected rate of return on the investor's portfolio, $\bar{r}_p$, is given by

$$\bar{r}_p = (1 - \alpha)r_f + \alpha\bar{r}_m$$
$$= r_f + \alpha[\bar{r}_m - r_f], \tag{1}$$

and the standard deviation of the rate of return on his portfolio, $\sigma(r_p)$, is given by

$$\sigma(r_p) = \alpha\sigma_m. \tag{2}$$

If equation 2 is solved for α and that quantity substituted into equation 1, the resulting relationship between the expected rate of return in a portfolio and its standard deviation (when the portfolio is a mixture of the market portfolio and a default-free asset) can be rewritten as

$$\bar{r}_p = r_f + \left[\frac{r_m - r_f}{\sigma_m}\right]\sigma(r_p). \tag{3}$$

A graphical representation of the relationship in equation 3 is shown in Figure 11-1, where line AD is the *capital market line*.

If an investor chose an α of 0 all his funds would be held in government securities and his expected return would be r_f and $\sigma(r_p) = 0$. This corresponds to point A in Figure 11-1. If an investor chose an α of 1, all his funds would be held in the market portfolio and his expected return would be $\bar{r}_m$ and $\sigma(r_p) = \sigma_m$. This corresponds to point C in Figure 11-1. An investor could also reach any point on the straight line from A to C by picking an appropriate value of α between 0 and 1.[1]

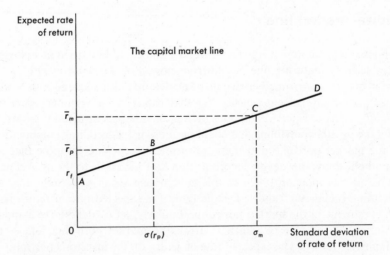

Figure 11-1

[1] The points to the right of point C on the market line correspond to values of α that are greater than 1. To reach such points, an investor must be able to borrow at the rate r_f. Suppose that this were the case and that an investor was willing to absorb a level of

The capital market line applies only to a very special category of portfolios, those consisting of mixtures of the market portfolio and of riskless assets.

security market line

The capital market line illustrates the relationships between the risk and expected return that an investor could realize by varying the proportion of the riskless asset and the market portfolio in his personal portfolio.

This is not the only way investors can adjust the composition of their portfolios in an effort to obtain a better combination of risk and expected return. Investors might vary the composition of their portfolios by increasing or decreasing their holdings of a particular risky security. If it were possible to achieve a better risk–return relationship by this technique then the market would not be in equilibrium since everybody would act to take advantage of the opportunity.

If v represents the equilibrium price of a security, then the rate of return that will be earned by holding the security for one period will be

$$r^* = \frac{w}{v} - 1 \tag{4}$$

where w is the sum of the dividends that will be received plus the end-of-period value of the security, and r^* is the rate of return on the equilibrium value of the security. The expectation of r^*, denoted by

$$\bar{r}^* = \frac{\bar{w}}{v} - 1 \tag{5}$$

is called the required rate of return.

If the market is in equilibrium, the required rate of return must satisfy the following relationship:

$$\bar{r}^* = r_f + \frac{\bar{r}_m - r_f}{\sigma_m^2} \text{Cov}(r^*, r_m). \tag{6}$$

---

risk corresponding to a value of $\sigma(r_p) = 2\sigma_m$. The investor could buy \$2 worth of the market portfolio for every dollar of equity he owned. He would obtain the necessary funds by borrowing an amount equal to his equity. In effect, he would be buying the market portfolio on a 50 per cent margin at an interest rate of r_f. The investor's expected return is given by equation 1 with α equal to 2. Similarly, the standard deviation of return to which he is subject is given by inserting $\alpha = 2$ into equation 2. Since both equations apply, it follows that equation 3 is also applicable.

We will define lambda to be equal to

$$\lambda = \frac{\bar{r}_m - r_f}{\sigma_m^2}$$

and substituting in equation (6) we obtain

$$\bar{r}^* = r_f + \lambda \, \text{Cov} \, (r^*, r_m). \tag{7}$$

Equations (6) and (7) measure the required rate of return from an asset, which may be any security or any portfolio of securities. On the right-hand side of the equation, $\text{Cov} \, (r^*, r_m)$ is the covariance between the rates of return on the equilibrium value of the security and the market portfolio, and λ is the market's return–risk trade-off rate for the period.

If the covariance between the rate of return from the individual security and the rate of return on the market portfolio is zero, then the equilibrium expected rate of return on the given security will equal the rate of return on a default-free asset, even if the particular security has a rate of return whose standard deviation is greater than zero. In fact, if a security could be found whose correlation with the market was negative, then its equilibrium expected rate of return could be less than the return received from a default-free asset. Negatively correlated investments are difficult to find.

For some purposes, it is convenient to compare the $\text{Cov} \, (r^*, r_m)$ for a particular security with the variance of the market portfolio by taking the ratio of these two quantities. This ratio, called the *beta coefficient* of the security, is

$$\beta = \frac{\text{Cov} \, (r^*, r_m)}{\sigma_m^2}. \tag{8}$$

A beta coefficient of unity indicates that a security has the same amount of systematic risk as the market portfolio. A beta coefficient greater (less) than unity indicates the security is riskier (safer) than the market portfolio.

required rate of return versus cost of capital [2]

Suppose that a one-period investment is available whose cost is c. The end-of-period-1 cash flow from the investment is x. Therefore the rate of return on

[2] The analysis in this section is adapted from Mark E. Rubinstein, "A Mean-Variance Synthesis of Corporate Financial Theory," *Journal of Finance*, XXVIII (March 1973), pp. 167–181.

cost for the investment is

$$r = \frac{x}{c} - 1$$

and the expected rate of return on cost is

$$\bar{r} = \frac{\bar{x}}{c} - 1$$

where $\bar{x}$ is the expected end-of-period-1 cash flow.

In capital budgeting practice a commonly used criterion for making accept or reject decisions is to compare the expected rate of return on cost for an investment with the firm's weighted average cost of capital (WACC). The WACC represents the required rate of return for the firm as a whole, and as its name suggests, is an average. Those who advocate this procedure recommend accepting the investment if its expected rate of return on cost exceeds or is equal to the firm's cost of capital. That is, accept if $r \geq$ WACC.

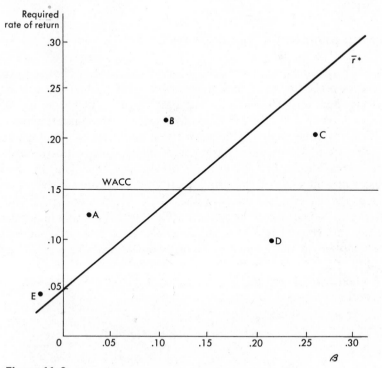

Figure 11-2

Figure 11-2 shows both the WACC and the required-return lines. The two lines imply different investment criteria; in each case the line is the boundary between the accept region (above the line) and the reject region (below the line).

For investments B and D both criteria lead to the same decisions. For investments A, C, and E, contradictory recommendations would result. Investments A and E would be rejected by the WACC criterion—but would be acceptable using the capital asset pricing model approach, even though E yields less than the default-free return. Investment C would be accepted using the WACC, but rejected using the CAPM approach.

Figure 11-2 illustrates one important limitation of the WACC approach: the fact that it does not take into account variations in the riskiness of different projects. The WACC approach tends to reject some low-risk projects like A that should be accepted because their rates of return are more than enough to compensate for their risk. The WACC approach tends to lead to the acceptance of high-risk projects, like C, whose expected rates of return are greater than the WACC, but not enough greater to compensate for the risk of the project.

making investment decisions

The theory of stock prices presented in this chapter can be applied to investment decisions if the assets in question have a life of only one period. We illustrate these applications here. The next chapter will illustrate how the theory can be applied to assets whose lives extend over multiple periods.

If the investment opportunities are economically independent, an accept or reject decision must be made for each investment. In this instance the criterion that should be used to make the decision is to compare the risk-adjusted present value of the cash flows from the investment with its cost c. Let v be the risk-adjusted present value. If $v - c$ is greater than or equal to zero, the investment should be accepted. If it is negative, it should be rejected. The quantity $(v - c)$ is the risk-adjusted counterpart, under conditions of uncertainty, of the net present value of the investment. Thus $v - c$ will be called the risk-adjusted net present value, RANPV.

To find the risk-adjusted present value of the cash proceeds we use the relationship,

$$v = \bar{y} - \lambda \operatorname{Cov}(y, r_m), \tag{9}$$

where $y = x/(1 + r_f)$.

Appendix 1 to this chapter shows how equation (9) is derived from equation (7).

EXAMPLE 1: Suppose that r_f is .08 and that the following facts apply to a one-period investment where two events may occur.

Event: n	Probability of Event: p	Value of r_m	Cash Flow x
1	.8	.20	432
2	.2	.00	108

From this we can compute $\bar{r}_m$ and σ_m^2.

n	p	r_m	pr_m	$r_m - \bar{r}_m$	$(r_m - \bar{r}_m)^2$	$p(r_m - \bar{r}_m)^2$
1	.8	.20	.16	.04	.0016	.00128
2	.2	.00	0	−.16	.0256	.00512
			$\bar{r}_m = .16$			$\sigma_m^2 = .00640$

The value of λ is

$$\lambda = \frac{\bar{r}_m - r_f}{\sigma_m^2} = \frac{.16 - .08}{.0064} = 12.5.$$

As here shown, if event 1 occurs the cash flows are $432 and if event 2 occurs the cash flows are $108.

The computations of $\bar{y}$ and Cov (y, r_m) follow:[3]

n	x	y	p	py	$(r_m - \bar{r}_m)$	$py(r_m - \bar{r}_m)$
1	432	400	.8	320	.04	12.8
2	108	100	.2	20	−.16	−3.2
				$\bar{y} = 340$		Cov $(y, r_m) = 9.60$

[3] The covariance between r_m and y, which is, by definition,

$$\sum p(y - \bar{y})(r_m - \bar{r}_m),$$

can be shown to equal

$$\sum py(r_m - \bar{r}_m).$$

The latter expression, which is computationally simpler, is used in the examples that follow.

We can now compute v:

$$v = \bar{y} - \lambda \, \text{Cov} \, (y, r_m)$$
$$= 340 - (12.5)(9.60) = 340 - 120 = \$220.$$

If the alternatives were to accept or reject, this investment would be acceptable if its cost were less than \$220.

A Simplified Calculation

The preceding calculation can be simplified. Let us define $s(n)$ to be the value today of an investment that will pay \$1 at time 1 if node n occurs. For $n = 1$, the value of $s(1)$ can be computed as follows.

n	x	y	p	py	$(r_m - \bar{r}_m)$	$py(r_m - \bar{r}_m)$
1	1	.92593	.8	.74074	.04	.02963
2	0	0	.2	0	−.16	0
				$\bar{y} = .74074$		$\text{Cov} \, (y, r_m) = .02963$

$$s(1) = \bar{y} - \lambda \, \text{Cov} \, (y, r_m)$$
$$= .74074 - (12.5)(.02963) = .74074 - .37037 = .37037.$$

A similar calculation for $n = 2$ will show that

$$s(2) = .55556.$$

To generalize these results let $p(n)$ be the probability of node n, and $r_m(n)$ the value of r_m at that node. Suppose an investment pays one dollar at time 1 if node n occurs and nothing otherwise. The present value of the expected cash flows from such an investment will be

$$\bar{y} = \frac{p(n)}{1 + r_f}.$$

The covariance between y and r_m for such an investment will be

$$\text{Cov} \, (y, r_m) = \frac{p(n)}{1 + r_f} [r_m(n) - \bar{r}_m].$$

Substituting the values for $\bar{y}$ and Cov (y, r_m) in equation (9), the value of such an investment will be

$$s(n) = \frac{p(n)}{1 + r_f} [1 - \lambda(r_m(n) - \bar{r}_m)]. \tag{10}$$

For example, $s(1)$ could be calculated directly using equation (10).

$$s(1) = \frac{.8}{1.08} [1 - (12.5)(.20 - .16)]$$

$$= (.74074)(1 - .5) = .37037.$$

Equation (10) is extremely important since it simplifies the computation of RAPV. The value $s(n)$ is a time-risk transformation factor that enables us to compute the risk-adjusted present value of a dollar at node n one time-period later. It is not dependent on there only being two outcomes. While v gives the risk-adjusted present value of all outcomes stemming from one node, $s(n)$ gives the risk-adjusted present value of one path stemming from a node.

To find the risk-adjusted present value of the investment we multiply the values of $s(n)$ by the cash flows and sum:

Event	$s(n)$	x	$xs(n)$
1	.3704	432	160
2	.5556	108	60
			$v = \$220$

This value of v agrees with the number obtained by using equation (9).

Equations (10) and (9) lead to the same solution, but (10) has the advantage of being easier to compute.

EXAMPLE 2: We will now consider an investment in which, again, two possible events may occur (labeled events 3 and 4). The value of r_f is now .03. The following facts apply:

Event: n	p	r_m	x
3	.3	.20	206
4	.7	.00	103

From this we can compute $\bar{r}_m$ and σ_m^2.

n	p	r_m	pr_m	$r_m - \bar{r}_m$	$(r_m - \bar{r}_m)^2$	$p(r_m - \bar{r}_m)^2$
3	.3	.20	.06	.14	.0196	.00588
4	.7	.00	.00	−.06	.0036	.00252
			$\bar{r}_m = .06$			$\sigma_m^2 = .00840$

The value of lambda is

$$\lambda = \frac{\bar{r}_m - r_f}{\sigma_m^2} = \frac{.06 - .03}{.0084} = 3.5714.$$

Using equation (10)

$$s(3) = \frac{p(n)}{1 + r_f} [1 - \lambda(r_m(n) - \bar{r}_m)] = \frac{.3}{1.03} [1 - 3.5714(.14)]$$

$$= .14563.$$

$$s(4) = \frac{.7}{1.03} [1 - 3.5714(-.06)] = .82524.$$

The risk-adjusted present value of the investment is

Event	$s(n)$	x	$xs(n)$
3	.1456	206	30
4	.8252	103	85
			$v = \$115$

The following calculations using the covariance also give $115.

n	p	x	y	py	$r_m - \bar{r}_m$	$py(r_m - \bar{r}_m)$
3	.3	206	200	60	.14	8.4
4	.7	103	100	70	−.06	−4.2
				$\bar{y} = 130$		Cov $(y, r_m) = 4.2$

The value of v is again $115:

$$v = \bar{y} - \lambda \text{ Cov } (y, r_m) = 130 - 3.5714(4.20) = 130 - 15 = \$115.$$

Instead of using equation (10) the values of $s(n)$ can be computed using equation (9) if we make the assumption that x is $1 with node n and zero otherwise. For example, for $n = 3$ we would have

n	p	x	y	py	$(r_m - \bar{r}_m)$	$py(r_m - \bar{r}_m)$
3	.3	1	.9709	.2913	.14	.0408
4	.7	0	0	0	−.06	0
				$\bar{y} = .2913$		Cov $(y, r_m) = .0408$

$$v = s(3) = \bar{y} - \lambda \operatorname{Cov}(y, r_m)$$
$$= .2913 - 3.5714(.0408) = .1456.$$

Comparable calculations for $s(4)$ again give a value of .8252.

If the investment earns cash flows of $1 with event 3 *and* event 4 we would expect the risk-adjusted present value to be $1/1.03 = \$.97087$, since there is zero risk ($1 will be received no matter what event occurs). Using the values of $s(3)$ and $s(4)$ we obtain $\$.97087$ for the RAPV.

Event	$s(n)$	x	$xs(n)$
3	.14563	$1	.14563
4	.82524	1	.82524
			$.97087

Conclusions

With risky cash flows we have to take both the time value and risk of the cash flows into consideration. We find that the values obtained from the use of equation (10) can be used as "prices" or transformation factors to find the risk-adjusted present value of cash flows to be received one period from now.

In the next chapter we will apply the models of this chapter to multi-period investments.

appendix 1

We want to show that equation (9) follows from equation (7).

$$v = y - \lambda \operatorname{Cov}(y, r_m). \qquad (9)$$

Starting with equation (7) we have

$$\bar{r}^* = r_f + \lambda \operatorname{Cov}(r^*, r_m).$$

We can substitute $\bar{x}/v - 1$ for $\bar{r}^*$, $x/v - 1$ for r^*, and then solve the equation for v. In doing this we take advantage of the fact that for any constant v,

$$\operatorname{Cov}\left(\frac{x}{v} - 1, r_m\right) = \frac{1}{v}\operatorname{Cov}(x, r_m).$$

Making these substitutions, equation (7) becomes

$$\frac{\bar{x}}{v} - 1 = r_f + \lambda\left(\frac{1}{v}\right)\operatorname{Cov}(x, r_m).$$

Adding one to both sides and multiplying by v gives

$$\bar{x} = (1 + r_f)v + \lambda \operatorname{Cov}(x, r_m)$$

therefore solving for v

$$v = \frac{\bar{x} - \lambda \operatorname{Cov}(x, r_m)}{1 + r_f}. \qquad (7.A)$$

Note that by definition

$$\frac{\bar{x}}{1 + r_f} = \bar{y}.$$

Also since $y = x/(1 + r_f)$, it follows that

$$\operatorname{Cov}(x, r_m) = (1 + r_f)\operatorname{Cov}\left(\frac{x}{1 + r_f}, r_m\right)$$

$$= (1 + r_f)\operatorname{Cov}(y, r_m).$$

Substituting these expressions into (7.A) gives

$$v = \frac{\bar{x}}{1 + r_f} - \lambda\frac{\operatorname{Cov}(x, r_m)}{1 + r_f}$$

$$= \bar{y} - \lambda\frac{(1 + r_f)\operatorname{Cov}(y, r_m)}{1 + r_f}$$

$$= \bar{y} - \lambda \operatorname{Cov}(y, r_m),$$

which is the desired result.

questions and problems

For problems 11-1 through 11-9, assume that $\bar{r}_m = .14$, $r_f = .08$, and $\sigma_m = .12$.

11-1. If an investor put half his funds in the market portfolio and half in treasury bills,

    a. What rate of return would you expect him to earn?

    b. What is the standard deviation of returns from his portfolio?

    c. Draw a rough graph with expected return on the vertical axis and standard deviation of return on the horizontal axis. Plot the market portfolio at point C and the investor's portfolio at point B on this graph.

    d. Find the slope of the capital market line.

11-2. If an investor wished to hold a portfolio consisting only of treasury bills and shares in the market portfolio, and he wanted an expected return of .12 per year, what proportion of his funds should be invested in the market portfolio? What is the standard deviation of returns from this portfolio?

11-3. On January 1, M.B. University had an endowment worth $100 million. Of this amount $25 million was invested in treasury bills, and $75 million was invested in the market portfolio. By the following December 31, MBU had earned $2 million in interest, and had received dividends of $3 million. These amounts were considered as "income" and used to pay the current expenses of the university. Except for "rolling over" treasury bills, no portfolio transactions were undertaken. Although on December 31 MBU's portfolio still held the same number of shares in the market portfolio, the market value of these shares had declined to $60 million because of a general decline in stock prices.

    a. What was the expected annual rate of return on MBU's portfolio on January 1, and its standard deviation?

    b. What was the actual rate of return earned?

11-4. Continuing problem 11-3, if no shift has occurred in the capital market line, what rate of return would be expected from the portfolio held by MBU on December 31?

If MBU wished to modify the composition of its December 31 portfolio so that the expected rate of return was the same as that of its January 1 portfolio, what transactions would be necessary?

11-5. Continuing problem 11-3,

   a. By how many standard deviations did the realized return on MBU's portfolio fall short of its expected return?

   b. If the distribution of rates of return can be approximated by a normal distribution, what is the probability of earning as little as this or less?

11-6. Suppose that it were possible for an investor to borrow at 8 per cent per year as much as $.75 for every dollar of stock he owned "free and clear." Could an investor having $100,000 in cash devise a portfolio consisting only of shares in the market portfolio and treasury bills for which the expected rate of return was 17 per cent?

If it is possible, describe the transactions that would be necessary; if not, explain why it is impossible.

11-7. A retired doctor wants to hold a portfolio consisting only of debt and stock in the market portfolio. He also wants the assurance that, even if the return on the market portfolio were two standard deviations below normal, the rate of return on his portfolio would be no less than −5 per cent. What portfolio would you recommend for him?

11-8. The covariance between the rate of return of the stock and the rate of return of the market index is .0192. What is the required rate of return of this stock?

11-9. What is the beta coefficient of the common stock described in problem 11-8?

11-10. If an investment is expected to temporarily depress both accounting income and the current market price of the stock, should the investment be undertaken if it is expected to have a beneficial long-run effect on stock prices?

11-11. Assume that the following facts exist:

	Default-Free Investment	Market Investment
Expected return	.07	.10
Standard deviation	0	.02

Compute the portfolio expected return and risk (standard deviation) if the investment is split .6 in the market and .4 in the default-free investment.

11-12. Continuing problem 11-11. For the information given determine the equations for the capital market line and the security market line for the investment. What are the slopes of the two lines?

11-13. Continuing problem 11-11. Assume that there is an investment j with a covariance of .00064 with the market. Determine the expected return required by the market.

11-14. Continuing problem 11-13. If the investment currently has an expected return of .15, what would you expect to happen?

11-15. Continuing problem 11-13. If the covariance of the investment with the market were −.00064, what would be the expected return required by the market?

11-16. For the information given in problem 11-13, compute the β of the investment. Using the β, compute the expected return required by the market.

11-17. If the β of a security is large, what does this imply about the expected change in value of the stock for small changes in the value of the market portfolio?

chapter 12

Theories that are right only 50 per cent of the
time are less economical than coin-flipping.

—George J. Stigler, *The Theory of Price* (New York:
Macmillan Publishing Co., Inc., 1966), p. 6. (Professor
Stigler assumes decisions with two outcomes.)

application of the capital asset pricing model to multiperiod investments

The capital asset pricing model was introduced, and its application to one-period investments illustrated, in Chapter 11. The present chapter suggests a method of using the capital asset pricing model to evaluate multiperiod investments. A risk-adjusted net present value factor (RAFVF) will be computed for each possible event (or tree diagram node), and this price will be applied to the cash flow of that node.

When we assumed certainty we applied present value factors to future cash flows to find present value equivalents. For example, with a .10 time value factor we applied a present value factor of .9091 to a cash flow of period 1 and .8264 to a cash flow of period 2 to find present value equivalents.

The procedure with uncertainty is exactly analogous. Prices are determined that take into consideration both time value and risk. The prices are time-value and risk-transformation factors that are analogous to the present-value factors used in the certainty situation. In this chapter the prices will be determined using the capital asset pricing model and the methods of calculation of Chapter 11.

Figure 12-1 shows the probabilities and the market returns for a two-period investment. The tree diagram provides a useful framework for analysis. For simplicity only two outcomes are allowed for each node.

Note that if a bad year occurs, the probability of a second bad year is high. The states of nature have been selected so that the market return can be only .2 or 0. Reference to Chapter 11 will show that the market return-risk trade-off

230

(λ) depends on the state of nature. Figure 12-1 combines the two one-period examples of Chapter 11 to make up a single two-period investment.

We will assume (consistent with the previous chapter) that

$r = .08$ for the first time period
$r = .08$ for the second time period if starting from node (1, 1)
$r = .03$ for the second time period if starting from node (2, 1).

Each node is numbered with two numbers separated by a comma. The first number is the node number (starting from the top) and the second number is the time period. Thus node (3, 2) is node 3 in time period 2. There is only one path through the tree diagram from the origin to a particular node.

In Chapter 11 we define $s(n)$ to be the risk-adjusted present value factor (RAPVF) for the nth node, and determined $s(1)$ to be .3707 and $s(2)$ to be .5552 for the first example and $s(3)$ to be .1459 and $s(4)$ to be .8253 for the second example. The cash flows are discounted one period.

Using the symbolism for multiperiod investments, $s(n, t)$, where n is the node number and t the time period, and the values from Chapter 11 we have

$$s(1, 1) = .3707 \qquad s(2, 2) = .5552$$
$$s(2, 1) = .5552 \qquad s(3, 2) = .1459$$
$$s(1, 2) = .3707 \qquad s(4, 2) = .8253$$

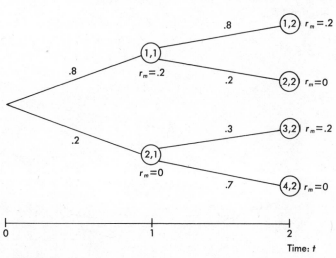

Figure 12-1

While we could use the $s(n, t)$ factors for single periods, it is somewhat easier to compute RAPVF's that transform the cash flows to values at time zero. Define $S(n, t)$ to be risk-adjusted present value at time zero of one dollar received at node n and time t. For the example we have

$$S(1, 1) = s(1, 1) = .3707$$
$$S(2, 1) = s(2, 1) = .5552$$
$$S(1, 2) = s(1, 1) \times s(1, 2) = .3707 \times .3707 = .1374$$
$$S(2, 2) = s(1, 1) \times s(2, 2) = .3707 \times .5552 = .2058$$
$$S(3, 2) = s(2, 1) \times s(3, 2) = .5552 \times .1459 = .0810$$
$$S(4, 2) = s(2, 1) \times s(4, 2) = .5552 \times .8253 = .4582$$

The logic of multiplying $s(2, 1)$ times $s(3, 2)$ to obtain $S(3, 2)$ is the same logic whereby we multiply .9091 times .9091 (where .9091 is the present value of $1 due in one time period) to obtain the present value of $1 due in two time periods. If a dollar at node $(3, 2)$ is worth .1459 at time 1, then it is worth .5552 times .1459 or .0810 at time zero, thus $S(3, 2) = .0810$.

Applying the RAPVF's

Now that we have determined the $S(n, t)'s$, the evaluation of an investment is exactly analogous to the net present value calculation. Figure 12-2 shows the cash flows of an investment that costs $300. The facts of Figure 12-1 also apply to Figure 12-2.

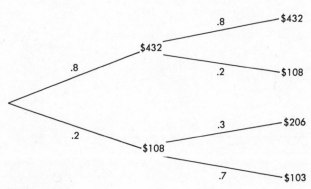

Figure 12-2

The risk-adjusted present value is

Node (n, t)	S(n, t)	Cash Flow	RAPV
1, 1	.3707	432	160
2, 1	.5552	108	60
1, 2	.1374	432	58
2, 2	.2058	108	22
3, 2	.0810	206	17
4, 2	.4582	103	47
		RAPV =	$364

Since the risk-adjusted present value is $364 and the cost is only $300 the investment is acceptable.

A SECOND EXAMPLE: Assume that an investment will generate $108 at nodes 1 and 2 of period 2, and $103 at nodes 3 and 4. These cash flows are represented in Figure 12-3. If node 1 occurs during period 1, the investor will know that he is to receive $108 for certain in period 2. He will also know the period 2 default-free interest rate, which will be 8 per cent in that case. So the future cash flows will be worth $100 at the end of period 1, at node 1.

If node 2 occurs during period 1, the investor will know that he is to receive only $103 for certain in period 2. He will also know the period 2 default-free interest rate, which will be 3 per cent in that case. So the future cash flows will be worth $100 at the end of period 1, at node 2.

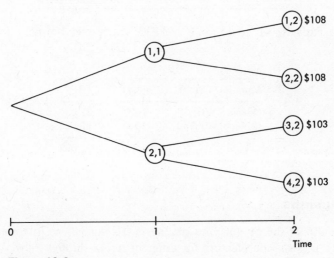

Figure 12-3

The value of the asset one period from now looks like this:

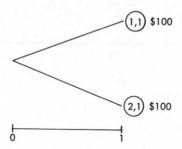

Since the interest rate in period one is 8 per cent, we would expect the asset to be worth $100/1.08 = 92.59$.

The same answer could be reached using risk-adjusted present value-factors on the period 2 cash flows.

Node (n, t)	$S(n, t)$	Cash Flows	RAPV
(1, 1)	.37037	0	0.00
(2, 1)	.55556	0	0.00
(1, 2)	.13717	108	14.81
(2, 2)	.20576	108	22.22
(3, 2)	.08091	103	8.33
(4, 2)	.45847	103	47.22
			$92.59

Alternatively, we could apply RAPVF's to the end-of-period one-asset values.

Node	$S(n, t)$	$v(n, t)$	RAPV
(1, 1)	.37037	100	37.037
(2, 1)	.55556	100	55.556
			$92.593

conclusions

Application of the capital asset pricing model enables us to compute risk-adjusted present-value factors for different nodes through time. While the presence of risk precludes the conventional compound interest calculations directly, indirectly we are taking into account the time value of money as well as the risk of the investment.

Once the RAPVF's have been computed, the calculations of the net value of an investment are analogous to the calculations that are made under the assumption of certainty. If the RAPV is greater than the cost of the investment, the investment is acceptable.

The computations of this and the previous chapter assume that the capital asset pricing model applies. Through time we can expect refinements in the model that will bring other factors into consideration than those described in these two chapters, but the basic principles and calculations described are likely to continue to be the foundation for the risk-adjusted present-value calculations. However, it is also important to realize that there are investors and firms for which the capital asset model does not apply, since the investors (owners) are not widely diversified. We will consider this type of situation in the next chapter.

problems

12-1. The following information applies to a one-period investment.

n	p	r_m	x
1	.3	.25	1,300
2	.7	.05	300

Assuming that $r_f = .06$, find the RAPV of the investment.

12-2. The following information applies to a one-period investment with $r_f = .06$. Find its RAPV.

n	p	r_m	x
1	.2	.25	1,900
2	.1	.25	100
3	.4	.05	600
4	.3	.05	-100

Compare the RAPV of this investment with the RAPV of the investment described in problem 12-1.

12-3. The following information applies to a two-period investment with $r_f = .06$. Find v.

t	n	p(n)	r_m	x
1	1	.3	.25	1,300
1	2	.7	.05	300
2	1	.09	.25	1,300
2	2	.21	.05	300
2	3	.21	.25	1,300
2	4	.05	.05	300

The tree diagram for this investment is as follows, with the cash proceeds for each time period shown on the appropriate branch.

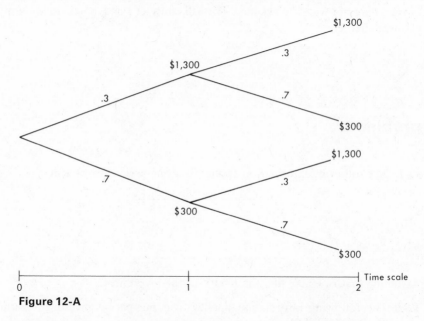

Figure 12-A

12-4. The following information applies to a two-period investment with $r_f = .06$. Find v.

t	n	p(n)	r_m	x
1	1	.3	.25	1,300
1	2	.7	.05	300
2	1	.09	.25	1,300
2	2	.21	.05	1,300
2	3	.21	.25	300
2	4	.49	.05	300

The tree diagram for this investment is as follows, with cash proceeds for each time period shown on the appropriate branch.

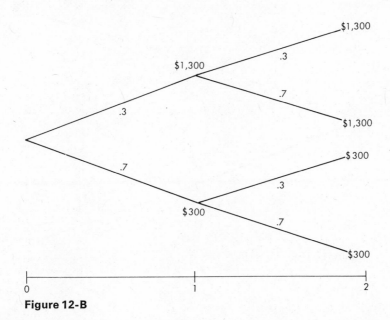

Figure 12-B

12-5. The following information applies to a two-period investment with $r_f = .06$. Find v.

t	n	$p(n)$	r_m	x
1	1	.3	.25	1,300
1	2	.7	.05	300
2	1	.09	.25	1,600
2	2	.21	.05	600
2	3	.21	.25	1,000
2	4	.49	.05	0

The tree diagram for this investment is as follows, with cash proceeds for each time period shown on the appropriate branch.

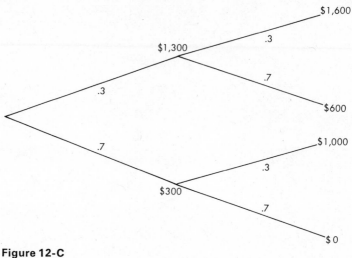

Figure 12-C

chapter 13

*The fundamental difficulty of uncertainty cannot
really be dodged ; and since it cannot be faced,
it must simply be ignored.*

—Robert M. Solow, *Capital Theory and the Rate of Return*
(Amsterdam: North-Holland Publishing Company, 1963), p. 15.

uncertainty and
undiversified investors

The previous two chapters have suggested how the capital asset pricing model
can be used as a guide to making investment decisions. The approach
described is reasonable if the following two conditions both apply:

1. The transaction costs that would be incurred in raising new capital
   are a relatively small percentage of the amount to be raised.
2. The objective of the decision makers is to maximize the market value
   of the stockholders' wealth.

In the present chapter we shall address ourselves to the problem of making
investment decisions under uncertainty when the second of these conditions
does not apply.

There is an analogy between the problems to be considered in this chapter
under conditions of uncertainty, and the problem of capital rationing
previously considered in Chapter 8 under conditions of certainty. Similarly,
there is an analogy between the circumstances considered in Chapters 2 to 4
under conditions of certainty and the circumstances considered in Chapters
11 and 12 under conditions of uncertainty. In Chapters 2 to 4, and again in
Chapters 11 and 12, it was possible to suggest criteria for making investment
decisions that are, in principle at least, objective. Market preferences are
used to evaluate alternatives. In Chapter 8 and again in this chapter, a
totally objective approach to investment decision making is not possible.
The subjective attitudes and objectives of the decision makers and owners of
the firm must be taken into account in deciding what investments should be
undertaken.

In Chapters 11 and 12 we argued that an appropriate criterion for making investment decisions would be to accept all independent investments for which the risk-adjusted net present value (RANPV) was greater than zero, that is, for which

$$\text{RANPV} = V - C \geq 0.$$

Now we shall claim, under the assumptions of this chapter, that the above relationship may not be sufficient for undertaking an investment.

Let us consider a situation where the management of a firm is unwilling to accept or reject investments on the basis of their effect on the market value of stockholder's wealth. This situation could occur when the stockholders of the firm are not perfectly diversified or when the management incorporates into the decision process other considerations than maximization of the common stock market value. It might be that the controlling stockholders are not able or willing to fully diversify their portfolios. Thus their interests are different from those of outside stockholders, and they act in their own self-interest rather than in the interests of the outside stockholders.

There are a number of reasons why the portfolios of management or controlling stockholders may not be as well diversified as the portfolios of other stockholders. A major asset of many managers is their knowledge and expertise about the company for which they work. This asset is nonmarketable. Its value depends on the continued existence of the firm; if the firm were to go out of business, the value of the manager's special expertise would evaporate. Such a manager may quite understandably give more weight to independent risks that could have a drastic effect on the continued existence of the particular firm for which he works, even though these risks are of little concern to stockholders whose portfolios are well diversified.

Another possibility is that management and the controlling stockholders may have more optimistic expectations about the future returns from "their" firm than do outside investors, and therefore the common stock of the firm may seem to offer them a higher expected rate of return relative to the risk involved than does the stock of other companies. Thus they are likely to hold a larger fraction of their marketable assets in the form of stock in the firm than do other investors. As a result, the rate of returns on their portfolios will be sensitive to statistically independent risks that affect their firm.

Still another possibility is that management and controlling stockholders derive benefits from their position that are not available to other stockholders. These benefits may take the form of higher salaries, the ability to charge certain of their consumption expenditures to the firm, or the prestige and power they obtain in the firm as a result of their control position. The continuation of such benefits depends on their continuing to hold a large amount of the stock in the firm that they control, thus providing the controlling stockholders with a reason for holding an undiversified portfolio. However, the heavily weighted portfolio results in these investors being more sensitive to events that could have a negative impact on the firm, even though these events are statistically independent of the rate of return on the market portfolio.

In the present chapter we offer suggestions as to how uncertainty might be taken into account in making investment decisions when the stockholders are undiversified investors or when considerations other than the maximization of the stockholders' wealth are thought to be relevant.

Given the present state of knowledge, these suggestions constitute our evaluation of what management can hope practically to accomplish in dealing with the uncertainty associated with such investment decisions. We are confident that as improvements are made in the underlying theoretical knowledge and in the computational techniques available to management, more efficient procedures will be developed.

attitudes toward risk

In a situation where shares of ownership in an investment are not tradable in a perfect capital market, or where investors are not perfectly diversified, attitude toward risk is an important factor that must be taken into account when considering investment opportunities that are subject to uncertainty. We shall discuss later the question of whose attitudes toward risk are relevant (for example, those of the decision makers or those of the persons financing the investment). For the purpose of introducing some basic ideas about risk preferences, we shall make the somewhat oversimplified assumption that the decision maker will also be required to finance the investment himself.

To illustrate the problem, let us suppose a potential investor has assets worth $5,000, all held in the form of a savings account earning 4 per cent. The investor considers that the probability is 1 that, if he holds his assets in a savings account for one year, he will have an asset worth $5,200 one year from now. That is, he considers the savings account to be a riskless asset.[1] Now suppose that he is faced with an investment opportunity that would require an immediate outlay of $5,000 and would return either $3,000 (with probability .2) or $10,000 (with probability .8) one year from now. If he accepts this opportunity, the expected cash flow one year from now will be $8,600 (that is, .2 × $3,000 + .8 × $10,000). The expected rate of return on this one-year investment will be 72 per cent, if we calculate the rate of return using the expected cash flow of one year from now. This is an attractive

[1] A savings account may be riskless in terms of cash flows (assuming that there is no possibility of default), but not in terms of purchasing power.

yield by ordinary standards. However, we cannot use the expected rate of return to decide the acceptability of this investment for this potential investor. It is necessary to establish his attitudes toward risk before we can decide whether he should accept or reject the investment, if he must finance it with his own funds.

The reader may be tempted to say that a reasonable way to make the decision is to compare the certain cash flow of $5,200 that would be realized if the investor kept his money in a savings account with the average or expected cash flow of $8,600 if he accepts the investment. The difficulty with this approach is that it buries the fact that at the end of the year the investor will have $3,000 or $10,000 if he accepts the risky investment compared to his initial assets of $5,000. The question that our potential investor cannot avoid is whether the dissatisfactions associated with the possibility of having only $3,000 next year, when he could have been sure of having $5,200, outweigh the satisfactions associated with the possibility that he may have $10,000.

The ability to make a decision under uncertainty depends on such comparisons, and requires knowledge of risk preferences or attitudes toward risk. Different investors might answer such questions differently, in which case we shall say that they have different risk preferences. And clearly the same investor may have different risk preferences at different times in his life or under different circumstances. Other investments already undertaken, his state of health, the number of persons dependent on him, and his chances of being unemployed next year are clearly factors that he will take into account in his decision.

A description of an investor's risk preferences is called a *utility function*. Just as subjective probabilities can be used to describe a person's attitude about the likelihood that some outcome will occur, so a utility function may describe his risk preferences.

A utility function assigns a number to each possible outcome of an uncertain event. The number assigned by a utility function can be interpreted as an index of the relative satisfaction the individual would derive if that outcome actually occurred. Table 13-1 illustrates the use of a utility function for the potential investor in the preceding example. Column 1 lists the possible outcomes that are involved in his choice measured in terms of net present value, and column 2 lists the utilities he assigns to each possible outcome.

If the utility function accurately describes the investor's risk preferences, he will make the choice that provides the highest expected utility. The calculation for this risky investment is presented in Table 13-1. In column 3 we list the probability of each outcome if the investor accepts either the bank account or the risky investment. In column 4 we list the product of the probability of each outcome multiplied by its utility. The expected utilities or

Table 13-1. Computation of Expected Utility

(1) Outcome: Net Present Values*	(2) Utility	(3) Probability	(4) Utility × Probability
Bank account 0	150	1.0	150
	Expected utility of bank account		150
Investment ($2,115) 4,615	100 200	.2 .8	20 160
	Expected utility of investment		180

* The analysis is made in terms of the net present values, using a discount rate of 4 per cent. The present value of the bank account (treating the initial balance as an outlay) is — $5,000 + $5,200 (.9615) = $0. With the risky investment the possible net present values are either — $5,000 + $3,000 (.9615) = — $2,115, or — $5,000 + $10,000 (.9615) = $4,615. The analysis could also have been carried out in terms of the possible net terminal values. The desirability of each outcome is the same whether we choose to measure it as a net present value or as a net terminal value.

the sums of these products for the two alternatives are also given in column 4. For the example given in this table a third party acting for the investor would choose the risky investment in preference to the certain outcome, because the former has a higher expected utility than the latter.

Suppose that we multiplied each of the utility numbers in column 2 by some positive number. Would this change the decision? The answer is that it would not. If we multiply each utility number in column 2 by 3, the expected utility for the risky investment would become 540 and the expected utility for the riskless investment would become 450. But the relative magnitudes of the two alternatives, and therefore the decision, would not change. Similarly, if we add or subtract the same number to or from every utility value in column 2, we will not change the decision. This means that two apparently different utility functions may actually describe the same risk preferences, just as the Fahrenheit and centigrade scales both measure the same quantity, temperature. By a combination of adding and multiplying by appropriate constants, one can convert temperature readings from one of these scales to the other. In exactly the same way, if one utility function can be derived from another by adding and multiplying by appropriate constants, the two utility functions actually measure the same risk preferences.

The utility measures in Table 13-1 are for one person at one moment in time. Our subject's risk preferences are conditioned by his current financial condition; if his financial condition were to change, we would expect that his utility measures for the particular outcomes shown would also change. Thus the utility function for an individual is a very unstable thing. Even if his financial condition were to remain unchanged, there may be other factors (such as health) that would also influence the utility function.

It is reasonable to ask at this point whether a utility function can always be derived that describes a person's attitudes toward risk. Certain kinds of attitudes toward risk in principle can be described by a utility function of the sort we have been describing. Several authors have described axioms or sets of postulates that are sufficient conditions for the existence of a utility function. That is, if a person's attitudes toward alternatives satisfy certain conditions, we know that his risk preferences can be described by a utility function.[2]

We have assumed that the outcomes may be described in terms of monetary consequences that are then translated into utility. It is possible other factors, such as the nature of the lottery, may be important to the decision maker. If a person enjoys being exposed to a certain kind of risk (say, because it makes him feel brave or clever), his risk preferences are not described by the utility function. For example, a poker player might get more satisfaction from winning $10 in a poker game than from another activity, say a lottery, that gave him equal chances of gains or losses. Intangibles such as this may have to be brought into the analysis, possibly in a qualitative manner.

Presumably, in most business situations, it is the possible monetary outcomes and their likelihood that are taken into account in analyzing risky decisions, and not the fun or excitement that may arise from being exposed to a risk of a specific nature, although such considerations may sometimes be relevant.

If changes in the purchasing power of money are important, it may be desirable to convert monetary values into dollars of constant purchasing power, that is, into real values rather than money values. For many purposes a utility function expressed in real values rather than money values may be more appropriate.

It is a convenience in terms of exposition to assume that risk preferences can be appropriately described by some utility function. We shall make this assumption throughout the remainder of our discussion. Whether or not this particular assumption is valid in the context of business decision making is not as important as the recognition that attitudes toward risk play a critical role in the process of making investment decisions under conditions of uncertainty.

[2] For a relatively simple explanation of these postulates and a proof that they are sufficient conditions for the existence of a utility function, the interested reader can consult W. J. Baumol, *Economic Theory and Operations Analysis*, 2nd ed. (Englewood Cliffs, N.J.: Prentice-Hall Inc., 1965), Chapter 22.

utility functions and business decision making

There are several questions that can be raised about the use of a utility function as an aid in business decision making:

1. Can an individual's utility function be obtained?
2. Even if an individual's utility function can be obtained, can we obtain the utility function of a group?
3. If we can obtain the utility function of a group, which group should be chosen for making the decisions of a corporation?
4. Is the use of a utility function inconsistent with wealth-maximizing objectives? What conditions are favorable for the use of a utility function, and when can wealth maximization be used without implicit or explicit consideration of utility?

Assuming that the preceding questions can be answered satisfactorily, there remains a question. Is the utility analysis an academic plaything, or is it a tool for the practical business decision maker? We argue that it is a practical tool either as an explicit procedure leading to a definite decision (accept if the utility of the investment is greater than the utility of $0), or as an implicit explanation of why the decision maker has to consider all possible events and not just the expected monetary value of an investment. Also, when we shift to portfolio analysis, the utility theory is implicit in the solution that is obtained.

Utility and the Individual

The mechanics of obtaining a utility function for an individual are well known, although it is possible for the individual to misunderstand the questions being posed, or to be inconsistent if a large number of points are obtained for the utility function.[3] However, the derived utility function should in a reasonable manner reflect the attitudes toward risk of the individual.

This utility function may in turn be used by a third party to make decisions involving risk for the individual whose function has been obtained. If the individual is making his own decisions, it is not necessary for him to determine his utility function. He knows better than us whether or not a particular investment is desirable, although we may be able to help him analyze the investment—for example, help him take time value into consideration. However, if we are required to make the decision without additional consultation

[3] See the last section of this chapter.

with the individual, we are more likely to make the decision consistent with the individual's wishes if we have his utility function than if we did not know his utility function. For example, assume that the individual has the opportunity to invest $4,000 and there are two possible outcomes with equal probability. He will receive $10,000 or $0 (that is, he will have $6,000 with probability .5 or lose $4,000 with probability .5). Each of us can make this type of decision for himself. However, you cannot effectively make this decision for another person without knowing his attitudes toward risk—that is, knowing his utility function or at least his utility for an additional $6,000 and the utility of a decrease in wealth of $4,000. The expected monetary value of the gamble is a positive $1,000, but this may be a poor guide for action if the loss of $4,000 will cause the individual to lose his home.

Utility and Groups

The construction of a utility function for an individual is well grounded in economic theory. There is less agreement about the construction of a utility function of a group of persons. It is agreed that we cannot just add the utility functions of each individual to obtain the group's utility function. One possibility would be to have the entire group answer the standard gambling questions posed to determine the utility function of an individual. The answers would depend on both the risk attitudes of the individual making up the group and their bargaining and political power. Some of the group (in fact all) may be unhappy at the resulting utility function.

But it is not fair to blame utility theory for the fact that group decision making has some difficulties not associated with decision making by individuals. If the group is making its own decisions, rather than arguing about artificial standard gambles, then the group could argue about the actual business decisions. The decisions they reach will indicate the nature of the utility function of the group. Investigating a series of business decisions reached by the group would be one effective means of arriving at a utility function for the group.[4]

If the group is actively making decisions, we do not have to determine its utility function. The appropriate attitudes toward risk are being applied directly in the decision process. As with individuals, the use of a utility function and formal analysis becomes important when the decision making (a selection of investments) is delegated to another person or group.

---

[4] One difficulty would be that, if the investments were relatively large, the undertaking of the investments in the past could influence the attitudes of the group toward undertaking additional investments of the same amount of risk. The utility function of changes in wealth is a conditional function and will change as decisions are made and as results of decisions are made known.

It may be that we can substitute an alternative procedure for the utility analysis. The group may describe the type of investments that are acceptable to it. For example, it may specify the requirement of a positive present value and no more than a .10 probability of losing $1 million or more. Other conditions would have to be specified, including the interaction with other investments, but the point is that a surrogate can be obtained for a utility function. There are alternative ways that we can attain much that the utility approach can accomplish, but this is not sufficient reason to reject the use of utility analysis.

whose attitudes?

The point has been made that, under conditions of uncertainty, subjective attitudes toward risk bearing should play an important role in investment policy. However, the issue of whose risk attitudes are relevant for a corporation remains. Any ongoing business affects the interests of a variety of groups, among them the owners, managers, workers, customers, and suppliers. These groups may consist of separate individuals or there may be considerable overlap. In a small family store or farm, the owners, managers, and workers may all be members of the same family. In such a case it is clearly the family's attitude toward risk that will be considered. In a large corporation, there is typically less overlap.

The traditional point of view is that where the owners are a distinct group a business is run primarily in the interests of the owners, except insofar as their freedom to make decisions in their own interest has been limited by laws, customs, or contractual arrangements with other interested parties.

In many business situations it is not sufficient to refer simply to the owners. For example, we might distinguish three subgroups. First, there may be the group of owners who actually control the business. These controlling owners may own a majority of the shares, or they may have a minority interest but a larger block than any other organized group of shareholders. In addition to those who have a controlling interest, there may be a much larger group of persons who have an ownership interest in the business but who do not, or cannot, control it. This latter group has an interest in the financial results insofar as they affect stockholders. Finally, the concept of owners might usefully be expanded, for some purposes, to include not only the present stockholders but also potential stockholders—in effect, the entire financial community. For example, while some investment or financial policies that a firm adopts might reduce the appeal of the stock to some of its present owners, at the same time they might increase the stock market value by making it more attractive to persons who are not currently owners.

If attitudes toward risk are to be considered in deciding what investments should be accepted, decision makers need a clear idea of whose attitudes toward risk are relevant and to what extent they should be considered. Suppose that the group whose attitudes toward risk are relevant in selecting investments has been defined. There still remain important questions of how to implement the investment decision. One difficulty with the current procedures of many firms for making decisions under uncertainty is that where there are operating divisions it is likely that different criteria for evaluating (or incorporating) risk are being used. It may be that operating management is rejecting as being too risky, investments that from the corporate standpoint would be very reasonable. One can imagine a credit officer of a bank rejecting a loan application because of the risk. However, from the point of view of the firm as a whole the loan may be a good investment. A second loan officer might be accepting loans that had too much risk from the point of view of the corporation. The element of personal judgment as to the likelihood of various events cannot be eliminated, but interpretation of the monetary consequences can at least be applied in a somewhat more consistent manner than is currently done.

It is suggested that a utility function be obtained from individuals to be used by other individuals managing the corporation. The fact that persons rather than the corporate entity are used to obtain the utility function should not be surprising (the corporation entity is a fictional being existing only to satisfy the wants and needs of people). The utility function is by necessity subjective, because we are dealing with reactions to gains and losses. Rather than destroying the usefulness of the concept, the subjectivity of the measure enhances its usefulness. We can take the monetary measures of the outcomes and transform them into utility measures that incorporate our attitudes toward the possible events. Another dimension is added to the available information to be used for making the decision.

If the group whose risk attitudes the decision makers wish to take into account is a relatively small, cohesive group with whom the decision makers can communicate directly (for example, if it were decided that investments should be selected in terms of the risk preferences of a small group of controlling stockholders or of an owner–manager or of the professional managers), the persons whose risk attitudes are relevant can be involved directly in the investment decision-making process. An attempt can be made to communicate the nature of the available risk alternatives and to obtain the reactions of the investors.

A second set of circumstances would obtain if it were decided that the relevant risk preferences were those of the present stockholders, but the stockholders were a large and diverse group with whom direct communication were not easily possible. Given present techniques we know of no one who has effectively implemented such an attempt.

A third possibility is that the relevant risk preferences would include those of all present or potential future owners. This is in some respects less difficult to implement than the second situation described. Assume that each stockholder has had ample opportunity to purchase the stock of other corporations (thus diversifying his portfolio, if he so wishes). In this situation, it may be appropriate for the corporation to use the procedures suggested in Chapters 11 and 12.

If the controlling group whose risk preferences are to be taken into account is also in a position to provide the financing necessary to implement their preferences, the risk preferences of the financial community as a whole decrease in importance. The primary considerations are what the controlling group's preferences are with respect to investment and financial policy (the market opportunities will influence these preferences). The situation is not much different when a relatively small amount of debt financing is required, because it will usually be possible to arrange small amounts of debt financing without severe restrictions on the controlling group's freedom of action.

Even when a firm is effectively controlled by some group that wishes to establish policies that reflect its own risk preferences, the response of the financial community will be relevant whenever a significant proportion of outside financing will be required, either immediately or in the foreseeable future.

If there is no cohesive group of stockholders seeking to exercise a controlling interest, and if the managers of the firm attempt to operate it in the best interests of the stockholders, the tastes and preferences of the financial community as a whole will be controlling. Among any large group of stockholders there will be individuals whose interests and preferences conflict with those of other stockholders. Management cannot hope to satisfy every individual stockholder. Those who are dissatisfied will tend to exercise their privilege of selling their stockholdings. Management can best discharge its interests to a diverse group of stockholders by undertaking policies that tend to lead to the highest sustainable market value for the company's common stock.

utility analysis and wealth maximizing

The term *wealth maximizing* is an approximate description of a decision process that accepts investments that have a positive expected present value. The classic example used to discredit the use of the expected monetary value decision rule is the St. Petersburg paradox. A fair coin is tossed until the first head, the winnings being equal to $\$2^n$, where n is the number of tosses required. The expected value of this gamble is infinite, but most of us would pay very little, say $\$8$, for the right to gamble.

Whether you consider the use of expected utility to be inconsistent with the objective of wealth maximizing depends on your interpretation of wealth maximization under conditions of uncertainty. Say you could buy a lottery as described (the St. Petersburg paradox) for $100. The expected monetary value is positive, but the probability of winning more than the $100 is very low and the probability of losing is high. Are we serving the wealth-maximizing objective by accepting this type of gamble?

A difficulty with a wealth-maximizing objective is that it is not clearly defined under conditions of uncertainty, unless it is defined in terms of expected value. But we know that expected value may be a poor guide to action.

In some situations the use of expected monetary value may be reasonable. Assume that a person of known repute approached you and proposed an investment that costs $1 and offers a payoff of $6 with a .5 probability and a payoff of $0 with .5 probability (the net expected monetary value of the investment is $2). Most of us would accept the investment. However, if the size of the investment were increased a millionfold, most of us would reject the investment. In the first situation the amounts are small, and we can easily absorb the possible loss. In the second case the amounts are large, and the possible loss could result in a mortgaging of our future for this and the next lifetime. With relatively small investments, statistically independent of other assets, and with a small variance of outcomes, the use of expected monetary value is a reasonable procedure. Some investments may turn out to be bad, but if the investments have positive net present values, and if they are small investments without too large a probability of loss, the use of expected monetary values may be a reasonable guide to action.

Now let us consider a large investment. This may be a machine-tool company of $200 million asset size that considers going into the automobile industry. In such a situation the use of expected monetary value may be misleading. If the investment does not turn out to be desirable, the entire future of the firm may be jeopardized. The distribution of possible events may be too spread out for the firm, despite a favorable expected value.

Essentially the same type of risk situation may develop with small investments if the investments are not statistically independent of each other. Consider a whole series of investments where each investment is $1, and we can undertake 1 million of these investments. The payoffs are $4 and $0 with .5 probability. If the investments are statistically independent, this is a very fine investment opportunity. If the investments are statistically dependent and we either win or lose on all 1 million investments, the risk of a large loss is much greater, and we might steer clear of this investment.

No matter how large the firm, there is some investment opportunity that it would not want to consider on a straight expected monetary value basis. The analysis of risk (that is, incorporating the consequences of the outcomes) could be performed by a utility analysis or by some other means, but it must be recognized that we cannot inspect one number (say, the yield of the investment or the expected monetary value) to make an investment decision. It is necessary to consider all possible outcomes and the probabilities of these outcomes. One method of systematically accomplishing this is a utility analysis.

For giant corporations it is sometimes difficult to imagine an investment that we could not judge on a straight expected monetary value basis. But even for such corporations there are investments (or classes of investments) of such magnitude that they give rise to the likelihood of events that could be disastrous to the firm. Incorporating this information into the analysis, rather than just using the maximization of wealth (or the expected monetary value criterion), can be done by the use of a utility analysis. Assume that an investment has the characteristic of resulting in a doubling of income or reducing income to approximately zero. Should this type of investment decision be made on an expected-value basis?

The expected-value decision criterion may at times be consistent with the wealth-maximization objective, but several things should be noted. The consistency holds true only in the long run and assuming we can repeat the trial many times. We are dealing with averages, and there is very little chance that the average event will actually occur on any trial (there may be no chance). In some cases, following the expected monetary value criterion will lead to bankruptcy (that is, ruin) and end of the "game." The possibility of this unhappy event is always present, and it is reasonable that this should affect our decision process. The objective "maximize the wealth of the owners" ignores the fact that this is a maximization of an average amount. This is not a sufficient description of the objectives of the investor. The maximization goal is reasonable, but the things being maximized should not be expected monetary values, but rather expected utility.

Investor diversification helps reduce the importance of the type of risk analysis described here; however, there are three important qualifications:

1. Not all investors in the corporation may have diversified portfolios; a risky decision may have a significant impact on the well-being of some of the stockholders. Management cannot assume that all stockholders possess well-diversified portfolios.

2. Even with the stock widely held, the corporation may encounter investments that the individual investor would reject if given the opportunity to invest in a proportion of the investment equal to the proportion of his investment in the firm. This can occur when the variance of the outcomes is large and there is a large probability of undesirable outcomes.

3. The management, workers, controlling stockholders, and communities where the major units of the firm are located all have an interest in the

well-being of the corporation, and they may not be able to diversify to the same extent as the average stockholder.

These important qualifications all point in the direction of utility analysis or some other formal incorporation of risk attitudes.

an illustration

Implementing investment decisions with uncertain outcomes can be very complicated. We shall illustrate a procedure, using an artificial situation, to make clear the basic steps. Assume that the time value of money is .05 and that we have been given the utility function of an individual. The following measures of utility of wealth for the different amounts of dollars apply:

Present Value of Wealth	Utility of Wealth
$1,500	-1,200
1,900	- 60
2,000	0
2,500	500
3,500	1,000
4,500	1,200

The investment is a two-period investment, with an immediate $500 outlay. At the end of the first period there is .5 probability of $0 and .5 probability of $1,050. At the end of the second period there is .8 probability of $0 and .2 probability of $2,205. The tree diagram (Figure 13-1) shows the possible outcomes. The expected present value is $400.

Present Value of Outcome		Probability		Expectation of Present Value
$2,500	×	.10	=	$250
500	×	.40	=	200
1,500	×	.10	=	150
- 500	×	.40	=	- 200
		Expected net present value		$400

Assume the investor currently has wealth of $2,000. We shall add each of the outcomes of the investment to $2,000 to determine the dollar outcomes. We will then convert the dollar outcomes to their utility counterparts to compute

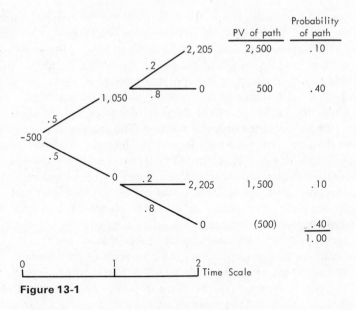

	PV of path	Probability of path
2,205	2,500	.10
0	500	.40
2,205	1,500	.10
0	(500)	.40
		1.00

Figure 13-1

the expected utility of wealth if the investment is undertaken. If the investment is rejected the value of the investor's wealth will be $2,000 with a probability of 1.0, and a utility of zero. Thus the expected utility of doing nothing is zero.

Outcome in Dollars	Wealth in Dollars	Utility of Wealth	Probability	Expectation of Utility
$2,500	$4,500	1,200	.10	120
500	2,500	500	.40	200
1,500	3,500	1,000	.10	100
−500	1,500	−1,200	.40	−480
			Expected utility −	60

The expected utility of wealth with the investment is less than the utility of $0 without the investment and we would choose the action "do nothing" with zero utility compared to the choice "invest." The negative utility of a loss of $500 outweighs the expected consequences of the other events.

The utility function provides a means of calculating the amount of dollar risk premium a decision maker would attach to a particular investment. In the preceding example undertaking the investment has an expected utility of −60. If a certain loss of $100 also has a utility of −60, a dollar loss of $100 is the certainty equivalent of the investment. The expected net present value of the investment is $400. The risk premium for any investment is the expected monetary value of the investment less the certainty equivalent of the investment. In this case, the risk premium is $500 [400 − (− 100)].[5]

Using this approach to decision making, we go beyond the application of intuition as a means of weeding the list of eligible investments. Attitudes toward risk are systematically incorporated into the analysis, and the procedure leads to a decision that is consistent with the feelings of the decision maker about the likelihood of the possible outcomes and the effect of the outcomes on the investor's financial position. The analysis as presented does leave out the value of immediate information about the outcomes compared with having to wait two periods for the final outcome. In the example which was illustrated, the investment would be rejected even if we assumed that we knew the results immediately. Thus it does not make a difference that we did not incorporate the information factor. If the investment had been marginally acceptable based on the expected utility computation, we would have had to incorporate a qualitative factor to take into account that we would have to wait two time periods before the final results were known.

In the preceding example we analyzed a situation in which there were four possible outcomes. Now assume that there are a large number of possible outcomes (possibly an infinite number of outcomes). This change would only modify the mechanics.

illustration of a derivation of a utility function

We shall illustrate one approach to deriving the utility function of an individual.

The first step is to assign two arbitrary amounts of utility to two arbitrary amounts of money wealth. For example, we shall arbitrarily choose $0 and $1 million and assign utilities of 0 and 1,000 to these two money amounts. The choice of these two points determines the scale of the utility function as well as its location.

The second step is to set up a sample lottery consisting of one lottery offering $X for certain and a second lottery offering the two amounts arbitrarily picked, each with .5 probability of occurring.

Lottery A	Lottery B
$X for certain	$0 with .5 probability
	$1,000,000 with .5 probability

[5] In a situation where there are a very large number of outcomes, we would shift to the use of continuous probability distributions. See the two appendixes to this chapter.

What amount X for certain causes you to be indifferent between lotteries A and B? If we set X equal to \$50, most of us would prefer lottery B. If we set X at \$5 million, all of us would prefer lottery A. After some introspection we might establish an amount for X equal to \$10,000. We then have

$$U(A) = U(B)$$
$$U(\$10,000) = .5U(\$0) + .5U(\$1,000,000)$$
$$U(\$10,000) = .5 \times 0 + .5 \times 1,000 = 500.$$

Thus the utility of \$10,000 is determined to be 500, and we have three points of the utility function. We can continue the process by substituting the \$10,000 for the \$1 million of lottery B. After obtaining several points, we may decide to find the utility of larger amounts by setting up the following two lotteries:

Lottery C	Lottery D
\$1,000,000 for certain	\$0 with .5 probability
	\$X with .5 probability

Assume that for you to be indifferent to the two lotteries X in lottery D must be equal to \$800 million.

$$U(\$1,000,000) = .5U(\$0) + .5U(\$800,000,000)$$
$$1,000 = .5 \times 0 + .5U(\$800,000,000)$$
$$U(\$800,000,000) = 2,000$$

The utility measure of \$800 million is 2,000. We can continue the process to obtain the utility measures of still larger amounts.

We must still determine utility measures for negative amounts of wealth. Lotteries of type E and F accomplish this.

Lottery E	Lottery F
\$0 for certain	\$10,000 with .5 probability
	\$X with .5 probability

If X were equal to or greater than \$0, we prefer lottery F; therefore, for us to be indifferent to E and F, X must be negative. Say X is equal to $-\$200$. We then have

$$U(\$0) = .5U(\$10,000) + .5U(-\$200)$$
$$0 = .5 \times 500 + .5U(-\$200)$$
$$U(-\$200) = -500.$$

We can continue this process and obtain the utility equivalents of other dollar outcomes.

nondiversified investors and the capital asset pricing model

A reading of this chapter makes clear the importance of the previous chapters in which we invoked the logic of the capital asset pricing model to obtain a reasonably well defined measure of the dollar risk adjustment. With the capital asset pricing model the risk preferences of the individual investor do not affect the desirability of an investment to be undertaken by a firm, since the market as a whole evaluates the worth of projects and sets the amount of the risk premium.

The capital asset pricing model can also be applied when investors are not well diversified, since the model will determine the market value of the project. This is relevant information to the nondiversified investor, even though the investor might still not undertake an investment, where the projected value change is greater than the cost, because the operation of the investment could lead to excessive risk to the corporate entity (and to the less-well-diversified investors).

appendix 1 computing the mean and variance of the distribution of present value

In a situation where the cash flows of an investment are uncertain and where we are able to predict the mean and variance of the cash flows of each time period, we can compute the mean and variance of the distribution of present values.[6]

We shall define the cash flow of period i to be a random variable y_i with mean $E(y_i)$ and Var (y_i).

We make use of two relationships, which hold for any probability distributions:

$$E(y_0 + y_1 + y_2 + \cdots + y_n) = E(y_0) + E(y_1) + \cdots + E(y_n),$$
$$E(cy) = cE(y).$$

[6] Also see F. S. Hillier, "The Derivation of Probabilistic Information for the Evaluation of Risky Investments," *Management Science*, April 1963.

If we let c equal $(1 + r)^{-i}$, we then have

$$E\left[\sum_{i=0}^{n} (1 + r)^{-i}y_i\right] = \sum_{i=0}^{n} (1 + r)^{-i}E(y_i).$$

If we let Y be the net present value of the investment, we have

$$Y = \sum_{i=0}^{n} (1 + r)^{-i}y_i$$

$$E(Y) = \sum_{i=0}^{n} (1 + r)^{-i}E(y_i).$$

EXAMPLE: Assume that the time value of money is .10.

Cash Flows

Period	Mean: $E(y_i)$	σ Standard deviation	Var (y_i)
0	− $1,800	$200	4×10^4
1	1,000	400	16×10^4
2	2,000	500	25×10^4

The expected present value is

Period	$E(y_i)$	$(1 + r)^{-i}$	$(1 + r)^{-i}E(y_i)$
0	−1,800	1.0000	−1,800
1	1,000	.9091	909
2	2,000	.8264	1,653
	Mean of the net present value distribution		762

For any variance

$$\text{Var}\,(cy) = c^2\,\text{Var}\,(y).$$

Also, if we assume the cash flows of successive periods are statistically independent, we know that

$$\text{Var}\,(y_0 + y_1 + \cdots + y_n) = \text{Var}\,(y_0) + \text{Var}\,(y_1) + \cdots + \text{Var}\,(y_n).$$

Thus, if $c = (1 + r)^{-i}$, we have

$$\text{Var}\,(c_0y_0 + \cdots + c_ny_n) = c_0^2\,\text{Var}\,(y_0) + \cdots + c_n^2\,\text{Var}\,(y_n),$$
$$\text{Var}\,(Y) = (1 + r)^{-0}\,\text{Var}\,(y_0) + (1 + r)^{-2}\,\text{Var}\,(y_1) + \cdots$$
$$+ (1 + r)^{-2n}\,\text{Var}\,(y_n).$$

Continuing the example and computing the variance of the net present-value distribution, we have the following:

Period	Var (y_i)	$(1 + r)^{-2i}$	$(1 + r)^{-2i}$ Var (y_i)
0	4×10^4	1.0000	4.00×10^4
1	16×10^4	.8264	13.22×10^4
2	25×10^4	.6830	17.08×10^4
			Var $(y) = 34.30 \times 10^4$

If the cash flows of each period except the initial period are unknown but we think that they will be equal, we would have

$$\text{Var (Benefits)} = \text{Var } [(1 + r)^{-1}y + (1 + r)^{-2}y + \cdots + (1 + r)^{-n}y]$$
$$= \text{Var } (B(n, r)y) = B(n, r)^2 \text{Var}(y).$$

In the context of the example, we would have the following:

Period	$(1 + r)^{-i}$
1	.9091
2	.8264
$B(n, r)$ =	1.7355
$B(n, r)^2$ =	3.01

If the variance of each period is assumed to be 16×10^4, we would have

$$B(n, r)^2 \text{ Var } (y) = 3.01 \times 16 \times 10^4 = 48.16 \times 10^4.$$

We could add this amount to the variance of the outlay (assuming independence between the outlay and the benefits):

$$\text{Var } (Y) = 4 \times 10^4 + 48.16 \times 10^4$$
$$= 52.16 \times 10^4.$$

Note that this variance is larger than the variance we obtained when we assumed independence. In this latter situation we had a special form of dependence. (Each result was equal.) We shall illustrate another type of dependence with a two-period example. If y_1 and y_2 are perfectly correlated (correlation coefficient equal to 1), we have

$$\text{Var } (y_1 + y_2) = \text{Var } (y_1) + \text{Var } (y_2) + 2\sigma_{y_1}\sigma_{y_2}$$
$$= \sigma_{y_2}^2 + 2\sigma_{y_1}\sigma_{y_2} + \sigma_{y_2}^2$$
$$= (\sigma_{y_1} + \sigma_{y_2})^2$$
$$\sigma_{y_1+y_2} = \sigma_{y_1} + \sigma_{y_2}.$$

In like manner, with perfect correlation

$$\text{Var}\,(c_1 y_1 + c_2 y_2) = (c_1 \sigma_{y_1} + c_2 \sigma_{y_2})^2$$
$$\sigma_{c_1 y_1 + c_2 y_2} = c_1 \sigma_{y_1} + c_2 \sigma_{y_2}.$$

It can be shown that the preceding relationship generalizes for n periods; thus if the cash flows are perfectly correlated

$$\sigma_{\text{Benefits}} = \sum_{i=1}^{n} (1 + r)^{-i} \sigma_{y_i},$$

$$\text{Var}\,(Y) = \left[\sum_{i=1}^{n} (1 + r)^{-i} \sigma_{y_i} \right]^2 + \text{Var}\,(y_0).$$

For the example being considered,

Period	σ_{y_i}	$(1 + r)^{-i}$	$(1 + r)^{-i}\sigma_{y_i}$
1	400	.9091	363.64
2	500	.8264	413.20
		σ_{Benefits} =	776.84
		$\sigma_{\text{Benefits}}^2$ =	60.35×10^4

$$\text{Var}\,(Y) = \sigma_{\text{Benefits}}^2 + \text{Var}\,(y_0)$$
$$= 60.35 \times 10^4 + 4 \times 10^4 = 64.35 \times 10^4.$$

appendix 2:
simulation of expected utility

When we have obtained the mean and variance of the probability distribution of the present values and are able to specify the nature of the distribution (for example, when we assume it is normal), we can follow a simulation process to determine the expected utility if we know the utility function of the individual. Figure 13-2 shows the wealth distribution and the utility function.

We want to determine the utility of wealth with mean $\bar{Y}$ and standard deviation σ_Y.

The procedure we shall follow is to go to a table of random normal deviates (which may also be generated on a computer) and enter the table

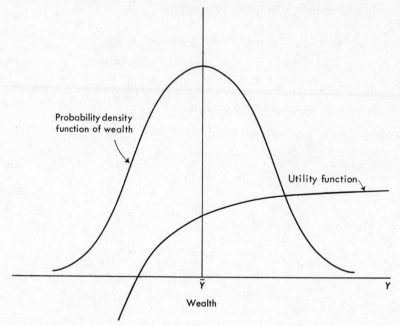

Probability density
function of wealth

Utility function

$\bar{Y}$

Wealth

Y

Figure 13-2

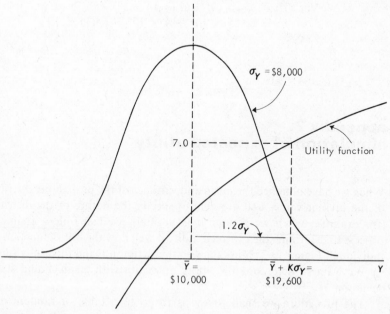

$\sigma_Y = \$8,000$

7.0

Utility function

$1.2\sigma_Y$

$\bar{Y} = \$10,000$

$\bar{Y} + K\sigma_Y = \$19,600$

Y

Figure 13-3

randomly. By taking a series of observations (that is, numbers from the table), we can determine the average utility of the wealth distribution.

Procedure:

1. Take a number, say k, from a table of standard normal deviates.
2. Convert k to wealth: $Y = \bar{Y} + k\sigma_Y$.
3. Go to Figure 13-3 and read the utility for Y wealth. This is one observation of utility.
4. Take n observations; obtain n utilities; divide the total of the n observations by n to obtain the mean utility of the wealth distribution.

EXAMPLE: Assume that the mean wealth, $\bar{Y}$, equals \$10,000 and the standard deviation of wealth, σ_Y, is \$8,000.

We take a random normal deviate and find it to be $+1.2$. The wealth observation is

$$Y = \bar{Y} + k\sigma_Y$$
$$= \$10,000 + 1.2(\$8,000) = \$19,600 = \text{first observation of wealth.}$$

The next step is to measure the utility of \$19,600 wealth. We see that the utility measure is 7. This is our first observation of utility. We would repeat this process many times to obtain a series of observations that would be summed and divided by the number of observations to obtain the expected utility of the wealth distribution. Thus we can simulate the expected utility value of the wealth distribution.

questions and problems

13-1. A person may estimate the expected cash flows of year 5 to be \$10,000. If this figure is used in the investment analysis, what assumption or assumptions are being made?

13-2. What is the maximum amount you would pay for the lottery of .5 probability of \$1,000 and a .5 probability of \$0? What does this imply about your utility function?

13-3. For you to be indifferent between the following two lotteries, what value of X must be inserted?

Lottery A	Lottery B
.5 probability of $1,000 .5 probability of $0	1.0 probability of $$X$

What does this imply about your utility function? Compare your value of X to the answer you gave to problem 13-2.

13-4. Would the utility function of a firm change after making an investment?

13-5. When is it reasonable to base decisions on the use of money (in the computations) and to ignore utility considerations?

13-6. In making a utility function for a corporation, how would you handle the situation where different corporate executives and owners have different utility functions?

13-7. If we did not try to incorporate utility considerations into the investment analysis, would the investment decisions of the firm still be affected by utility functions of the individual corporate executives, assuming some degree of decentralization?

13-8. If the firm is small enough for the president to make all the decisions, is it necessary to make a formal analysis using utility functions? Explain.

13-9. If we do not know the exact probabilities of the events that may occur, is it still reasonable to use the utility analysis? Is it reasonable to compute the expected monetary value?

13-10. The following utility function of Mr. Jay will be used for problems 13-10 and 13-11.

Dollars of Wealth	Utility Measure
− 3,000	−3,000
− 1,000	−1,000
− 600	− 500
− 500	− 350
0	0
100	100
500	150
1,000	200
2,000	350
4,000	500
10,000	1,000

Assume that there is a gamble which has .5 probability of $10,000 and .5 probability of $0.

Required: (a) What is the utility measure of the gamble? (b) What is the amount that Mr. Jay would be willing to accept for certain to cause him to be indifferent to the choice between the gamble and the certain amount? (c) What is the expected monetary value of the gamble?

13-11. Assume that there is a gamble which has a .5 probability of $4,000 and .5 probability of $1,000.

Required: (a) What is the utility measure of the gamble? (b) What is the amount that Mr. Jay would be willing to accept for certain to cause him to be indifferent to the choice between the gamble and the certain amount? (c) What is the expected monetary value of the gamble?

13-12. The following problem attempts to illustrate the simulation of the mean utility of a cash flow that has a normal probability density function.

The outcomes of a period are normally distributed with a mean of $100,000 and a standard deviation of $20,000. Four random deviations from the mean were obtained (in an actual simulation the number of observations would be much larger).

$$d$$

.40
1.35
− .83
2.50

The following values were obtained from the utility function:

Dollars	Utility Measures
0	0
83,400	10,000
108,000	15,000
110,000	16,000
127,000	19,000
150,000	20,000

Required: (a) Compute the four outcomes. (b) Using the utility function, determine the utility observation for each outcome. (c) Determine the expected utility of the observations. (d) Determine the certainty equivalent.

13-13. Assume the following utility function for the newly formed ABC Corporation.

Dollars	Utility Measure
−20,000	−400
−10,000	−100
0	0
7,200	80
8,600	90
10,000	100
18,600	140
20,000	150
30,000	190
35,800	200
40,000	220
60,000	240

a. Should the corporation accept an investment that requires an outlay of $10,000 and that will either involve a complete loss or generate cash flows of $30,000 within one week (each possibility has a .5 probability)?

b. What would be your recommendation if the probabilities were .65 of failure and .35 of success?

13-14. Assume the same utility function as in problem 13-13.

a. Should the ABC Corporation undertake the following investment? Assume that a .05 discount rate is appropriate.

Period	Cash Flow
0	−10,000
1	0 with .5 probability
	30,000 with .5 probability

b. What would be your recommendation if the probabilities were .6 of failure and .4 of success?

13-15. Assume the same utility function as in problem 13-13. The ABC Corporation has been offered an investment that costs $20,000. The investment has .5 probability of not generating any cash the first day and .5 probability of generating $30,000. It also can generate $0 or $30,000 with the same probabilities the second day. The amount received on the second day is statistically independent of the amount received on the first day. Should the firm accept the investment?

13-16. Assume the same situation as in problem 13-15, except that the transactions take place in successive years instead of days. The discount rate is .05. Should the firm accept the investment?

13-17. Assume the same investment as in problem 13-15, except that the cash flows of the second day will be the same as for the first day. Should the firm accept the investment?

13-18. Assume that the cash flows of an investment are as follows:

Period	Mean Value	Standard Deviation
0	−8,000	500
1	10,000	1,000
2	10,000	2,000

Compute the mean, variance, and standard deviation of the net present-value distribution. Assume that the cash flows of each period are independent. Use a .05 rate of discount.

13-19. Determine whether the following investment is acceptable. Explain briefly your computations and assumptions.

Period	Cash Flows
0	($1,000)
1	.5 probability of $2,100 cash flow
	.3 probability of $1,050
	.2 probability of $0

The firm has a cost of money of .05. The utility function of the corporation has the following values (interpolate if you need other values).

Money	Utility
−1,000	−300
0	0
500	50
1,000	70
1,050	75
1,300	85
1,500	90
2,000	100
2,100	101
3,000	125

13-20. The cash flows of an investment are independent and have the following distributions:

Period	Mean	Variance
0	−1,600	2,500
1	1,000	4,000
2	1,000	10,000

(a) Assume that the appropriate rate of discount is .05. Compute the mean and variance of the distribution of the net present values of cash flows. (b) Change the assumptions of part (a) to be that the cash flow of the second period will be the same as those of period 1 (there is dependency). Compute the mean and variance of the distribution of the net present values of cash flows. Ignore the preceding description of period 2 specifying a variance of 10,000.

13-21. The ABC Company can invest $1 million. The two possible payoffs occurring immediately are as follows:

Probability	Payoff
.5	$ 0
.5	2,600,000

(a) If you were in charge of making this decision would you accept? Explain. (b) Assume that you can make two investments similar to that described above and own .5 of each investment. Would you accept this alternative? Do you prefer it to the possibility of investing the entire $1 million in one investment?

13-22. It has sometimes been argued that net present value is "more sensitive" than the yield of an investment to variations in the cash-flow estimates. For example, suppose that an immediate outlay of $3.859 million produces proceeds of $1 million per year for fifteen years and an additional end-of-life salvage value that might be from $0 to $4.4 million. With a discount rate of 9 per cent the net present values would range from $4.2 million to $5.4 million (a variation of about 25 per cent). The yield would range from 25 per cent, if there is no salvage, to 26 per cent if there is the maximum recovery of salvage (a variation of only 4 per cent).

If sensitivity is measured by the percentage of variation in the measure of investment worth for a given range of variation in the cash-flow estimates, would you agree that in general net present value is a more sensitive measure of investment worth than yield?

part III

This part of the book consists of a series of miscellaneous topics that explicitly or implicitly assume certainty. They are important but not essential to a basic understanding of capital budgeting, and thus are separated from the introductory certainty material of Part I.

In Chapter 14 we study the buy or lease decision, and suggest a method of analysis for this very important decision.

In Chapter 15 we attempt to reconcile the decision to invest and the measurement of costs and benefits after the investment is completed. The depreciation measurement presented has significance for measuring the performance of managers.

Although the basic capital budgeting principles are applicable when there is the prospect of inflation, in Chapter 16 we offer suggestions on how to apply these principles when the risk of inflation is high.

In Chapter 17, a solution to the timing problem, which is contained in both growth-period decisions and decisions involving replacement of equipment, is offered.

In Chapter 18, we consider how private investments might be evaluated from the point of view of their effects on the national economy.

Chapter 19 considers the special problems that occur if a firm has a choice of several types of equipment and faces fluctuations in demand.

chapter 14

buy or lease

When we use the term *lease* in this chapter, we shall be referring to a financial type of lease, that is, a lease where the firm has a legal obligation to continue making payments for a well-defined period of time. We are excluding from consideration the type of lease where an asset is acquired for a short period of time to fill a temporary need and then leasing is stopped. (A familiar example of this latter type of lease is the renting of an automobile at an airport.) We shall first deal with leases where there is a buy or lease option and the firm has already made the decision to acquire the asset. In this situation the buy or lease decision becomes a financing decision. We shall then discuss the situation where the firm must decide whether or not to buy, lease, or do nothing. We shall conclude that many financial leases are very similar to debt and should be treated in essentially the same manner as debt. A legally oriented person would be able to point out the differences between a lease and debt (especially when there is a failure to pay the required payments), but we shall concentrate on the similarities, and the decision maker can bring the differences into the analysis in a qualitative manner if he so wishes.

borrow or lease: the financing decision

We shall first assume a zero tax rate and analyze the financial aspects of the lease versus buy decision. Assume that a company is considering the lease or purchase of a piece of equipment. The firm has decided to acquire the equipment. The equipment will incur operating costs and will generate revenues that are unaffected by whether or not the equipment is leased or purchased. Thus for any lease or buy decision there will be many cash flows that are common to both decisions. There are, however, differences in the cash flows related to the method of financing the equipment. On the one hand, we have the cash flows associated with buying, and, on the other, the cash flows associated with leasing. Assume that the equipment costs $100,000, and we can borrow the $100,000 at a cost of .05 per year or we can lease the equipment at a cost of $28,201 per year. Should we lease or buy, assuming that the equipment has an expected life of four years? Because we have decided to acquire the asset, the only decision is the type of financing. The cash flows of the two financing alternatives are as follows:

		Period				
		0	1	2	3	4
Buy and		+ $100,000	− $5,000	− $5,000	− $5,000	− $5,000
borrow	A	− 100,000				− 100,000
Lease	B		− 28,201	− 28,201	− 28,201	− 28,201
Difference	A − B	$ 0	$23,201	$23,201	$23,201	$23,201
(buy minus						− $100,000
lease)						

The present value of the cash outlays with leasing is $28,201 times the present value of an annuity for four periods using an interest rate of .05:

$$\$28,201 \times 3.5460 = \$100,000.$$

The present value of the cash outlays associated with buying are also $100,000 and in this situation we are indifferent between leasing and buying.

We can take the differences of the cash flows of borrowing and leasing and compute the rate of return of this stream. The rate of interest that makes the present value of the cash flows equal to zero is .05. Because this is a loan type of cash-flow sequence (positive flows followed by negative), the lower the yield, the more desirable the cash flows.

Cash Flow		Present-Value Factor		Present Value
+ $23,201	×	3.5460	=	$82,270
− 100,000	×	.8227	=	− 82,270
				0

To obtain an investment type of cash-flow pattern, we can multiply the differential cash flows by − 1. We have outlays of $23,201 for four years and a one-period return of $100,000. In this case we could say that leasing yields a rate of return of .05 compared to buying and borrowing (the higher the yield, the better leasing is compared to buying and borrowing). Because we can borrow at a cost of .05, we are indifferent between buying and borrowing and leasing.

There is no reason why we have to choose the method of repayment that is illustrated. For example, we could repay the $100,000 loan using equal annual payments of $28,201. Because the cash flows of leasing and financing by borrowing would be exactly the same, the computation of a return rate on the differences would not have any meaning in this latter situation. We would again be indifferent between borrowing and leasing.

In general, if the discount rate used in the analysis is the same as the interest rate that the firm would have to pay if it actually attempted to finance the purchase of the asset by a loan, the particular loan repayment schedule chosen will not affect the present value of the loan. Suppose that an amount K is borrowed, and interest of r per cent is paid on the principal plus accrued interest outstanding. Using r as the discount rate, we find that the present value of the payments required to repay the loan will always be K, whatever loan repayment schedule is chosen.

The purpose of this phase of the analysis is to determine whether the proposed lease is financially attractive. Because the lease is presumed to require a contractually predetermined set of payments, it is reasonable to compare the lease with an alternative type of financing available to the company that also required a contractually predetermined set of payments, that is, a loan. In this analysis we are only determining whether leasing or borrowing is preferable.

Now assume that the lease payments are $29,000 per year, and the debt is repaid at the end of four years. The cash flows of the two financing alternatives are as follows:

		Period				
		0	1	2	3	4
Buy and		− $100,000	− $ 5,000	− $ 5,000	− $ 5,000	− $ 5,000
borrow	A	+ 100,000				− 100,000
Lease	B		− 29,000	− 29,000	− 29,000	− 29,000
Difference	B − A		− $24,000	− $24,000	− $24,000	− $ 24,000
(lease minus						
buy)						+ $100,000

The rate of return of this investment stream from leasing instead of buying (and borrowing) is approximately .03, and we would want to borrow and buy rather than lease, because a .03 rate of return is not acceptable for an investment when the cost of borrowing is .05.

Although we can compute and interpret the yield of the financial type of cash flow, the interpretation is somewhat difficult. Is a high yield good or bad for the cash-flow difference? Another procedure would be to compute the present values of the two series of cash flows. With any discount rate greater than .03, the present value of the lease will be greater than the present value of buying and borrowing. When we use .05 as the rate of discount, the present value of buying and borrowing is

$$
\begin{aligned}
\$5,000 \times 3.5460 &= \$ \ 17,730 \\
\$100,000 \times .8227 &= \underline{\ \ \ 82,270} \\
&\quad \ \ \$100,000
\end{aligned}
$$

The present value of leasing is

$$\$29,000 \times 3.5460 = \$102,834.$$

Comparing the two present values, we see that the cost of borrowing is less than the cost of leasing (assuming lease payments of $29,000 per year) and that if the asset is acquired it should be purchased, not leased.

Using a .05 discount rate, we previously computed the present values of the borrow and lease alternatives, where the lease payments were $28,201 per year, and found that the present values of both alternatives were $100,000 and we would be indifferent between leasing and borrowing.

The conclusions to this point can be summarized as follows: We can buy a piece of equipment for $100,000; it has an expected life of four years. The firm could borrow the money to finance the purchase at an interest cost of 5 per cent. The equipment could also be acquired through a lease. If the annual lease payments were $28,201 per year for four years, there would be no financial cost advantage or disadvantage to leasing, because the present value of the lease payments at 5 per cent is equal to the amount that would have to be borrowed to finance the purchase through borrowing. If the lease payments were greater than $28,201 per year (say, $29,000), the lease would have a financial cost disadvantage. Similarly, if the lease payments required were less than $28,201, it could be shown that the lease would have a financial cost advantage.

leasing and financial leverage

An objection to the financial analysis can be considered at this point. Suppose that an analysis along the lines described led to the conclusion that the lease had a financial cost advantage, but that the firm has the $100,000 cash available with which it can purchase the asset. One can imagine a company treasurer objecting as follows: "I agree that the lease incorporates very favorable financial terms. However, if we acquire the asset by leasing, we will be adding to the burden of fixed charges (including interest, debt repayment, other leases, and noncancellable overhead) that the company must bear. Entering into this lease would add to these fixed charges. For that reason I would prefer that we purchase the equipment outright if we decide to acquire it at all."

One can sympathize with the treasurer's desire not to increase fixed charges, and still disagree with his conclusion about the lease. He is correct in saying that, if the funds are used to purchase the asset, fixed financing charges will not increase. However, fixed charges could also be kept constant if the company leases the asset rather than buys it by applying the $100,000 available for purchase to a reduction in other fixed charges, say, by repaying some debt.

Accepting or rejecting a lease does not necessarily imply an increase or decrease in total fixed charges. A company can accept a financially advantageous lease without increasing its fixed charges. If the analysis indicates a financial disadvantage to the lease, and if the equipment is to be acquired at all, it should be bought. Whether the funds for the purchase should be obtained from debt, equity, or some mixture is a separate decision.

The analysis we have presented may be used to decide whether direct borrowing with an explicit debt security is more desirable or less desirable than leasing. We have not attempted to present an analysis here that proves debt is more or less attractive than other types of financing.

The analysis we have presented cannot be used to decide whether or not the asset should be acquired. Nor can it be used to decide whether the firm should have more or less financial leverage. If it has been decided that acquiring the use of the equipment is desirable, the analysis can be used to determine whether to buy or lease the equipment. The specific actions that should be taken will depend on whether or not additional financial leverage

Exhibit 14-1. Appropriate Actions Depending on the Desirability of a Lease, and on the Desirability of Additional Financial Leverage

Additional Leverage Is	Lease Is	
	Desirable	Undesirable
Desirable	Lease equipment	Buy equipment and borrow
Undesirable	Lease equipment and repay existing debt	Buy equipment

is desirable. The appropriate actions, assuming it has been decided that acquiring the use of the equipment is desirable, are summarized in Exhibit 14-1.

The analysis of this section is incomplete in two respects. It cannot tell us whether the equipment should be acquired at all, and it cannot tell us whether additional financial leverage is desirable.

The preceding analysis assumes a zero tax rate. It is necessary to take income taxes into consideration to make the analysis more realistic because income taxes will tend to influence the choice.

buy or lease with taxes

Let us now consider the effects of a corporate income tax of 40 per cent. With an income tax we shall want to put all cash flows on an after-tax basis, and because interest expense is deductible for tax purposes, we shall use an after-tax discount rate. If a discount rate of 5 per cent was appropriate on a before-tax basis for borrowed funds, the corresponding after-tax rate can be assumed to be $(1 - .4).05 = .03$.

Because lease payments are a deductible expense in computing income subject to taxes, annual payments of $28,201 per year will become after-tax cash flows of $(1 - .4)$28,201, or $16,921, per year. The present value of the after-tax lease payments, using a 3 per cent discount rate, will be $16,921 $\times$ 3.7171, or $62,897.

The cost of the equipment is $100,000, and we shall consider borrowing that amount in order to finance purchase of the machine. The exact pattern of after-tax cash flows will depend on the debt repayment schedule. If the lender charges 5 per cent per year, equal payments of $28,201 per year for four years would be one repayment schedule sufficient to repay the interest and principal on the loan. To put these cash flows on an after-tax basis for the borrower, we need to determine for each year how much of this amount will be considered a payment of interest and how much a repayment of principal. Only the interest expense portion is allowable as an expense for tax purposes. A different repayment schedule would lead to a different pattern of after-tax cash flows; but provided interest was computed on the remaining debt balance, the present value of the after-tax cash flows required to repay the principal and interest of the loan will always be $100,000. For example, suppose that the firm pays interest at $5,000 per year for four years and repays the principal in a lump sum at the end of the fourth year. The after-tax interest payments are $3,000 for each year.

$$\begin{array}{rl} \$ \quad 3,000 \times 3.7171 & = \$ \ 11,151 \\ \$100,000 \times \quad .88849 & = \quad 88,849 \\ \hline & \$100,000 \end{array}$$

We want to compute the cash flows of buying. If we subtract the present value of the positive cash flows associated with borrowing (plus $100,000) from the present value of the after-tax cash payments (a negative $100,000), we find that borrowing has a zero present value. The present value of the cash flows of buying and borrowing is the $100,000 immediate cost of the asset.

If we compare the purchase price of the asset with the present value of the lease payments, there appears to be an advantage in favor of the lease, when taxes are taken into effect. However, depreciation expenses have not yet been considered. If the equipment is leased, the lessee cannot deduct depreciation. If the equipment is purchased, the right to deduct depreciation expense for tax purposes is also obtained. With a tax rate of 40 per cent, each dollar of depreciation expense will save $.40 of taxes. The present value of the tax savings resulting from depreciation will depend on the timing of the depreciation expense. If depreciation is charged on a straight-line basis over a four-year period, the value of the tax savings each year will be $10,000 (.4 × $25,000), and the present value of the tax savings will be $10,000 × 3.7171 = $37,171. Subtracting this from the cost of the investment gives a net present value of after-tax cash flows of $62,829 for the borrow-and-buy decision. This is slightly less than the present value of the lease payments ($62,897).

If a more rapid method of depreciation were used, there would be a more clearly defined advantage in favor of buying. For example, if the twice-straight-line, declining-balance method of depreciation were used, the present value of the tax savings could be computed, using Appendix Table D. With an interest rate of 3 per cent and a life of four years, the present value of the tax deduction privilege is as follows: $100,000 × .4 × .946539 = $37,862. Subtracting this amount from $100,000 gives a net present value of $62,138 for buying and borrowing, which is $759 less than that for leasing.

The tax savings that result from charging depreciation if the asset is owned are not contractual in nature as are the other cash flows we are considering. However, frequently there is nearly as little uncertainty associated with the amount and timing of these cash flows as there would be in the case of a contract. Regardless of whether the particular piece of equipment performs as anticipated, the right to charge depreciation expense will generate tax savings as long as the firm as a whole has taxable income. Even if the firm does not have taxable income in any particular year, the tax-loss carry-forward and carry-back provisions of the law provide a high degree of assurance that tax savings will result, although their timing might change slightly.

The preceding analysis made the lease-and-buy alternatives comparable by including financial-type cash flows in the purchase-decision analysis. This is reasonable because lease payments are a special type of debt, with special tax treatment. The entire amount of payment may be deducted in computing taxable income, unlike the conventional debt for which only interest is deductible for tax purposes.

One important difference in buying, compared to leasing, is that the firm that buys an asset owns the asset at the end of the time period of the lease. To the extent that the asset has net value at that time, this is also a net cash flow for the buy analysis. This difference will be illustrated when we discuss the buy–lease analysis for acquisition of land.

risk considerations in lease versus borrow decisions

We began this chapter by suggesting that many leases are essentially financing instruments, comparable to debt contracts. It is desirable to consider the risks associated with the financial decisions (borrow or lease) we have been considering.

For practical purposes it may be reasonable, in some circumstances, to treat the financial cash flows as being free of any uncertainty. This assumption will not always be valid, as we shall see. If the likelihood of any substantial deviation from our predictions is very small, the time and cost involved in any detailed analysis of the uncertainties may not be worth the effort. The main justification for treating these financial cash flows as essentially certain for practical purposes is that their amounts and timing are largely determined by legal contracts that the firm acquiring the asset will have to fulfill. The lease contract determines the amounts and timing of the lease payments; the debt contract determines the amounts and timing of the debt repayments by the firm acquiring the asset. The depreciation expense charges allowed for tax purposes are not contractual, but they are fixed by law and in the presence of a large amount of other income and stable tax rates are reasonably certain.

Given a specific set of contracts, it might be possible to analyze the cash flows under various foreseeable alternatives. What would happen if the firm could not meet the legal requirements? Would it be declared bankrupt? Could the lease be terminated earlier? Could the loan be extended or renewed, or is it callable?

Possible changes in the corporate income tax rates are worth considering. If a decrease in the corporate income tax rates is anticipated, it will tend to raise the after-tax cash flows for any of the alternatives considered. However, the effect of this increase on the net present value of any alternative will be somewhat offset by the fact that a decrease in tax rates will also tend to increase the appropriate after-tax discount rate and to decrease the value of the depreciation deductions, thus changing the relative desirability of buying or leasing. Some leases specify a minimum term and contain an option allowing the lessee to extend the lease for a longer time period, if he desires. In these circumstances, uncertainty about how long the capital asset will be needed may influence the choice between leasing or buying.

The effects of these sources of uncertainty could be analyzed in detail if such an analysis were considered worthwhile. The following section illustrates such an analysis when there is uncertainty about how long the asset will be needed.

leases with uncertain lives

Suppose that a piece of equipment is needed. The initial cost of the equipment, if it is bought, is $100,000. The equipment can be used for up to four years. After that time, a physical replacement would be necessary, which would cost an additional $100,000. The asset will be depreciated on a straight-line basis. If at any time the asset is no longer needed, it can be sold for its book value. The before-tax cost of borrowing is five per cent, and a corporate income tax rate of 40 per cent is applicable.

If the equipment is purchased, the cost will depend on how long it is needed. Table 14-1 shows how the present value of the costs and the equivalent annual costs of owning the equipment will vary with the length of time that it is needed.

Suppose that the equipment is also available on a lease basis. The lease requires rental payments of $28,333 per year [equal to (.6)($28,333) = $17,000 after taxes]. The lease is for a period of four years. It can be canceled by the lessee at the end of any annual period. There is a penalty of $5,000 if the lease is canceled at the end of the first year, but no penalty if canceled in later years. The lessor cannot cancel the lease.

Table 14-2 compares the present value of the costs of owning versus leasing for periods of from one to four years.

Table 14-1. Present Values and Equivalent Annual Costs of Owning Equipment for t Years

Item	Length of Time Equipment Is Owned (t)			
	1	2	3	4
Present value of purchase, outlays	$100,000	$100,000	$100,000	$100,000
Present value of tax shield from depreciation	9,709	19,135	28,286	37,171
Present value of salvage	72,816	47,130	22,879	0
Net present value of costs	17,475	33,735	48,835	62,829
Equivalent annual costs for t years	17,999	17,630	17,265	16,902

Table 14-2.   Present Values of Costs of Owning and Leasing

	Number of Years Equipment is Used			
	1	2	3	4
Owning	$17,475	$33,735	$48,835	$62,839
Leasing	19,417	32,529	48,086	63,191

If it were certain how long the equipment would be needed, Table 14-2 could be used to decide whether to lease or buy. For example, if the equipment were needed for four years, it would be less expensive to buy it. Suppose that four years is the most probable length of time the equipment will be needed. Although buying is less expensive if the equipment is needed for four years, it does not follow that buying is the best decision.

A better approach is to calculate the expected present value of the two alternatives of buying or leasing. This requires assigning a probability to each year to reflect the likelihood that the equipment will be needed for that length of time, but not longer. Table 14-3 illustrates the necessary calculations for a hypothetical set of probabilities. On an expected-value basis, the costs of leasing are less than the costs of buying.

The risks associated with the alternatives, buying or leasing, are illustrated more clearly if one calculates for each year the amount by which the cost of each alternative exceeds the cost of the best alternative. This excess cost is called an *opportunity loss*. The calculations are illustrated in Table 14-4.

The opportunity-loss calculations clearly indicate buying is preferable if the equipment will be needed for either two or three years; otherwise, leasing is less expensive. The decision that minimizes the expected opportunity loss will also be the same decision that minimizes the expected present value of the costs. The difference between expected present values of buying minus leasing (from Table 14-3) is $48,281 − 48,150 = $131. This is the same as the

Table 14-3.   Expected Present Values of Leasing Versus Buying

Number of Years Equipment Will Be Used	Probabilities	Buying		Leasing	
		Present Value of Costs	Expected Present Value	Present Value of Costs	Expected Present Value
1	.1	$17,475	$ 1,747	$19,417	$ 1,942
2	.2	33,735	6,747	32,529	6,506
3	.3	48,835	14,651	48,086	14,426
4	.4	62,839	25,136	63,191	25,276
	1.0		$48,281		$48,150

Table 14-4. Expected Opportunity Losses of Leasing Versus Buying

Number of Years Equipment Will Be Used	Probability	Buying Opportunity Loss	Buying Expected Value	Leasing Opportunity Loss	Leasing Expected Value
1	.1	$ 0	$ 0	$1,942	$194
2	.2	1,206	241	0	0
3	.3	749	225	0	0
4	.4	0	0	352	141
	1.0		$466		$335

difference between the expected opportunity losses (from Table 14-4) of buying minus leasing, or $466 − 335 = $131.

This analysis is correct if the need for the equipment in a given year is statistically independent of the rate of return on the market portfolio. However, if the need for the equipment is correlated with the return on the market portfolio, a more complex analysis using the approach described in Chapter 12 would be needed.

is the equipment worth acquiring?

In the previous sections we have shown that the present value of the cost (using twice-straight-line depreciation) of acquiring the equipment is $62,138 if it is bought, and $62,897 if leased. To decide whether it is worth buying the equipment, we need to compare the present value of the benefits with the net cost of $62,138.

Suppose that the equipment has a life of four years and would lead to before-tax cash savings of $30,000 per year. The after-tax cash savings are $(1 − .4) \times \$30,000$, or $18,000 per year. The present value of the tax savings that would result from the right to charge depreciation expense on the equipment has already been calculated and subtracted from the purchase price of the equipment, so these tax savings should not be considered again.

Using the after-tax interest rate of 3 per cent, we find that the present value of the savings from operating the machine is

$$\$18,000 \times 3.7171 = \$66,908.$$

Subtracting the present value of the costs of equipment from the present value of the savings, we have a net present value of $4,770 (that is, $66,908 − $62,138), indicating that we can accept the machine on a borrow-and-buy basis.

In situations such as this, we may be able to estimate the cost of acquiring the asset with a high degree of confidence, whereas the savings that would result from having the use of the asset are subject to considerable uncertainty. If the firm has not had experience with similar equipment, there may be some question as to whether the savings in cost per unit of product (or other measure of the rate of usage) will be as high as anticipated. In addition, there may be some uncertainty about the number of units of product that will be needed and about the equipment's anticipated life. For these and other reasons, a decision about whether or not the machine should be acquired will to a great extent depend upon management's judgments.

leasing of land

In making investment decisions we generally separate the cash outlay (the investment) from the financing (the source of the cash). The two are tied together by the use of a given rate of discount that measures the time value of money for the firm.

In leasing decisions involving land it may not always be possible to separate an investment from its financing, as they frequently become interwoven. In fact, in some situations it is not clear whether the land is being purchased or leased. Assume a situation where land is being leased but the company leasing the land can acquire the land for a nominal price at the end of twenty years. Are the lease payments for the use of the land, or are they for the use of money during the twenty-year period plus payments for the land?

We shall assume the following situation: Company A owns land and has offered to lease it to Company B at a cost of $80,242.65 per year for twenty years. After the twenty years A retains the land, assuming B leases.

B is a very large, stable company, and A considers a lease with B to be the equivalent of a certain cash flow. Using the current long-term debt rate of .05, B finds the before-tax present value of the $80,242.65 to be $1 million.

A has offered to sell the land to B for $1 million. (A would not be taxed on this transaction.) Should B buy? B can obtain long-term funds at a cost of .05. These funds would have to be repaid at the end of twenty years. B's tax rate is .40, and B has taxable income.

B's analysis is as follows:

Cost of Leasing

The after-tax cost of leasing is obtained by multiplying the lease by the tax and present-value factors.[1]

$$\text{After-tax cost of leasing} = (\$80,242.65) \times .60 \times 14.8775$$
$$= \$716,286.$$

[1] $B(20 \ .03) = 14.8775.$

Cost of Buying

If we ignore the method of financing, the cost of buying is the immediate outlay of $1 million.

Alternatively, we can compute the cost for the twenty years as being equal to the present value of the interest of $50,000 a year plus the $1 million at maturity. Discounted at .05, this has a present value equal to $1 million, and the cost of buying is again $1 million. But this calculation is before taking taxes into consideration.

B must compare the after-tax cost of borrowing with the after-tax cost of leasing, which is $716,000. The after-tax cost of borrowing is $1 million.

$$\$50,000 \times 14.8775 \times .60 = \$ \ \ 446,300$$
$$\$1,000,000 \times .5537 = \ \ \ \ 553,700$$
$$\overline{\$1,000,000}$$

The after-tax cost of leasing is less than the after-tax cost of borrowing. This is not surprising, as the entire payment of the lease is tax deductible (thus with a lease only .6 of the amount paid is included as an outlay), but only the interest payments are deductible for tax purposes if we borrow.

There is a tax advantage in repaying the $1 million via a lease compared to repaying the $1 million outlay via a debt if we buy. However, in considering the buy decision we ignored the value of land at the end of the twenty years. Adding this to the cash flow of the twentieth year may affect the decision.

We will compare the $716,000 after-tax cost of leasing with the $1 million after-tax cost of buying and borrowing and compute the break-even value of land (at the end of twenty years). Let X be the value of the land after twenty years.

$$\$716,000 = \$1,000,000 - X(1 + .03)^{-20}$$
$$\$284,000 = .5537X$$
$$X = \$513,000$$

Based on the after-tax computation, if the land is expected to have a value of less than $513,000, we should lease; otherwise we should buy.

We can compare the two alternatives year by year. Assume that the land will be worth its present purchase price at the end of twenty years. The lease plan does not have a buy option.

The after-tax cash flows (in dollars) are as follows:

	Year				
	1	2	3 ⋯	20	
Lease	− $48,146	− $48,146	− $48,146	− $ 48,146	
Buy	− 30,000	− 30,000	− 30,000	− 30,000	interest
				−1,000,000	repayment of debt
				+1,000,000	value of land
Difference (lease − buy)	− $18,146	− $18,146	− $18,146	− $ 18,146	

The $18,146 is the extra cost (per year) of leasing compared to buying. Assuming that the land does not depreciate in value through time, the advantage is clearly with buying. If the lease payment was $50,000 per year before tax, there would be indifference between buying and leasing.

Changing the timing of the debt repayment would not change the basic conclusion as long as the interest rate of the loan and the discount rate were equal.

Lease and Buy

There is an additional complication. Suppose that Company B can lease and then buy the land for $300,000 at the end of twenty years. A lease decision is preferable, based on the after-tax economic analysis. However, the Internal Revenue Service will probably object to the deduction of the lease payment for tax computations and will consider a large part of the cash outlay as being a payment for the land (which it is).

Conclusions

Leasing of land is a possible method of financing the use of land. If we remove the mystery from the decision process, we find that leasing may be more desirable than purchasing if there exists a difference of opinion relative to the value of land upon termination of the lease. If Company A thinks the value of land will be increasing, it may lease to B at a price that seems low to B, if B thinks the value of the land will decrease. To the extent that the Internal Revenue Service allows lease payments for land to be deductible when there is an option to buy at a reduced price (that is, a price less than the expected market price) at the termination of the lease, there may be a tax advantage to leasing land. But this tax advantage cannot be automatically assumed, as it is likely that the lease payments will be interpreted to be a purchase payment, and thus not deductible for tax purposes.

questions and problems

Problems 14-1 to 14-6 are tied together and should be done consecutively. Assume a zero tax rate.

14-1. The ABC Company has contracted to make three lease payments of $10,000 each for the use of a piece of equipment. The first payment is to be made immediately and the other payments are to be made in successive years. Assume that the cost of debt is .05.

Required: Determine the debt equivalent of the lease payments.

14-2. Refer to problem 14-1. If we could borrow $28,000 and buy the equipment being leased, should we purchase it or lease it?

14-3. A piece of equipment costs $28,000 and has indicated cash flows of $10,200 a year for three years. The cash flows are received at the *beginning* of each year. With a time value of money of .10, is the investment desirable?

14-4. Assume that $18,000 could be borrowed with the funds being paid back as follows:

Period	
0	
1	$10,000
2	10,000

Refer to problem 14-3. Is the investment now desirable?

14-5. Refer to problem 14-3. If we could lease the equipment for $10,000 a year, with the first payment due immediately, would the equipment be desirable?

14-6. Refer to problems 14-3 and 14-4. If we could lease the equipment for $10,000 a year, would it be more desirable to buy and borrow or to lease the equipment?

14-7. The RSV Company can finance the purchase of a new building costing $1 million with a .05 bond that would pay $50,000 interest per year. Instead of buying the building, the company can lease it for $95,000 per year, the first payment being due one period from now. The building has an expected life of twenty years. The company has a zero tax rate.

Required: Should the company borrow and buy or lease?

14-8. The CDE Company is considering leasing a piece of equipment. There are three lease payments of $10,000 due at the end of each of the next three years. The equipment is expected to generate cash flows of $10,500 per year. Assume that the cost of debt is .05 and the income tax rate is .40.

Required: Combining the investment and its financing, prepare an analysis that shows the net present value of leasing.

14-9. Assume that the equipment of problem 14-8 can be purchased at a cost of $27,232.

Required: Should the equipment be purchased? Use sum-of-the-years'-digits method of depreciation for tax purposes. Use a discount rate of .03, but exclude the financing from the cash flows.

14-10. Assume that the life of a piece of equipment is uncertain, but that management believes that the probabilities of it having different lives and the present values of cash flows for buying and leasing for different assumed lives are as follows:

Assumed Life	Probability	Present Value (Buying)	Present Value (Leasing)
1	.2	− $20,000	− $ 2,000
2	.3	0	4,000
3	.4	20,000	10,000
4	.1	40,000	16,000
	1.0		

Required: Is it more desirable to buy or lease?

14-11. *The Rocky Boat Company*

The Rocky Boat Company is considering the purchase of a business machine. The alternative is to rent it. The purchase price of the machine is $100,000. The rental per year of the same machine is $30,000. The $30,000 includes all repairs and service. If the machine is purchased, a comparable service contract can be obtained for $1,000 a year.

The salesman of the Business Machine Corporation has cited evidence indicating that the expected useful service life of this machine is five years.

The appropriate rate of discount of the firm is 5 per cent per year. If rented, the company may cancel the lease arrangement with one month's notice.

Required: Prepare a comprehensive analysis for the controller of the Rocky Boat Company, indicating whether it is more desirable to purchase or rent. Assume a tax rate of zero.

14-12. The Rocky Boat Company (see problem 14-11) has purchased the machine on January 1, 1971. How should the machine be depreciated for tax purposes? Assume that a life of five years is acceptable to the Internal Revenue Service and that the tax rate is 52 per cent. The net salvage value of the machinery is zero, because the removal costs are expected to be equal to the salvage proceeds. Use a .05 discount rate. (a) Prepare an analysis backing up your answer. (b) Recompute the investment decision of problem 14-11, taking income taxes into consideration and assuming that a five-year life is valid.

14-13. The Able Company was approached by a salesman from the Rochester Machine Tool Corporation. Rochester had developed a machine that could mechanize an Able Company operation now performed by hand. The machine cost $30,000, had a life expectancy of three years, and could save Able Company $14,000 per year in labor costs. Able Company estimated that its hurdle rate was 10 per cent. Its analysis of the cash flows that would result from using the machine is given in Table 14-5. Able Company was subject to a 50 per cent corporate profit tax, and the machine would be depreciated on a straight-line basis for three years.

Subjecting the purchase price and cash savings from using the machine to a present-value analysis, illustrated in Table 14-6, the Able Company decided it was not profitable to buy the machine.

When the Rochester Machine Tool salesman heard of the decision, he offered the machine to Able on the basis of a three-year lease. The lease payments required were $11,223 per year. The salesman pointed out that the extra $3,669 the company would pay if it leased the machine just covered the interest costs on the purchase price over a three-year period at 6 per cent. Able figured that the lease payments of $11,223 were $2,777 less than the saving in labor cost. Half the difference would go to the government in extra taxes, but the company would be ahead by $1,388 per year (half of $2,777) and no capital outlay was involved. They decided to lease the machine.

Table 14-5. Cash Savings from Buying New Machine

Annual reduction in labor expense	$14,000
Increased income tax liability before allowing for depreciation	−7,000
Tax saving from depreciation charge of $10,000 per year	5,000
Annual increase in cash flow from using machine	$12,000

Table 14-6.   Cash Flow Analysis from Buying Machine

		Present-Value Factor	
Year	Cash Flow	(10% cost of capital)	Present Value
0	($30,000)	1.0000	− $30,000
1	12,000	.9091	10,909
2	12,000	.8264	9,917
3	12,000	.7513	9,016
	$ 6,000	—	− $ 158

Table 14-7 A.   Cash Flows from Buying Machine and Borrowing Purchase Price from Bank at 6 Per Cent

		Year	
Item	1	2	3
Reduction in labor expense	$14,000	$14,000	$14,000
Increased interest expense	−1,800	−1,235	− 635
Increase in income tax before allowing for depreciation	−6,100	−6,383	− 6,683
Tax savings from depreciation	5,000	5,000	5,000
Cash flows from operations	11,100	11,382	11,682
Repayment of loan principal	−9,423	−9,988	−10,589
Net cash flows	$ 1,677	$ 1,394	$ 1,093

Table 14-7 B.   Comparison of Present Values from Leasing Versus Buying and Borrowing

	Lease		Buy and Borrow		Present-
Year	Cash Flows*	Present Values	Cash Flows†	Present Values	Value Factors (10%)
1	$1,388	$1,262	$1,677	$1,525	.9091
2	1,388	1,147	1,394	1,152	.8264
3	1,388	1,043	1,093	821	.7513
	$4,164	$3,452	$4,164	$3,498	

* ($14,000 − 11,223) × .5 = $1,388.
† See Table 14-7A.

Only one Able executive disagreed. He felt that the company could borrow the money to pay for the machine from its regular banking connections and save even more money. His calculations are presented in Table 14-7. He was overruled because the other executives felt it was not wise for the company to incur any more debt.

Should Able buy or lease or neither?

14-14. The ABC Company can purchase a new data-processing machine for $35,460 or rent it for four years at a cost of $10,000 per year. The estimated life is four years. The machine will result in a saving in clerical help of $11,000, compared to the present manual procedure. The corporation has a hurdle rate of .10 and a cost of available debt of .05. The incremental tax rate is .52. Assume that the .07 tax credit does not apply. The following analysis was prepared for the two alternatives:

			Year			
Buy	0	1	2	3	4	Total
1. Outlay	− $35,460					
2. Savings before tax		$11,000	$11,000	$11,000	$11,000	
3. Depreciation*		17,730	8,865	4,432	4,432	
4. Taxable income (2 − 3)		(6,730)	2,135	6,568	6,568	
5. Tax on savings (.52 of income)		(3,500)	1,110	3,415	3,415	
6. Net cash flow (2 − 5)		14,500	9,890	7,585	7,585	
7. Present-value factors (using .10)		.9091	.8264	.7513	.6830	
8. Present values (6 × 7)	− $35,460	$13,182	$ 8,173	$ 5,699	$ 5,181	− $3,225

* Assume the depreciation of each year for tax purposes is computed, using the twice-straight-line method of depreciation.

		Year		
Lease	0	1	2	3	4
Gross savings		$11,000	$11,000	$11,000	$11,000
Lease payments		− 10,000	− 10,000	− 10,000	− 10,000
Savings before taxes		1,000	1,000	1,000	1,000
Income tax		520	520	520	520
Net savings		$ 480	$ 480	$ 480	$ 480

"Buy" was rejected because the net present value was minus $3,225. The lease alternative was accepted because the present value of the savings is positive for any positive rate of discount.

Required: Comment on the decision to lease. Prepare a report for the president of your firm on the relative merits of leasing and buying of depreciable assets and land.

14-15. The ABC Company has decided to acquire a piece of equipment but has not yet decided to buy or lease. The lease payments would be $33,670 paid annually at the end of each year. If purchased, the equipment would be financed with debt costing .05, which can be repaid at any rate desired. The life of the equipment is three years. The lease is a firm commitment to make three payments. There is no salvage value. Should the firm lease or buy–borrow?

14-16. Continuing problem 14-15. Assume that the firm has not yet decided to purchase (or lease) the equipment. The benefits (known with certainty) are $35,000 per year. The firm has a hurdle rate of .10. There are no taxes. The firm will use .05 debt if the asset is purchased. Should the firm buy or lease? The firm can still lease at $33,670 per year.

14-17. Continuing problem 14-15. Assume that the lease terms are $33,049 and the firm can also borrow at .05 (the repayment would be $33,049 per year). Without taxes the firm is indifferent to borrowing and leasing. If the tax rate is .4, does this make buy–borrow or lease relatively more desirable?

14-18. The ABC Company has $10 million of debt outstanding, which pays .05 (that is, $500,000) interest annually. The maturity date of the securities is twenty years from the present.

Assume that a new twenty-year security could be issued which would yield .04 per year. The issue costs would be $800,000, and the call premium on redemption of the old bonds is $100,000.

Assume a zero tax rate for this company. The hurdle rate of the firm is .10.

Required: Should the present bonds be refunded?

14-19. Continuing problem 14-18. How would your answer be modified if the maturity date of the new issue were thirty years instead of twenty years?

14-20. The BCD Company has $10 million of debt outstanding, which pays .06 annually. The maturity date of the securities is twenty years from the present.

Assume that new securities could be issued which would have the same maturity date. The issue costs of the new securities would be $2.7 million; there is no call premium on the present debt. Assume a zero tax rate.

Required: Determine the rate of interest or yield rate of new securities at which the firm would just break even if they refunded. Determine to the nearest per cent.

14-21. The National Money Company, in deciding whether to make or buy, considers only direct labor and direct material as being relevant costs. The sum of these two cost factors is compared with the cost of purchasing the items, and a decision is made on this basis.

Required: Appraise the make or buy procedure of the National Money Company.

14-22. The Ithaca Manufacturing Company has excess capacity and is considering manufacturing a component part that is currently being purchased. The estimate of the cost of producing one unit of product is as follows:

Direct labor	$2.00
Material	3.00
Variable overhead	1.00
Fixed overhead (based on accounting procedures of a generally accepted nature)	2.50
	$8.50

The average increase in net working capital that will be required if the item is produced internally is $50,000.

The firm uses 100,000 of the parts per year. The unit cost of purchasing the parts is $6.05. Assume a zero tax rate.

Required: Should the company make or buy?

14-23. The York State Electric Corporation has $100 million of debentures outstanding, which are currently paying interest of 5.5 per cent ($5.5 million) per year. The bonds mature in twenty-four years.

It would be possible currently to issue thirty-year debentures of like characteristics that would yield 5 per cent. The firm considers its cost of capital to be 8 per cent. The marginal tax rate is .4.

The analysis in Table 14-8 has been prepared.

Required: Should the firm refund? Explain briefly.

14-24. The Bi-State Electric and Gas Corporation has $25 million of debentures outstanding, which are currently paying interest of 4.5 per cent ($1.125 million) per year. The bonds mature in twenty-four years.

It would be possible to currently issue thirty-year debentures of like characteristics that would yield 4 per cent. The firm considers its hurdle rate to be 8 per cent. The marginal tax rate is .50.

Table 14-8. York State Electric Refunding Calculations

	Before Taxes	After Taxes
Cash Outlays		
Premium at $50 per $1,000	$5,000,000	$3,000,000
Duplicate interest for thirty-day call period less interest received on principal at 1.4% due to temporary investment	300,000	180,000
Refunding expense (80% of $250,000, total expense of new issue based on remaining life of old issue of twenty-four years)	200,000	120,000
Call expense	50,000	30,000
Less tax saving due to immediate write-off of unamortized debt discount and expense		(20,000)
Total cash outlay of refunding		$3,310,000
Interest Calculations		
Annual interest—old issue at 5.5%	$5,500,000	$3,300,000
Annual interest—new issue at 5%	5,000,000	3,000,000
		300,000
Total after-tax interest—old issue—discounted at 8% for twenty-four years* (present value = 10.5288)		34,700,000
Total after-tax interest—new issue—discounted at 8% for twenty-four years (present value = 10.5288)		31,600,000
Total after-tax discounted interest savings resulting from refunding		$3,100,000
Total after-tax cash outlay of refunding		3,310,000
Net savings due to refunding at effective interest rate of 5%		$ (210,000)

* The remaining life of the old issue.

The following analysis has been prepared:

Cash Outlays	Before Taxes	After Taxes
Premium at $52 per $1,000	$1,300,000	$650,000
Duplicate interest for thirty-day call period less interest received on principal at 2% due to temporary investment	54,000	27,000
Refunding expense (80% of $220,000 total expense of new issue based on remaining life of old issue of twenty-four years)	176,000	88,000
Call expense	25,000	12,500
Less tax saving resulting from immediate write-off of unamortized debt discount and expense		−18,000
		$759,500

Required: Should the firm refund? Explain.

chapter 15

What you're saying, then, is that just because all the professionals in the field believe it, it must be right. If this were really true, the world is flat.

—Joel Segall. From the Autumn 1969 *Newsletter* of the Graduate School of Business, University of Chicago.

accounting concepts consistent with present-value calculations

Much of the economic analysis of evaluating prospective capital investments relies heavily on concepts such as cash flows and their net present value. This is in contrast to the usual accounting practice where the investment review emphasizes such concepts as revenue, depreciation, income, and return on investment. The purpose of this chapter is to show that the discounted cash flow approach and the main accounting concepts can be reconciled, provided that the accounting concepts are appropriately defined.

economic depreciation

If we are given the cash-flow stream associated with an asset and an appropriate interest rate and method of compounding, we can define the net present value of the cash flows associated with the asset during all succeeding time periods, and denote this present value as $V(t)$. $V(0)$ is the present value at time 0 (end of zero period) and $V(1)$ is the present value at time 1.

The economic depreciation of the asset during period t will be defined as the change in present values during this period. That is, $D(t)$ is the depreciation of period t, and if there is no new external investment during the period, $D(t)$ is defined as

$$D(t) = V(t - 1) - V(t).$$

Let $I(t)$ be defined as an investment type of cash flow occurring in period t. This is a negative cash flow that is incurred because the present value of the positive cash flows associated with the action is sufficiently large to warrant the expenditure. If there are investment-type cash flows encountered in period t, we have

$$I(t) + D(t) = V(t - 1) - V(t)$$

or

$$D(t) = V(t - 1) - V(t) - I(t),$$

where $I(t)$ is a negative quantity.

We shall assume zero investment after the initial period unless we explicitly describe a different situation.

In the usual case, where the present values have declined over the period, depreciation will be a positive quantity. If the present values increase during the period, depreciation will be negative, and we shall refer to the negative value of depreciation as appreciation. If $N(t)$ is the cash flow from operations of the t period (positive for inflows and negative for outflows), the income of the period is defined as the cash flow from operations of the period minus the depreciation of the period.[1] That is, if income is denoted by $Y(t)$ then

$$Y(t) = N(t) - D(t).$$

Return on investment can be defined as the ratio of the income of the period to the present value of the asset at the end of the previous period. If r is the discount rate used in this analysis, it will be shown that each period's return on investment will be equal to r.[2] That is,

$$\frac{Y(t)}{V(t - 1)} = r$$

if $V(t - 1) \neq 0$.

Initially, we shall assume that the cash flow pattern is such that, at the rate of interest used for discounting, the net present value of the cash flows is zero at all times before the period in which the first (nonzero) cash flow occurs. Suppose that this first cash flow occurs at the end of period 0. Then the preceding assumption means that the net present value of the cash flows at the end of period 0 is equal to the initial outlay.

To illustrate these concepts, suppose that the discount rate is 5 per cent and that interest is compounded annually. The cash flows associated with a

[1] This is not exact but will be close enough for purposes of this chapter. See H. Bierman, Jr., "A Further Study of Depreciation," *The Accounting Review*, April 1966, pp. 271–274.
[2] This equality is proved later in the chapter.

hypothetical asset are as follows. It is convenient to assume that the cash flows occur at the end of the period indicated.

Period	End-of-Period Cash Flow
0	− $54.47
1	20.00
2	10.00
3	30.50

The calculations of the net present values of the remaining cash flows at various points in time are illustrated in Table 15-1. The calculations of depreciation, income, and return on investment are illustrated in Exhibit 15-1.

Table 15-1. Calculation of Net Present Value of an Asset at Various Points in Time ($r = .05$, compounded annually)

Period	End-of-Period Cash Flow	Present-Value Factor	Present Value
1	$20.00	.9524	$19.05
2	10.00	.9070	9.07
3	30.50	.8638	26.35
			54.47 = $V(0)$
2	10.00	.9524	9.52
3	30.50	.9070	27.66
			37.18 = $V(1)$
3	30.50	.9524	29.05 = $V(2)$
			0 = $V(3)$

Exhibit 15-1. Depreciation, Income, and Return on Investment in Each Period for Asset Described in Table 15-1.

$$D(1) = \$54.47 - 37.18 = \$17.29$$
$$D(2) = \$37.18 - 29.05 = \$8.13$$
$$D(3) = \$29.05 - 0 = \$29.05$$
$$Y(1) = \$20.00 - 17.29 = \$2.71$$
$$Y(2) = \$10.00 - 8.13 = \$1.87$$
$$Y(3) = \$30.50 - 29.05 = \$1.45$$
$$r = Y(1)/V(0) = 2.71/54.47 = .05$$
$$r = Y(2)/V(1) = 1.87/37.18 = .05$$
$$r = Y(3)/V(2) = 1.45/29.05 = .05$$

Now suppose that the first cash flow occurs at the end of period 1, and assume that the net present value of the cash flows at the end of period 0 is 0. The concept of return on investment will be undefined for period 1 and for any other periods for which the net present value was 0 at the end of the preceding period.

Period	End-of-Period Cash Flow
0	0
1	− $54.47
2	20.00
3	10.00
4	30.50

Cash Flow	$0	− $54.47	$20.00	$10.00	$30.50
$V(t)$	$V(0) = 0$	$V(1) = 54.47$	$V(2) = 37.18$	$V(3) = 29.05$	$V(4) = 0$
$D(t)$	0	0	17.29	8.13	29.05
Time	0	1	2	3	4

Table 15-2. Calculation of Net Present Value of an Asset at Various Times ($r = .05$)

Period	End-of-Period Cash Flow	Present-Value Factor	Present Value
0	0	1.0000	0
1	− $54.47	.9524	− $51.87
2	20.00	.9070	18.14
3	10.00	.8638	8.64
4	30.50	.8227	25.09
			$0.00 = V(0)$
2	20.00	.9524	19.05
3	10.00	.9070	9.07
4	30.50	.8638	26.35
			$54.47 = V(1)$
3	10.00	.9524	9.52
4	30.50	.9070	27.66
			$37.18 = V(2)$
4	30.50	.9524	$29.05 = V(3)$
			$0 \quad = V(4)$

Exhibit 15-2.   Depreciation, Income, and Return on Investment
in Each Period for Asset Described in Table 15-2.

$$
\begin{aligned}
D(t) &\ V(t-1) - V(t) - I(t) \\
D(1) &= \$0 - 54.47 - (-54.47) = -54.47 + 54.47 = \$0 \\
D(2) &= \$54.47 - 37.18 = \$17.29 \\
D(3) &= \$37.18 - 29.05 = \$8.13 \\
D(4) &= \$29.05 - 0 = \$29.05 \\
Y(1) &= \$0 - 0 = \$0 \\
Y(2) &= \$20.00 - 17.29 = \$2.71 \\
Y(3) &= \$10.00 - 8.13 = \$1.87 \\
Y(4) &= \$30.50 - 29.05 = \$1.45 \\
r &= Y(2)/V(1) = 2.71/54.47 = .05 \\
r &= Y(3)/V(2) = 1.87/37.18 = .05 \\
r &= Y(4)/V(3) = 1.45/29.05 = .05
\end{aligned}
$$

The calculations of the net present values of the remaining cash flows at various points in time are illustrated in Table 15-2. The calculations of depreciation, income, and return on investment are illustrated in Exhibit 15-2.

We can express each of the concepts used in terms of the basic cash flows. The present value of the asset at the end of any period t can be expressed as follows:

$$V(t) = \sum_{i=t+1}^{\infty} (1+r)^{-i+t}[N(i) + I(i)].$$

The corresponding expression for period $t-1$ is

$$V(t-1) = \sum_{i=t}^{\infty} (1+r)^{-i+t-1}[N(i) + I(i)].$$

Therefore

$$V(t) = (1+r)V(t-1) - N(t) - I(t).$$

We can express depreciation in period t in terms of $V(t-1)$ and $N(t)$.

$$
\begin{aligned}
D(t) &= V(t-1) - V(t) - I(t) \\
&= V(t-1) + N(t) - (1+r)V(t-1) + I(t) - I(t) \\
&= N(t) - rV(t-1)
\end{aligned}
$$

Income in period t can be written as

$$
\begin{aligned}
Y(t) &= N(t) - D(t) \\
&= N(t) - N(t) + rV(t-1) \\
&= rV(t-1).
\end{aligned}
$$

It follows that the return on investment (r) will be equal to $Y(t)/V(t-1)$ (in this example r is both the time value of money and the yield of the investment) except when $V(t-1) = 0$.

assets with positive present values

In the preceding example we assumed that, before the first cash flow occurs, the net present value of the cash flows associated with the asset is 0. (The yield of the investment is equal to the time value of money.) We shall now consider investment opportunities whose present value is positive. How can we measure income and depreciation in such cases?

The example presented earlier will serve to illustrate this case if we assume that the cash flow associated with the asset in period 1 is $-\$45.00$ rather than $-\$54.47$. The calculation of the present value of the cash flows at the 5 per cent rate of interest is shown in Table 15-3, as are the calculations of depreciation, income, and return on investment for period 1, applying mechanically the definitions and relationships introduced so far. The calculations for

Table 15-3. Computations for Period 1

Period	Cash Flow	Present Value Factor (5%)	Present Value
1	− $45.00	.9524	− $42.87
2	20.00	.9070	18.14
3	10.00	.8638	8.64
4	30.50	.8227	25.09

$$\$ 9.00 = V(0)$$
$$54.47 = V(1)$$
$$37.18 = V(2)$$
$$29.05 = V(3)$$
$$0 = V(4)$$

$$D(1) = V(0) - V(1) - I(1) = \$9.00 - 54.47 + 45.00 = -\$.47$$
$$Y(1) = N(1) - D(1) = \$0 - (-.47) = \$.47$$
$$r = \frac{Y(1)}{V(0)} = \frac{0.47}{9.00} = .05$$

Exhibit 15-3. Depreciation for Each Period

Cash Flow	$0	− $45.00	$20.00	$10.00	$30.50
V(t)	V(−1) = 0	V(0) = 9.00	V(1) = 54.47	V(2) = 37.18	V(3) = 29.05	V(4) = 0
D(t)	0	− 9.00	− .47	17.29	8.13	29.05
Time	−1	0	1	2	3	4

periods 2 through 4 are not shown because they are identical to those presented in Table 15-2.

In addition to the preceding values, we need $V(-1)$, that is, the value one period before we discover the investment. Assuming that $V(-1) = 0$, we then have $D(0) = V(-1) - V(0) = 0 - 9.00 = -9.00$. Thus for period 0 we have $9 of appreciation.

This procedure would present $9 of additional income (appreciation) at time 0 and $.47 of appreciation for period 1 and for each year of operations that follows; the return on investment calculations would show a 5 per cent return as before.[3] Because the depreciation is based on value decreases and the value of the asset at time 1 is $54.47, we find that in years 2 through 4 a total of $54.47 ($9.47 more than cost) is charged to depreciation expense. This seems to violate the accounting convention that an asset should be depreciated on the basis of its original cost, but it should be remembered that in periods 0 and 1 we recorded $9 and $.47 of negative depreciation (appreciation).

We have taken into account that the asset in question has a net present value of $9 as of time 0 and $9.47 at time 1, immediately before expending the $45. That is, the asset's cost is $9.47 less than the present value at time 1 of the cash inflows it provides. The net present value has been interpreted as a gain obtainable from the asset, over and above the normal return implied in the discount rate being used. The $9.47 measures the present value of the unrealized extra profits at time 1 that will be obtained by owning the asset. It results in an asset increase and an increase in the stockholders' ownership. One can interpret the resulting extra depreciation as deriving from the fact that an increase in the asset has been gradually charged to depreciation expense as the cash flows occur and the asset changed from a long-lived investment to cash.

An alternative approach would be to use a higher discount rate in calculating depreciation. If a discount rate is chosen that makes the net present value of the asset equal to 0 as of time 0, and depreciation is calculated using the change in present values at this discount rate, then the total depreciation charge will equal the cash outlay associated with the asset, and the return on investment in each year will be equal to the discount rate used. In this case a discount rate of 15 per cent compounded annually will make the net present value equal to 0. The calculations of the net present values at the end of each period are given in Table 15-4 and additional calculations in Exhibit 15-4.

The use of a higher discount rate (presumably higher than that at which the firm could lend or borrow money) solves some problems but leaves others unsolved. Suppose that the asset whose cash flows were described in Table 15-4 and the one whose cash flows are given in Table 15-2 represented inde-

---

[3] We could start accounting for the investment at time 1, in which case we would have appreciation over cost of $9.47 instantaneously at time 1 and the remainder of the analysis would be identical to that shown.

Table 15-4.   Calculation of Net Present Value of an Asset
at Various Times ($r = .15$)

Period	Cash Flow	Present-Value Factor (15%)	Present Value
1	−$45.00	.8696	− $39.13
2	20.00	.7561	15.12
3	10.00	.6575	6.57
4	30.50	.5718	17.44
			$0 = V(0)$
2	20.00	.8696	17.39
3	10.00	.7561	7.56
4	30.50	.6575	20.05
			$45.00 = V(1)$
3	10.00	.8696	8.70
4	30.50	.7561	23.06
			$31.76 = V(2)$
4	30.50	.8696	$26.52 = V(3)$
			$0 = V(4)$

Exhibit 15-4.   Depreciation, Income, and
Return on Investment in
Each Period for Asset
Described in Table 15-4

$$D(1) = \$0 - 45.00 - 45.00 = \$0$$
$$D(3) = \$45 - 31.76 = \$13.24$$
$$D(3) = \$31.76 - 26.52 = \$5.24$$
$$D(4) = \$26.52 - 0 = \$26.52$$
$$Y(1) = \$0 - 0 = \$0$$
$$Y(2) = \$20.00 - 13.24 = \$6.76$$
$$Y(3) = \$10.00 - 5.24 = \$4.76$$
$$Y(4) = \$30.50 - 26.52 = \$3.98$$
$$r = Y(2)/V(1) = 6.76/45.00 = .15$$
$$r = Y(3)/V(2) = 4.76/31.76 = .15$$
$$r = Y(4)/V(3) = 3.98/26.52 = .15$$

pendent investments available simultaneously to the same company. Perhaps both investments would be accepted. Because they offer identical benefits, the asset described in Table 15-3 is just as valuable as that described in Table 15-2, but it would be carried on the company's books at a lower value. This practice would tend to destroy the usefulness of the return-on-investment calculation as a managerial control device. Suppose that two managers are in charge of the

Exhibit 15-5.   Income and Return on Investment Calculations
                for Asset with Positive Net Present Value

Period 2

Revenue	$20.00
Less: Depreciation of original cost	13.24

Income (based on cost of asset)	6.76
Less: Reduction in unrealized capital gain of asset	4.05

Income (based on value of asset)	2.71

$$\frac{\text{Income (based on cost of asset)}}{\text{Depreciated cost of asset}} = \frac{6.76}{45.00} = 15\%$$

$$\frac{\text{Income (based on value of asset)}}{\text{Depreciated value of asset}} = \frac{2.71}{54.47} = 5\%$$

---

two assets. If both do as well as expected with their assets (that is, achieve the cash flows predicted for their assets), one will have a low return on investment and the other a higher return on investment. Thus the return on investment measures not their operating ability, but the ability (or luck) of whoever originally uncovered the investment opportunities.

We can adjust the first procedure illustrated for those who do not want to recognize the unrealized appreciation as income. Suppose that the asset is carried on the books under two headings: (1) cost of the asset, and (2) the difference between the present value and the cost of the asset. The cost would be reduced each period by a depreciation expense computed by taking the change in the present value of the cash flows, using the yield (the interest rate that makes the present value of the investment equal to 0). The difference between the value and the cost would be reduced each year by an additional amount calculated so that the total of the two asset accounts equaled the value of the asset. The incomes and returns on investment for the investment in period 2 are shown in Exhibit 15-5.

An alternative interpretation would be to define the depreciation of the period to be the decrease in value ($17.29) and then recognize that a portion of the unrealized gain recognized prior to the beginning of operations has

Exhibit 15-6.   Income Based on Cost

Period 2

Revenue	$20.00
Less: Depreciation based on value decrease	17.29

Income (based on value)	2.71
Plus: Capital gain considered to be realized	4.05

Income based on cost	6.76

Table 15-5. Computation of Incomes

Period	Revenue	Depreciation (based on value)	Income (based on value)	Realized Gain	Income (based on cost)
0	—				
1	—				
2	$20	$17.29	$2.71	$4.05	$ 6.76
3	10	8.13	1.87	2.89	4.76
4	30.50	29.05	1.45	2.53	3.98
	$60.50	$54.47	$6.03*	$9.47	$15.50

* This measure of income omits the $9.00 of period 0 and the $.47 of period 1 (appreciation of the investment) on the grounds that these gains have not been realized.

Table 15-6. Computation of Realized Capital Gains*

Period	Depreciation (based on value)	Depreciation (based on cost)	Realized Gain
2	$17.29	$13.47	$4.05
3	8.13	5.24	2.89
4	29.05	26.52	2.53
	$54.47	$45.00	$9.47

* We could also have taken the difference in incomes resulting from the use of the two methods of depreciation. Identical results would be obtained.

been realized in period 2. The amount of the realized gain is equal to the difference between the depreciation of the investment cost using the yield of the investment and the depreciation based on value using the time value of money. Exhibit 15-6 shows the incomes for this interpretation.

The two incomes presented in Exhibit 15-6 are the same as the incomes presented in Exhibit 15-5, although the interpretation is somewhat different and their order is reversed.

Table 15-5 shows the computation of the incomes for each period and Table 15-6 the computation of the realized capital gains.

tax effects

The preceding discussion applies if there are no income taxes, or if the cash flows and the discount rates used are on an after-tax basis. In general, the value of an asset or investment opportunity will depend on the tax status of the investor. Thus it may be profitable for the investor who undertakes an investment to sell the resulting asset to another investor whose tax status is different.

Consider the asset described in Table 15-3. After the expenditure of $45,

Table 15-7.   Value of an Asset to an Investor in the 40 Per Cent Tax
Bracket If It Is Held

Before-Tax Cash Flow	Depreciation for Taxes	Taxable Income	Income Tax	After-Tax Cash Flow	Present-Value Factor	Present Value
$20.00	$15.00	$ 5.00	$2.00	$18.00	.9709	$17.48
10.00	15.00	(5.00)	(2.00)	12.00	.9426	11.31
30.50	15.00	15.50	6.20	24.30	.9151	22.24
$60.60	$45.00	$15.50	$6.20	$54.30		$51.02

the value of the future cash flows from the asset will be worth $54.47 to investor B, if B is not subject to income taxes. Suppose that the original investment has been made by A, that A is subject to a marginal tax rate of 40 per cent on his taxable income, and that taxable income is computed using straight-line depreciation on the cost of the asset. Since A is subject to a tax rate of 40 per cent, if the before-tax interest rate is .05, A's after-tax interest rate will be .03. Table 15-7 shows the present value of A's after-tax cash flows from the asset at a discount rate of .03, provided he retains the asset.

Suppose that A arranges to sell the asset at time 0 to B for $54.47. A is subject to a capital gains tax at the rate of 20 per cent on the $9.47 difference between this selling price and his cost of $45. His after-tax proceeds are $45 + (9.47)(.8) = $52.58. Thus A has a net gain of $1.56 from selling the asset immediately, instead of retaining it.

An even better strategy may be for A to wait until the beginning of the last year of the asset's life. At that time the present value of the remaining cash flows to B will be ($30.50)(.9524) = $29.05. If A can sell the asset for that price and pay a capital gains tax on the difference between its depreciated cost ($15.00) and the selling price, his after-tax proceeds from the sale will be $15 + (.8)(14.05) = $26.24. In that case, the present value of the cash proceeds to A will be as follows:

Table 15-8.   Value of an Asset to an Investor in
the 40 Per Cent Tax Bracket If It Is
Sold After Two Periods

Period	After-Tax Cash Flow	Present Value Factor	Present Values
1	$18.00	.9709	$17.48
2	12.00	.9426	11.31
2	26.24	.9426	24.73
			§53.52

The present value in this case is $2.50 greater than if A did not sell.

Even when different investors are subject to different tax rates, opportunities for transactions motivated by differences in tax status would be eliminated if taxable income were determined by using depreciation based on value. When this convention is adopted, two investors who expect the same before-tax cash flows from an asset will assign it the same value at each point in time, even though each investor values the asset by discounting the after-tax flows it could generate for him.[4]

As an example, suppose that an investor is subject to income taxes at a rate of 40 per cent. Taxable income is defined as the change in the present value of the future cash flows from an asset. If interest payments for such a taxpayer are tax deductible and the interest received is included in taxable income, such a taxpayer would use an after-tax rate of .03 if the before-tax interest rate was .05.

Now consider the asset whose before-tax cash flows are described in Table 15-3. The table also shows the value of the asset at various points in time and the income in period 1. The income for subsequent periods is shown in Exhibit 15-2. The before-tax cash flow and income data are reproduced for convenience in Table 15-9, which shows the tax of each period and the after-tax cash flows, assuming that the definition of income is based on the change in the present value of the asset.

In Table 15-10, the after-tax cash flows and the after-tax discount rate of .03 are used to calculate the value of the asset at various times. At each time, the value of the asset is the same, whether the calculations are done on a before-tax or after-tax basis (compare Tables 15-3 and 15-10).

It is also worth noting that, when the before-tax figures are used and income is computed using changes in value, the return on investment in each period is equal to .05, the discount rate. Since the value of the investment is the same, but the after-tax income of each period is 40 per cent smaller than the before-tax income, the after-tax return on investment in each period will equal .03, the after-tax discount rate.

Table 15-9.   Income Tax and After-Tax Cash Flows When Taxable Income Is Defined in Present-Value Terms

Period	End-of-Period Before-Tax Cash Flow	Income (based on value)	Tax	End-of-Period After-Tax Cash Flow
1	− $45.00	$ .47	$ .19	− $45.19
2	20.00	2.71	1.08	18.92
3	10.00	1.87	.75	9.25
4	30.50	1.45	.58	29.92

[4] See P. A. Samuelson, "Tax Deductibility of Economic Depreciation to Insure Invariant Valuation," *Journal of Political Economy*, 72, Dec. 1964, pp. 604–606.

Table 15-10. Calculation of Net Present Value of an Asset
Based on After-Tax Cash Flows ($r = .03$)

Period	End-of-Period, After-Tax Cash Flow	Present-Value Factor	Present Value
1	− $45.19	.9709	− $43.87
2	18.92	.9426	17.83
3	9.25	.9151	8.46
4	29.92	.8885	26.58
			9.00 = $V(0)$
2	18.92	.9709	18.37
3	9.25	.9426	8.72
4	29.92	.9151	27.38
			54.47 = $V(1)$
3	9.25	.9709	8.98
4	29.92	.9426	28.20
			37.18 = $V(2)$
4	29.92	.9709	29.05 = $V(3)$
			0 = $V(4)$

conclusions

In this chapter we have presented a set of accounting concepts that are consistent with present-value calculations. When these concepts are used, the return on investment of an asset can be related to the rate of discount used in the present-value calculations. Furthermore, if these concepts were used for income tax purposes, the value of an asset would be the same for all investors, even though investors were not all in the same tax bracket. In such a world, we could determine the value of an asset using before-tax cash flows and be sure that the value would not change if we recomputed it using an after-tax flow. In practice, the definitions of income used for tax purposes have little relationship to income definitions suggested in this chapter. This emphasizes the need to make all decisions on the basis of after-tax cash flows.

questions and problems

15-1. An asset costs $17,355 and will earn proceeds of $10,000 a year for two years. The cash is received at the end of each period. The time value of money is .10.

Required: (a) Compute the yield of the investment. (b) Compute the depreciations in value of the asset, the incomes, and returns on investment for the two years of life.

15-2. An asset costs $25,619 and will earn proceeds of $10,000 in year 1 and $20,000 in year 2. The time value of money is .10.
Required: (a) Compute the yield of the investment. (b) Compute the depreciations in value of the asset, the incomes, and returns on investment for the two years of life.

15-3. An asset costs $26,446 and will earn proceeds of $20,000 in year 1 and $10,000 in year 2. The time value of money is .10.
Required: (a) Compute the yield of the investment. (b) Compute the depreciations in value of the asset, the incomes, and the returns on investment for the two years of life.

15-4. An asset costs $20,000 and earns proceeds of $11,000 in year 1 and $10,500 in year 2. The time value of money is .05.
Required: (a) Compute the yield of the investment. (b) Compute the depreciations in value of the asset, the incomes, and returns on investment for the two years of life.

15-5. An asset costs $20,000 and will earn proceeds of $12,000 in year 1 and $11,000 in year 2. The time value of money is .10.
Required: (a) Compute the yield of the investment. (b) Compute the depreciations in value of the asset, the incomes, and the returns on investment for the two years of life.

15-6. An asset costs $15,777 and will earn cash proceeds of $10,000 a year for two years, the first payment to be received two years from now. The sales will be made at the end of periods 1 and 2 and the collections at the end of periods 2 and 3. The time value of money is .10.
Required: Compute the depreciations, the incomes, and returns on investment for the life of the investment.

15-7. An asset costs $8,454 at time 0 and an additional $8,000 at time 1. It will earn proceeds of $10,000 a year for two years, the first payment to be received two years from now. The time value of money is .10.
Required: Compute the depreciations, the incomes, and returns on investment for the life of the investment.

15-8. Continuing problem 15-7. What is the value of the investment at time 1 (after the second investment) if the actual investment outlay was only $5,000 at time 0 and $4,000 at time 1? What is the value at time 2? Assume that the expected benefits are unchanged.

15-9. The tax laws allow accelerated depreciation. Assume that an investment has equal cash flows in each year over its entire life.

Required: Without taxes, what timing of depreciation expense would you recommend to measure income appropriately? What does this imply about the tax depreciation deduction?

15-10. An investment costs $14,059 and has expected cash flows of

0	1	2
− $14,059	$10,000	$5,000

The time value of money of the firm is .05. Management wants a system for reappraising capital budgeting decisions. (a) Assume that the accounting measures of expense (except for depreciation) and revenues would be the same as the preceding. Prepare statements of income and return on investment that would be reasonable tools for reappraisal of the decisions. (b) Assume that the cash flows just indicated apply, but the accounting measure of net revenue in period 1 is $14,762 and the net revenue in period 2 is $0. What is the depreciation of periods 1 and 2?

15-11. The XYZ Company wants to know the cost of a new building it has constructed. It paid the builder an advance of $2 million and paid the remainder when the building was completed two years later (total amount paid to the builder was $3 million). (a) Determine the cost, assuming that the building was financed with .05 debentures. (b) Determine the cost, assuming that the building was financed entirely by stock.

15-12. The company has an investment opportunity that offers $1 million of cash flows a year for perpetuity. It requires a cash outlay of $19.6 million for plant and equipment and the necessary inventory. It is estimated that an additional $500,000 of cash will have to be carried as a compensating balance during the period of the investment. The company has a time value of money of .05.

Required: Is the investment acceptable?

15-13. The Allen Company is faced with the decision whether to buy or rent data-processing equipment. The initial outlay for the equipment is $380,000 if purchased. The rentals are $100,000 per year and are cancellable on one month's notice by the Allen Company. Similar service contracts may be obtained if the equipment is purchased or rented.

The time value of money is 10 per cent. The income tax rate is zero.

The best estimate of service life is five years, but an analysis of the life of equipment of a similar nature indicates that the life may be as follows:

Year	Probability (%)
1	0
2	1
3	2
4	25
5	40
6	30
7	2
8	0

Required: Should the equipment be purchased or rented?

15-14. High Voltage Electric Company has $10 million of debt outstanding, which pays 7 per cent interest annually. The maturity date of the securities is fifteen years from the present. There are $100,000 of bond issue costs and $200,000 of bond discount currently on the books.

Assume that a fifteen-year security could be issued which would yield 6 per cent annually. The issue costs on the new issue would be $300,000, and the call premium on the old issue would be $500,000. (a) The company has a 10 per cent cost of capital. Assume a zero tax rate. Should the old bonds be replaced with new securities? (b) Assume a discount rate of 7 per cent. What would be your answer?

15-15. Referring to problem 15-14, how would your answer be affected by the possibility of interest rates decreasing in the future and the new bonds being issued for a thirty-year period?

15-16. The Giant Motor Car Company is considering the size that would be most desirable for its next assembly plant. We shall assume that there are the following two alternatives:

	Large Plant	Small Plant
Initial costs	$20,000,000	$4,000,000
Out-of-pocket cost savings per year, assuming the assembly of different numbers of cars per year		
100,000 cars		1,000,000
200,000 cars	...	
300,000 cars	2,000,000	
400,000 cars	4,000,000	

A forecast of car sales indicates the following demand for automobiles assembled in this plant:

First year after completion of the plant	100,000 cars
Second year after completion of the plant	200,000
Third year after completion of the plant	200,000
Fourth year after completion of the plant	300,000
Fifth year and thereafter for the expected life of the plant of twenty years	400,000

The company has a cost of money of 10 per cent. For purposes of this problem assume an income tax rate of zero.

Required: Which one of the two plants is the more desirable?

chapter 16

capital budgeting and inflation

The basic principles of capital budgeting are applicable when there is a risk of inflation as well as when the risk of inflation is negligible. However, it is not always easy to apply these principles correctly when the risk of inflation is of primary importance. The purpose of the present chapter is to offer some suggestions about how to consider inflation in an effective manner. When inflation is possible, future cash flows may differ not only in their timing but in their purchasing power, and we may want to determine whether money flows or purchasing power flows are more useful in describing the outcomes of an investment and in making decisions about alternative investments. In addition, selecting an appropriate discount rate in the presence of inflationary risks is more complex.

what is inflation?

In a dynamically growing economy, price changes take place constantly. In the highly organized markets for securities and for some commodities, it is normal for prices to change from one transaction to the next. In other cases— for example, most real estate leases—prices (rents, in the case of a lease) are fixed by contract for a period of years. Sometimes the price of a particular good or service may exhibit an upward or downward trend that can last for months, years, or even decades.

The price changes that are the result of shifts in the supply or demand for particular goods and services do not imply any change in the general price level. Increases in the price of some goods or services will be offset by decreases in others, so that the average level of prices may remain more or less constant.

A change in the average price level takes place if there is a strong tendency for all prices to move up or down in proportion to one another. Inflation is a rise in the average price level; deflation is a decline in the average price level. In the United States, price-level changes have tended to be inflationary during most of the last half-century; during the preceding half-century, the price-level changes tended to be deflationary.

Although the idea of an average price level is a useful tool, it is important to be aware of its limitations. The statisticians who construct price-level indexes must decide what goods to include in the index and what weight to assign to each. A commonly used index, the consumer price index, is designed to measure the average price of the goods consumed by an average-sized middle-income urban family. It is a reasonable measure for this purpose, but the price level it records may not accurately reflect the buying habits of large low-income rural families or of a business enterprise. Many families and almost all business organizations will have important components of their revenues or expenses whose movements are not closely tied to the average price level of consumer goods in the short run, or even in the long run. In these circumstances careful consideration of the prices of specific goods and services of particular importance to the decision makers is required. In evaluating capital budgeting decisions a businessman must consider not only the possible effects of inflation, but also the effect of long-run trends in the relative prices of his products and of his important categories of expenditures.

This point is particularly important because the prices of many of the most important goods and services purchased by businessmen are not directly included in the commonly used price indexes. Labor is the prime example. Wage and salary payments are a major expense item for almost every business. Yet wage rates are not directly included in price indexes used to measure the rate of inflation or deflation. However, labor costs are reflected in the costs of the consumption goods and services that are included in the price indexes.

Up to this point we have described investments in terms of cash flows. If the price level rises, the purchasing power of a dollar will decline. For some purposes it may be equally useful to measure the costs and benefits of an investment in terms of dollars of constant purchasing power. Suppose that an investment will return $100 this year and $100 next year. If the price level rises 4 per cent between now and next year (the price index is 100 for this year and 104 for next year), the $100 to be received next year will have a purchasing power in terms of this year's dollar of $100/1.04 = $96.15.

To distinguish in this chapter between cash flows measured in dollars and cash flows measured in terms of purchasing power, the former will be referred to as money cash flows and the latter as real cash flows. The symbol $R\$$ will be used to denote real cash flows. Thus, in the example used in the previous paragraph, R$96.15 is the real cash flow of the investment next year.

real cash flows and money flows

The process of analyzing a capital investment project involves at least two distinct steps. First, the costs and benefits of the project must be described in some meaningful way. Second, the costs and benefits must be evaluated in terms of the goals and objectives of the decision maker. In each of these steps the decision maker has a choice of whether money cash flows or real cash flows will be used.

It has long been recognized that one of the disadvantages of an unstable price level is that it makes the task of appropriately analyzing the economic advantages and disadvantages of different alternatives more difficult and complex. In the present chapter it is our intention to illustrate with specific examples techniques that may be used to take the possibility of inflation into account.

Although capital budgeting decisions may be made using either money or real flows, there may be differences in our ability to estimate the necessary inputs, the costs and benefits of an investment project. Generally, if revenues or costs are mainly determined by market forces in the period in which the outlays are made or the revenues received, estimates in terms of real cash flows are likely to be more accurate than estimates of money flow. But if future costs and revenues are determined by immediate decisions, by income tax considerations, or by long-term contractual relationships, estimates in terms of money flows are likely to be more accurate.

Money values are converted into real values by dividing the monetary value by an appropriate price-index relative. For example, suppose that an investment promises to return $100 per year for the next two years and that the cash proceeds measured in money values are certain. At 9 per cent, the present value of the monetary value is $175.91. Suppose that the price index for the current period is 140; it is expected to be 145.6 next year and 151.424 the following year. We wish to convert the money values in all three years to real values in terms of this year's price level. To do this the first step is to construct price-index relatives for each of the three years. A price-index relative is a ratio of two price-index values. The value in the numerator is the value of the price index for the year in which the cash flows will occur. The denominator is the price index of the base period (the real values are to be expressed in terms of the purchasing power of that period). In this case the price-index relatives are $140/140 = 1$ for the current period, $145.6/140 = 1.04$ for next year, and $151.424/140 = 1.0816$ for the following year.

To convert money values to real values, the money values for a given period are divided by the price-index relative for that period. The real value of the $100 to be received next year is R$96.154 ($100/1.04) and the real value of the $100 to be received the following year is R$92.456 ($100/1.0816).

Suppose that a firm is considering investing $10,000 in a machine that has a useful life of five years. For simplicity, assume that for tax purposes the machine will be depreciated (zero salvage) on a straight-line basis over its life. With the machine, one worker using 2,000 pounds of raw materials per year can produce 1,600 units of product per year. In current prices the machine will cost $10,000, the worker, $8,000 per year, and the raw material $2 per pound. The firm is subject to a combined federal and state corporate income tax rate of 60 per cent. The product can be sold for $10 per unit.

In each of the five years, if there are no changes in any of these prices, the cash flow will be as follows:

Revenues 1,600 × $10	$16,000
Labor expense	8,000
Raw material expense	4,000
Income taxes	1,200
Net cash flow	$ 2,800

However, even with no change in the general price level, these assumptions may not be valid. For example, assume labor expense will rise by 2 per cent per year even if there is no change in the price level. Labor expense in year 5 will be approximately 10 per cent higher ($1.02^5 = 1.104$). This will increase labor expense by $800, reduce tax payments by $480, and reduce the cash flow by $320 to $2,480 for year 5.

Now suppose that the price level is 10 per cent higher in year 5 and that this price-level change is reflected in strictly proportional changes in the product and raw material prices. Suppose also that labor expense is 10 per cent higher than it would have been without inflation, that is, $9,680 per year. Calculating the cash flow in year 5 under these assumptions, we have the following:

Revenues: 1,600 × $11	$17,600
Labor expense: 8,000 × 1.1 × 1.1	9,680
Raw material expense	4,400
Income taxes	912
Net cash flow	$ 2,608

If we assume an upward drift in labor expense and if the decision maker is concerned only with money outcomes, he may conclude that inflation is to his advantage. His money cash flow is $128 higher in year 5, with a 10 per cent increase in the price level than without it ($2,608 compared to $2,480).

Table 16-1. Examples of Effects of Price Level and Labor
Expense Changes on Money and Real Cash Flows

Assumptions			
Real wages	No change	+10%	+10%
Price level	No change	No change	+10%
Money cash flows			
Revenues	$16,000	$16,000	$17,600
Expenses			
Labor expenses	8,000	8,800	9,680
Raw material	4,000	4,000	4,400
Income taxes	1,200	720	912
Net cash flow	$ 2,800	$ 2,480	$ 2,608
Real cash flows	R$ 2,800	R$ 2,480	R$ 2,371

But with a 10 per cent inflation the money cash flow of $2,608 in year 5 is equivalent, in purchasing power, to $(1/1.10)(\$2,608) = R\$2,371$. It is this amount that should be compared to $2,480, which will be received (real and money cash flow) without inflation. With inflation the decision maker's real cash flow is R$109 less than without inflation.

Table 16-1 is intended to illustrate the importance of making realistic assumptions about how specific prices are likely to change, with or without inflation.

inflation and the discount rate

We have previously argued that the discount rate is an appropriate means of adjusting for time value. In the present section we shall discuss the choice of discount rates in the presence of possible changes in the price level. Imagine that there are two types of bonds, both issued and fully guaranteed by the government. The first bond is a money income bond. It promises to pay the holder $100 per year indefinitely. The second bond is a real income bond. It promises to pay the holder R$100 per year indefinitely. That is, the real income bond will pay $100 this year, and the real value of $100 next year and in every future year indefinitely. For example, if in some future year the price level rises to 140 (based on a level of 100 now), the real income bond will pay the holder $140 in that year. The real value of that $140 payment will be $\$140/1.40 = R\$100$. Similarly, if the price level declined to 85 in some future year (based on a level of 100 now), the real income bond would pay the holder only $85 in that year, because that sum would have a value of R$100 ($\$85/.85 = R\$100$).

For an investor whose utility depends on money income, the money income bond is a safe asset, with no significant uncertainty. However, for such an investor, the real income bond is a risky asset, because the money value of the payments one will receive from holding it are uncertain.

By contrast, for the investor whose utility depends on real income, the real income bond is a safe asset. However, for such an investor, the money income bond is a risky asset, because the real value of the money payments one will receive from it are uncertain.

It is interesting to note that both bonds could be described as "default free" in that there is no risk that the bond issuer will fail to live up to his contract. Moreover, if one could be certain that no price-level changes were going to take place, the two bonds would be identical; both would pay $100 and $R\$100$ in each future year.

If uncertainty about the future price level is allowed, it may be tempting to jump to the conclusion that the investor interested in money income will buy the money income bond and that the investor interested in real income will buy the real income bond. Whether this conclusion is valid depends on many things, including the price of each bond and risk preferences.

Suppose that the money income bond is selling for $1,250 and that simultaneously the real income bond is selling for $2,000. These prices refer to bonds that return $100 in money and real income, respectively, per annum.

The annual money return on the money income bond is 8 per cent and the annual real return on the real income bond is 5 per cent. In both cases the returns quoted are calculated in the units to which the bond refers. Suppose that it is known in advance that the price level is going to rise steadily at the rate of 3 per cent per year. Let us calculate the present value of the investment alternatives open to investors interested in real returns and those interested in money returns.

For the investor interested in money income one alternative is to buy the money income bond. This returns 8 per cent in money terms. If he wants to compare this alternative with the real income bonds, the investor may transform the real income of the real income bonds into money income, calculate the present value of the money income stream at 8 per cent (the interest rate on default-free money income streams), and compare the present value of the proceeds with the present value of the money income bond. The calculations are as follows:

Period	Real Cash Flow	Price-Level Relative	Money Cash Flow	Money Present-Value Factor	Money Present Value
1	$R\$100$	(1.03)	$\$103$	$(1.08)^{-1}$	$\$95.37$
2	100	$(1.03)^2$	$100(1.03)^2$	$(1.08)^{-2}$	90.91
3	100	$(1.03)^3$	$100(1.03)^3$	$(1.08)^{-3}$	86.74
$\vdots$					
n	100	$(1.03)^n$	$100(1.03)^n$	$(1.08)^{-n}$	$100 \times \dfrac{(1.03)^n}{(1.08)^n}$

In each line in the table the present-value factor is of the form $(1.03)^n/$ $(1.08)^n$. This ratio may be approximated by $1/(1 + .08 - .03)^n = 1/(1.05)^n$.[1] The present value of the money income received from the real income bond is equal to the present value of an infinite sequence of receipts growing at 3 per cent and discounted at 5 per cent, which is approximately $2,000. Because the present value of the money proceeds using 8 per cent as the discount rate is approximately equal to the cost of the real income bond, the money rate of return the investor would earn on the real income bond is approximately 8 per cent.

In the absence of uncertainty the money income investor would be indifferent between the money income bond and the real income bond. If there were uncertainty about future price levels, the money income investor might prefer the money bond; its return will be 8 per cent, whereas the money return of the real income bond is uncertain, although it is expected to return 8 per cent in money terms.

Now let us consider the investment alternatives available to the investor whose utility depends on the real cash flows he receives. This investor will wish to compare both bonds in terms of the real cash flows they provide.

One alternative is to buy the real income bond with a real return of 5 per cent per year. If he wants to compare this alternative with money income bonds, the money cash flows of the money income bond must be transformed into real cash flows. Then these real cash flows should be discounted at the time value of real money, which is 5 per cent in this example. The calculations are as follows:

Period	Money Cash Flow	Price-Level Adjustment Factor	Real Cash Flow	Real Present-Value Factor	Real Present Value
1	$100	$\dfrac{1}{(1.03)}$	$\dfrac{100}{1.03}$	$\dfrac{1}{1.05}$	R$92.46
2	100	$\dfrac{1}{(1.03)^2}$	$\dfrac{100}{(1.03)^2}$	$\left(\dfrac{1}{1.05}\right)^2$	85.50
3	100	$\dfrac{1}{(1.03)^3}$	$\dfrac{100}{(1.03)^3}$	$\left(\dfrac{1}{1.05}\right)^3$	79.05
$\vdots$					
n	100	$\dfrac{1}{(1.03)^n}$	$\dfrac{100}{(1.03)^n}$	$\left(\dfrac{1}{1.05}\right)^n$	$\dfrac{100.00}{(1.03)^n(1.05)^n}$

In the real present-value column each line in the table for year n is of the form $\$100/(1.03)^n(1.05)^n$. The product $(1.03)^n(1.05)^n$ is approximately equal

---

[1] The exact value is .04854, not .05. If we used continuous price level and interest, functions .05 would be exact since $e^{-.08t} \times e^{.03t} = e^{-.05t}$.

to $(1.03 + .05)^n = (1.08)^n$.[2] Each \$100 in the infinite series is being multiplied by $(1.08)^{-i}$ and the sum of this series is approximately $R\$1,250$. Thus the value of the money income bond is approximately equal to its cost, and the real rate of return of the money income bond is 5 per cent.

In the absence of uncertainty, in this situation the real income investor would be indifferent between the money income bond and the real income bond. If there were uncertainty about future price levels, the real income investor might prefer the real income bond, because its real cash flows will be certain. For the real income investor, uncertainty about the future price levels creates uncertainty about the real present value of the money income bond and reduces its desirability, although the real expected return of the money income bond is the same as for the real income bond.

Certain features of this example have general applicability. First, the appropriate discount rate depends on whether money or real cash is being discounted. Before discounting a series of money flows they should be adjusted for future price-level changes into real cash values if the discount factor being used is a default-free rate that refers to real income flows (such as the 5 per cent used above). Alternatively, we may convert real cash flows into money terms if a default-free rate, such as the 8 per cent rate in the preceding example, is used.

Second, the degree of uncertainty associated with an investment may depend on the goals of the investor as well as the characteristics of the investment. If there is uncertainty about future price-level changes, one cannot arbitrarily say that one of the two bonds used in this example is safer or provides a more certain return than the other. It depends on the objective of the investor. A business firm that wants to raise additional funds and has available the alternatives of issuing real income bonds or money income bonds has a decision analogous to that of the investor.

In the American economy, no commonly available securities exactly correspond to real income bonds. But if the United States economy continues to be as inflation inclined in the future as it has been in the postwar period, there will be a desire for such securities.

The example used in this section of the chapter assumed that the expected real rates of return on both money income bonds and real income bonds were the same (when expectations about inflation are taken into account). There are strong economic forces in the real world that tend to produce this result. If the expected real return on money income bonds was less than on real income securities (such as stocks), two processes would be set in motion. First, investors interested in real returns would sell their money income bonds and buy real income securities (stocks). Second, security issuers concerned with the real cost of raising funds would tend to refinance by substituting money bonds for stocks. Both processes would tend to raise the real return

---

[2] The product $(1.03)^n(1.05)^n$ is equal to $(1.0815)^n$.

on money income bonds, and lower the real return on stocks. In a society in which most security holders are interested in real income, these processes are likely to continue until the real returns on the two types of securities are nearly equal.

If the expected real return on the two types of securities is equal when investors expect inflation, the initial yield (interest divided by investment) will be higher for money income bonds than for real income securities. This is illustrated in the example by the fact that a money income bond costs only $1,250 whereas a real income bond costs $2,000. In the absence of inflation both provide the same $100 cash flow per year and if no inflation were expected both bonds might sell for the same price.

It is traditionally assumed that for corporate issuers the average cost of debt is less than the cost of equity, and the investors in stock expect a higher return than investors in bonds because stocks have more risk. Although this assumption has been valid in the past, an important implication of the analysis in this chapter is that this traditional relationship between the costs of debt and equity need not necessarily continue.

The traditional relationship between the relative costs of debt and equity is based on the belief that debt is safer than stock because it has a definite and prior claim on income (and assets), whereas equity is riskier than debt because its claim is indefinite and residual. This relative evaluation is reasonable in a society in which the risk of depressions and recessions (most of which is borne by equity holders and employees) is great and in which price inflation is not an important factor. However, investors may some day conclude that the risks of periodic spells of inflation are considerable and that the risks of severe recessions or depressions, and resultant business failure, are relatively minor. If so, they may also decide that from a long-term point of view, the risks associated with owning a diversified portfolio of common stock are less than those of owning debt securities not protected from inflation. When these decisions are reflected in market prices, it is possible that the required expected monetary returns from debt will exceed the required expected returns from equity. This implies that the inflation risk of the debt might tend to balance the financial and business risk of stock, and that someday investors might prefer the risk characteristics of stock.

questions and problems

16-1. Assume that the price level is expected to increase by .05 in the coming year. What return do you have to earn on an investment of $100 to earn .06 on your investment in terms of real purchasing power?

16-2. A one-year $100 debt security is issued to yield .10. It is expected that there will be .08 inflation during the next year. What return, in real terms, will the security earn if the prediction of price-level change actually is fulfilled?

16-3. A three-year $100 debt security is issued to yield .10 ($133.10 will be paid after three years). It is expected that there will be .08 inflation per year during the time period. What return, in real terms, will the security earn if the prediction of price-level change actually occurs?

16-4. Which is more risky, a mortgage bond or common stock of a large oil company? Explain.

16-5. The ABC Company is building a plant that is expected to cost $10 million to service the capacity needs of the firm for the next three years. For another $2 million it can build excess capacity that is expected to fill the needs for an additional seven years. It is expected that it would cost $3 million to make the identical changes three years from now. The firm's cost of money is .10. Should the excess capacity be purchased?

16-6. The ABC Company is considering an investment costing $1 million that is expected to yield .04. Debt funds can be obtained to finance this investment at a cost of .05. The justification offered for the investment is that there is expected to be inflation; thus there will be a gain at the expense of the bondholders (they will be holding fixed dollar claims). The .04 yield of the investment includes appropriate adjustments in cash flows because of the expected inflation. The lives of the investment and the debt are comparable. Can the investment be justified?

16-7. Prepare an example or an explanation that indicates why each of the following is an insufficient description of the goals of a profit-seeking organization: (a) maximize profits or earnings per share; (b) maximize the price per share of the common stock now; (c) maximize the price per share of the common stock in the future; (d) maximize sales (or percentage of the market).

16-8. The ABC Company has opened 100 new stores. It has incurred a great deal of expenses associated with opening the stores, and the stores have not yet built up enough clientele to be profitable. However, the stores are operating at profit levels exceeding expectations and there are indications that they will be very profitable in the future. It is obvious that the stock market has not yet digested this latter fact, and the stock of the company is currently depressed compared to management's appraisal of value. The company has the opportunity to acquire an additional fifty stores this year, but to do so will require new stockholder capital acquired from the market (it has borrowed all it feels it is prudent to borrow and cannot obtain more capital from its current stockholders). Without the new capital the stockholders can expect to earn an equivalent annual yield of .15 on the current market value of their investment (assume that there is $100 million or 1 million shares of stock outstanding). The stock is currently selling at $100 per share and paying a $6 per share dividend. The earnings are $7.50 per share ($7.5 million in total).

The new investments would require $10 million to be obtained by issuing 100,000 new shares of common stock. The investment would return $1.2 million per year available for dividends for perpetuity. The stockholders desire a .08 return per year on their incremental investments.

Required: (a) Should the corporation issue the new shares and undertake the investment? (b) What would be your recommendation if the corporation had the necessary cash already available?

16-9. Continuing problem 16-8. Change the statement of the problem so that the present stockholders can expect to earn dividends of $6 per share or an equivalent annual yield of .06 for perpetuity, unless the new investment is undertaken. Should the new investment be undertaken?

16-10. Continuing problem 16-8. Change the statement of the problem so that the present stockholders can expect to earn $8 million, or an equivalent return of .08 per year on the current market value of their investment, if the new investment is not undertaken. Should the new investment be undertaken?

16-11. The ABC Company can borrow and lend funds at an interest rate of .08. It can invest $11 million in a risky project that on the average will lead to net cash flows of $1 million per year. A consultant has suggested that the firm use its cost of capital of .10 in computing the present value of the investment. The investment's life is extremely long. Insurance can be purchased that will guarantee the $1 million per year. Should the investment be undertaken? How much could the firm afford to pay for the insurance?

16-12. The ABC Company currently has outstanding $1 million of .05 debt with a maturity of two years. The only way it can finance a $500,000 investment would be by refinancing the $1 million with $1.5 million of .08 debt, also maturing in two years. The investment would pay $55,000 in year 1 and $555,000 in year 2 (the investment has a yield of .11). The firm has a cost of capital of .10:

Cost of equity	.12 × .5 = .06
Cost of debt	.08 × .5 = .04
	.10

Should the investment be accepted?

chapter 17

Bill Shankly, manager of Liverpool's defending champions in the English Soccer League, comments: "The way some people talk about modern football [soccer], anyone would think the results of just one game was a matter of life and death. They don't understand. It's much more serious than that."

—*The New York Times, p. 7. January 13, 1974.*

investment timing

In this chapter the term timing will be used to refer to decisions about when a new investment should be undertaken and when an investment should be terminated. For certain categories of investment decisions, the question of when to start is critical. An investment may seem desirable if the only alternatives considered are to accept or reject the investment now. However, if the alternative of undertaking the investment at a later time is possible, that may be preferable to accepting the investment now. In principle, the timing problem could be handled by considering a mutually exclusive set of alternatives: undertaking the investment now, or undertaking it one period from now, or two periods from now, and so on. But more efficient techniques for approaching this problem are available. We shall consider some of these in this chapter.

Frequently, in making investment decisions the useful life of the investment must be determined. This can be accomplished in at least two ways. First, the desirability of an investment may be affected by the estimate of its useful life. Thus the estimated profits from growing trees are critically affected by assumptions about when they will be harvested. Second, the decision to undertake an investment may require terminating an existing investment. Planting a new crop of trees may require harvesting the existing stand of trees; or buying a new car may require selling the old one. In these cases the salvage value of the existing investment, the costs incurred, and the revenues that might be received if it were not scrapped now will influence the decision of when to undertake the new investment.

In timing problems the relationships among the cost and revenue streams of the various alternatives are frequently complex. But the basic principles

320

at work are not difficult to understand. To help focus on the basic principles, we begin with a simple example of a class of situations in which timing problems are important, but no investment decision is involved.

basic principles of when to start and stop a process

In Figure 17-1, the curve R represents the contribution to overhead (revenues minus variable costs) that will be generated at time t of a day if the business is operating. The line F represents the fixed costs that could be avoided if the business were not operating at time t. On the X axis time is measured from zero to twenty-four hours.

Let us first make the assumption that the business must operate continuously around the clock if it operates at all. For example, a private water works company may be obliged to operate twenty-four hours a day if it operates at all, even though the contribution to overhead produced during certain night-time hours does not even cover the avoidable fixed costs of the time period. In these circumstances there is no timing problem, and it will be economically desirable to operate only if the total area under the R curve exceeds the total area under the F curve over the entire cycle of operations.

In some situations the manager is free to decide when to operate and when to shut down. For example, the owner of a supermarket may not be obliged to operate on a twenty-four-hour basis. In this situation, considering only explicit revenues and costs, the enterprise should operate only during the interval in which the contribution to overhead from operations exceeds the avoidable fixed costs of operating. In Figure 17-1 this interval extends from t_1 to t_2. The operations should start at t_1 and cease at t_2, since between these points $R \geqq F$; in other words, the contribution exactly equals or is larger than the avoidable fixed costs.

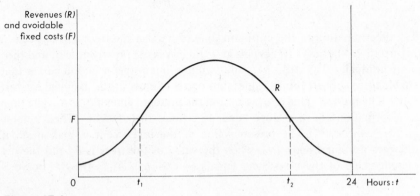

Figure 17-1

The conclusion from these illustrations is that if there is a choice about when to start and stop an operation, it should be started when revenues equal costs and are rising; and it should be stopped when revenues equal costs and are falling.

As we shall see, this simple rule is really applicable to all the situations considered in this chapter. In applying the rule, the conceptual difficulties center on identifying the relevant revenues and costs.

growth-type investments[1]

Suppose that a firm owns a tract of land and is considering planting a crop of trees. It wishes to determine the net present value of that investment. Since the net present value will depend on when the trees are harvested, an estimate of that date is required. If the firm makes the investment, it is prepared to harvest the trees when the net present value of the investment is maximized. Let

$f(t)$ = net revenue (net of all finishing expenses) obtainable if the trees are harvested in year t.

$f'(t)$ = slope of $f(t)$, that is, the rate at which the obtainable net revenue is changing with time.

i = market rate of interest.

C = cost of planting trees.

e^{-it} = present-value factor for time t.

P = net present value of the investment.

The net present value of the investment if the trees are harvested at time t is

$$P(t) = -C + e^{-it}f(t). \tag{1}$$

The determination of the optimum time to harvest the trees can be seen in Figure 17-2. The curve $f(t)$ begins at 0 and increases, rapidly at first, and then more gradually. The paths a_0a_1 and b_0b_1 are time-transformation curves that enable us to convert future values into present values at the assumed interest rate i. The present value of a_1 is a_0, and the present value of b_1 is b_0. The time transformations have a slope equal to i times their height. (Their heights are a_0e^{it} and b_0e^{it}.) The present value of the investment is maximized if the trees are harvested at t_2, when the value of the trees is b_1 and the net present value of the investment equals $(-C + b_0)$. At t_2 the $f(t)$ curve is

[1] This section is based in part on Harold Bierman, Jr., "The Growth Period Decision," *Management Science*, 14, No. 6, Feb. 1968.

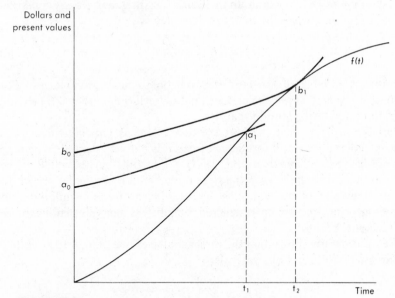

Figure 17-2

tangent to the time-transformation curve. It follows that the slope of the $f(t)$ curve is $if(t_2)$ at t_2. Thus the value of t at which the present value of the investment is maximized must satisfy the condition that

$$f'(t) = if(t). \tag{2}$$

Recall that $f'(t)$ is the increase in the value of the trees per year. Thus the condition for an optimum is that the increase in the value of the trees must equal the interest rate times the value of the trees.

In terms of the criteria for stopping referred to in the previous section, the increase in the value of the trees if they are not harvested corresponds to the revenues, and the interest on the value of the trees corresponds to the fixed cost that can be avoided by harvesting.

The rule considered previously for deciding when to harvest ignores the value of the land on which the trees are planted. If additional land of comparable quality is available in any desired amount at no cost, the economic value of the land is zero, and it need not be considered in deciding when to harvest trees growing on it.

Ordinarily, the value of the land must be considered. Suppose that if the trees were harvested the cleared land would be worth an amount $V(t)$ at time t. In that case the avoidable fixed costs incurred if the trees are allowed to grow include both the interest on the value of the standing trees and the interest on the value of the land. In these circumstances, a necessary condition that should be met when the trees are harvested is

$$f'(t) = i[f(t) + V(t)].$$ (3)

Of course, the value of the land depends on its best available use. For example, if the best use of the cleared land is for farming, then $V(t)$ should reflect the value of the land in that use.

Suppose however that the best use of the land is growing trees. Then although equation 3 is still formally correct, it is not very helpful. When the trees are harvested depends on the value of the land; but the value of the land will depend on how often the trees growing on it can be harvested. In this case the value of the land must be determined on the assumption that the trees growing on it are harvested and replanted at intervals that maximize the value of the land.

We have already shown that the present value of one crop of trees, if they are harvested at the end of t years, is

$$P(t) = -C + f(t)e^{-it}.$$

Assume that the trees are replanted every T years and that we want to determine the optimum value of T. Let $V(T)$ be the present value of the land under these circumstances. Then $V(T)$ is determined as follows:

$$V(T) = P(T) + P(T)e^{-iT} + P(T)e^{-i2T} + P(T)e^{-i3T} + \cdots.$$

Summing this infinite series,

$$V(T) = \frac{P(T)}{1 - e^{-iT}} = \frac{-C + f(T)e^{-iT}}{1 - e^{-iT}}.$$ (4)

We want to select the value of T that maximizes $V(T)$. It can be shown that the value of T that maximizes $V(T)$ satisfies the following relationship:

$$f'(T) = i[f(T) + V(T)].$$ (5)

In practice, the best way to determine the optimum value of T is by trial and error, using equation 4. Equation 5 is basically the same as equation 3, but in deriving equation 5 we have given an explicit method of determining the value of the land in its use for growing trees. Equation 5 can be interpreted as follows: a crop of trees should be allowed to grow until the annual increase in its value declines to the point where it is equal to the market interest rate times the sum of the value of the current stand of trees plus the present value of the future crops of trees that could be grown on the land if the present crop were harvested now.

tree farm example

Suppose that the net realizable value of a crop of trees on a particular parcel of land as a function of their age is given by the following equation:

$$f(t) = -350 + 60t - .5t^2, \quad \text{for } 10 \le t \le 30. \tag{6}$$

Assuming a continuously compounded rate of interest of 5 per cent per year, Table 17-1 shows the net realizable value of the trees from one growth cycle at various ages, their percentage rates of growth, and their present value. If the value of the land is ignored, the trees would be allowed to grow until the rate of increase in their value declines below 5 per cent (in year 23). This is the age at which the present value of the realizable value of the trees is maximized.

Suppose however that after the trees were harvested the land could be sold for $500 or converted to some other use whose value was $500. In that case the amount realized when the trees were harvested would be $500 + f(t)$.

Table 17-1.

Age of Trees t	Realizable Value f(t)	Annual Increment in Value f'(t)	Rate of Increase in Value f'(t)/f(t)	Present-Value Factor e^{-it}	Present Value $f(t)e^{-it}$
10	$200	$50	.2500	.6065	$121.30
11	250	49	.1960	.5770	144.25
12	298	48	.1611	.5448	162.35
13	346	47	.1358	.5220	180.61
14	392	46	.1173	.4966	194.67
15	438	45	.1027	.4724	206.91
16	482	44	.0913	.4493	216.56
17	526	43	.0817	.4274	224.81
18	568	42	.0739	.4066	230.95
19	610	41	.0672	.3867	235.89
20	650	40	.0615	.3679	239.14
21	690	39	.0565	.3499	241.43
22	728	38	.0522	.3329	242.35
23	766	37	.0483	.3166	242.52*
24	802	36	.0449	.3012	241.56
25	837	35	.0418	.2865	239.80
26	872	34	.0390	.2725	237.62

* Maximum present value.

Table 17-2.

Age of Trees t	Realizable Value of Land and Trees 500 + f(t)	Annual Increment in Value f'(t)	Rate of Increase in Value $\dfrac{f'(t)}{500 + f(t)}$	Present-Value Factor e^{-it}	Present Value $e^{-it}[500 + f(t)]$
10	$ 700	$50	.0714	.6065	$424.55
11	750	49	.0653	.5770	432.75
12	798	48	.0602	.5448	434.75
13	846	47	.0556	.5220	441.61
14	892	46	.0516	.4966	442.97
15	938	45	.0480	.4724	443.11*
16	982	44	.0448	.4493	441.21
17	1,026	43	.0419	.4274	438.51
18	1,068	42	.0393	.4066	434.25
19	1,110	41	.0369	.3867	429.24
20	1,150	40	.0348	.3679	423.09
21	1,190	39	.0328	.3499	416.38

* Maximum present value.

Table 17-2 shows the appropriate calculations in this case. Under these circumstances it would pay to harvest the trees when they are between the fourteenth and fifteenth year. After that time the rate of increase in the value of the trees is less than 5 per cent of the amount that could be realized by cutting the trees and putting the land to some other use.

If the most economical use of the land is to grow trees, the value of the

Table 17-3.

Age of Trees t	Net Present Value of One Crop of Trees Growing for t Years $P(t) = -50 + e^{-it}f(t)$	Annuity Factor $\dfrac{1}{1 - e^{-it}}$	Value of Land $\dfrac{P(t)}{1 - e^{-it}} = V(t)$
10	$ 71.30	2.54	$181.10
11	94.25	2.36	222.82
12	112.35	2.20	246.81
13	130.61	2.09	273.25
14	144.67	1.99	287.39
15	156.91	1.90	297.41
16	166.56	1.82	302.46
17	174.81	1.75	305.29*
18	180.95	1.69	304.94
19	185.89	1.63	303.09
20	189.14	1.58	299.22

* Maximum present value.

Table 17-4.

t	V(t)	f(t)	f'(t)	$\dfrac{f'(t)}{V(t) + f(t)}$
10	$181.10	$200	50	.1312
11	222.82	250	49	.1036
12	246.81	298	48	.0881
13	273.25	346	47	.0759
14	287.39	392	46	.0677
15	297.39	438	45	.0612
16	302.46	482	44	.0561
17	305.29	526	43	.0517*
18	304.94	568	42	.0481
19	303.09	610	41	.0449
20	299.22	650	40	.0421

* Closest to .05.

land in this use must be determined. But the value of the land depends on the frequency at which crops are harvested and the costs of planting a new crop. Table 17-3 shows the value of the land when crops are harvested at various ages, if the cost of planting is $50. This is an application of equation 4. Harvesting in year 17 maximizes the present value of the land.

Table 17-4 applies equation 5 to this situation. Both equations 4 and 5 result in an optimum life of seventeen years per crop.

equipment replacement

The question of when to replace an existing piece of equipment with another machine that will perform the same function is very similar to the question of when to harvest a crop of trees. One difference is that in the case of trees we are seeking to maximize the net present value of the revenues that we can receive from the land, whereas in the equipment-replacement problem we are seeking to minimize the net present value of the costs that will be incurred from owning and operating a sequence of machines.

In the machine problem, the costs incurred by retaining the existing machine are the costs of operating it for the current period (including any necessary repairs and maintenance), the decline in its salvage value during the current period, and the interest on the current salvage value of the existing machine. If the machine is retained for one additional period, we benefit by delaying for that length of time the costs of acquiring and operating all subsequent replacement machines. The magnitude of the latter cost is measured by the market interest rate times the present value of the costs of acquiring and operating all subsequent replacements. This present value will depend critically on how long each subsequent replacement equipment is retained. Thus the decision about when to replace the current machine requires an estimate of the economic value of its anticipated replacements, just as the decision about when to harvest a crop of trees depends on the future use that will be made of the land occupied by the trees.

questions and problems

17-1. Why may a supermarket stay open during certain hours even though fixed operating costs are not recovered in these hours?

17-2. The formulation

$$f'(t) = rf(t) \quad \text{or} \quad r = \frac{f'(t)}{f(t)},$$

where r is the internal rate of return, is sometimes suggested (let growth continue until r is maximized). Using the example of the chapter, with land free, what does this imply about the growth period? What is the deficiency of the solution?

17-3. Trees growing in value at .15 per year are currently worth $1,000,000 The land itself (without the trees) is worth $5,000,000 now and one year from now. Money is worth .10. Should the trees be harvested now?

17-4. What is your answer to problem 17-3 if the trees are growing at .20 per year and money is worth .05?

17-5. A grove of trees can be harvested at time 1 or time 2 with the following results:

| Harvest at Time | Period | | | Rate of Return |
	0	1	2	
1	− $1,000	$1,400		.40
2	− 1,000		$1,822.50	.35

Money has a time value of .05. At what time should the trees be harvested? The land has no alternative use.

chapter 18

Without development there is no profit, without
profit no development.

—Joseph A. Schumpeter, *Theory of Economic Development*
(Cambridge, Mass.: Harvard University Press, 1934), p. 154

evaluating private investment proposals: a national economic point of view

In the other chapters we have been concerned with methods of evaluating the economic worth of proposed investment projects from the point of view of the managers or owners of a business. An investment proposal that appears desirable to the business that proposes it may be considered to be unattractive from the point of view of a government that tries to measure the investment's impact on the country. Similarly, a proposal that is unattractive to a business may be considered to be attractive to the government. The purpose of the present chapter is to introduce the reader to some of the differences between evaluating investment projects from a business point of view and from a national economic point of view.

Many executives in private business corporations will encounter situations in which to do their jobs effectively they must understand how investments are evaluated from a national economic point of view. In many countries it is necessary to obtain government approval before an important business investment can be undertaken. This is particularly likely in some of the less-developed countries of the world, but it is by no means limited to such countries. A businessman contemplating an investment in such a country must be prepared to justify his investment not only to his board of directors but to officials from a finance ministry or a government planning office. These officials will be more interested in the cost and benefits from a national point of view than in the profitability to the corporation. However, many principles of economic analysis relevant to evaluating investments from the point of view of the owners are also relevant to evaluating investments from a national economic viewpoint.

Most businessmen would want to give some attention to the effects an investment might have on groups other than the owners of the business proposing it. In recent years, for example, American businessmen have been called upon to cooperate in helping to solve the balance of payments problems of the United States. It is not difficult to cite examples in which business investments that were economic from the point of view of the business organization proposing them were opposed by others because of water pollution, air pollution, or detrimental effects on scenic values.

The primary considerations to be incorporated in an evaluation of investments from a national economic point of view are

1. How large are the net benefits that would be derived from the proposed investment?
2. Who would receive the benefits?
3. By what means would the benefits become available to the recipients?

The first question refers to matters of economic efficiency. The second refers to matters of income distribution. The relevance of these two questions should be fairly clear. The relevance of the third question may be less apparent. The means by which benefits are distributed to a group may influence the satisfaction they derive from the benefits. It seems likely, for example, that both American farmers and countries that derive foreign exchange from exports of basic commodities would prefer an increase in income resulting from a higher price for the commodities they sell, to an equal increase in income in the form of a grant that has the characteristics of an unearned gift.

Although in principle the answers to all three questions are relevant to deciding on the value of a proposed investment, we shall concentrate in this chapter on the computations that must be made in order to measure the size of the net benefits.

In the following discussion we shall assume that we begin with an investment proposal that has already been analyzed from the point of view of its profitability to the owners of the business, using the procedures suggested earlier. The process of adjusting this analysis to a national economic point of view can be thought of as consisting of three basic steps.

In evaluating investments a businessman uses market prices to estimate the relevant cash flows. However, for a variety of reasons, market prices may not reflect opportunity costs of resources used or the opportunity value of the production. Whenever there is a systematic and material difference between the market price and these opportunity prices, the latter should be substituted for corresponding market prices. This substitution would be applicable to most investments, and its materiality would be particularly important in developing countries where the importance of investment decisions is magnified because of the crucial need for investments.

A second type of adjustment is necessary when an investment is so large, relative to the markets in which its factors of production will be purchased or in which its products will be sold, that acceptance of the investment will appreciably change the relevant market price or opportunity price of one or more of the resources used or produced. When this is the case, neither the market prices, or the opportunity costs that would have prevailed without the project, nor the prices with the project will exactly measure the benefits or costs of accepting the project. In these circumstances we should use a price in between the price that would have prevailed without the project and the price that will prevail with it.

Some investment projects will lead to changes in the efficiency of other economic activities in the society. Such changes in efficiency may be beneficial or detrimental. In either case it is desirable to take them into account when evaluating the economic worth of investments from a national point of view.

The following sections discuss each of the preceding adjustments in some detail.

discrepancies between market prices and opportunity prices

The opportunity price or cost of a resource is the value of the resource used in its most valuable manner. In a competitive market there is a strong tendency for market prices to represent opportunity prices. Customers will tend to purchase additional units of a product whenever the value of the product to them is more than the price. Similarly, producers will tend to produce an additional unit whenever the price of an additional unit is greater than the extra cost of producing it (where cost is the opportunity cost of the factors of production). In equilibrium, under these conditions, the price of a commodity will measure both the value of an additional unit to customers and the incremental cost of producing it.

Monopoly Pricing

When a commodity is being produced under monopolistic (or oligopolistic) conditions, market prices are likely to differ from opportunity prices. A firm in a monopolistic position will find that it can increase its profits by pricing its products at something more than the extra cost of producing an additional unit. The market price will represent the marginal value of the commodity to the marginal user, but not generally the cost of producing an additional unit.

If an investment proposal involves using factors of production purchased from a monopolistic firm, a better measure of the cost of the project, from a national economic point of view, can be obtained by substituting an estimate of the marginal cost of the products for the actual market prices.

Unemployed Resources

If in the absence of the project a resource would be unemployed, and if the resource cannot be stored, the appropriate opportunity price for using that resource in the project may be zero. In some countries there is considerable unemployment and underemployment of resources, particularly unskilled labor. If a person who would otherwise be unemployed is put to work as a result of a new investment project, the wages he will be paid may considerably overstate the true opportunity cost of using him in this particular project. In fact, the opportunity to work may have a positive value taking into consideration the morale of the unemployed workers. With some particularly unpleasant or dangerous work the opportunity price may be greater than zero. More importantly, if labor must be induced to move from one location to another or be retrained, there may be some significant opportunity costs in employing the labor, even if the alternative would be to leave it unemployed. In addition to the direct cost of moving the workers, there may be costs associated with providing housing, schools, and various government facilities for the additional population at the new location. These are costs that might be avoided if the workers remained in their old location. Even allowing for such costs the market wage rates are likely to overestimate the opportunity cost of unskilled labor in countries where there is chronic unemployment.

Foreign Exchange Shortages

So far we have considered cases when the market price for using a resource was higher than its opportunity price. There are also important cases when the market price is liable to be less than the opportunity cost of employing a resource. An important example involves the use of imported goods or services. The official exchange rate may not properly measure the opportunity price of foreign exchange. If a businessman imports a commodity, the price he pays is likely to be the world market price converted to domestic prices at the official exchange rate. The opportunity cost for foreign exchange is a better estimate of the cost to the country of using foreign exchange in this way. Some projects may produce goods for export. The value of a foreign exchange earned by the exports may be underestimated when the official exchange rate is used. The investment project may produce goods that are not exported but are substitutes for imported goods. Such goods may save foreign exchange by reducing the amount that would have otherwise been imported. Again the value of the foreign exchange saving should be estimated by using an opportunity price for an exchange rate to compute the value of the imports rather than the official exchange rate.

Savings Versus Consumption

Ordinarily, in attempting to evaluate an investment project we measure the extra income (the benefits less the costs) that would be generated by the project, but we do not concern ourselves with how this income would be used. A justification for stopping with a measure of income is that, if the recipients are free to allocate income in any manner they desire, the opportunity value of an additional dollar used for savings will have the same value as an additional dollar used for consumption. In some less-developed countries this assumption may not be valid at the national level. If the country's economic development is inhibited by low levels of savings and investment, an increment of income saved and invested may be of greater value in promoting the economic interests of the country than an increment of income used for current consumption. In these circumstances it might be desirable to go beyond simply measuring the income generated by a project and to attempt to estimate how that income is likely to be used. The proportion of income that goes into savings may be given more weight than the proportion going into current consumption. The addition value attached to income that is saved and reinvested can be thought of as an opportunity price for savings.

Taxes

A major difference between the way investments would be evaluated from the point of view of the businessman and from the point of view of a national economy is related to the treatment of taxes. The businessman will be concerned only with the after-tax cash flows associated with the investment. This is correct from the national point of view if the taxes are really prices charged for services rendered to the business by government bodies. Examples are tax assessments covering services such as water, sewage, police, and fire protection. Such taxes need to be deducted, but they may require adjustment, as it is unlikely that they reflect the additional cost of providing the additional services used as a result of the investment. Expenditures reflecting the costs of providing such services are a proper deduction from the benefits of an investment from the national economic point of view.

Most tax payments, however, cannot usefully be thought of as payments for identifiable quantities of services rendered a particular business. A large fraction of taxes collected in any country is likely to be used for such things as health, education, and national defense (or paying for past wars). A business may benefit from such services in a general way, but there is not likely to be an identifiable relationship between the amount of taxes paid by the business and the amount of benefit received. Because this is the case, from the national economic point of view, the costs and benefits of an investment should be analyzed on an individual investment basis with an attempt to measure the cost of the government services to be used and the contribution of the investment to the financing of these services.

We have previously mentioned that, if a country's ability to achieve its economic goals is inhibited because savings are too low to finance the desired level of investment, it may be reasonable to attach a high opportunity price to that portion of the project's income that is channeled into savings. Government savings might be used to finance either its own investment projects or those of the private sector. If a government devoted a proportion of its tax revenues to savings and if political or administrative complications did not prevent the effective use of these savings, the extra revenues generated by a new investment project might have more value in contributing to the country's economic goals than the same amount of funds retained in the hands of consumers. This analysis suggests than an opportunity price may in some situations be assigned to government tax revenues. This will increase the measure of benefits associated with investments that generate tax revenues.

indivisibilities

If a project is large relative to the markets of the country so that the operation of the project would change the market prices of one or more of the inputs purchased or of the products being produced, the net benefits of the project to a nation may not be properly measured using market prices. This may be true even when the market prices represent the opportunity costs of using the resources consumed in the project and the opportunity values of the resources produced. This special evaluation problem arises if for some technological reason the investment must be undertaken on at least a certain minimum scale, large enough so that some of the relevant prices would change as a result of building the project. There are many situations where a series of small incremental investments is not feasible technologically. A jet airport runway must be of a certain minimum size; a dam cannot stop halfway across a river; and a railroad must have at least one set of tracks, preferably with reasonable starting and ending locations.

Suppose that a hydroelectric project results in a 25 per cent increase in electric output and that a 50 per cent reduction in the price of electricity results in a sufficient expansion of the use of electricity to absorb this extra power. Even if the new price of electricity appropriately measures both the marginal cost of producing an extra unit of electricity and the marginal value of the extra unit in its various uses, the benefits of the investment cannot be measured in terms of revenues collected. Under the assumptions given, accepting the project would lead to a 37.5 per cent reduction in total revenues collected by the electric power generating system. If revenues were used as a measure of the benefits, one might conclude that the 25 per cent increase in output led to a reduction in total benefits.

One difficulty in this case arises because the price at which all the electricity is sold tells how much one more increment of electricity would be worth when added to the existing supply. In fact, the project added not one small increment to the supply but a very large increment. Consumers as a group would have been willing to pay more for the output of the project. The value of this additional increment, expressed as a price per unit, will be an amount somewhere between the market price that would have prevailed without the project and the market price that will prevail with it.

The appropriate measure of benefits in such cases is illustrated in Figure 18-1. The vertical axis measures the price per unit, and the horizontal axis measures the rate of consumption in kilowatts per year. The curve ee is a market demand curve for electricity. Each point on the curve shows the quantity people would purchase at the corresponding price. Suppose that without the project a quantity OA would be produced (the marginal cost is AB) and sold at a price of AB. The total revenue collected under these circumstances is measured by the rectangle $OABS$. With the project, an additional quantity

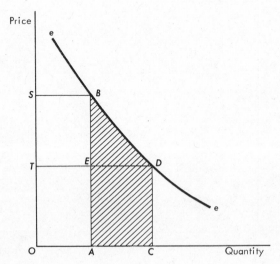

Figure 18-1

AC would be produced (with a marginal cost of CD). The market price will now be CD per unit. If all units are sold at that price, the total revenue collected with the new project would be measured by the rectangle $OCDT$. The additional amount that consumers are willing to pay for an increment of AC units of additional electricity, if the alternative were to do without this increment, is measured by the shaded area $ACDB$. It is this shaded area rather than the change in total revenues that properly measures the extra benefits from having this increment of electricity.

It is still necessary to subtract from these benefits an appropriate measure of the extra costs of providing this electricity. A problem similar to the revenue calculation occurs if a new investment project would materially change the prices of some of the resource inputs used in the project. Figure 18-2 presents an example of this sort. Suppose that in a country with only one steel mill it is proposed to build a second steel mill. Both the old and the new steel mills will require metallurgists. With just one steel mill OG metallurgists would be employed in the old mill at a salary of GH. The curve ss represents the potential supply of metallurgists at various salary levels. With the new mill, let us suppose that the total number who will be required in both the old and new mill increased by an amount GI. (The exact amount of the increase will depend on the demand curve of the product.) To increase the supply by this amount, it will be necessary to pay a wage equal to IJ. The total wage bill for metallurgists with one steel mill is given by the area $OGHL$. The total wage bill for metallurgists with two steel mills is given by the area $OIJK$ However, the excess of the large area over the small area does not properly measure the extra cost to the country of obtaining the metallurgists required

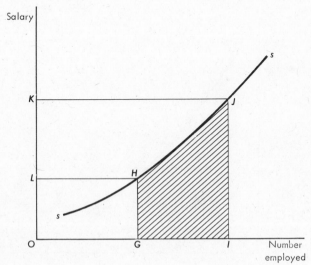

Figure 18-2

for the new mill. These extra costs are measured by the shaded area *GIJH*. The additional monetary payments that would in fact be paid to metallurgists if the new mill were built are transfers of income (in this case from the owners of the steel mill to the metallurgists) in excess of the minimum needed to increase the supply of metallurgists.[1] The actual wages would be used by a private owner of the mill, including the excess incentive to the workers; it should not be included in evaluating the new mill from the national economic point of view.

external effects

An investment project may adversely affect the productivity of resources employed in other economic activities or the welfare of the population. To the extent that such changes are compensated for through market or legal institutional arrangement, their effect will tend to be included in the private benefit–cost evaluation of the investment. If the institutional arrangements do not provide for appropriate monetary compensation, these effects should be taken into account by incorporating implicit costs or benefits in evaluating the investment.

Suppose that a factory will produce a large amount of dirt and smoke. Consumers living where the dirt settles will spend more time dusting their furniture and more time and money cleaning clothes. Breathing the polluted air may even shorten their lives. In the absence of an appropriate tax on the factory that reduces its profit and compensates consumers for the additional expense and trouble, the smoke would be an uncompensated external diseconomy that should be taken into account in evaluating a project from the national point of view.

In other cases an investment may directly affect the productivity of resources employed in other enterprises. If a farmer installs drainage tiles on his field, the productivity of some of his neighbors' fields receiving the runoff may also be increased. An oil company drilling a wildcat well on its own land may provide valuable information about the possibility of oil on adjacent land that it does not control. Sometimes a drilling company is able to obtain compensation from its neighbors for the value of this information in the form of a payment toward the cost of the well, but generally there is no compensation for this type of information. A private utility may build a dam to generate electricity. An uncompensated effect of the dam might be to reduce the danger of flooding on downstream land. Unless it owned the land, the utility would not count this as a benefit derived from its investment. From the national point of view, decreased flood damage is a benefit attributable to the dam.

[1] For the minimum amount to take place, a discriminatory wage system would have to be used.

investments by governments

Governments facing investment decisions have exactly the same basic problem as business managers, that is, measuring the costs and benefits of each period and transforming them all back to the present so that one measure of value may be obtained.

The public servant does have a somewhat more difficult problem of measuring benefits because he knows he should include the social benefits (and costs) of the project. The business manager may choose to take refuge in profit maximization of the firm and not include the social costs and benefits. (We are not saying that this position is desirable.)

Government projects are not without risk, so the government worker is also faced with the necessity of making a risk analysis. The position of a national government is analogous to that of a well-diversified investor when it comes to evaluating project risk. Primary attention must be focused on the systematic risk of the project.

The choice of interest rate is an interesting problem. The government has two basic choices:

1. Its borrowing rate.
2. The opportunity cost to the economy as measured by the cost of funds to business or the required return the firms are using.

The borrowing rate of the government is attractive because it is objectively measured and easily determined. Unfortunately, the rate itself is frequently a result of decisions of government (or near government) officials and may not reflect the opportunity cost of investments to the economy.

The second measure considered is the cost of funds to firms (or their required return); this measure is attractive, but again the information is difficult to obtain. Firms use a wide range of hurdle rates and frequently include risk adjustments. The rate used to take time value of money into account should not include a risk factor. Risk should be analyzed as explained in Chapters 11 and 12.

An added complication is the fact that business firms are taxed and government entities are not. Thus the investments of government should be placed on the same tax basis as the investments of corporations. This also means that the discount rate used by the government body should be on the same tax basis as the business firm.

For example, if we assume that investors require a return of .06 for both debt and stock, and if there is a .48 corporate tax rate, the following represents the cost of capital calculation:

	Before-Tax Required Return	Tax Rate	After-Tax Return to Cor-poration	Return to Investor	Tax Saving from Interest	After-Tax Cost to Cor-poration
Debt	.0600	.48	.0600	.0600	.0288	.0312
Stock	.1154	.48	.0600	.0600	—	.0600

	After-Tax Cost	Capital Structure	Weighted Average
Debt	.0312	.4	.0125
Stock	.0600	.6	.0360
			.0485

To make its discount rate equivalent, the government body would compute a before-tax required return. Thus its time value of money would be as follows:

	Before-Tax Required Return	Capital Structure	Weighted Average
Debt	.0600	.4	.024
Stock	.1154	.6	.069
			.093

Although the .093 required return is higher than the .0485 after-tax return of the business firms, it must be remembered that we are placing the government required return on a before-tax basis that is equal to the before-tax required return of the business firm. There is also a difference in the way benefits are measured. The private firm will apply its after-tax required return to the after-tax cash flows from the investment. If the government uses an equivalent before-tax discount rate, it should be applied to the before-tax benefits of the project. As was explained in Chapter 15, if the definition of income for tax purposes is consistent with present value concepts, the value of the project will be the same whether it is measured by applying the after-tax rate discount rate to the after-tax cash flows, or by applying the before-tax discount rate to the before-tax cash flows.

The argument may be made that the required return of government should be lowered because the benefits of a business firm are incorrectly measured (omitting social costs) and the benefits of government enterprises are under-stated (omitting social benefits). These facts may require an adjustment, but the adjustment should not be in the form of changing the required time-value factor. Also, if either of the .06 required returns included a risk factor, this factor should be excluded by the government in discounting for time. Risk considerations should be incorporated as described in Chapters 11 and 12.

cost–benefit analysis

The use of the term *cost–benefit analysis* to describe the valuation of government projects is widespread. Although the term might well refer to several different procedures, the usual interpretation is a ratio of the present value of benefits to the present value of costs. This is, of course, the same calculation that we described as the index of present value.

We were critical of the present-value index as a method of ranking investments and all the criticisms carry over to the cost–benefit calculation. However, its use is appropriate and beneficial if

1. All investments are accepted whose benefit–cost ratio is greater than 1
2. All the benefits and costs are instantaneous; the best investment is the investment that has the largest ratio. (The other investments can then be undertaken.)
3. The best investment is "continuous" in the sense that we can invest all the funds in it.
4. Only investments with benefit–cost ratios greater than 1 are accepted; then at least the government has chosen an acceptable investment. (It may not be the best.)
5. The computation of the benefit–cost ratio initiated a calculation of the benefits and costs of the investment.

conclusions

It is apparent that different analyses of the desirability of investments may be appropriate for managerial decision making and for decision making where the objective is to take the national economic point of view into consideration. We have suggested several adjustments that might be made to the analysis prepared by the business manager. These adjustments generally require subjective judgments by the analyst.

The business manager might wish for a laissez-faire attitude on the part of government and for the government planners to allow any investment deemed desirable by a person willing to bet his fame or fortune, but the institutional fact remains that in many countries the considerations described in this chapter are relevant.

It is obvious that the businessman should be aware of factors taken into consideration by the government planning organization when it attempts to decide whether or not a private investment project should be approved. In like manner the planning organization that is not aware of the factors considered by the business manager (or owner) in making his investment decision is at a severe disadvantage.

The discussion in this chapter of adjustments that can be made to investment project proposals to make them reflect the projects' effects on the national economy should not be interpreted as a recommendation by the authors that governments should institute controls over private investment activity. A full discussion of this issue is beyond the scope of this book, although some points might be mentioned. Market prices may imperfectly measure the national economic benefits of a project, but it does not follow that a system of investment controls would be preferable. Market prices have the advantage of being relatively objective; their use facilitates decentralized decision making and prompt adjustment to changed circumstances. At best, direct government controls have the disadvantage of adding to the time and expense needed to implement investment decisions. There is no guarantee that an attempt to estimate the national economic benefits of a project, requiring as it does a high level of analytical ability and a detailed knowledge of many sectors of the national economy, possibly influenced by political considerations, will in practice produce an estimate that is consistently closer to the true measure than the unadjusted private estimate.

questions and problems

18-1. There are three purchasers of a product; each is willing to pay the following amounts for one unit per period:

Purchaser	Price He Is Willing to Pay
A	$10 (for first unit)
A	8 (for second unit)
B	7
C	5

There are four suppliers; each is willing to supply one unit per period at the following prices or higher:

Supplier	Price
W	$12
X	10
Y	9
Z	8 (for second unit)
Z	7 (for first unit)

Assume that the preceding prices for the suppliers also represent their marginal costs.

Required: (a) At what price would you expect the product to sell, and how many units would you expect to be sold per period? (b) What total (maximum) revenue would the purchasers of the product be willing to pay? At what total cost would the suppliers be willing to sell? (c) Assume that A sold for $18 two units it had purchased. What profit would it report? (d) From the point of view of the economy, what would be the change in position as a result of A buying and selling two units? (e) How much could a planner invest to make it possible for A to buy the two units?

18-2. A major investment project will employ 100,000 workers. Presently 40,000 of these workers are employed, but the remainder are unemployed. Those that are employed are currently earning $20 million per year; it is expected that they will earn $60 million per year when the new project begins operation. The other workers will earn $30 million.

It will cost $2 million to retrain the workers for their new jobs and $1 million to move them to new living locations. The cost of new governmental and service facilities at their new location will be $10 million.

Required: Describe how the preceding information would be incorporated into the investment analysis from the point of view of the economy.

18-3. The exchange rate for a country is 2 yen for $1. A piece of equipment for an investment project will cost $100,000 or 200,000 yen. The country is short of dollars and wants to conserve its present supply. The planning board wants to choose between two alternative plans: (a) One suggestion is to use an effective exchange rate of 4 yen to $1. (b) Another suggestion is to use a higher discount rate for investments requiring the use of dollars than for investments using only domestic resources. For example, .08 could be used for the former and .04 for the latter. It is felt that there are current uses for dollars that will return, on a present-value basis, $2 for every $1 invested.

Required: How would you evaluate the desirability of the equipment?

18-4. The country of Rajah has hired a firm of American consultants to decide on the desirability of a private corporation building a steel mill. The net annual benefits are computed to be $200 million and $90 million on an after-tax basis. (The taxes are excise and income taxes.) The consultants computed the present value using the $90-million-a-year benefits.

Required: Comment on the computation of the annual benefits.

18-5. Assume that the appropriate time discount for money is 5 per cent on a before-tax basis and that the income tax rate is 40 per cent. An investment opportunity is available requiring an outlay of $10,000 in year 0 and producing proceeds of $10,500 in year 1.

Required: Compute the present value on a before-tax and after-tax basis.

18-6. The before-tax cash flows are the same as in problem 18-5, but the outlay of $10,000 in period 0 is chargeable to expense for tax purposes in period 0.

Required: Compute the before-tax and after-tax cash flows.

18-7. The Eastern University has been offered a foundation grant of $2 million to establish a program in the administration of the arts. Although the program has been judged to be acceptable from an academic point of view, the president of the university does not want to accept the grant if it will drain resources from ongoing programs.

The following analysis of the program costs has been prepared:

	Annual Costs
Two professors of specialized interests	$ 60,000
Support of research personnel	40,000
Fringe benefits	9,000
Office space and other overhead	10,000
Student support	30,000
Administration	11,000
Overhead	20,000
Total	$180,000

Required: Should the president accept the grant?

18-8. The Airplane Company has a cost-plus-fixed-fee contract with the Air Force to build superjet transports. The government will buy any additional equipment that is needed and that is justified on a cost-saving basis.

The incremental tax rate for the company is .4.

The company has computed the following labor saving for a new piece of equipment that costs $18,334:

Time Period	
1	2
$10,000	$10,000 before tax
6,000	6,000 after tax

The company has an after-tax time value of money of .05, and the federal government has a time value of money of .04.

Required: Should the equipment be purchased?

18-9. In 1963 the United States Steel Corporation completed for the U.S. government "A Techno-Economic Survey of a Proposed Integrated Steel Plant at Bokaro, Bihar State, India."

The following quotations are taken from the study:

Profitability—Operations of the plant at Step I levels alone would be unprofitable even though operations are projected at full capacity following completion of start-up. . . . Each year of the projected period produces a cash deficit which reaches $270 million in 10 years or an average annual deficit of $27 million.

Presumably, government of India loans will cover these deficits.

Upon examination of the profitability of Bokaro it is evident that the heavy burden of excise duties and large interest payments on loans are the greatest influences on the results. Production costs on the other hand indicate that Bokaro could be a relatively low cost steel producer based upon the facilities proposed and the assumptions made with respect to raw materials, manpower and managerial control.

The projected Bokaro expansion in Step II to 2.5 million ingot tons, with operations beginning four years after start of Step I production, will result in profitable operations when close to 100 per cent of capacity is reached and will remain profitable thereafter.

Since the government of India is assumed to own the mill, it is relevant to mention that during the 20-year period an estimated $1.0 billion of revenue would accrue to the government of India from the Bokaro operation, through excise duties on ingots, finished steel products, and coal chemical by-products. Income taxes paid by Bokaro would give the government an estimated $0.5 billion. In addition, the "surcharge," of difference between the retention price and selling price, would amount to about $1.2 billion during the same period and would accrue to the government.

The selling price is the price paid by a plant's customers, the retention price the amount it is permitted to keep. Both are set by the government.

Required: Discuss how the items described should affect the analysis of the Bokaro steel plant.

18-10. The time value of money is 6 per cent in country R and 8 per cent in country P. Country P will not allow foreigners (from country R) to invest directly in country P. Country R is a rich country. Country P is poor. R has a foreign-aid program and it is considering two mutually exclusive proposals for helping country P. These are (a) make a gift of $5 million to country P; (b) make a $20 million loan to country P. Interest on the loan will be 5 per cent, paid annually, with the principal to be repaid in a lump sum after twenty years.

You are a congressman in country R and you will have to vote for one or the other of these two proposals. Assume no uncertainty. Justify your answer, using the net present-value method.

Required: (a) Which alternative should you favor if you want to minimize the cost to country R of the aid it is providing to country P? (b) Which alternative should you favor if you want to maximize the benefit received by country P from R's foreign-aid program?

18-11. A state housing authority will lend funds at a cost of .05 to universities in the state to build student dormitories. The Private University has a proven need for dormitories, expected to cost $50,000,000, that would qualify for the state loans. The board of trustees of Private has consistently followed a policy of borrowing no more than .4 of the cost of any facility and using the university's own resources for the remainder of the cost. There is $50,000,000 of endowment available (legally) for this type of construction, and members of the Board have argued that it should be used. Some argue that while $20,000,000 could be borrowed, they fear the degree of risk that would be associated with having a facility financed with 100 per cent debt.

The current interest rate on long-term industrial bonds is .08 and long-term U.S. government bonds are earning .07.

Required: If you were advising the president of the university and the board of trustees, what would you recommend? What would you recommend if the university did not have the $20,000,000 of cash available for construction?

18-12. The U.S. government has offered to assist a foreign government. For the construction of roads, it will lend $20,000,000 to be repaid 40 years from now. For the first twenty years no interest will be paid, and then .03 interest will be paid per year (first payment twenty-one years from today).

The long-term borrowing rate for the U.S. government is .07.

Required: A Senate committee is investigating the cost of foreign aid. Prepare a statement for the committee.

chapter 19

There is less in this than meets the eye.—

—Attributed to Tallulah Bankhead. *Familiar Quotations* by
J. Bartlett (1955).

fluctuating rates of output

Special problems occur if a firm is faced with a choice of two or more types
of equipment to produce a product, and if there will be fluctuations in the
rate of output at which the equipment will be operated. The fluctuations in
output may be the result of seasonal fluctuations in demand (which cannot
be fully offset by storage), or the fluctuations may result because the rate of
output needed is increasing or decreasing through time. We shall illustrate
the case in which the fluctuations are due to seasonal factors. A similar
analysis would apply if demand were growing or falling.

When there are fluctuations in the rate of output, the amount of productive
capacity needed will be determined by the peak rate of output required. The
seasonal pattern will determine whether the average amount produced during
the year is a high or low percentage of the available capacity.

When there are several types of equipment available, some types may
have higher fixed costs, but lower variable costs, than others. If only one type
of equipment can be used, the choice will depend on the average percentage
of capacity used. For plants that operate at a high average percentage of
capacity, equipment with high fixed costs and low variable costs is likely to
have lower total costs. If the seasonal fluctuations are such that the plant
operates at a low average percentage of capacity during the year, the equipment with lower fixed costs and higher variable costs is more likely to have
lower total costs.

To determine the capacity needed and the average percentage of capacity
at which the plant will be operated, the seasonal pattern of production must
be known. This information is contained in the following table for a hypothetical example.

The maximum rate of production of 6,000 units per quarter occurs during
the July–September quarter, and a plant with this capacity is needed. But the
annual average rate of production will be only 4,000 units per quarter. So

Period	Required Production (Units per Quarter)
January–March	2,000
April–June	5,000
July–September	6,000
October–December	3,000
Total annual production	16,000
Average production per quarter	4,000

the average fraction of capacity at which the plant will operate is 4,000/6,000 or .67. We will assume the 6,000 unit demand has to be met.

Suppose that there is a choice between manual and semiautomatic equipment, but only one type can be used. The basic cost data are as follows:

Type of Equipment	Fixed Costs per Quarter for a Capacity of 1,000 Units per Quarter	Variable Costs of Production per Unit
Manual	$ 80	$1.00
Semiautomatic	$330	.50

The total fixed costs will be determined by the capacity needed; the total variable costs are the product of the variable costs per unit times the number of units of capacity times the average fraction of capacity used. Denoting the latter by p, the average total costs (per quarter) for the production of 6,000 p units utilizing six units of manual equipment are

$$6(\$80) + (\$1)(6,000)p = \$480 + \$6,000p.$$

The average total costs per quarter for a plant utilizing six units of semiautomatic equipment and producing 6,000 p units of product are

$$(6)(330) + (\$.50)(6,000)p = \$1,980 + \$3,000\,p.$$

Setting the two expressions for total cost equal and solving for p, we can determine the breakeven fraction of capacity:

$$480 + 6,000p = 1,980 + 3,000p$$

$$p = \frac{1,500}{3,000} = .50.$$

Thus the semiautomatic equipment is preferred if the fraction of capacity utilized exceeds .5, and the manual equipment if the fraction of capacity utilized is less than .5. Since the actual fraction of capacity to be utilized is .67, the semiautomatic plant would be preferred.

Suppose that fully automatic equipment were also available at a fixed cost of $555 per quarter for a capacity of 1,000 units per quarter. The variable costs per unit are $.25. The total cost of a fully automatic plant would be

$$(6)(\$555) + (\$.25)(6,000)p = \$3,330 + 1,500p.$$

The breakeven point between the semiautomatic and fully automatic equipment is

$$1,980 + 3,000p = 3,330 + 1,500p$$
$$p = \frac{1,350}{1,500} = .90.$$

Thus fully automatic equipment cannot be justified, unless the average fraction of capacity utilized is at least .9.

Given a required capacity of 6,000 units per quarter, the breakeven points can be expressed in terms of average production per quarter. Between manual and semiautomatic equipment, the breakeven point is $(.5)(6,000) =$ 3,000 units per quarter. Between semiautomatic and fully-automatic equipment, the breakeven point is $(.9)(6,000) = 5,400$ units per quarter. Since the actual average rate of production required is 4,000 units per quarter, if only one type of equipment can be utilized, semiautomatic equipment would be preferred. The analysis could also be performed using the fixed costs per year and the capacity for a year. The value of p would not be changed.

Figure 19-1 shows the breakeven points among these three types of equipment, for a plant with a capacity of 6,000 units per quarter.

Optimum Equipment Mix

So far we have assumed that only one type of equipment can be utilized. But in some circumstances several types of equipment can be used in the same plant or productive system. For example, a power-generating system may contain atomic energy generating capacity, fossil fuel capacity, and gas turbine capacity.

In designing a plant that contains several types of equipment, the objective is to have the correct amount of each type of equipment so as to minimize costs. Once a plant has been constructed, it must be operated in the most economical way possible. This requires utilizing the equipment with the lowest variable costs per unit to the maximum extent possible (that is, to its capacity) before resorting to equipment with higher variable costs per unit.

Suppose that we consider the problem of designing an optimum plant to meet the required rates of production specified in the previous model, where

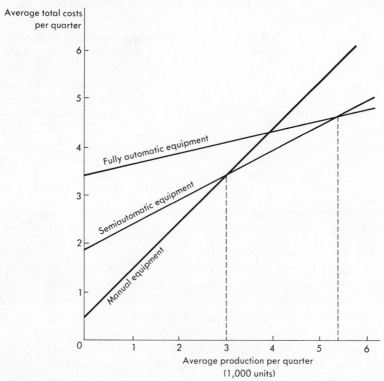

Figure 19-1

the required capacity of 6,000 units per quarter can be divided up among the three types of equipment, manual, semiautomatic, and fully automatic, in whatever amounts are considered desirable.

Note that four rates of production occur. In order of size they are 2,000, 3,000, 5,000, and 6,000 units per quarter. Based on these rates of production, the required capacity can be divided into four incremental components of 2,000, 1,000 ($=3,000 - 2,000$), 2,000 ($=5,000 - 3,000$), and 1,000 ($=6,000 - 5,000$) units each.

The first component of 2,000 units of capacity will be used to meet the lowest rate of production and all higher rates. The second component of 1,000 units will be utilized whenever the rate of production is 3,000 per quarter or more.

Similarly, the third and fourth components will be utilized only when the rate of production equals or exceeds 5,000 or 6,000 units per quarter, respectively.

With the equipment divided into these four components, we can construct an operating plan for the plant to indicate which equipment component is to be utilized each quarter. This plan is presented in Table 19-1.

Table 19-1.   Seasonal Production Plan Using Multiple Equipment
              Components

		Equipment component number: Capacity			
		1 2,000	2 1,000	3 2,000	4 1,000
Quarter	Required Production	Amount to Be Produced from Each Component			
Jan.–March	2,000	2,000	0	0	0
April–June	5,000	2,000	1,000	2,000	0
July–Sept.	6,000	2,000	1,000	2,000	1,000
Oct.–Dec.	3,000	2,000	1,000	0	0
Total production		8,000	3,000	4,000	1,000
Average rate of production		2,000	750	1,000	250
Fraction of capacity utilized		1.00	.75	.50	.25

The last line in the production plan table shows, for each equipment
component, what fraction of that component's capacity will be used. Given
the breakeven points that have already been calculated, it is now possible to
determine what type of equipment should be utilized for each component.
The first component will be utilized all the time. Since fully automatic
equipment has the lowest cost when its rate of utilization is .9 or better,
fully automatic equipment should be used for the first component of 2,000
units. The rate of utilization for the second component of 1,000 units is .75.
At this rate of utilization, semiautomatic equipment has the lowest costs.
The third component will be utilized at a rate of .5. At this rate of utilization,
the costs of semiautomatic and manual equipment are the same; so either of
these types of equipment could be used for this 2,000 units of capacity. The
utilization rate for the fourth component will be only .25, so manual equipment should be chosen for this 1,000 units of capacity.

   Suppose that the plant is designed to contain 2,000 units of automatic
equipment, 3,000 units of semiautomatic equipment, and 1,000 units of
manual equipment. The average total costs per quarter for this plant can be
computed as follows:

Type of Equipment	Capacity	Fixed Costs	Rate of Utilization	Variable Costs	Total Costs
Fully automatic	2,000	$1,100	1.00	$ 500	$1,600
Semiautomatic {	1,000	330	.75	375	705
	2,000	660	.50	500	1,160
Manual	1,000	80	.25	250	330
	6,000	$2,170		$1,290	$3,795

By comparison, the best plant that could be constructed utilizing only one type of equipment would contain only semiautomatic equipment. The average total costs per quarter for such a plant would be

$$6(\$330) + (.5)(\$4,000) = \$1,980 + \$2,000 = \$3,980.$$

Thus a plant with an optimum mix of equipment would reduce costs by $185 per quarter compared to a plant with only one type of equipment (assuming no efficiencies in spare parts and maintenance arising from using one type of equipment).

questions and problems

19-1. A new plant is to be built to produce widgets. Three types of facilities are available: fully automated, semiautomated, and manual. All three facilities have the same expected life and produce widgets that are identical in every respect. Only the cost characteristics of the three types of facilities vary. The fixed and variable costs for each type of facility are shown in Table 19-2. All costs are on an after-tax basis, and fixed costs are expressed in terms of equivalent monthly after-tax cash flows, after allowing for tax savings from depreciation.

To prevent thefts, each widget is produced with the customer's name engraved on it. The name must be engraved before the widget is assembled. This makes it impractical to maintain an inventory of completed widgets. Instead, production must take place after orders are received. Since demand follows a seasonal pattern, widget production is seasonal as well. The anticipated seasonal pattern of demand (and production) is described in Table

Table 19-2. Cost Characteristics of Alternative
Types of Widget Production Facilities

Facility Type	Fixed Cost per Month for Enough Capacity to Produce Q_{max} Widgets per Month	Variable Cost per Widget
Fully automated	$20Q_{max}$	$25
Semiautomated	$14Q_{max}$	35
Manual	$6Q_{max}$	60

Table 19-3. Estimated Demand

Month	Estimated Demand
January	100
February	100
March	300
April	400
May	600
June	500
July	400
August	400
September	300
October	200
November	200
December	100

Estimated annual demand	3,600 widgets/year
Average monthly demand $(\bar{Q}) = \dfrac{3,600}{12} = 300$ widgets per month	

19-3. The peak demand is 600 units per month, and a capacity sufficient to meet this peak demand is needed.

Suppose that the plant to be built can contain only one type of facility:

a. Using the demand forecast in Table 19-3, which type of facility should be chosen?

b. If Table 19-3 were modified by raising estimated demand in all months from March through August to 600 units per month, which type of facility should be chosen?

c. If peak demand (and therefore the required capacity) remained at 600 units per month (Q_{max}), how low would average monthly demand $(\bar{Q})$ have to fall before the manual facility would be chosen?

d. Let the total monthly cost of using the ith type of facility be

$$T_i = Q_{max}F_i + \bar{Q}V_i, \tag{1}$$

where T_i = total monthly cost of the ith facility,

   F_i = fixed cost per month for enough capacity to produce one widget per month using the ith facility,

   V_i = variable cost per unit for the ith facility,

   Q_{max} = maximum level of demand per month (equals required capacity),

   $\bar{Q}$ = average level of demand (widgets per month).

Make a rough graph with T_i on the vertical axis and $\bar{Q}$ on the horizontal axis. Sketch in equation 1 for each of the three facilities on this graph, using $Q_{max} = 600$ and the values of F_i and V_i from Table 19-2.

e. What generalizations can you make about the levels of $\bar{Q}$ at which each type of facility would be preferred?

f. The following equation was obtained from equation 1 by dividing both sides by Q_{max}, and letting $v = \bar{Q}/Q_{max}$.

$$\frac{T_i}{Q_{max}} = F_i + pV_i \tag{2}$$

Make a rough graph with T_i/Q_{max} as the vertical axis and p as the horizontal axis. Sketch in equation 2 on this graph for each of the three facilities, using the values of F_i and V_i from Table 19-2.

g. Does this graph suggest any further generalizations about the type of facility that would be preferred in problems of this type?

19-2. Continuing problem 19-1. Suppose that a widget plant can be constructed that contains more than one type of facility.

a. A widget plant has been constructed that contains six types of facilities. There are 100 units of capacity of each type. In terms of variable costs per widget, facility 1 has the lowest cost, facility 2 the next lowest cost, and so on. You are in charge of scheduling production in this plant and responsible for meeting each month's required production, while minimizing variable costs. Plan your production schedule by completing the following table to show for each month the number of units to be produced in each type of facility.

Month	Required Production	Amount to Be Produced in Facility No.					
		1	2	3	4	5	6
Jan.	100						
Feb.	100						
March	300						
April	400						
May	600						
June	500						
July	400						
Aug.	400						
Sept.	300						
Oct.	200						
Nov.	200						
Dec.	100						
	3,600						

b. For each of the six types of facilities, compute the fraction of that facility's annual capacity which you plan to utilize.

c. If you were designing this plant and had available only the three types of facilities described in problem 19-1, how many units of capacity of each of the three types would you choose in order to minimize total costs? Of the year's production of 3,600 widgets, how many would be produced in each type of facility?

d. Compute the average total cost per month (averaged over a whole year) for the plant design you chose. Compare these costs with the best plant you could devise using only one type of facility.

19-3. *The Algone Case*

Memorandum
TO: Y. P. Student
          Economic Evaluation Manager
          Wedoodit Chemical Corporation
FROM: I. M. Selfmade, President

As you know, the research and development department of our company has developed a new product that we are considering marketing under the brand name of Algone. Algone is an unstable liquid that must be kept under pressure at an extremely low temperature, of approximately $-200°F$. Above this temperature it decomposes within a few minutes. Algone has only one important known commercial application. When a quarter pound of Algone is sprayed through a specially designed applicator onto the feathers of a freshly killed chicken, the feathers completely disappear within seconds. There are no harmful side effects and the product has been approved for use by the Food and Drug Administration.

Wedoodit Chemical is considering two alternative means of exploiting this new product. One possibility is to sell the exclusive rights to the patent to the Chiselem Corporation, which would produce and market Algone. The alternative is for Wedoodit to build a plant to produce the product itself. Chiselem has offered us a straight cash payment of $1 million for the patent rights.

The attached memoranda from the Market Research Manager and the Engineering Manager provide a basis for evaluating the profit potential of Algone if Wedoodit undertakes to manufacture and market the product itself. I expect you as economic evaluation manager, to specify the type of equipment that would be needed for the most profitable manufacturing facility to produce Algone, to present cash flow estimates for the operation of this facility and to make a recommendation as to whether or not Wedoodit should sell its patent rights to Algone.

As you know, we have estimated our cost of capital to be 8 per cent, and it is company policy to exploit all available investment opportunities that can earn us at least that much.

We are subject to income taxes of 54 per cent on incremental income, consisting of 52 per cent federal and 2 per cent state corporate income tax rates.

Memorandum
TO:　　　I. M. Selfmade
　　　　　President
　　　　　Wedoodit Chemical Corporation
FROM:　　V. Gotfigures
　　　　　Market Research Manager
SUBJECT:　Market Potential for Algone

Total Market
　The only significant potential commercial use for Algone is to remove feathers from chickens (broilers) being processed for market. This requires ¼ lb of Algone per bird. Approximately 2 billion chickens are consumed in the United States each year. Poultry consumption has been growing rapidly in the last decade as a result of improved technology and lower costs. However, no further growth in this market is expected. The effects of increased population will be offset by growing competition from turkeys and increased consumption of beef as a result of higher consumer incomes.
　About half of the poultry are processed in plants in very low cost labor areas where Algone would be more expensive than other means of removing feathers, or in plants whose layout is not easily converted to this process. Therefore, we expect the total market potential for this process to amount to 1 billion birds per year for the foreseeable future. This would require 250 million lb of Algone annually, or about 1 million lb per working day (based on a five-day week and fifty working weeks in the year).

Market Share
　Although Algone is patented, news of our discovery has already leaked out to competitors, who are developing similar products not covered by our patents. We are certain to have competitors soon after we begin production. The high capital costs of producing this product and the large potential market will prevent any one firm from dominating the market. We expect to be able to gain and hold 10 per cent of the total U.S. market, equivalent to 25 million lb annually.

Price
　Because alternative means of removing chicken feathers are easily available, a market demand for Algone would be very elastic at prices above 12 cents per pound. It is difficult to know how low the price might go, as this would depend on the costs of our competitors and the danger the industry might overexpand, making the business unprofitable for all concerned. Prices below 8 cents per pound would almost certainly be unprofitable. We estimate the price level will fluctuate around 10 cents, and recommend using that figure for planning purposes. All price quotations are F.O.B. our plant; customers to absorb freight.

Fluctuations in Demand
　Fluctuations in demand are particularly important because Algone is an unstable compound. It cannot be stored except at prohibitive costs. The

product must be shipped the same day it is produced. The effective market area for our plant will be limited to those customers who can receive product no more than twenty-four hours after it leaves the plant. The plant will have to operate Saturday through Thursday, because product shipped on Friday would be received on Saturday and would partly decompose by Monday. Poultry processing plants do not operate Saturdays or Sundays.

Poultry consumption does not fluctuate very much seasonally. But poultry processing *plants* normally operate only a half-day on Friday. Our production of Algone would be correspondingly lower on Thursdays.

Thus a plant that expects to have an average daily output of 100,000 lb should expect a product fluctuation as follows:

Day of Week	Daily Production (*lb*)
Sunday through Wednesday	111,000
Thursday	55,000
Average daily production	100,000

Memorandum
TO: I. M. Selfmade
FROM: W. E. Triedit
            Manager of Engineering
            Design and Pilot Plant Operations Department
            Wedoodit Chemical Corporation

A plant location has been selected for the Algone project in consultation with Market Research and Traffic Departments. Land and associated development costs (nondepreciable) would be $100,000. We hold a ninety-day option on the site.

Two methods of producing Algone have been devised and pilot plant tested. Summary cost figures follow:

Method	Equipment and Installation per 1,000 Lb of Daily Capacity	Variable Material and Operating Expense per 1,000 Lb of Algone Produced
A	$80,000	$ 5
B	$34,000	$45

Either type of equipment would last for ten years and the costs of equipment and installation would be entirely depreciable. No salvage is expected. Variable costs do not include any depreciation and are on a before-tax basis.

In addition to the equipment listed, capital costs for office, shipping, and miscellaneous utilities would amount to $20,000 per 1,000 lb of maximum daily output. The variable costs of operating these facilities are included in the variable costs of methods A and B.

It would be possible to design a plant that would include a provision for producing Algone by both methods A and B in whatever proportions seem desirable. For example, a 50,000-lb daily maximum production could be achieved in a facility having a capacity of 30,000 lb using method A and 20,000 lb using method B. There are no significant shutdown or start-up costs for either method of production.

A plant with a daily output capacity up to 125,000 lb per day could expect fixed costs (for property taxes, insurance, plant guards, etc.) of about $100,000 per year (excluding depreciation). These costs would all require cash outlays and could be charged to expense for income tax purposes. A plant this size would also require working capital (inventories, accounts receivable, and cash) of about $50,000.

19-4. The DEF Company uses a batch process method to produce product S. The product is very perishable so inventories are small, and production is geared closely to current sales. There are two seasons for product S, each season lasts six months. The DEF company has been producing and selling product S at the rate of 30 million units per month during the busy season— which lasts for six months. During the six-month slow season production and sales are only 10 million units per month.

The company is convinced it could sell an additional 5 million units per month during the six-month busy season if additional capacity were available. There is no question that these additional sales would be profitable. There is a question of what type of production equipment should be installed.

The company has a choice between two types of equipment. The batch process equipment is the same as the equipment currently in use. The continuous process equipment was developed a few years ago. Both types are known to be reliable and to produce equally high quality products. Cost data are given below.

Cost Item	Batch	Continuous
Equivalent annual fixed costs: Dollars per year per unit of capacity capable of producing one unit of product per month.	2.20	5.00
Variable costs of producing one unit of product.	0.90	0.50

a. What action would you recommend to the DEF Company if there were no costs savings or salvage values associated with scrapping existing batch capacity?

b. What action would you recommend if fixed costs of 1.00 per year per unit of capacity could be avoided by scrapping existing batch capacity?

part IV

This part of the book consists of three chapters. In Chapter 20 we illustrate how a mixture of investments changes the risk of an investment portfolio, and how the probability of ruin may be affected by an investment strategy.

In Chapters 21 and 22 we make use of matrix notation (which is described in Chapter 21). In Chapter 21 we present models for portfolio analysis and in Chapter 22 a programming approach to capital rationing is developed. Although we do not consider any of these three chapters to be essential for operational decisions at the firm level, they can provide useful insights. Chapter 22 is particularly useful, since it provides a comparison against which rules of thumb for ranking independent investments can be judged.

chapter 20

*But no one has ever won contemporary acclaim
as a hero for wise economy and rationality, nor is
his name celebrated in history books or attached
to magnificent dams—our modern equivalent of
pyramids.*

—J. Hirshleifer, J. C. DeHaven, J. W. Milliman, *Water Supply,
Economics, Technology, and Policy.* (The Rand Corporation,
The University of Chicago Press, 1960), pp. v-vi.

using investment portfolios
to change risk*

introduction

In previous chapters we have stressed that different combinations of investments involve different risks. In recent years the analysis of risk has tended to
focus on two moments of the probability distribution of returns, the mean
and variance.[1] In this chapter we first consider the effect on the variance of
an investment fund of adding dependent investments.[2] Second, the effect of
investment strategy on the probability of ruin is investigated.

Let us consider the investing of I dollars in two investments, X and Y,
with identical means but the investments are not statistically independent.
We are investing α (where α is a decimal fraction between 0 and 1) in X and

---

* Part of this chapter is adapted from an article originally published in the *Journal
of Financial and Quantitative Analysis*, June 1968.
[1] See H. M. Markowitz, *Portfolio Selection: Efficient Diversification of Investments* (New
York: John Wiley & Sons, Inc., 1959) and W. F. Sharpe, "Capital Asset Prices: A
Theory of Market Equilibrium Under Conditions of Risk," *The Journal of Finance*,
Sept. 1964, pp. 425–442; or W. F. Sharpe, "A Simplified Model for Portfolio Analysis,"
Management Science, Jan. 1963, pp. 277–293. The appropriateness of using only means
and variances may well be questioned. The fact that there are ready markets for puts,
calls, warrants, and convertible bonds suggests that skewness and higher moments are
also relevant.
[2] See P. A. Samuelson, "General Proof That Diversification Pays," *Journal of Financial
and Quantitative Analysis*, March 1967, pp. 1–13, for a sophisticated discussion and
proof of the usefulness of diversification.

$1 - \alpha$ in Y. The total variance of our investment is a function of α. If $\alpha = 1$, and Var (P) is the variance of the total portfolio, then

$$\text{Var}(P) = \text{Var}(X).$$

If $\alpha = 0$,

$$\text{Var}(P) = \text{Var}(Y).$$

With α invested in X, the total variance of the investment is [3]

$$\text{Var}(P) = \alpha^2 \, \text{Var}(X) + (1 - \alpha)^2 \, \text{Var}(Y) + 2\rho\alpha(1 - \alpha)\sigma_X\sigma_Y.$$

Taking the derivative of Var (P) with respect to α,

$$\frac{d\text{Var}(P)}{d\alpha} = 2\alpha \, \text{Var}(X) - 2(1 - \alpha) \, \text{Var}(Y) + (2 - 4\alpha)\rho\sigma_X\sigma_Y.$$

Setting the first derivative equal to 0,

$$2\alpha \, \text{Var}(X) + 2\alpha \, \text{Var}(Y) - 4\alpha\rho\sigma_X\sigma_Y = 2 \, \text{Var}(Y) - 2\rho\sigma_X\sigma_Y.$$

To minimize the variance of the investment, we want α to be

$$\alpha = \frac{\text{Var}(Y) - \rho\sigma_X\sigma_Y}{\text{Var}(X) + \text{Var}(Y) - 2\rho\sigma_X\sigma_Y} = \frac{\sigma_Y(\sigma_Y - \rho\sigma_X)}{\text{Var}(X) + \text{Var}(Y) - 2\rho\sigma_X\sigma_Y}$$

$$= \frac{\text{Var}(Y) - \text{Cov}(X, Y)}{[\text{Var}(X) - \text{Cov}(X, Y)] + [\text{Var}(Y) - \text{Cov}(X, Y)]}.$$

This solution is valid only if the values of α are in the interval $0 \leq \alpha \leq 1$, because negative real investments are not generally possible.

EXAMPLE: X and Y are imperfectly correlated with identical means.

$$\text{Var}(Y) = 3{,}600; \sigma_Y = 60$$
$$\text{Var}(X) = 2{,}500; \sigma_X = 50$$

---

[3] It should be recalled that

$$\text{Var}(X + Y) = \text{Var}(X) + \text{Var}(Y) + 2\,\text{Cov}(X, Y)$$
$$= \text{Var}(X) + \text{Var}(Y) + 2\rho\sigma_X\sigma_Y,$$

where ρ is the correlation coefficient of X, Y, and $-1 \leq \rho \leq 1$. Also Var $(\alpha X) = \alpha^2$ Var (X) and Cov $(\alpha X, Y) = \alpha$ Cov (X, Y).

$\rho = .4$. The covariance is equal to $.4 \times 60 \times 50 = 1,200$.

$$\alpha = \frac{\sigma_Y(\sigma_Y - \rho\sigma_X)}{\text{Var}(X) + \text{Var}(Y) - 2\rho\sigma_X\sigma_Y}$$

$$= \frac{60(60 - .4 \times 50)}{2,500 + 3,600 - 2 \times .4(60)(50)} = \frac{60 \times 40}{6,100 - 2,400}$$

$$= \frac{2,400}{3,700} = .64$$

If $\rho = 0$, as would occur if X and Y are independent, we have

$$\alpha = \frac{\text{Var}(Y)}{\text{Var}(X) + \text{Var}(Y)}.$$

Assume that $\rho = 1$, as would occur if the investments are perfectly correlated. With identical means we would choose that investment with the smaller variance. (Because the investments are perfectly positively correlated, there is no advantage in diversification.)

If $\rho = -1$, we have

$$\alpha = \frac{\sigma_Y(\sigma_Y + \sigma_X)}{\sigma_X^2 + \sigma_Y^2 + 2\sigma_X\sigma_Y} = \frac{\sigma_Y(\sigma_Y + \sigma_X)}{(\sigma_X + \sigma_Y)^2} = \frac{\sigma_Y}{\sigma_Y + \sigma_X}.$$

EXAMPLE:

$$\sigma_X^2 = 1 \qquad \sigma_X = 1 \qquad \rho = -1$$

$$\sigma_Y^2 = 4 \qquad \sigma_Y = 2 \qquad \alpha = \frac{\sigma_Y}{\sigma_X + \sigma_Y} = \frac{2}{1+2} = \frac{2}{3}$$

$$\text{Var}(P) = \left(\frac{4}{9} \times 1\right) + \left(\frac{1}{9} \times 4\right) - \left(2 \times \frac{2}{3} \times \frac{1}{3} \times 2 \times 1\right) = \frac{8}{9} - \frac{8}{9} = 0$$

The variance of the portfolio is equal to zero if $\frac{2}{3}$ of the funds are invested in X and $\frac{1}{3}$ in Y.

If, in addition to the investments being perfectly negatively correlated ($\rho = -1$), the Var (X) equals Var (Y), then $\alpha = \frac{1}{2}$:

$$\alpha = \frac{\text{Var}(Y) + \text{Var}(Y)}{\text{Var}(Y) + \text{Var}(Y) + 2\,\text{Var}(Y)} = \frac{1}{2} \quad \text{or} \quad \alpha = \frac{\sigma_Y}{\sigma_Y + \sigma_X} = \frac{1}{2}.$$

The variance of the investment will be equal to 0:

$$\text{Var}(P) = \frac{1}{4}\text{Var}(Y) + \frac{1}{4}\text{Var}(Y) - 2\left(\frac{1}{2}\right)\left(\frac{1}{2}\right)\text{Var}(Y)$$

$$= \frac{1}{2}\text{Var}(Y) - \frac{1}{2}\text{Var}(Y) = 0.$$

The next step in the analysis is to recognize that the different investments have different yields. One would expect that the decrease in variance resulting from investment in several assets would result not only in decreased variance but also in decreased expected return. Some form of utility analysis would be useful to choose the set of outcomes that is most desirable.

sufficient conditions for investing in one asset to minimize the variance

We have established that to minimize the variance we should set α equal to

$$\alpha = \frac{\text{Var}(Y) - \text{Cov}(X, Y)}{[\text{Var}(X) - \text{Cov}(X, Y)] + [\text{Var}(Y) - \text{Cov}(X, Y)]}.$$

This relationship holds if the resulting value of α is in the interval $0 \leq \alpha \leq 1$. This means that we cannot allocate more than 100 per cent of our funds to one of the investments. Next we shall determine the values of ρ, σ_X, and σ_Y that would lead to an extreme solution, that is, a solution with $\alpha = 0$ or $\alpha = 1$. In either of these cases, all our funds would be allocated to one of the investments. Because the designation of one of the two investments as investment X is abitrary, we shall assume that the labels have been chosen so that the standard deviation of investment Y is at least as large as the standard deviation of X. That is, $\sigma_X \leq \sigma_Y$. All our funds would be allocated to investment X if $\alpha = 1$. To see under what conditions this would occur, we set $\alpha = 1$ in the preceding equation and simplify:

$$\text{Var}(X) - \text{Cov}(X, Y) + \text{Var}(Y) - \text{Cov}(X, Y) = \text{Var}(Y) - \text{Cov}(X, Y),$$
$$\text{Var}(X) = \text{Cov}(X, Y).$$

Substituting σ_X^2 for $\text{Var}(X)$ and $\rho\sigma_X\sigma_Y$ for $\text{Cov}(X, Y)$ the preceding equality will hold if either of the following conditions are true:

$$\sigma_X = 0$$

or

$$\rho = \frac{\sigma_X}{\sigma_Y}.$$

In general, if $\rho \geq \sigma_X/\sigma_Y$, then $\alpha = 1$.

EXAMPLE: Suppose that $\text{Var}(X) = 1$, $\text{Var}(Y) = 9$, and $\rho = \frac{1}{2}$. Then $\sigma_X/\sigma_Y = \frac{1}{3}$. Since ρ is larger than $\frac{1}{3}$, $\alpha = 1$, and all funds should be invested in X to minimize the variance of returns.

In this example,

$$\begin{aligned}
\text{Cov}(X, Y) &= \rho\sigma_X\sigma_Y \\
&= (\tfrac{1}{2})(1)(3) \\
&= 1.5.
\end{aligned}$$

Using the general formula for this situation, we obtain a nonfeasible solution:

$$\begin{aligned}
\alpha &= \frac{\text{Var}(Y) - \text{Cov}(X, Y)}{[\text{Var}(X) - \text{Cov}(X, Y)] + [\text{Var}(Y) - \text{Cov}(X, Y)]} \\
&= \frac{9 - 1.5}{[1 - 1.5] + [9 - 1.5]} \\
&= \frac{7.5}{7} = 1.07.
\end{aligned}$$

The standard deviations, σ_X and σ_Y, can never be negative, and if σ_X or σ_Y are 0, then r must also equal 0. If $\sigma_X > 0$, $\sigma_Y > 0$, and $\rho < 0$, the investments are negatively correlated. If they are negatively correlated, there will always be some combination of the two investments that will have a lower variance than either investment by itself.

These results and those in the previous sections can be summarized in the following schedule, which assumes that $\sigma_Y \geq \sigma_X > 0$.

Values of ρ	Value of α (proportion in X)
$\rho = -1$	$\alpha = \dfrac{\sigma_Y}{\sigma_X + \sigma_Y}$
$-1 < \rho < 0$	$\dfrac{\sigma_Y}{\sigma_X + \sigma_Y} < \alpha < \dfrac{\text{Var}(Y)}{\text{Var}(X) + \text{Var}(Y)}$
$\rho = 0$	$\alpha = \dfrac{\text{Var}(Y)}{\text{Var}(X) + \text{Var}(Y)}$
$0 < \rho < \dfrac{\sigma_X}{\sigma_Y}$	$\dfrac{\text{Var}(Y)}{\text{Var}(X) + \text{Var}(Y)} < \alpha < 1$
$\rho \geq \dfrac{\sigma_X}{\sigma_Y}$	$\alpha = 1$

risk-free and default-free investments

We can point to government bonds as being default free. However, they are subject to risk arising from changing interest rates and changing price levels. Thus we could say that the expected monetary return from a $1,000 invest-ment in government bonds is $50, with a variance of 0, or we could measure the return in terms of purchasing power. The variance of the purchasing power return is not 0.

EXAMPLE

	Money Terms		Purchasing Power	
	Mean	Variance	Mean	Variance
Government bonds	50	0	40	400
Common stock	100	900	80	1,600

If we measured results in terms of money, we would invest the entire amount in bonds to minimize the variance. When we consider the purchasing power of the two investments, it is not obvious that we should invest only in bonds to minimize the variance of the return. Continuing the preceding example, assume that the correlation coefficient of the returns of bonds and stocks is .4. To minimize the variance, we might invest $\frac{128}{136}$ of our assets in bonds and $\frac{8}{136}$ in stocks.[4] (This choice is not optimum because it ignores the effect on risk caused by the difference in means.) Our expected return measured in terms of purchasing power would then be

$$.04 \times \frac{128}{136} = .0376$$

$$.08 \times \frac{8}{136} = .0047$$

Expected return = .0423

4

$$\alpha = \frac{\text{Var}(Y) - \rho\sigma_x\sigma_y}{\text{Var}(X) + \text{Var}(Y) - 2\rho\sigma_x\sigma_y} = \frac{1,600 - .4(20)(40)}{400 + 1,600 - .8(20)(40)} = \frac{128}{136}.$$

The variance is

$$\left(\frac{128}{136}\right)^2 400 + \left(\frac{8}{136}\right)^2 1,600 + 2(.4)\left(\frac{128}{136}\right)\left(\frac{8}{136}\right) 20 \times 40 = 396.$$

The expected return in terms of dollars unadjusted for purchasing power would be

$$.05 \times \frac{128}{136} = .0471$$

$$.10 \times \frac{8}{136} = \underline{.0059}$$

$$\text{Expected return} = .0530$$

It is interesting to note that the default-free rate of .05 associated with government bonds has more risk than the .053 return associated with the mixture of bonds and stocks.[5] This conclusion has implications when we choose the rate of interest to be used for discounting for time. The magnitude of the difference is affected by the sign and size of the correlation coefficient between bonds and stock. The desirability of adding stock to decrease risk is increased if ρ is negative or 0; but ρ may be positive. We may be able to increase the expected yield and decrease the variance of the real return by investing in stocks as well as bonds.

independent identical investments

In addition to diversification (by acquiring investments with different risk characteristics) we can change the risk characteristics of an investment, if there are other independent investments with equivalent characteristics, by pooling of risk. We accomplish the risk pooling by spreading our investment fund over several investments. (The investments are exactly alike, but the results are independent.) It should be noted that we do not change the expected monetary value of the investment by the suggested procedure, but we do change the probabilities of several possible gains or losses. If the variance of each investment is Var (X_i) for our full investment of S dollars, and if we invest S/n in each of n types of these investments, we have for the variance of the portfolio

$$\text{Var}(P) = \text{Var}\left(\frac{X_1}{n}\right) + \text{Var}\left(\frac{X_2}{n}\right) + \cdots + \text{Var}\left(\frac{X_n}{n}\right)$$

$$= \sum_{i=1}^{n} \text{Var}\left(\frac{X_i}{n}\right)$$

$$= \frac{1}{n^2} \sum_{i=1}^{n} \text{Var}(X_i).$$

[5] This conclusion was pointed out to the authors by K. L. Hastie when he was a graduate student at Cornell. See K. L. Hastie, "The Determination of Optimal Investment Policy," *Management Science*, Aug. 1967, pp. 757–774.

Because all Var (X_i) are equal and all X_i independent, we have

$$\sum_{i=1}^{n} \text{Var } X_i = n \text{ Var } (X)$$

$$\text{Var } (P) = \frac{1}{n} \text{Var } (X).$$

EXAMPLE: Assume that we have a large number of independent investments, all with the following characteristics:

Probability	Consequence
.5	1,000
.5	0

The expected outcome for any one investment is $500 and the variance is 250,000.

X	$\bar{X}$	$(X - \bar{X})^2$	$P(X)$	$P(X)(X - \bar{X})^2$
1,000	500	$500^2 = 250,000$	.5	125,000
0	500	$500^2 = 250,000$	.5	125,000
			Var $(P) =$ Var $(X) =$	250,000

If instead of investing in one unit of investment we split our investment between two units (the outcomes are independent), the variance is

$$\text{Var } (P) = \frac{1}{n} \text{Var } (X) = \frac{1}{2} \times 250,000 = 125,000.$$

X	$\bar{X}$	$(X - \bar{X})^2$	$P(X)$	$P(X)(X - \bar{X})^2$
1,000	500	$(500)^2 = 250,000$	.25	62,500
500	500	$0 = 0$	.50	0
0	500	$(500)^2 = 250,000$	.25	62,500
			Var $(P) =$	125,000

Now assume that we invest in four different units:

X	$\bar{X}$	$(X - \bar{X})^2$	$P(X)$	$P(X)(X - \bar{X})^2$
1,000	500	250,000	1/16	15,625
750	500	62,500	4/16	15,625
500	500	0	6/16	0
250	500	62,500	4/16	15,625
0	500	250,000	1/16	15,625

$$\text{Var } (P) = 1/4 \text{ Var } (X) = \frac{250,000}{4} = 62,500$$

Table 20-1 shows how the variance of the portfolio is decreased as other independent identical investments are added to the portfolio.

We can keep reducing the variance by investing in more different types of investments. However, this policy would result in increased transaction costs and costs of information. Also, we have assumed that each investment has identical expected returns. In the real world one might have to accept lower yields as more investments were introduced.

These examples have important implications for the art of decision making. If we start with a desirable but risky investment, we can change the risk characteristics by investing in not one, but several of these investments (each with independent outcomes). Assume that the investment is an oil well. We can drill with 100 per cent ownership and have .5 probability of not striking oil. If instead of drilling one well, we only purchase .25 of the well, but purchase four wells; there is now .0625 probability of complete failure. We can change the drilling of the oil well from an investment with very risky

Table 20-1. Variance
of *n* Investments

Number of Equal Independent Investments	Variance of Portfolio
1	250,000
2	125,000
4	62,500
5	50,000
10	25,000
25	10,000
50	5,000
100	2,500
200	1,250

characteristics to one that is somewhat safer, the probabilities of the extreme outcomes being reduced.[6]

By now the reader may have observed that the adage "don't put all your eggs in one basket" has justification if we want to minimize the risk of losing all. But there is a price to be paid, because we also reduce the likelihood of the best possible outcome occurring.

investment strategy and the probability of ruin[7]

The previous section considered the effect on the probability of zero gains of investing in a different number of independent investment opportunities. We shall now investigate more systematically the effect on the probability of ruin of varying the size of the outlays and the objective. We shall have to make some simplifying assumptions. It is essential that these assumptions be kept in mind, because the transferral of the conclusions derived from the model to the real world will depend on how closely the real-world situation fits the assumptions. Unfortunately, real-world problems are generally complex.

The assumptions that will be made for all the models of this section are the following:

1. The investments are statistically independent of each other.
2. There are two possible outcomes to each investment (win or lose).
3. The outlays for each investment are the same.
4. The probabilities of each investment are identical to those of the other investments.

It is frequently stated that the law of large numbers will ensure success if a large number of gambles is undertaken. This is inexact and requires explanation. If many independent trials are undertaken in a process where the probabilities of the two possible events are the same for each trial, the law of large numbers applies. It states that the number of successes S_n divided by the number of trials n will differ from the true probability of a success p by a very small amount.[8]

---

[6] We are assuming that the outcomes of drilling are statistically independent.

[7] The material in this section is to a great extent based on William Feller, *An Introduction to Probability Theory and Its Applications* (New York: John Wiley & Sons, Inc., 1950), pp. 185–191, 233–237, 311–318.

[8] An algebraic expression of the law of large numbers is given by Feller, *op. cit.*, p. 141:

$$P\left\{ \left| \frac{S_n}{n} - p \right| < \epsilon \right\} \to 1.$$

"As n increases, the probability that the average number of successes deviates from p by more than preassigned ϵ tends to zero" (p. 141).

EXAMPLE: The true probability of a success is .6 and a failure is .4, and 100 million independent trials are undertaken. The law of large numbers says that the number of successes divided by the 100 million will be very close to .6.

$$\frac{S_n}{n} \rightarrow p \quad \text{or} \quad \frac{S_n}{100,000,000} \rightarrow .6$$

It is important to note that the law of large numbers makes no claim that the number of successes will be close to the expected number of successes. In the preceding example the expected number of successes is 60 million, but the actual number of successes is likely to be considerably different from 60 million.

It is interesting to compute the variance of the number of successes for the type of process being discussed:

$$\text{Var}(S_n) = npq = np(1 - p)$$
$$= 100,000,000 \times .6 \times .4 = 24,000,000.$$

The variance of the proportion of successes is

$$\text{Var}\left(\frac{S_n}{n}\right) = \frac{1}{n^2}\text{Var}(S_n) = \frac{1}{n^2}(npq) = \frac{pq}{n}$$
$$= \frac{.24}{100,000,000}.$$

Inspection of the two variances that we have computed helps us to understand the law of large numbers. As n increases, the variance S_n/n, the proportion of successes, decreases, and the probability of S_n/n being very close to p increases. However, as n increases the variance of the number of successes S_n increases, and the actual number of successes resulting from the 100 million trials may be considerably different from the 60 million expected number of successes.

A firm investing in a large number of independent investments with identical probability distributions may be able to make an estimate of the proportion of successes with a considerable amount of confidence (assuming that we know the value of p), but the number of successes may differ considerably from the expected number of successes. This is indicated by the variance being equal to npq and increasing as n increases.

If the probability of a success (or failure) is very small, the number of trials needed for the law of large numbers to hold may be astronomical. For example, if the probability of winning $1 million was $1/1,000,000$ and the cost of playing is $1, the investment is fair. Assume that the investment is made 1 million times. We might expect the law of large numbers to hold, but it does not. Instead of the proportion of successes being close to 1/1,000,000 with probability 1, the following probabilities hold[9]:

Number of Successes	Proportion of Successes	Probability
0	$\dfrac{0}{1,000,000}$	.368
1	$\dfrac{1}{1,000,000}$	.368
2	$\dfrac{2}{1,000,000}$	.184
3	$\dfrac{3}{1,000,000}$	.061
4	$\dfrac{4}{1,000,000}$	.015

It becomes apparent that we need additional tools to analyze risk-type situations. Feller has analyzed these under the topic heading of "random walk" or "gambler's ruin."

Ruin with Absorbing Barriers

The first situation involves an investor who plays until he has no more funds or has all the funds committed to the game (that is, he reaches either of two absorbing barriers).

We shall need the following symbols:

p = probability of winning a trial.
p_z = probability of winning if the investor starts with z units of money.
q = probability of losing a trial ($p + q = 1$).
q_z = probability of losing if the investor starts with z.
z = investor's initial capital.
$a - z$ = opponent's initial capital.
a = total capital committed to the game $[z + (a - z) = a]$.

Figure 20-1 shows a portion of the investing process, assuming that we

[9] The probabilities are computed using the Poisson probability distribution:

$$p(k) = \frac{e^{-np}(np)^k}{k!} = \frac{e^{-1}}{k!}$$

since $np = 1$.

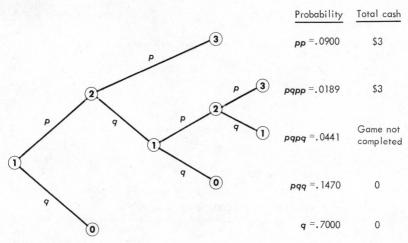

Figure 20-1

start with $1 and our opponent starts with $2. On each trial we either win or lose $1. The tree shows our progress. If we reach 3 or 0, the game is ended.

If we carried the tree far enough we could compute the probability of ruin (that is, $0) and the probability of winning (that is, $3), although we would always have a little probability unaccounted for because the game could be carried still farther. In the preceding example let q be .7 and p be .3; we would then have the following:

	Probability of Results	Economic Results
$pp =$	.0900	$3
$pqpp =$	.0189	$3
$pqpq =$	.0441	Game not completed
$pqq =$	.1470	$0
$q =$	.7000	$0

There is .8470 probability of ruin, .1089 probability of $3 winnings, and .0441 probability remaining to be distributed. The actual q_z is .886.

Fortunately, there are easier methods of solution. We define q_0 as equal to 1 and q_a as equal to 0 (that is, if we have lost all our funds, the probability of failure is 1; if we have all the funds, the probability of failure is 0). Next we establish the following difference equation:

$$q_i = pq_{i+1} + qq_{i-1}.$$

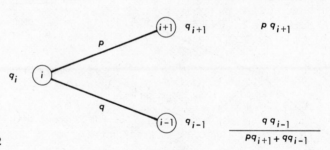

Figure 20-2

Figure 20-2 helps explain the preceding relationship:

$$q_0 = 1,$$
$$q_1 = pq_2 + qq_0,$$
$$q_2 = pq_3 + qq_1,$$
$$\vdots$$
$$q_a = 0.$$

The solution to the preceding difference equations and the boundary conditions gives the following formula for computing the probability of ruin if p is not equal to q.

$$q_z = \frac{\left(\dfrac{q}{p}\right)^a - \left(\dfrac{q}{p}\right)^z}{\left(\dfrac{q}{p}\right)^a - 1}$$

Applying this formula to a situation where $a = 3$, $z = 1$, $p = \frac{2}{3}$, $q = \frac{1}{3}$, and bets of \$1 are made for each trial,

$$\frac{q}{p} = \frac{\frac{1}{3}}{\frac{2}{3}} = \frac{1}{2}.$$

We find the probability of ruin to be

$$q_z = \frac{\left(\frac{1}{2}\right)^3 - \left(\frac{1}{2}\right)^1}{\left(\frac{1}{2}\right)^3 - 1} = \frac{\frac{1}{8} - \frac{1}{2}}{\frac{1}{8} - 1} = \frac{3}{7} = .43.$$

If the probability of losing on each trial changed from $\frac{1}{3}$ to $\frac{2}{3}$, the probability of ruin would change from .43 to .86.

$$p = \tfrac{1}{3}$$
$$q = \tfrac{2}{3}$$
$$\frac{q}{p} = \frac{\frac{2}{3}}{\frac{1}{3}} = 2$$

$$q_z = \frac{(2)^3 - (2)^1}{(2)^3 - 1} = \frac{8 - 2}{8 - 1} = \frac{6}{7} = .86$$

If we leave p and q unchanged but change a to 10 and z to 9 (that is, we are rich and our opponent poor), the probability of our ruin decreases from .86 to .50.

$$q_z = \frac{\left(\frac{q}{p}\right)^a - \left(\frac{q}{p}\right)^z}{\left(\frac{q}{p}\right)^a - 1} = \frac{2^{10} - 2^9}{2^{10} - 1}$$

$$= \frac{1{,}024 - 512}{1{,}024 - 1} = \frac{512}{1{,}023} = .50$$

An increase in our capital relative to our opponent's capital has changed the probability of ruin from .86 to .50, whereas the probability of losing on any one trial remained constant at $\frac{2}{3}$.

If $p = q = \frac{1}{2}$, it is necessary to return to the difference equations and obtain a new solution. We would now find that the probability of ruin is

$$q_z = 1 - \frac{z}{a}, \quad \text{if} \quad q = p.$$

In embarking upon a two-person struggle over a given "market," it is desirable, from the point of view of minimizing the probability of ruin, to enter the fray with more capital than your opponent. The relative size of your capital compared to your opponent's capital will greatly influence the probability of ruin.

Even though the assumptions of the model are restrictive, it does have some lessons for corporate managers. A small firm challenging a large firm to a set of gambles (say, battling the large firm in a large number of separate markets) is at a disadvantage. Even if the probability of success for each trial is .5, the probability of ruin for the smaller firm will be greater than it will be for the large firm. For example, if the smaller firm has $1 million to commit to the struggle and the larger firm $9 million, the probability of ruin for the smaller firm is .9. (Remember the assumptions of the model, including the fact that the one firm wins an amount equal to what the other loses and that is all.) The competing firms could increase the market and both firms would benefit from the competition, or the trials might not be independent with identical probability distributions, and p equal to q equal to $\frac{1}{2}$, in which case the preceding computations would not hold.

Games Against Nature

The previous situation assumed two opponents with finite capital playing against each other. We shall now assume that you are playing against an infinitely rich opponent, which we shall call nature, although it might also be called the economy or the stock market. Your stake remains z, but the resources of nature are assumed to be infinite. The total resources committed to the game are infinite.

We shall consider two situations. If p is greater than q, we find that the basic equation for the probability of ruin simplifies to

$$q_z = \frac{\left(\frac{q}{p}\right)^\infty - \left(\frac{q}{p}\right)^z}{\left(\frac{q}{p}\right)^\infty - 1} = \left(\frac{q}{p}\right)^z, \quad p > q.$$

If q is equal to or greater than p, the probability of ruin approaches 1. In a situation where the probability of losing is greater than the probability of winning on one trial, and we are playing a very rich opponent, the strategy of playing until we have $0 or win all is a very poor strategy. In fact, the probability of ruin approaches 1.

One way of changing the probability of ruin is to determine how much money we want to win and stop when we have attained those winnings. In this situation the wealth of nature effectively changes from infinite wealth to the amount we want to win.

EXAMPLE: Assume that an opponent is infinitely rich, but we will stop after we have won $2. Our stake is $4 and we bet $1 each trial with a probability of $\frac{2}{3}$ of winning $1 and a probability of $\frac{1}{3}$ of losing.

$$p = \tfrac{2}{3} \qquad z = 4$$
$$q = \tfrac{1}{3} \qquad a - z = 2$$
$$\frac{q}{p} = \frac{1}{2} \qquad a = 6$$

$$q_z = \frac{(\tfrac{1}{2})^6 - (\tfrac{1}{2})^4}{(\tfrac{1}{2})^6 - 1} = \frac{\tfrac{1}{64} - \tfrac{1}{16}}{\tfrac{1}{64} - 1} = \frac{\tfrac{3}{64}}{\tfrac{63}{64}} = \frac{1}{21}$$

By limiting our desired winnings to \$2, we have decreased the probability of ruin from $\frac{1}{16}$ to $\frac{1}{21}$.

Another method of changing the probability of ruin is to change the size of the bet. Let us assume that we halve the bet we have been making. This is equivalent to doubling our initial capital and the total amount in the game. Let q_z^* be the new probability of ruin. We then have

$$q_z^* = \frac{\left(\frac{q}{p}\right)^{2a} - \left(\frac{q}{p}\right)^{2z}}{\left(\frac{q}{p}\right)^{2a} - 1} = q_z \left[\frac{\left(\frac{q}{p}\right)^{a} + \left(\frac{q}{p}\right)^{z}}{\left(\frac{q}{p}\right)^{a} + 1} \right].$$

If the probability of losing is greater than the probability of winning ($q > p$), the last right-hand term (the fraction) is larger than 1; thus $q_z^* > q_z$. We can increase the probability of ruin by decreasing the size of our bets if $q > p$. We can decrease the probability of ruin by increasing the size of our bets. Thus, if the game is advantageous to the opponent, our strategy should be to bet the largest amount on one trial consistent with our winning objectives. The opposite strategy holds if the game is advantageous to us.

The combination of strategies of entering the game with a large stock of capital, limiting the desired winnings, and investing in accordance with rules previously described relative to the size of bets can greatly affect the probability of ruin and thus the probability of winning. Feller writes of the story of a man who visited Monte Carlo yearly and for a period of ten years always came away a winner. He attributed his success to magic powers, but actually it resulted from going with a large amount of cash and desiring only a modest winnings (about .1 of the stake). The probability of success in any one year was approximately .9 and the probability of winning in all ten years was approximately .37.[10]

conclusions

Assuming that the expected values of all investments are the same, a person desiring to avoid risk should search for investments that are negatively correlated. Having exhausted this possibility, the second means of reducing risk is to find independent investments and bring them all into the investment portfolio (being limited only by information and transaction costs). Risk can be reduced by adding investments that are positively correlated as long as the extent of correlation is less than σ_X/σ_Y, assuming that the investments have identical means. It becomes apparent that a model neglecting information and transaction costs and unrealistically assuming that all

[10] See Feller, *op. cit.*, p. 315.

investments have the same mean might lead to an excessive amount of diversification. To arrive at a realistic recommendation for portfolio policy, one must include these factors. Nevertheless, it is interesting to note the incentives that exist for including a wide range of types of investments in a portfolio if the objective is simply to reduce the variance of the total investment.

Despite the limitations of the assumptions, do the ideas of "gambler's ruin" carry over into the business world?

The fact that probability of ruin is a function of the size of our capital and that we can influence the effective size of our capital by changing the size of our investment has implications even in situations that do not exactly fit the model.

The following would seem to be generally valid for investments, although by changing the facts significantly each could be shown to be incorrect.

1. Set a realistic goal for winnings and do not try to bankrupt nature unless you believe that p is significantly greater than q for each trial.
2. If q is greater than p for each trial, bet large amounts and reduce the number of trials. (This means placing all your eggs in one basket.)
3. If p is greater than q for each trial, bet small amounts and increase the number of trials. (This results in diversification of investment.)

Expectations relative to the probabilities of winning and losing should affect the investment strategy.

It is interesting that a corporation maintaining liquid assets affects z and affects the probability of ruin to some extent. Thus a strong liquid asset position may be partially justified by a desire to avoid ruin.

questions and problems

20-1. Investments X and Y have the same means. Other information is as follows:

$$\text{Var}\,(X) = 2,500, \qquad \sigma_X = 50,$$
$$\text{Var}\,(Y) = 8,100, \qquad \sigma_Y = 90.$$

Required: What percentage of the investment should be placed in X to minimize the variance of the sums of the two investments if the correlation coefficient is (a) 0, (b) .1, (c) .5, (d) .9, (e) 1, (f) −1.

20-2. Assume that we have a large number of independent investments all with the same mean, and a variance of 1 million if we invest all our funds in one investment type.

Required: Compute the variance, assuming that we split our investment into (a) two different investments, (b) four different investments, (c) ten different investments, (d) 1,000 different investments.

20-3. The Standard Oil Company of California is considering drilling a well in a new field. To what extent does the law of large numbers apply? To what extent do the models described in the chapter apply?

20-4. Assume that trials are independent, the probability of winning on each trial is .5, we either win or lose $1 on each trial, and there are 1 million trials.

Required: (a) What is the expected number of successes (winning trials)? (b) What is the expected proportion of successes? (c) What is the variance for the distribution for number of successes? The standard deviation? (d) What is the variance for the distribution of the proportion of successes?

20-5. Does the law of large numbers explain why a large corporation is less likely to go bankrupt than a small firm in the same type of business?

20-6. The probability of winning a lottery on one trial is 10^{-5}. The cost of playing is $1 and the payoff is $100,000 every time you win. Assume that you will play 100,000 times.

Required: (a) Does the law of large numbers apply? (b) Compute the probability of winning $0, $100,000, $200,000, and so on.

20-7. Assume that you have $2 and your opponent has $1. The probability of your winning $1 for a $1 bet is .9. Draw a tree diagram and use it to compute the approximate probabilities of your winning and losing.

20-8. Assume that you have $4,000 and your opponent has $1,000. You will bet $1,000 each trial (you will be $1,000 richer or poorer after each trial). The probability of your winning on each trial is $\frac{3}{5}$.

Required: (a) What is the probability of your ruin? (b) What is the probability of your ruin if $p = \frac{1}{2}$?

20-9. Assume the same situation as in problem 20-8 except that you have $1,000 and your opponent has $4,000.

Required: (a) What is the probability of your ruin? (b) What is the probability of your ruin if $p = \frac{1}{2}$?

20-10. Assume that your opponent's resources are infinite. You have enough capital for five trials. The probability of your winning on each trial is .6. You will win or lose the amount of your bet.

Required: (a) What is the probability of your ruin? (b) What is the probability of your ruin if the probability of winning on a trial is .5? (c) Assume that you have $4 and you will stop after net winnings of $1. With a probability of winning on a trial of .6, what is the probability of ruin? Each bet is $1.

20-11. Assume that you have $2 and your opponent has $4. The probability of your winning is $\frac{2}{3}$. You win or lose the amount of your bet.

Required: Compute the probability of ruin assuming that (a) you bet $1 each trial; (b) you bet $2 each trial; (c) you bet $.50 each trial.

20-12. If you had a friend going to Monaco to gamble, other than the advice "don't gamble," what would you suggest?

20-13. As an investor in the stock market should you buy all one stock or diversify? Explain.

chapter 21

models for portfolio analysis

matrix notation

A matrix is a rectangular array of numbers that is very useful for the presentation of numerical data and their mathematical manipulation. In particular, many properties of portfolios and of relations among the securities in a portfolio that are awkwardly expressed in ordinary algebraic notation can be expressed very conveniently and compactly in terms of matrices. In the present chapter only certain elementary properties of matrices are introduced and their applications to portfolio problems illustrated. Matrices can also be used in many other applications that are not discussed here, such as the solution of systems of simultaneous linear equations.[1]

We shall enclose an array of numbers in brackets, [ ], to indicate a matrix. Also, we shall use uppercase letters to designate matrices that are not vectors.

$$A = \begin{bmatrix} a_{11} & a_{12} & a_{13} & a_{14} \\ a_{21} & a_{22} & a_{23} & a_{24} \\ a_{31} & a_{32} & a_{33} & a_{34} \end{bmatrix}$$

Matrix A has 3 rows and 4 columns; thus we say A is of order 3×4, or, equivalently, A is 3×4.

[1] For additional applications see S. R. Searle and W. H. Hausman, *Matrix Algebra for Business and Economics* (New York: John Wiley & Sons, Inc., 1970).

The symbol a_{23} refers to the element in the second row and third column and the symbol a_{ij} refers to the element of the ith row and the jth column.

Vectors and Scalars

A matrix consisting of a single column is called a *column vector* and is designated by a lowercase letter; for example,

$$x = \begin{bmatrix} a_{11} \\ a_{21} \\ a_{31} \end{bmatrix} = \begin{bmatrix} 5 \\ -8 \\ 3 \end{bmatrix}$$

is a column vector. A matrix that is a single row is a *row vector*. We use a prime after the letter to indicate a row vector. If x is the column vector referred to above, x' is the row vector:

$$x' = \begin{bmatrix} 5 & -8 & 3 \end{bmatrix}.$$

For clarity in reading, commas are sometimes inserted between the elements of a row vector.

In general, if A is any matrix, the *transpose* of A, denoted A', is obtained from A by letting the rows of A become the columns of A'. Thus if

$$A = \begin{bmatrix} 1 & 2 \\ 3 & 4 \\ 5 & 0 \end{bmatrix}, \quad \text{then} \quad A' = \begin{bmatrix} 1 & 3 & 5 \\ 2 & 4 & 0 \end{bmatrix}.$$

A matrix with one row and one column is a single number and is called a *scalar*. The elements of the matrices in this chapter will all be scalars.

Matrix Multiplication

Ordinary arithmetic deals with a class of objects called numbers (scalars) and with operations such as addition, multiplication, and division that can be performed on pairs of these objects. The result of applying an arithmetic operation to a pair of numbers is valid if the rules of arithmetic are followed. For example, the operation $6 \div 2$ leads to a valid result. But the operation $6 \div 0$ is undefined and does not lead to a valid or meaningful result. In an analogous manner we can define a type of arithmetic in which the objects being manipulated are matrices instead of ordinary numbers.

Just as one number can be divided into another only if the divisor is not 0, two matrices can be multiplied only if the appropriate conditions hold. Assume that we want to multiply two matrices, A and B. When the number of columns in A equals the number of rows in B, the matrices are said to be conformable for multiplication for the product AB. The product AB has the same number of rows as A and the same number of columns as B. If A is $r \times c$ and B is $c \times s$, AB will be $r \times s$. (The first letter is the number of rows; the second letter is the number of columns.) The ijth element of the product AB is the sum of products of the elements of the ith row of A with those of the jth column of B. If the first row of A is $[1 \quad 2]$ and the second column of B is $[\begin{smallmatrix}2\\2\end{smallmatrix}]$, the element in the first row and the second column of AB is $(1 \times 2) + (2 \times 2) = 5$.

EXAMPLE: Let

$$A = \begin{bmatrix} 1 & 2 \\ 3 & 4 \\ 5 & 0 \end{bmatrix}, \qquad B = \begin{bmatrix} 3 & 2 & 1 \\ 0 & 2 & 0 \end{bmatrix}.$$

Since A is 3×2 and B is 2×3, the product AB exists and is of order 3×3.

$$AB = \begin{bmatrix} 1 & 2 \\ 3 & 4 \\ 5 & 0 \end{bmatrix} \begin{bmatrix} 3 & 2 & 1 \\ 0 & 2 & 0 \end{bmatrix} = \begin{bmatrix} 3 & 6 & 1 \\ 9 & 14 & 3 \\ 15 & 10 & 5 \end{bmatrix}$$

The product BA is of order 2×2, and is not equal to AB.

$$BA = \begin{bmatrix} 3 & 2 & 1 \\ 0 & 2 & 0 \end{bmatrix} \begin{bmatrix} 1 & 2 \\ 3 & 4 \\ 5 & 0 \end{bmatrix} = \begin{bmatrix} 14 & 14 \\ 6 & 8 \end{bmatrix}$$

In ordinary arithmetic, multiplication can be applied to two or more numbers. For example, $(2 \times 3) \times 4 = 2 \times (3 \times 4) = 24$. A similar rule holds for matrix multiplication. If A, B, and C are three matrices, if AB are conformable for multiplication, and if BC are conformable for multiplication, then

$$(AB)C = A(BC).$$

For example, let A and B be the matrices referred to above and let

$$C = \begin{bmatrix} 2 \\ 0 \\ 1 \end{bmatrix}.$$

The matrix product ABC can be computed in either of two ways. We can compute the matrix AB and premultiply C by it:

$$\begin{bmatrix} 3 & 6 & 1 \\ 9 & 14 & 3 \\ 15 & 10 & 5 \end{bmatrix} \begin{bmatrix} 2 \\ 0 \\ 1 \end{bmatrix} = \begin{bmatrix} 7 \\ 21 \\ 35 \end{bmatrix}.$$

Alternatively, we can first compute BC.

$$\begin{bmatrix} 3 & 2 & 1 \\ 0 & 2 & 0 \end{bmatrix} \begin{bmatrix} 2 \\ 0 \\ 1 \end{bmatrix} = \begin{bmatrix} 7 \\ 0 \end{bmatrix}$$

The result can then be premultiplied by A.

$$\begin{bmatrix} 1 & 2 \\ 3 & 4 \\ 5 & 0 \end{bmatrix} \begin{bmatrix} 7 \\ 0 \end{bmatrix} = \begin{bmatrix} 7 \\ 21 \\ 35 \end{bmatrix}$$

The answer is the same and independent of the order in which the multiplication is performed.

If A and B are two matrices of the same order, the sum or difference of the two matrices results in a new matrix of the same order. The elements of the new matrix are the sums or differences of the corresponding elements of the the original matrices. Thus, if

$$A = \begin{bmatrix} 1 & 7 & 4 \\ 2 & 8 & 6 \\ 3 & 9 & 5 \end{bmatrix}, \quad B = \begin{bmatrix} -1 & 2 & 1 \\ 3 & 4 & -2 \\ 0 & -8 & 4 \end{bmatrix},$$

then

$$A + B = \begin{bmatrix} 0 & 9 & 5 \\ 5 & 12 & 4 \\ 3 & 1 & 9 \end{bmatrix} \quad \text{and} \quad A - B = \begin{bmatrix} 2 & 5 & 3 \\ -1 & 4 & 8 \\ 3 & 17 & 1 \end{bmatrix}.$$

expected return of investments

The matrix notation just introduced can be used to describe the expected values of a set of investments made under conditions of uncertainty. For example, suppose that a businessman is considering the two investments described in the following table.

**Returns of Two Investments
Under Two States of Nature**

	States	
Investment	1	2
x	.13	.07
y	.06	.10
State probabilities	.5	.5

To illustrate the calculation of expected returns, we can form a matrix in which each row represents one investment and each column the outcome of the investment in a particular state. Thus

$$D = \begin{bmatrix} .13 & .07 \\ .06 & .10 \end{bmatrix}.$$

Next we form a vector p whose elements are the probabilities of the states.

$$p = \begin{bmatrix} .5 \\ .5 \end{bmatrix}$$

Postmultiplying the matrix by the vector gives values that we shall define as the expected returns of each investment.

$$Dp = \begin{bmatrix} .13 & .07 \\ .06 & .10 \end{bmatrix}\begin{bmatrix} .5 \\ .5 \end{bmatrix} = \begin{bmatrix} .10 \\ .08 \end{bmatrix} = \bar{r}$$

The elements of the vector $\bar{r}$ are the expected returns of the investments. A similar result obtains if we take the transpose of both the vector and the matrix and premultiply the matrix by the vector.

$$p'D' = [.5 \quad .5]\begin{bmatrix} .13 & .06 \\ .07 & .10 \end{bmatrix} = [.10 \quad .08] = \bar{r}'$$

variances and covariances of investment rates of return

Portfolio analysis uses matrices whose elements are the variance and covariances of the rates of return from the set of investments under consideration. If x_i is the rate of return of investment x in state i, and p_i is the probability of the state, then $\bar{x}$, the expected value of x, is

$$\bar{x} = \sum_{i=1}^{n} x_i p_i$$

and the variance of the rate of return of x is

$$\text{Var}(x) = \sum_{i=1}^{n} p_i(x_i - \bar{x})^2.$$

If y_i denotes the rate of return of investment y under state i, then the co-variance of x and y is defined as

$$\text{Cov}(x, y) = \sum_{i=1}^{n} p_i(x_i - \bar{x}_i)(y_i - \bar{y}).$$

The variance–covariance matrix for these two investments is a square matrix whose elements are the variances and covariances of the corresponding investments, placed as follows:

$$V = \begin{bmatrix} \text{Var}(x) & \text{Cov}(x, y) \\ \text{Cov}(x, y) & \text{Var}(y) \end{bmatrix}.$$

To calculate V we first construct a matrix A whose elements are deviations between the rate of return of an investment under a particular state, and the expected return of the investment. In general, A will be a rectangular matrix with as many rows as there are investments in the set under consideration, and as many columns as there are states of nature. In the present example

$$A = \begin{bmatrix} (x_1 - \bar{x}) & (x_2 - \bar{x}) \\ (y_1 - \bar{y}) & (y_2 - \bar{y}) \end{bmatrix}.$$

In terms of D and $\bar{r}$, A can be written as

$$\begin{aligned} A &= D - \bar{r}[1 \quad 1] \\ &= \begin{bmatrix} .13 & .07 \\ .06 & .10 \end{bmatrix} - \begin{bmatrix} .10 \\ .08 \end{bmatrix}[1 \quad 1] \\ &= \begin{bmatrix} .13 & .07 \\ .06 & .10 \end{bmatrix} - \begin{bmatrix} .10 & .10 \\ .08 & .08 \end{bmatrix} = \begin{bmatrix} .03 & -.03 \\ -.02 & .02 \end{bmatrix}. \end{aligned}$$

Now let P be a square matrix with as many rows (and columns) as there are states, and with the state probabilities on the main diagonal and zeros everywhere else. In this case

$$P = \begin{bmatrix} .5 & 0 \\ 0 & .5 \end{bmatrix}.$$

Then

$$
\begin{aligned}
V &= APA' \\
&= \begin{bmatrix} .03 & -.03 \\ -.02 & .02 \end{bmatrix}\begin{bmatrix} .5 & 0 \\ 0 & .5 \end{bmatrix}\begin{bmatrix} .03 & -.02 \\ -.03 & .02 \end{bmatrix} \\
&= \begin{bmatrix} .015 & -.015 \\ -.01 & .01 \end{bmatrix}\begin{bmatrix} .03 & -.02 \\ -.03 & .02 \end{bmatrix} \\
&= \begin{bmatrix} .0009 & -.0006 \\ -.0006 & .0004 \end{bmatrix} = \begin{bmatrix} \text{Var}(x) & \text{Cov}(x,y) \\ \text{Cov}(x,y) & \text{Var}(y) \end{bmatrix}.
\end{aligned}
$$

expectation and variance of portfolio returns

In the previous sections we showed how a vector containing the expected rates of return of a pair of investments and a square matrix containing the variances and covariances of these rates of return can be calculated. The basic information required to make these calculations is the rate of return of each investment for each state of nature that can occur and the probability of each state. Although in the numerical example used there were only two investments and two states of nature, the same basic procedure can be applied to any number of investments and any number of states. It can also be used to compute the variances and covariances of the present values.

Once a vector containing the expected rate of return of each security and a variance–covariance matrix for these rates of return have been calculated, it is possible to calculate the expected return and variance of any particular portfolio that can be constructed from these securities, without going back to the original state probability data.

Suppose that there are n different securities and that we wish to consider a portfolio in which a proportion x_i of the total available funds is invested in security i. Let x be a vector whose elements are the n values x_i. Let $\bar{r}$ be a vector whose elements are the expected returns of the investments, and V be the variance–covariance matrix for these rates of return. Let $E(R)$ be the expected return per dollar invested in the portfolio, and $\text{Var}(R)$ be the variance of return of the portfolio. Then

$$E(R) = x'\bar{r},$$
$$\text{Var}(R) = x'Vx.$$

To simplify the arithmetic we shall use integer returns that are not realistic but are easier to work with than fractional returns. For example, let

$$\bar{r} = \begin{bmatrix} 10 \\ 8 \end{bmatrix}, \qquad x = \begin{bmatrix} .6 \\ .4 \end{bmatrix}, \qquad V = \begin{bmatrix} 4 & -1 \\ -1 & 2 \end{bmatrix},$$

$$E(R) = x'\bar{r} = [.6 \quad .4]\begin{bmatrix} 10 \\ 8 \end{bmatrix} = 6 + 3.2 = 9.2,$$

$$\text{Var}(R) = [.6 \quad .4]\begin{bmatrix} 4 & -1 \\ -1 & 2 \end{bmatrix}\begin{bmatrix} .6 \\ .4 \end{bmatrix}$$

$$= [.6 \quad .4]\begin{bmatrix} 2 \\ .2 \end{bmatrix} = [1.2 + .08] = 1.28.$$

The variance of the portfolio is less than the variance of either investment. We can also compute the variance using the basic relationship:

$$\text{Var}(R) = x_1^2 \text{Var}(r_1) + x_2^2 \text{Var}(r_2) + 2x_1 x_2 \text{Cov}(r_1 r_2)$$
$$= .36 \times 4 + .16 \times 2 + 2 \times .6 \times .4 \times (-1)$$
$$= 1.44 + .32 - .48 = 1.28.$$

sharpe's single index model

In two closely related articles, W. F. Sharpe presented a simplified portfolio analysis model that has led to much significant work in both portfolio analysis and capital budgeting.[2] In the first of these articles, "A Simplified Model for Portfolio Analysis," Sharpe presents an approach that greatly reduces the effort required to estimate the variance–covariance matrix for a set of investments. To appreciate the contribution of this article, consider the number of items to be estimated if 100 different securities are being analyzed. First, the variance of each of the 100 securities must be estimated. Second, the covariance of each security with every other one must be estimated. There are 4,950 different covariances.[3] Sharpe's procedure requires the estimation of $(n + 1)$ variances.

Instead of proceeding directly to calculate the large number of covariances Sharpe's model assumes that the return from each security can be related to the level of a general market index. When the relationship of each security to

[2] W. G. Sharpe, "A Simplified Model for Portfolio Analysis," *Management Science*, Jan. 1963, pp. 277–293, and "Capital Asset Prices: A Theory of Market Equilibrium Under Conditions of Risk," *The Journal of Finance*, Sept. 1964, pp. 425–442.

[3] If there are n different securities, there are $\frac{n}{2}(n - 1)$ covariances.

the market index is specified, the covariances of the securities with each other can be easily calculated.

The return of ith security is defined as being equal to

$$r_i = a_i + b_i d + c_i,$$

where r_i is the return of the ith security, a_i and b_i are parameters determined by regression analysis, d is the index of general business activity, and c_i is a random element with variance q_i. The market index is equal to

$$d = a_{n+1} + c_{n+1},$$

where c_{n+1} is a random element with variance q_{n+1}. The vector of the proportion invested in each security is

$$p' = [x_1, x_2, x_3 \cdots, x_n].$$

We shall augment the vector p' by the term x_{n+1} to obtain the vector x':

$$x' = [x_1, x_2, x_3, \cdots, x_n, x_{n+1}],$$

where x_{n+1} is defined as being equal to

$$x_{n+1} = \sum_{i=1}^{n} x_i b_i$$

or in vector notation

$$x_{n+1} = p'b$$

and

$$\sum_{i=1}^{n} x_i = 1.$$

An explanation for including the term x_{n+1} is contained in Appendix 1 to this chapter.

All the random elements c_i are assumed to have the following characteristics:

$$E(c_i) = 0,$$
$$E(c_i c_j) = 0,$$

if $i \neq j$, for all i, j from 1 to $n + 1$. Since Cov $(c_i c_j) = E(c_i c_j) - E(c_i)E(c_j)$, all Cov $(c_i c_j) = 0$.[4]

The variance–covariance matrix of the random elements, c_i, is a square matrix Q, with nonzero elements only on the main diagonal:

$$
Q = \begin{bmatrix} q_1 & & & & \\ & q_2 & & & \\ & & \cdot & & \\ & & & \cdot & \\ & & & q_n & \\ & & & & q_{n+1} \end{bmatrix}.
$$

We have the following vectors:

$$
\begin{aligned}
a' &= [a_i, a_2, \ldots, a_n, a_{n+1}], \\
b' &= [b_1, b_2, \ldots, b_n], \\
c' &= [c_1, c_2, \ldots, c_n, c_{n+1}], \\
p' &= [x_1, x_2, \ldots, x_n], \\
x' &= [x_1, x_2, \ldots, x_n, x_{n+1}].
\end{aligned}
$$

The expected return of a portfolio is

$$
E(R) = x'a.
$$

The variance of the portfolio is

$$
\mathrm{Var}\,(R) = x'Qx.
$$

EXAMPLE:

$$
\begin{array}{lll}
r_1 = 50 + .8d + c_1 & q_1 = 100 & x_1 = .5 \\
r_2 = 40 + .1d + c_2 & q_2 = 60 & x_2 = .1 \\
r_3 = 20 - .2d + c_3 & q_3 = 20 & x_3 = .4 \\
d = 40 + c_4, & q_4 = 2{,}500 &
\end{array}
$$

SOLUTION:

$$
x_{n+1} = p'b = [.5 \quad .1 \quad .4]\begin{bmatrix} .8 \\ .1 \\ -.2 \end{bmatrix} = .33
$$

---

[4] Strictly speaking, Cov $(c_i c_{n+1}) = 0$; but the deviation from zero is not important. See E. F. Fama, "Risk, Return and Equilibrium: Some Clarifying Comments," *Journal of Finance*, 23, March 1968, pp. 29–40.

The expected return is

$$E(R) = x'a = [.5 \quad .1 \quad .4 \quad .33] \begin{bmatrix} 50 \\ 40 \\ 20 \\ 40 \end{bmatrix} = 50.2.$$

The variance of the portfolio is

$$\text{Var}(R) = x'Qx = [.5 \quad .1 \quad .4 \quad .33] \begin{bmatrix} 100 & & & \\ & 60 & & \\ & & 20 & \\ & & & 2{,}500 \end{bmatrix} \begin{bmatrix} .5 \\ .1 \\ .4 \\ .33 \end{bmatrix}$$

$$= [.5 \quad .1 \quad .4 \quad .33] \begin{bmatrix} 50 \\ 6 \\ 8 \\ 825 \end{bmatrix}$$

$$= 25 + .6 + 3.2 + 272.25 = 301.05.$$

It can be shown (see chapter Appendix 2) that the implicit covariance between r_i and r_j is[5]

$$\text{Cov}(r_i r_j) = b_i b_j q_{n+1} \qquad \text{if } i \neq j$$

and the

$$\text{Var}(r_i) = b_i^2 q_{n+1} + q_i \qquad \text{if } i = j.$$

Continuing the example, the implicit covariances of the returns are[6]

$$\text{Cov}(r_1 r_2) = .8 \times .1 \times 2{,}500 = 200$$
$$\text{Cov}(r_1 r_3) = .8 \times (-.2) \times 2{,}500 = -400.$$
$$\text{Cov}(r_2 r_3) = .1 \times (-.2) \times 2{,}500 = -50.$$

Implicit in the Sharpe model is a distinction between two components of the risk associated with an investment. One of these components refers to the

---

[5] Also see K. J. Cohen and J. A. Pogue, "An Empirical Evaluation of Alternative Portfolio-Selection Models," *The Journal of Business*, April 1967, pp. 166–193, for this derivation and others.

[6] If we redefine Q so as to omit q_{n+1}, the variance–covariance matrix is $V = bb'q_{n+1} + Q$ and $\text{Var}(R) = p'Vp$.

risk that occurs because of the relation between the return of the investment with the market index. Changes in the market index reflect changes in the level of business conditions generally. This component of risk is called the systematic risk. A second component of risk is unique to the particular investment.

The two components are reflected in the formula for the variance of the return of a single investment and the formula for the covariance. These formulas, which we derive in chapter Appendix 2, are

$$\text{Var}\,(r_i) = b_i^2 q_{n+1} + q_i,$$
$$\text{Cov}\,(r_i r_j) = b_i b_j q_{n+1},$$

where q_{n+1} is the variance of the market index and q_i is the variance of security i's return around its expected value for a given level of the market index, and b_i shows the average relationship between a change in the market index and a change in the return of the individual investment. (b_j is the same measure for a different security.)

The quantity Var (r_i) can be called an indicator of the total risk of security i. Intuitively, one might expect that if investors dislike risky securities, an increase in either component of risk would decrease the attractiveness of a security and thus require it to earn a higher return in order to be competitive. Given the variance of the market index, q_{n+1}, the total risk of security i will tend to increase if either q_i is increased or if b_i is increased.[7]

However, to determine the effect on the portfolio's risk of adding more of a security, we must determine the covariances of this investment and the other investments currently held. (The signs of b_i and b_j are important.)

The risk of a security is evaluated by an investor not on the basis of its total risk, but on the basis of the risk it contributes to the security owner's portfolio. Unless a given security is a relatively large part of a portfolio, the change in the riskiness of the portfolio that results from adding more of the security to the portfolio depends more on the size of the covariance between the return of the security and the return of the portfolio than on the size of the variance.

The main practical significance of the Sharpe model for capital budgeting is that it strongly suggests that in evaluating the riskiness of capital investments from the point of view of shareholders we should concentrate our attention not on the total variance of the investment proposal, but on its interaction with the other investments. The sign and size of the product $b_i b_j$ is extremely important (or equivalently, the covariance is important). Chapters 11 and 12 made use of this principle.

---

[7] Only an increase in b_i will lead to a higher expected rate of return. The expected return of a security is $E(r_i) = a_i + b_i(a_{n+1})$.

conclusions

In this chapter we presented models for computing the mean and variance of a portfolio. Markowitz has defined an efficient frontier of investments in terms of a portfolio that with a given variance has the largest mean, or with a given mean has the smallest variance. Using the concepts of this chapter supplemented by programming techniques, we can compute the mean and variances of different sets of investments[8] and find efficient investments.

Unfortunately, the real world is not a mean–variance world, but is more complex, because other factors (or, more exactly, higher moments of the probability distribution of outcomes) are likely to be relevant to the decision maker.

Despite the limitations of the models presented, they represent progress in the art of investment decision making. Through the years we have moved from the rules of thumb, such as payback and a naïve return on investment, to the discounted cash flow procedures (present value and rate of return), and finally to considerations of risk. Risk was first approached from the point of view of the individual investment; finally it was recognized that the statistical interaction of investments (the correlation of investments) and the risk of the portfolio were more important than the risk of the individual investment.

The old tools of investment decision making are still being used and will be used in the future, but they will be supplemented by techniques that enable the manager to grasp better the consequences of his decisions.

appendix 1: the expected return of a portfolio

We want to explain the use of x_{n+1} in the computation of the expected return: $E(R) = x'a$. Let

$$r_1 = a_1 + b_1 d + c_1,$$
$$r_2 = a_2 + b_2 d + c_2,$$
$$r_3 = a_3 + b_3 d + c_3,$$
$$d = a_4 + c_4,$$
$$E(d) = a_4,$$
$$p' = [x_1, x_2, x_3].$$

[8] H. M. Markowitz, "Portfolio Selection," *Journal of Finance*, March 1952, pp. 77–91; or *Portfolio Selection: Efficient Diversification of Investments*, Cowles Foundation Monograph No. 16 (New York: John Wiley & Sons, Inc., 1959).

The expected returns are

$$E(r_i) = a_i + b_i E(d) = a_i + b_i a_4,$$
$$E(r_1) = a_1 + b_1 a_4,$$
$$E(r_2) = a_2 + b_2 a_4,$$
$$E(r_3) = a_3 + b_3 a_4.$$

The expected return for the portfolio is

$$E(R) = x_1(a_1 + b_1 a_4) + x_2(a_2 + b_2 a_4) + x_3(a_3 + b_3 a_4)$$
$$= a_1 x_1 + a_2 x_2 + a_3 x_3 + a_4 \sum_{i=1}^{n} x_i b_i.$$

The term a_4 is being multiplied by an amount that has been defined to be x_4, or x_{n+1}; thus

$$E(R) = a_1 x_1 + a_2 x_2 + a_3 x_3 + a_4 x_4$$
$$= x'a.$$

appendix 2
covariance between investment rates of return

We can calculate the covariance between the rates of return of any pair of investments i and j as follows. First the expression for the relationship between investment i and the market index is noted.

$$r_i = a_i + b_i d + c_i$$

In this relationship we substitute the expression for d.

$$r_i = a_i + b_i(a_{n+1} + c_{n+1}) + c_i$$

Taking expected values

$$E(r_i) = a_i + b_i a_{n+1}.$$

The deviation between any particular return and its expected value is

$$r_i - E(r_i) = a_i + b_i(a_{n+1} + c_{n+1}) + c_i - a_i - b_i a_{n+1}$$
$$= b_i c_{n+1} + c_i.$$

A similar expression exists for every security. The covariance between the returns of the ith and jth security is

$$\text{Cov}(r_i, r_j) = E[(b_i c_{n+1} + c_i)(b_j c_{n+1} + c_j)]$$
$$= E[b_i b_j c_{n+1}^2 + b_i c_{n+1} c_j + b_j c_{n+1} c_i + c_i c_j].$$

Since $E(c_i) = E(c_j c_{n+1}) = E(c_i c_{n+1}) = 0$, we have

$$\text{Cov}(r_i, r_j) = b_i b_j q_{n+1} + E(c_i c_j).$$

If $i \neq j$, then $E(c_i c_j) = 0$, and

$$\text{Cov}(r_i, r_j) = b_i b_j q_{n+1}.$$

If $i = j$, then

$$\text{Cov}(r_i, r_i) = b_i^2 q_{n+1} + q_i = \text{Var}(r_i).$$

questions and problems

21-1. Assume that the expected returns and variance–covariance matrix for two securities in a portfolio are

$$\bar{r} = \begin{bmatrix} .20 \\ .10 \end{bmatrix}, \qquad V = \begin{bmatrix} .04 & -.01 \\ -.01 & .02 \end{bmatrix}.$$

Compute the expected return and variance for

a. $x' = [1, 0]$
b. $x' = [0, 1]$
c. $x' = [.3, .7]$

21-2. There are two investments (A and B) that will have the following returns for the specified states.

	States		
Investment	1	2	3
A	.40	.20	.00
B	.00	.30	.30
State probabilities	.5	.4	.1

Required: Compute the expected return of investing .8 in A and .2 in B. Also compute the variance–covariance matrix.

21-3. Consider a portfolio with two securities with the following characteristics:

$$r_1 = 50 + .8d + c_1 \quad \text{and} \quad q_1 = 100,$$
$$r_2 = 40 - .1d + c_2 \quad \text{and} \quad q_2 = 50,$$
$$d = 20 + c_3 \quad \text{and} \quad q_3 = 2{,}500.$$

Required: Calculate the expected return and variance of the return for the following portfolios:

a. $x_1 = 1, x_2 = 0$
b. $x_1 = .4, x_2 = .6$

chapter 22

*If a man will begin with certainties, he shall end in
doubt; but if he will be content to begin with
doubts, he shall end in certainties.*

—Francis Bacon, *Advancement of Learning*, v. 8 (ed. 1605).
From *Oxford Dictionary of Quotations*, 2nd ed. (New York:
Oxford University Press, Inc., 1959).

capital rationing: a programming approach

We argue that a firm cannot rank independent investments using any of the conventional methods of evaluating investments (rate of return, present value, profitability index, index of present value, and so on). However, businessmen do claim that capital rationing does exist (there are more desirable investments than there are funds available for investment), and they want a solution of the problem. There follows a solution that uses a programming approach.[1] An effort is made to find the set of investments through time that maximizes the present value of future dividends. We find that it is not necessary to rank individual investments, but rather the firm can choose the best set of investments.

basic problems of ranking investments

Consider a situation where a firm has a capital budget limited to $10,000 and has the following two investment opportunities:

[1] H. M. Weingartner in *Mathematical Programming and the Analysis of Capital Budgeting Problems*, (Englewood Cliffs, N.J.: Prentice-Hall, 1963) and "Capital Budgeting of Interrelated Projects: Survey and Synthesis," *Management Science*, March 1966, made the initial breakthroughs in this area. Weingartner's solution was modified by W. J. Baumol and R. D. Quandt in "Investment and Discount Rates Under Capital Rationing —A Programming Approach," *The Economic Journal*, June 1965. More recently, W. T. Carleton has built on the Weingartner and Baumol–Quandt models in "An Analytical Model in Long-Range Financial Planning," *Journal of Finance*, May 1970, and "Linear Programming and Capital Budgeting Models: A New Interpretation," *Journal of Finance*, Dec. 1969.

	Period			Net	
	0	1	2	Present Value (.05)	Yield
x_1	− $10,000		$12,100	$975	.10
x_2	− 10,000	$11,400		857	.14

Using present values and assuming that the time value of money is .05, the firm would choose x_1. However, if it chooses x_1, the opportunity cost of funds is .10; and if either .10 or .14 is used as the opportunity cost, x_2 is preferred to x_1.

Now add the information that in period 1 the firm can invest in investment x_3 that costs $11,400 and will pay $12,540 in period 2 (it has a present value of $517 and a yield of .10). It is feasible to invest in both x_2 and x_3. The joint investment will have a present value of $1,374, which is higher than the present value of investing only in x_1.

In a capital-rationing situation the time value of money cannot be used as a discount rate for individual investments since it does not represent the opportunity cost of funds. However, when we incorporate all sequential investments, this opportunity cost is taken into account, and the time value of money can be used to discount terminal values of all alternatives back to the present. Since the alternatives are all being multiplied by the same constant, the final result is not changed; the analysis could just as well be done using terminal values.

Although not exactly the same as the process that will be described next (dividends will be discounted back), the preceding example does illustrate what we are trying to accomplish in the capital-rationing model. The objective of the section to follow is to develop a systematic procedure for arriving at a solution to the type of problem illustrated here, that is, to determine the optimum set of investments.

a programming approach: the primal

We shall assume that the objective of the firm is to maximize the present value of the dividends of the firm and that there is no adjustment for risk. The capital-rationing problem will be solved by maximizing the present value of the dividends generated by the investments. Initially, we shall set no limitations on dividend policy (other than that dividends must be non-negative).

We shall define the rate of interest to be used for accomplishing the discounting of dividends to be a default-free market rate (a risk adjustment would be added or subtracted from the resulting present value if the investment were not risk neutral).

We shall initially illustrate a situation in which it is not necessary to consider investing the funds in short-term securities, but later this assumption will be relaxed. In addition, we shall assume that all investments are continuous (any amount may be invested in any investment), and the yields of all investments considered are larger than the cost of new funds.

In matrix notation we then have

$$\text{Maximize} \quad Z = a'D$$
$$\text{subject to}$$
$$Cx + D \le M,$$
$$x, D \ge 0,$$

where a = time-value-factors vector (a' is a row vector),

D = dividend vector,

C = matrix of cash flows (outlays are positive and inflows are negative), the rows are the cash flows of each period and the columns are the cash flows of each investment,

M = column vector of cash available from outside sources,

x = column vector indicating the number of units invested in each investment.

In summation notation, assuming J different investments and a planning horizon of T periods, we would have

$$\text{Max} \quad Z = \sum_{t=0}^{T} a_t D_t$$

subject to

$$\sum_{j=1}^{J} C_{jt} x_j + D_t \le M_t, \qquad t = 0, 1, \ldots, T,$$
$$x_j, D_t \ge 0.$$

Let us consider the example solved previously:

	Cash Flows Investment		
Period	x_1	x_2	x_3
0	− $10,000	− $10,000	$ 0
1	0	11,400	− 11,400
2	12,100		12,540

Assume that .05 is the default-free rate of interest. We have

$$a' = (a_0 \quad a_1 \quad a_2) = (1.05^0 \quad 1.05^{-1} \quad 1.05^{-2}),$$
$$D' = (D_0 \quad D_1 \quad D_2),$$

$$C = \begin{bmatrix} 10{,}000 & 10{,}000 & 0 \\ 0 & -11{,}400 & 11{,}400 \\ -12{,}100 & 0 & -12{,}540 \end{bmatrix},$$

$$x' = (x_1 \quad x_2 \quad x_3).$$

If $x_1 = 1$, then one unit or \$10,000 is invested in investment $j = 1$ (investment X_1). Since financing of \$10,000 is available only at time 0, we have

$$M' = (M_0 \quad M_1 \quad M_2) = (10{,}000 \quad 0 \quad 0).$$

The primal is

$$\text{Max} \quad Z = a'D = (1.05^0 \quad 1.05^{-1} \quad 1.05^{-2}) \begin{pmatrix} D_0 \\ D_1 \\ D_2 \end{pmatrix}$$

Subject to

$$\begin{bmatrix} 10{,}000 & 10{,}000 & 0 \\ 0 & -11{,}400 & +11{,}400 \\ -12{,}100 & 0 & -12{,}540 \end{bmatrix} \begin{bmatrix} X_1 \\ X_2 \\ X_3 \end{bmatrix} + \begin{bmatrix} D_0 \\ D_1 \\ D_2 \end{bmatrix} \leq \begin{bmatrix} 10{,}000 \\ 0 \\ 0 \end{bmatrix},$$
$$x_j, D_t \geq 0.$$

Completing the matrix multiplication,

$$\text{Max} \quad Z = \sum_{t=0}^{2} a_t D_t = \sum_{t=0}^{2} (1.05)^{-t} D_t$$

subject to

$$10{,}000x_1 + 10{,}000x_2 + 0x_3 + D_0 \leq 10{,}000,$$
$$0x_1 - 11{,}400x_2 + 11{,}400x_3 + D_1 \leq 0,$$
$$-12{,}100x_1 + 0x_2 - 12{,}540x_3 + D_2 \leq 0.$$

If

$$x_1 = D_0 = D_1 = 0,$$
$$x_2 = 1,$$
$$x_3 = 1,$$
$$D_2 = 12{,}540,$$

the value of the objective function is

$$Z = 1.05^{-2} \times 12{,}540 = \$11{,}374$$

and the constraints are satisfied. No other solution is better. The solution may be found using standard linear programming techniques.

If x_1 and x_2 were mutually exclusive investments, there would be an additional restraint, such as

$$x_1 + x_2 \leq 1.$$

If any of the x_i have to be integers, the problem would be solved using integer programming.

the dual

The dual of the problem can also be formulated (see the chapter appendix for the derivation):

$$\begin{aligned}
\text{Minimize} \quad & Z = M'k \\
\text{subject to} \quad & \\
& C'k \geq 0, \\
& k \;\; \geq 0, \\
& k \;\; \geq a.
\end{aligned}$$

The values of the k vector set values for additional amounts M_t. Thus, if $k_0 = 1.10$, this would mean that one more dollar to invest in period 0 would have a present value of \$1.10.

In the example the dual would be

$$\text{Min} \quad Z = (10{,}000 \quad 0 \quad 0) \begin{pmatrix} k_0 \\ k_1 \\ k_2 \end{pmatrix}$$

subject to

$$\begin{bmatrix} 10{,}000 & 0 & -12{,}100 \\ 10{,}000 & -11{,}400 & 0 \\ 0 & +11{,}400 & -12{,}540 \end{bmatrix} \begin{pmatrix} k_0 \\ k_1 \\ k_2 \end{pmatrix} \geq 0,$$

$$k \geq a.$$

interpretation of dual variables

Assume that k_t is the value of an additional dollar of investment in period t and k_{t+1} is the value in period $t + 1$.

Let r_{t+1} be the opportunity cost, or the firm's time-value factor for the time period $t + 1$. Then

$$\frac{k_{t+1}}{k_t} = (1 + r_{t+1})^{-1}$$

or

$$1 + r_{t+1} = \frac{k_t}{k_{t+1}}.$$

EXAMPLE: Assume that

$$k_t = 1.265,$$
$$k_{t+1} = 1.10.$$

Then

$$1 + r_{t+1} = \frac{1.265}{1.100} = 1.15$$

and

$$r_{t+1} = .15.$$

Funds have a higher opportunity cost in period t than in period $t + 1$; thus a dollar would have to earn .15 to justify transferring it to period $t + 1$.

$$k_t = 1.10,$$
$$k_{t+1} = 1.265,$$

then

$$1 + r_{t+1} = \frac{1.100}{1.265} = .8696,$$

$$r_{t+1} = -.1304.$$

It is better to transfer a dollar to period $t + 1$ even if the transferral has a negative return (the opportunity to invest at a default-free rate would preclude this negative return from happening).

expanded model

The preceding formulation did not allow for the retention of cash (or more accurately the investment in short-term securities). We shall now expand the investment set to $J + T$ investments in order to allow such investments. We shall assume that an investment of x_{J+t} in period t will result in x_{J+t}/a_1 in period $t + 1$. The matrix formulation will be identical to that already presented, but the x vector and the C matrix will be different. On completion of the matrix multiplication, we will have in the constraints of period t

$$C_{1t}x_1 + C_{2t}x_2 + \cdots + C_{Jt}x_J + x_{J+t} - \frac{x_{J+t-1}}{a_1} + D_t = M_t.$$

other constraints

Many other constraints may be added. For example, one can specify dividends for a period of years, making the dividends up to some given time period constants and then letting the dividends after that time period be a function of the earlier dividend policy (if the early dividends are set too high, there will be no feasible solution).

In addition to specifying a desired dividend policy, management may also specify other artificial goals, such as earnings per share or total earnings for each year. The impact of different investments on earnings would have to be computed and a restraint equation established.

Again it is possible that no set of investments or dividend policies will enable us to satisfy the earnings constraint. In this situation the planner must return to top management and explain the difficulty (one practical solution is to revise the effect on earnings by changing the accounting procedures).

The more constraints that are added, or the more that the D vector is specified, the more drag there is on Z. Each constraint tends to reduce the maximum feasible Z. This does not necessarily mean that constraints are undesirable. If the constraint reduces risk or in some other way enhances the value of the common stock, it is possible for Z to go down and the value of the stockholder's holdings to go up. Nevertheless, management should know the cost in terms of expected present value of adding a constraint.

conclusions

It is possible to formulate the capital-rationing situation as a linear (or integer) programming problem. Although this does not enable the firm to rank investments, it does lead to a selection of the best set of investments.

The procedure described in this chapter does have one very important limitation—the large amount of information required. It implies that management is willing and able to describe the investment opportunities of the future. Perhaps the most important contributions of the model are that it sets a standard by which rules of thumb must be compared and sets an objective. Rather than ranking investments, management should seek the set of sequential investments through time that will maximize the stockholder's well-being.

appendix
derivation of the dual[2]

The primal is

$$\text{Max} \quad Z = a'D$$

subject to

$$Cx + D \le M,$$
$$x, D \ge 0.$$

We want to show that the dual is

$$\text{Min} \quad Z = M'k$$

subject to

$$C'k \ge 0,$$
$$k \ge a.$$

Let

$$Y = \begin{pmatrix} x \\ D \end{pmatrix}, \quad V = \begin{pmatrix} 0 \\ a \end{pmatrix}, \quad B = (C\,I),$$

[2] John McClain and Vithala Rao assisted with this derivation.

where I is the identity matrix. Then

$$BY = (C\ I)\binom{x}{D} = Cx + D.$$

Since $V'Y = (0 \quad a')\binom{x}{D} = a'D$, we now have, using the basic definitions of the relationships of a primal and dual,

Primal	Dual
Max $V'Y$	Min $M'k$
subject to	subject to
$BY \leq M$,	$B'k \geq V$,
$Y \geq 0$.	$k \geq 0$.

Substituting back to the terms originally used,

Primal

Max $a'D$
subject to
$$Cx + D \leq M,$$
$$x \geq 0,$$
$$D \geq 0.$$

Dual

Min $M'k$
subject to
$$\binom{C'}{I}(k) \geq \binom{0}{a} \quad \text{or} \quad C'k \geq 0,$$
$$Ik \geq a \quad \text{or} \quad k \geq a.$$

questions and problems

22-1. Illustrate why one cannot rank independent investments by their rates of return.

22-2. Illustrate why one cannot rank independent investments by their present values.

22-3. Illustrate why one cannot rank independent investments by their indexes of present value (present value of benefits divided by present value of costs).

22-4. Does IBM have a situation that can be described as "capital rationing"? Explain.

22-5. Describe the informational requirements for the programming solution to capital rationing.

appendix tables

Table A. Present Value of $1.00

$$(1 + r)^{-n}$$

n/r	1.0%	1.1%	1.2%	1.3%	1.4%
1	.990099	.989120	.988142	.987167	.986193
2	.980296	.978358	.976425	.974498	.972577
3	.970590	.967713	.964847	.961992	.959149
4	.960980	.957184	.953406	.949647	.945906
5	.951466	.946769	.942101	.937460	.932847
6	.942045	.936468	.930930	.925429	.919967
7	.932718	.926279	.919891	.913553	.907265
8	.923483	.916201	.908983	.901829	.894739
9	.914340	.906232	.898205	.890256	.882386
10	.905287	.896372	.887554	.878831	.870203
11	.896324	.886620	.877030	.867553	.858188
12	.887449	.876973	.866630	.856420	.846339
13	.878663	.867431	.856354	.845429	.834654
14	.869963	.857993	.846200	.834580	.823130
15	.861349	.848658	.836166	.823869	.811766
16	.852821	.839424	.826251	.813296	.800558
17	.844377	.830291	.816453	.802859	.789505
18	.836017	.821257	.806772	.792556	.778604
19	.827740	.812322	.797205	.782385	.767854
20	.819544	.803483	.787752	.772345	.757253
21	.811430	.794741	.778411	.762433	.746798
22	.803396	.786094	.769181	.752649	.736487
23	.795442	.777541	.760061	.742990	.726318
24	.787566	.769081	.751048	.733455	.716290
25	.779768	.760713	.742142	.724042	.706401
26	.772048	.752437	.733342	.714750	.696648
27	.764404	.744250	.724646	.705578	.687029
28	.756836	.736152	.716054	.696523	.677544
29	.749342	.728143	.707563	.687585	.668189
30	.741923	.720220	.699173	.678761	.658963
35	.705914	.681883	.658692	.636311	.614712
40	.671653	.645586	.620554	.596516	.573432
45	.639055	.611221	.584624	.559210	.534924
50	.608039	.578685	.550775	.524237	.499002

n is the number of time periods.
r is the discount rate defined for the same unit of time as n.

n/r	1.5%	1.6%	1.7%	1.8%	1.9%
1	.985222	.984252	.983284	.982318	.981354
2	.970662	.968752	.966848	.964949	.963056
3	.956317	.953496	.950686	.947887	.945099
4	.942184	.938480	.934795	.931127	.927477
5	.928260	.923701	.919169	.914663	.910184
6	.914542	.909155	.903804	.898490	.893213
7	.901027	.894837	.888696	.882603	.876558
8	.887711	.880745	.873841	.866997	.860214
9	.874592	.866875	.859234	.851667	.844175
10	.861667	.853224	.844871	.836608	.828434
11	.848933	.839787	.830748	.821816	.812988
12	.836387	.826562	.816862	.807285	.797829
13	.824027	.813545	.803207	.793010	.782953
14	.811849	.800734	.789781	.778989	.768354
15	.799852	.788124	.776579	.765215	.754028
16	.788031	.775712	.763598	.751684	.739968
17	.776385	.763496	.750834	.738393	.726171
18	.764912	.751473	.738283	.725337	.712631
19	.753607	.739639	.725942	.712512	.699343
20	.742470	.727991	.713807	.699914	.686304
21	.731498	.716526	.701875	.687538	.673507
22	.720688	.705242	.690143	.675381	.660949
23	.710037	.694136	.678607	.663439	.648625
24	.699544	.683205	.667263	.651708	.636531
25	.689206	.672446	.656109	.640185	.624662
26	.679021	.661856	.645142	.628866	.613015
27	.668986	.651433	.634358	.617746	.601585
28	.659099	.641174	.623754	.606823	.590368
29	.649359	.631077	.613327	.596094	.579360
30	.639762	.621139	.603075	.585554	.568558
35	.593866	.573747	.554328	.535584	.517492
40	.551262	.529970	.509521	.489879	.471013
45	.511715	.489534	.468336	.448074	.428708
50	.475005	.452183	.430479	.409837	.390203

Table A.   Present Value of $1.00 (cont'd)

n/r	2.0%	2.1%	2.2%	2.3%	2.4%
1	.980392	.979432	.978474	.977517	.976562
2	.961169	.959287	.957411	.955540	.953674
3	.942322	.939556	.936801	.934056	.931323
4	.923845	.920231	.916635	.913056	.909495
5	.905731	.901304	.896903	.892528	.888178
6	.887971	.882766	.877596	.872461	.867362
7	.870560	.864609	.858704	.852846	.847033
8	.853490	.846826	.840220	.833671	.827181
9	.836755	.829408	.822133	.814928	.807794
10	.820348	.812349	.804435	.796606	.788861
11	.804263	.795640	.787119	.778696	.770372
12	.788493	.779276	.770175	.761189	.752316
13	.773033	.763247	.753596	.744075	.734684
14	.757875	.747549	.737373	.727346	.717465
15	.743015	.732173	.721500	.710993	.700649
16	.728446	.717114	.705969	.695008	.684228
17	.714163	.702364	.690772	.679382	.668191
18	.700159	.687918	.675902	.664108	.652530
19	.686431	.673769	.661352	.649177	.637237
20	.672971	.659911	.647116	.634581	.622302
21	.659776	.646338	.633186	.620314	.607716
22	.646839	.633044	.619556	.606368	.593473
23	.634156	.620023	.606219	.592735	.579563
24	.621721	.607271	.593169	.579408	.565980
25	.609531	.594780	.580400	.566382	.552715
26	.597579	.582547	.567906	.553648	.539761
27	.585862	.570565	.555681	.541200	.527110
28	.574375	.558829	.543720	.529032	.514756
29	.563112	.547335	.532015	.517138	.502691
30	.552071	.536078	.520563	.505511	.490909
35	.500028	.483169	.466894	.451183	.436015
40	.452890	.435482	.418759	.402694	.387259
45	.410197	.392502	.375586	.359415	.343955
50	.371528	.353763	.336864	.320788	.305494

Table A. Present Value of $1.00 (cont'd)

n/r	2.5%	2.6%	2.7%	2.8%	2.9%
1	.975610	.974659	.973710	.972763	.971817
2	.951814	.949960	.948111	.946267	.944429
3	.928599	.925887	.923185	.920493	.917812
4	.905951	.902424	.898914	.895422	.891946
5	.883854	.879555	.875282	.871033	.866808
6	.862297	.857266	.852270	.847308	.842379
7	.841265	.835542	.829864	.824230	.818639
8	.820747	.814369	.808047	.801780	.795567
9	.800728	.793732	.786803	.779941	.773146
10	.781198	.773618	.766118	.758698	.751357
11	.762145	.754013	.745976	.738033	.730182
12	.743556	.734906	.726365	.717931	.709603
13	.725420	.716282	.707268	.698376	.689605
14	.707727	.698131	.688674	.679354	.670170
15	.690466	.680440	.670569	.660851	.651282
16	.673625	.663197	.652939	.642851	.632928
17	.657195	.646390	.635774	.625341	.615090
18	.641166	.630010	.619059	.608309	.597755
19	.625528	.614045	.602784	.591740	.580909
20	.610271	.598484	.586937	.575622	.564537
21	.595386	.583318	.571506	.559944	.548627
22	.580865	.568536	.556481	.544693	.533165
23	.566697	.554129	.541851	.529857	.518139
24	.552875	.540087	.527606	.515425	.503537
25	.539391	.526400	.513735	.501386	.489346
26	.526235	.513061	.500229	.487729	.475554
27	.513400	.500059	.487077	.474445	.462152
28	.500878	.487387	.474272	.461522	.449127
29	.488661	.475036	.461803	.448952	.436470
30	.476743	.462998	.449663	.436723	.424169
35	.421371	.407232	.393581	.380400	.367673
40	.372431	.358183	.344494	.331341	.318702
45	.329174	.315042	.301530	.288609	.276254
50	.290942	.277097	.263923	.251388	.239459

Table A. Present Value of $1.00 (cont'd)

n/r	3.0%	3.1%	3.2%	3.3%	3.4%
1	.970874	.969932	.968992	.968054	.967118
2	.942596	.940768	.938946	.937129	.935317
3	.915142	.912481	.909831	.907192	.904562
4	.888487	.885045	.881620	.878211	.874818
5	.862609	.858434	.854283	.850156	.846052
6	.837484	.832622	.827793	.822997	.818233
7	.813092	.807587	.802125	.796705	.791327
8	.789409	.783305	.777253	.771254	.765307
9	.766417	.759752	.753152	.746616	.740142
10	.744094	.736908	.729799	.722764	.715805
11	.722421	.714751	.707169	.699675	.692268
12	.701380	.693260	.685241	.677323	.669505
13	.680951	.672415	.663994	.655686	.647490
14	.661118	.652197	.643405	.634739	.626199
15	.641862	.632587	.623454	.614462	.605608
16	.623167	.613566	.604122	.594833	.585695
17	.605016	.595117	.585390	.575830	.566436
18	.587395	.577224	.567238	.557435	.547810
19	.570286	.559868	.549649	.539627	.529797
20	.553676	.543034	.532606	.522388	.512377
21	.537549	.526706	.516091	.505700	.495529
22	.521893	.510869	.500088	.489545	.479235
23	.506692	.495508	.484582	.473906	.463476
24	.491934	.480609	.469556	.458767	.448236
25	.477606	.466158	.454996	.444111	.433497
26	.463695	.452142	.440888	.429924	.419243
27	.450189	.438547	.427217	.416190	.405458
28	.437077	.425361	.413970	.402894	.392125
29	.424346	.412571	.401133	.390023	.379231
30	.411987	.400166	.388695	.377564	.366762
35	.355383	.343516	.332055	.320988	.310300
40	.306557	.294885	.283669	.272890	.262530
45	.264439	.253140	.242334	.231999	.222114
50	.228107	.217304	.207021	.197235	.187920

Table A. Present Value of $1.00 (cont'd)

n/r	3.5%	3.6%	3.7%	3.8%	3.9%
1	.966184	.965251	.964320	.963391	.962464
2	.933511	.931709	.929913	.928122	.926337
3	.901943	.899333	.896734	.894145	.891566
4	.871442	.868082	.864739	.861411	.858100
5	.841973	.837917	.833885	.829876	.825890
6	.813501	.808801	.804132	.799495	.794889
7	.785991	.780696	.775441	.770227	.765052
8	.759412	.753567	.747773	.742030	.736335
9	.733731	.727381	.721093	.714865	.708696
10	.708919	.702106	.695364	.688694	.682094
11	.684946	.677708	.670554	.663482	.656491
12	.661783	.654158	.646629	.639193	.631849
13	.639404	.631427	.623557	.615793	.608132
14	.617782	.609486	.601309	.593249	.585305
15	.596891	.588307	.579854	.571531	.563335
16	.576706	.567863	.559165	.550608	.542190
17	.557204	.548131	.539214	.530451	.521838
18	.538361	.529084	.519975	.511031	.502250
19	.520156	.510699	.501422	.492323	.483398
20	.502566	.492952	.483532	.474300	.465253
21	.485571	.475823	.466279	.456936	.447789
22	.469151	.459288	.449643	.440208	.430981
23	.453286	.443328	.433599	.424093	.414803
24	.437957	.427923	.418129	.408567	.399233
25	.423147	.413053	.403210	.393610	.384248
26	.408838	.398700	.388823	.379200	.369825
27	.395012	.384846	.374950	.365318	.355943
28	.381654	.371473	.361572	.351944	.342582
29	.368748	.358564	.348671	.339060	.329723
30	.356278	.346105	.336231	.326648	.317346
35	.299977	.290007	.280378	.271077	.262093
40	.252572	.243002	.233803	.224960	.216460
45	.212659	.203616	.194965	.186689	.178772
50	.179053	.170613	.162578	.154929	.147646

Table A.   Present Value of $1.00 (cont'd)

n/r	4.0%	4.1%	4.2%	4.3%	4.4%
1	.961538	.960615	.959693	.958773	.957854
2	.924556	.922781	.921010	.919245	.917485
3	.888996	.886437	.883887	.881347	.878817
4	.854804	.851524	.848260	.845012	.841779
5	.821927	.817987	.814069	.810174	.806302
6	.790315	.785770	.781257	.776773	.772320
7	.759918	.754823	.749766	.744749	.739770
8	.730690	.725094	.719545	.714045	.708592
9	.702587	.696536	.690543	.684607	.678728
10	.675564	.669103	.662709	.656382	.650122
11	.649581	.642750	.635997	.629322	.622722
12	.624597	.617435	.610362	.603376	.596477
13	.600574	.593117	.585760	.578501	.571339
14	.577475	.569757	.562150	.554651	.547259
15	.555265	.547317	.539491	.531784	.524195
16	.533908	.525761	.517746	.509860	.502102
17	.513373	.505054	.496877	.488840	.480941
18	.493628	.485162	.476849	.468687	.460671
19	.474642	.466054	.457629	.449364	.441256
20	.456387	.447698	.439183	.430838	.422659
21	.438834	.430066	.421481	.413076	.404846
22	.421955	.413127	.404492	.396046	.387783
23	.405726	.396856	.388188	.379718	.371440
24	.390121	.381226	.372542	.364063	.355785
25	.375117	.366211	.357526	.349054	.340791
26	.360689	.351788	.343115	.334663	.326428
27	.346817	.337933	.329285	.320866	.312670
28	.333477	.324623	.316012	.307638	.299493
29	.320651	.311838	.303275	.294955	.286870
30	.308319	.299556	.291051	.282794	.274780
35	.253415	.245033	.236935	.229113	.221556
40	.208289	.200434	.192882	.185621	.178641
45	.171198	.163952	.157019	.150386	.144038
50	.140713	.134111	.127824	.121839	.116138

Table A.   Present Value of $1.00 (cont'd)

n/r	4.5%	4.6%	4.7%	4.8%	4.9%
1	.956938	.956023	.955110	.954198	.953289
2	.915730	.913980	.912235	.910495	.908760
3	.876297	.873786	.871284	.868793	.866310
4	.838561	.835359	.832172	.829001	.825844
5	.802451	.798623	.794816	.791031	.787268
6	.767896	.763501	.759137	.754801	.750494
7	.734828	.729925	.725059	.720230	.715437
8	.703185	.697825	.692511	.687242	.682018
9	.672904	.667137	.661424	.655765	.650161
10	.643928	.637798	.631732	.625730	.619791
11	.616199	.609750	.603374	.597071	.590840
12	.589664	.582935	.576288	.569724	.563241
13	.564272	.557299	.550419	.543630	.536931
14	.539973	.532790	.525710	.518731	.511851
15	.516720	.509360	.502111	.494972	.487941
16	.494469	.486960	.479571	.472302	.465149
17	.473176	.465545	.458043	.450670	.443421
18	.452800	.445071	.437482	.430028	.422709
19	.433302	.425498	.417843	.410332	.402964
20	.414643	.406786	.399086	.391538	.384141
21	.396787	.388897	.381171	.373605	.366197
22	.379701	.371794	.364060	.356494	.349091
23	.363350	.355444	.347717	.340166	.332785
24	.347703	.339813	.332108	.324586	.317240
25	.332731	.324869	.317200	.309719	.302422
26	.318402	.310582	.302961	.295533	.288295
27	.304691	.296923	.289361	.281998	.274829
28	.291571	.283866	.276371	.269082	.261991
29	.279015	.271382	.263965	.256757	.249753
30	.267000	.259447	.252116	.244997	.238087
35	.214254	.207201	.200385	.193801	.187438
40	.171929	.165475	.159270	.153302	.147564
45	.137964	.132152	.126590	.121267	.116172
50	.110710	.105540	.100616	.095926	.091459

n/r	5.0%	5.1%	5.2%	5.3%	5.4%
1	.952381	.951475	.950570	.949668	.948767
2	.907029	.905304	.903584	.901869	.900158
3	.863838	.861374	.858920	.856475	.854040
4	.822702	.819576	.816464	.813367	.810285
5	.783526	.779806	.776106	.772428	.768771
6	.746215	.741965	.737744	.733550	.729384
7	.710681	.705961	.701277	.696629	.692015
8	.676839	.671705	.666613	.661566	.656561
9	.644609	.639110	.633663	.628268	.622923
10	.613913	.608097	.602341	.596645	.591009
11	.584679	.578589	.572568	.566615	.560729
12	.556837	.550513	.544266	.538096	.532001
13	.530321	.523799	.517363	.511012	.504745
14	.505068	.498382	.491790	.485292	.478885
15	.481017	.474197	.467481	.460866	.454350
16	.458112	.451187	.444374	.437669	.431072
17	.436297	.429293	.422408	.415640	.408987
18	.415521	.408461	.401529	.394720	.388033
19	.395734	.388641	.381681	.374853	.368153
20	.376889	.369782	.362815	.355986	.349291
21	.358942	.351838	.344881	.338068	.331396
22	.341850	.334765	.327834	.321052	.314417
23	.325571	.318521	.311629	.304893	.298309
24	.310068	.303064	.296225	.289547	.283025
25	.295303	.288358	.281583	.274973	.268525
26	.281241	.274365	.267664	.261133	.254768
27	.267848	.261052	.254434	.247990	.241715
28	.255094	.248384	.241857	.235508	.229331
29	.242946	.236331	.229902	.223654	.217582
30	.231377	.224863	.218538	.212397	.206434
35	.181290	.175350	.169609	.164062	.158701
40	.142046	.136739	.131635	.126726	.122004
45	.111297	.106630	.102163	.097887	.093793
50	.087204	.083150	.079289	.075610	.072106

Table A. Present Value of $1.00 (cont'd)

n/r	5.5%	5.6%	5.7%	5.8%	5.9%
1	.947867	.946970	.946074	.945180	.944287
2	.898452	.896752	.895056	.893364	.891678
3	.851614	.849197	.846789	.844390	.842000
4	.807217	.804163	.801125	.798100	.795090
5	.765134	.761518	.757923	.754348	.750793
6	.725246	.721135	.717051	.712994	.708964
7	.687437	.682893	.678383	.673908	.669466
8	.651599	.646679	.641801	.636964	.632168
9	.617629	.612385	.607191	.602045	.596948
10	.585431	.579910	.574447	.569041	.563690
11	.554911	.549157	.543469	.537846	.532285
12	.525982	.520035	.514162	.508361	.502630
13	.498561	.492458	.486435	.480492	.474627
14	.472569	.466343	.460204	.454151	.448184
15	.447933	.441612	.435387	.429255	.423215
16	.424581	.418194	.411908	.405723	.399636
17	.402447	.396017	.389695	.383481	.377371
18	.381466	.375016	.368681	.362458	.356347
19	.361579	.355129	.348799	.342588	.336494
20	.342729	.336296	.329990	.323807	.317747
21	.324862	.318462	.312195	.306056	.300044
22	.307926	.301574	.295359	.289278	.283328
23	.291873	.285581	.279431	.273420	.267543
24	.276657	.270437	.264363	.258431	.252637
25	.262234	.256096	.250107	.244263	.238562
26	.248563	.242515	.236619	.230873	.225271
27	.235605	.229654	.223859	.218216	.212720
28	.223322	.217475	.211788	.206253	.200869
29	.211679	.205943	.200367	.194947	.189678
30	.200644	.195021	.189562	.184260	.179111
35	.153520	.148512	.143673	.138996	.134475
40	.117463	.113095	.108893	.104851	.100963
45	.089875	.086124	.082533	.079094	.075802
50	.068767	.065585	.062553	.059665	.056912

Table A. Present Value of $1.00 (cont'd)

n/r	6%	7%	8%	9%	10%	11%
1	0.9434	0.9346	0.9259	0.9174	0.9091	0.9009
2	0.8900	0.8734	0.8573	0.8417	0.8264	0.8116
3	0.8396	0.8163	0.7938	0.7722	0.7513	0.7312
4	0.7921	0.7629	0.7350	0.7084	0.6830	0.6587
5	0.7473	0.7130	0.6806	0.6499	0.6209	0.5935
6	0.7050	0.6663	0.6302	0.5963	0.5645	0.5346
7	0.6651	0.6227	0.5835	0.5470	0.5132	0.4817
8	0.6274	0.5820	0.5403	0.5019	0.4665	0.4339
9	0.5919	0.5439	0.5002	0.4604	0.4241	0.3909
10	0.5584	0.5083	0.4632	0.4224	0.3855	0.3522
11	0.5268	0.4751	0.4289	0.3875	0.3505	0.3173
12	0.4970	0.4440	0.3971	0.3555	0.3186	0.2858
13	0.4688	0.4150	0.3677	0.3262	0.2897	0.2575
14	0.4423	0.3878	0.3405	0.2992	0.2633	0.2320
15	0.4173	0.3624	0.3152	0.2745	0.2394	0.2090
16	0.3936	0.3387	0.2919	0.2519	0.2176	0.1883
17	0.3714	0.3166	0.2703	0.2311	0.1978	0.1696
18	0.3503	0.2959	0.2502	0.2120	0.1799	0.1528
19	0.3305	0.2765	0.2317	0.1945	0.1635	0.1377
20	0.3118	0.2584	0.2145	0.1784	0.1486	0.1240
21	0.2942	0.2415	0.1987	0.1637	0.1351	0.1117
22	0.2775	0.2257	0.1839	0.1502	0.1228	0.1007
23	0.2618	0.2109	0.1703	0.1378	0.1117	0.0907
24	0.2470	0.1971	0.1577	0.1264	0.1015	0.0817
25	0.2330	0.1842	0.1460	0.1160	0.0923	0.0736
26	0.2198	0.1722	0.1352	0.1064	0.0839	0.0663
27	0.2074	0.1609	0.1252	0.0976	0.0763	0.0597
28	0.1956	0.1504	0.1159	0.0895	0.0693	0.0538
29	0.1846	0.1406	0.1073	0.0822	0.0630	0.0485
30	0.1741	0.1314	0.0994	0.0754	0.0573	0.0437
35	0.1301	0.0937	0.0676	0.0490	0.0356	0.0259
40	0.0972	0.0668	0.0460	0.0318	0.0221	0.0154
45	0.0727	0.0476	0.0313	0.0207	0.0137	0.0091
50	0.0543	0.0339	0.0213	0.0134	0.0085	0.0054

n/r	12%	13%	14%	15%	16%	17%
1	0.8929	0.8850	0.8772	0.8696	0.8621	0.8547
2	0.7972	0.7831	0.7695	0.7561	0.7432	0.7305
3	0.7118	0.6931	0.6750	0.6575	0.6407	0.6244
4	0.6355	0.6133	0.5921	0.5718	0.5523	0.5337
5	0.5674	0.5428	0.5194	0.4972	0.4761	0.4561
6	0.5066	0.4803	0.4556	0.4323	0.4104	0.3898
7	0.4523	0.4251	0.3996	0.3759	0.3538	0.3332
8	0.4039	0.3762	0.3506	0.3269	0.3050	0.2848
9	0.3606	0.3329	0.3075	0.2843	0.2630	0.2434
10	0.3220	0.2946	0.2697	0.2472	0.2267	0.2080
11	0.2875	0.2607	0.2366	0.2149	0.1954	0.1778
12	0.2567	0.2307	0.2076	0.1869	0.1685	0.1520
13	0.2292	0.2042	0.1821	0.1625	0.1452	0.1299
14	0.2046	0.1807	0.1597	0.1413	0.1252	0.1110
15	0.1827	0.1599	0.1401	0.1229	0.1079	0.0949
16	0.1631	0.1415	0.1229	0.1069	0.0930	0.0811
17	0.1456	0.1252	0.1078	0.0929	0.0802	0.0693
18	0.1300	0.1108	0.0946	0.0808	0.0691	0.0592
19	0.1161	0.0981	0.0829	0.0703	0.0596	0.0506
20	0.1037	0.0868	0.0728	0.0611	0.0514	0.0433
21	0.0926	0.0768	0.0638	0.0531	0.0443	0.0370
22	0.0826	0.0680	0.0560	0.0462	0.0382	0.0316
23	0.0738	0.0601	0.0491	0.0402	0.0329	0.0270
24	0.0659	0.0532	0.0431	0.0349	0.0284	0.0231
25	0.0588	0.0471	0.0378	0.0304	0.0245	0.0197
26	0.0525	0.0417	0.0331	0.0264	0.0211	0.0169
27	0.0469	0.0369	0.0291	0.0230	0.0182	0.0144
28	0.0419	0.0326	0.0255	0.0200	0.0157	0.0123
29	0.0374	0.0289	0.0224	0.0174	0.0135	0.0105
30	0.0334	0.0256	0.0196	0.0151	0.0116	0.0090
35	0.0189	0.0139	0.0102	0.0075	0.0055	0.0041
40	0.0107	0.0075	0.0053	0.0037	0.0026	0.0019
45	0.0061	0.0041	0.0027	0.0019	0.0013	0.0009
50	0.0035	0.0022	0.0014	0.0009	0.0006	0.0004

Table A.   Present Value of $1.00 (cont'd)

n/r	18%	19%	20%	21%	22%	23%
1	0.8475	0.8403	0.8333	0.8264	0.8197	0.8130
2	0.7182	0.7062	0.6944	0.6830	0.6719	0.6610
3	0.6086	0.5934	0.5787	0.5645	0.5507	0.5374
4	0.5158	0.4987	0.4823	0.4665	0.4514	0.4369
5	0.4371	0.4190	0.4019	0.3855	0.3700	0.3552
6	0.3704	0.3521	0.3349	0.3186	0.3033	0.2888
7	0.3139	0.2959	0.2791	0.2633	0.2486	0.2348
8	0.2660	0.2487	0.2326	0.2176	0.2038	0.1909
9	0.2255	0.2090	0.1938	0.1799	0.1670	0.1552
10	0.1911	0.1756	0.1615	0.1486	0.1369	0.1262
11	0.1619	0.1476	0.1346	0.1228	0.1122	0.1026
12	0.1372	0.1240	0.1122	0.1015	0.0920	0.0834
13	0.1163	0.1042	0.0935	0.0839	0.0754	0.0678
14	0.0985	0.0876	0.0779	0.0693	0.0618	0.0551
15	0.0835	0.0736	0.0649	0.0573	0.0507	0.0448
16	0.0708	0.0618	0.0541	0.0474	0.0415	0.0364
17	0.0600	0.0520	0.0451	0.0391	0.0340	0.0296
18	0.0508	0.0437	0.0376	0.0323	0.0279	0.0241
19	0.0431	0.0367	0.0313	0.0267	0.0229	0.0196
20	0.0365	0.0308	0.0261	0.0221	0.0187	0.0159
21	0.0309	0.0259	0.0217	0.0183	0.0154	0.0129
22	0.0262	0.0218	0.0181	0.0151	0.0126	0.0105
23	0.0222	0.0183	0.0151	0.0125	0.0103	0.0086
24	0.0188	0.0154	0.0126	0.0103	0.0085	0.0070
25	0.0160	0.0129	0.0105	0.0085	0.0069	0.0057
26	0.0135	0.0109	0.0087	0.0070	0.0057	0.0046
27	0.0115	0.0091	0.0073	0.0058	0.0047	0.0037
28	0.0097	0.0077	0.0061	0.0048	0.0038	0.0030
29	0.0082	0.0064	0.0051	0.0040	0.0031	0.0025
30	0.0070	0.0054	0.0042	0.0033	0.0026	0.0020
35	0.0030	0.0023	0.0017	0.0013	0.0009	0.0007
40	0.0013	0.0010	0.0007	0.0005	0.0004	0.0002
45	0.0006	0.0004	0.0003	0.0002	0.0001	0.0001
50	0.0003	0.0002	0.0001	0.0001	0.0000	0.0000

Table A. Present Value of $1.00 (cont'd)

n/r	24%	25%	26%	27%	28%	29%
1	0.8065	0.8000	0.7937	0.7874	0.7813	0.7752
2	0.6504	0.6400	0.6299	0.6200	0.6104	0.6009
3	0.5245	0.5120	0.4999	0.4882	0.4768	0.4658
4	0.4230	0.4096	0.3968	0.3844	0.3725	0.3611
5	0.3411	0.3277	0.3149	0.3027	0.2910	0.2799
6	0.2751	0.2621	0.2499	0.2383	0.2274	0.2170
7	0.2218	0.2097	0.1983	0.1877	0.1776	0.1682
8	0.1789	0.1678	0.1574	0.1478	0.1388	0.1304
9	0.1443	0.1342	0.1249	0.1164	0.1084	0.1011
10	0.1164	0.1074	0.0992	0.0916	0.0847	0.0784
11	0.0938	0.0859	0.0787	0.0721	0.0662	0.0607
12	0.0757	0.0687	0.0625	0.0568	0.0517	0.0471
13	0.0610	0.0550	0.0496	0.0447	0.0404	0.0365
14	0.0492	0.0440	0.0393	0.0352	0.0316	0.0283
15	0.0397	0.0352	0.0312	0.0277	0.0247	0.0219
16	0.0320	0.0281	0.0248	0.0218	0.0193	0.0170
17	0.0258	0.0225	0.0197	0.0172	0.0150	0.0132
18	0.0208	0.0180	0.0156	0.0135	0.0118	0.0102
19	0.0168	0.0144	0.0124	0.0107	0.0092	0.0079
20	0.0135	0.0115	0.0098	0.0084	0.0072	0.0061
21	0.0109	0.0092	0.0078	0.0066	0.0056	0.0048
22	0.0088	0.0074	0.0062	0.0052	0.0044	0.0037
23	0.0071	0.0059	0.0049	0.0041	0.0034	0.0029
24	0.0057	0.0047	0.0039	0.0032	0.0027	0.0022
25	0.0046	0.0038	0.0031	0.0025	0.0021	0.0017
26	0.0037	0.0030	0.0025	0.0020	0.0016	0.0013
27	0.0030	0.0024	0.0019	0.0016	0.0013	0.0010
28	0.0024	0.0019	0.0015	0.0012	0.0010	0.0008
29	0.0020	0.0015	0.0012	0.0010	0.0008	0.0006
30	0.0016	0.0012	0.0010	0.0008	0.0006	0.0005
35	0.0005	0.0004	0.0003	0.0002	0.0002	0.0001
40	0.0002	0.0001	0.0001	0.0001	0.0001	0.0000
45	0.0001	0.0000	0.0000	0.0000	0.0000	
50	0.0000					

n/r	30%	31%	32%	33%	34%	35%
1	0.7692	0.7634	0.7576	0.7519	0.7463	0.7407
2	0.5917	0.5827	0.5739	0.5653	0.5569	0.5487
3	0.4552	0.4448	0.4348	0.4251	0.4156	0.4064
4	0.3501	0.3396	0.3294	0.3196	0.3102	0.3011
5	0.2693	0.2592	0.2495	0.2403	0.2315	0.2230
6	0.2072	0.1979	0.1890	0.1807	0.1727	0.1652
7	0.1594	0.1510	0.1432	0.1358	0.1289	0.1224
8	0.1226	0.1153	0.1085	0.1021	0.0962	0.0906
9	0.0943	0.0880	0.0822	0.0768	0.0718	0.0671
10	0.0725	0.0672	0.0623	0.0577	0.0536	0.0497
11	0.0558	0.0513	0.0472	0.0434	0.0400	0.0368
12	0.0429	0.0392	0.0357	0.0326	0.0298	0.0273
13	0.0330	0.0299	0.0271	0.0245	0.0223	0.0202
14	0.0253	0.0228	0.0205	0.0185	0.0166	0.0150
15	0.0195	0.0174	0.0155	0.0139	0.0124	0.0111
16	0.0150	0.0133	0.0118	0.0104	0.0093	0.0082
17	0.0116	0.0101	0.0089	0.0078	0.0069	0.0061
18	0.0089	0.0077	0.0068	0.0059	0.0052	0.0045
19	0.0068	0.0059	0.0051	0.0044	0.0038	0.0033
20	0.0053	0.0045	0.0039	0.0033	0.0029	0.0025
21	0.0040	0.0034	0.0029	0.0025	0.0021	0.0018
22	0.0031	0.0026	0.0022	0.0019	0.0016	0.0014
23	0.0024	0.0020	0.0017	0.0014	0.0012	0.0010
24	0.0018	0.0015	0.0013	0.0011	0.0009	0.0007
25	0.0014	0.0012	0.0010	0.0008	0.0007	0.0006
26	0.0011	0.0009	0.0007	0.0006	0.0005	0.0004
27	0.0008	0.0007	0.0006	0.0005	0.0004	0.0003
28	0.0006	0.0005	0.0004	0.0003	0.0003	0.0002
29	0.0005	0.0004	0.0003	0.0003	0.0002	0.0002
30	0.0004	0.0003	0.0002	0.0002	0.0002	0.0001
35	0.0001	0.0001	0.0001	0.0000	0.0000	0.0000
40	0.0000	0.0000	0.0000			
45						
50						

n/r	36%	37%	38%	39%	40%	41%
1	0.7353	0.7299	0.7246	0.7194	0.7143	0.7092
2	0.5407	0.5328	0.5251	0.5176	0.5102	0.5030
3	0.3975	0.3889	0.3805	0.3724	0.3644	0.3567
4	0.2923	0.2839	0.2757	0.2679	0.2603	0.2530
5	0.2149	0.2072	0.1998	0.1927	0.1859	0.1794
6	0.1580	0.1512	0.1448	0.1386	0.1328	0.1273
7	0.1162	0.1104	0.1049	0.0997	0.0949	0.0903
8	0.0854	0.0806	0.0760	0.0718	0.0678	0.0640
9	0.0628	0.0588	0.0551	0.0516	0.0484	0.0454
10	0.0462	0.0429	0.0399	0.0371	0.0346	0.0322
11	0.0340	0.0313	0.0289	0.0267	0.0247	0.0228
12	0.0250	0.0229	0.0210	0.0192	0.0176	0.0162
13	0.0184	0.0167	0.0152	0.0138	0.0126	0.0115
14	0.0135	0.0122	0.0110	0.0099	0.0090	0.0081
15	0.0099	0.0089	0.0080	0.0072	0.0064	0.0058
16	0.0073	0.0065	0.0058	0.0051	0.0046	0.0041
17	0.0054	0.0047	0.0042	0.0037	0.0033	0.0029
18	0.0039	0.0035	0.0030	0.0027	0.0023	0.0021
19	0.0029	0.0025	0.0022	0.0019	0.0017	0.0015
20	0.0021	0.0018	0.0016	0.0014	0.0012	0.0010
21	0.0016	0.0013	0.0012	0.0010	0.0009	0.0007
22	0.0012	0.0010	0.0008	0.0007	0.0006	0.0005
23	0.0008	0.0007	0.0006	0.0005	0.0004	0.0004
24	0.0006	0.0005	0.0004	0.0004	0.0003	0.0003
25	0.0005	0.0004	0.0003	0.0003	0.0002	0.0002
26	0.0003	0.0003	0.0002	0.0002	0.0002	0.0001
27	0.0002	0.0002	0.0002	0.0001	0.0001	0.0001
28	0.0002	0.0001	0.0001	0.0001	0.0001	0.0001
29	0.0001	0.0001	0.0001	0.0001	0.0001	0.0000
30	0.0001	0.0001	0.0001	0.0001	0.0000	
35	0.0000	0.0000	0.0000	0.0000		
40						
45						
50						

Table A. Present Value of $1.00 (cont'd)

n/r	42%	43%	44%	45%	46%	47%	48%
1	0.7042	0.6993	0.6944	0.6897	0.6849	0.6803	0.6757
2	0.4959	0.4890	0.4823	0.4756	0.4691	0.4628	0.4565
3	0.3492	0.3420	0.3349	0.3280	0.3213	0.3148	0.3085
4	0.2459	0.2391	0.2326	0.2262	0.2201	0.2142	0.2084
5	0.1732	0.1672	0.1615	0.1560	0.1507	0.1457	0.1408
6	0.1220	0.1169	0.1122	0.1076	0.1032	0.0991	0.0952
7	0.0859	0.0818	0.0779	0.0742	0.0707	0.0674	0.0643
8	0.0605	0.0572	0.0541	0.0512	0.0484	0.0459	0.0434
9	0.0426	0.0400	0.0376	0.0353	0.0332	0.0312	0.0294
10	0.0300	0.0280	0.0261	0.0243	0.0227	0.0212	0.0198
11	0.0211	0.0196	0.0181	0.0168	0.0156	0.0144	0.0134
12	0.0149	0.0137	0.0126	0.0116	0.0107	0.0098	0.0091
13	0.0105	0.0096	0.0087	0.0080	0.0073	0.0067	0.0061
14	0.0074	0.0067	0.0061	0.0055	0.0050	0.0045	0.0041
15	0.0052	0.0047	0.0042	0.0038	0.0034	0.0031	0.0028
16	0.0037	0.0033	0.0029	0.0026	0.0023	0.0021	0.0019
17	0.0026	0.0023	0.0020	0.0018	0.0016	0.0014	0.0013
18	0.0018	0.0016	0.0014	0.0012	0.0011	0.0010	0.0009
19	0.0013	0.0011	0.0010	0.0009	0.0008	0.0007	0.0006
20	0.0009	0.0008	0.0007	0.0006	0.0005	0.0005	0.0004
21	0.0006	0.0005	0.0005	0.0004	0.0004	0.0003	0.0003
22	0.0004	0.0004	0.0003	0.0003	0.0002	0.0002	0.0002
23	0.0003	0.0003	0.0002	0.0002	0.0002	0.0001	0.0001
24	0.0002	0.0002	0.0002	0.0001	0.0001	0.0001	0.0001
25	0.0002	0.0001	0.0001	0.0001	0.0001	0.0001	0.0001
26	0.0001	0.0001	0.0001	0.0001	0.0001	0.0000	0.0000
27	0.0001	0.0001	0.0001	0.0000	0.0000		
28	0.0001	0.0000	0.0000				
29	0.0000						
30							
35							
40							
45							
50							

Table B.   Present Value of $1 Received per Period

$$\frac{1 - (1 + r)^{-n}}{r}$$

n/r	1.0%	1.1%	1.2%	1.3%	1.4%
1	.99010	.98912	.98814	.98717	.98619
2	1.97040	1.96748	1.96457	1.96167	1.95877
3	2.94099	2.93519	2.92941	2.92366	2.91792
4	3.90197	3.89237	3.88282	3.87330	3.86383
5	4.85343	4.83914	4.82492	4.81076	4.79667
6	5.79548	5.77561	5.75585	5.73619	5.71664
7	6.72819	6.70189	6.67574	6.64975	6.62391
8	7.65168	7.61809	7.58473	7.55158	7.51864
9	8.56602	8.52432	8.48293	8.44183	8.40103
10	9.47130	9.42070	9.37048	9.32066	9.27123
11	10.36763	10.30732	10.24751	10.18822	10.12942
12	11.25508	11.18429	11.11414	11.04464	10.97576
13	12.13374	12.05172	11.97050	11.89007	11.81041
14	13.00370	12.90971	12.81670	12.72465	12.63354
15	13.86505	13.75837	13.65286	13.54852	13.44531
16	14.71787	14.59780	14.47911	14.36181	14.24587
17	15.56225	15.42809	15.29557	15.16467	15.03537
18	16.39827	16.24934	16.10234	15.95723	15.81398
19	17.22601	17.06167	16.89955	16.73961	16.58183
20	18.04555	17.86515	17.68730	17.51196	17.33908
21	18.85698	18.65989	18.46571	18.27439	18.08588
22	19.66038	19.44598	19.23489	19.02704	18.82237
23	20.45582	20.22353	19.99495	19.77003	19.54869
24	21.24339	20.99261	20.74600	20.50348	20.26498
25	22.02316	21.75332	21.48814	21.22752	20.97138
26	22.79520	22.50576	22.22148	21.94228	21.66803
27	23.55961	23.25001	22.94613	22.64785	22.35505
28	24.31644	23.98616	23.66218	23.34438	23.03260
29	25.06579	24.71430	24.36975	24.03196	23.70079
30	25.80771	25.43452	25.06892	24.71072	24.35975
31	26.54229	26.14691	25.75980	25.38077	25.00962
32	27.26959	26.85154	26.44249	26.04222	25.65051
33	27.98969	27.54851	27.11709	26.69519	26.28255
34	28.70267	28.23789	27.78368	27.33977	26.90587
35	29.40858	28.91977	28.44237	27.97608	27.52058
40	32.83469	32.21950	31.62051	31.03722	30.46915
45	36.09451	35.34358	34.61463	33.90692	33.21972
50	39.19612	38.30136	37.43540	36.59715	35.78557

n/r	1.5%	1.6%	1.7%	1.8%	1.9%
1	.98522	.98425	.98328	.98232	.98135
2	1.95588	1.95300	1.95013	1.94727	1.94441
3	2.91220	2.90650	2.90082	2.89515	2.88951
4	3.85438	3.84498	3.83561	3.82628	3.81699
5	4.78264	4.76868	4.75478	4.74094	4.72717
6	5.69719	5.67784	5.65859	5.63943	5.62038
7	6.59821	6.57267	6.54728	6.52204	6.49694
8	7.48593	7.45342	7.42112	7.38904	7.35716
9	8.36052	8.32029	8.28036	8.24070	8.20133
10	9.22218	9.17352	9.12523	9.07731	9.02976
11	10.07112	10.01330	9.95598	9.89913	9.84275
12	10.90751	10.83987	10.77284	10.70641	10.64058
13	11.73153	11.65341	11.57604	11.49942	11.42353
14	12.54338	12.45415	12.36583	12.27841	12.19189
15	13.34323	13.24227	13.14241	13.04363	12.94592
16	14.13126	14.01798	13.90600	13.79531	13.68588
17	14.90765	14.78148	14.65684	14.53370	14.41206
18	15.67256	15.53295	15.39512	15.25904	15.12469
19	16.42617	16.27259	16.12106	15.97155	15.82403
20	17.16864	17.00058	16.83487	16.67147	16.51033
21	17.90014	17.71711	17.53674	17.35900	17.18384
22	18.62082	18.42235	18.22689	18.03439	17.84479
23	19.33086	19.11649	18.90549	18.69782	18.49341
24	20.03041	19.79969	19.57276	19.34953	19.12995
25	20.71961	20.47214	20.22887	19.98972	19.75461
26	21.39863	21.13399	20.87401	20.61858	20.36762
27	22.06762	21.78543	21.50837	21.23633	20.96921
28	22.72672	22.42660	22.13212	21.84315	21.55958
29	23.37608	23.05768	22.74545	22.43925	22.13894
30	24.01584	23.67882	23.34852	23.02480	22.70749
31	24.64615	24.29017	23.94152	23.60000	23.26545
32	25.26714	24.89190	24.52460	24.16503	23.81300
33	25.87895	25.48416	25.09793	24.72007	24.35035
34	26.48173	26.06708	25.66168	25.26529	24.87767
35	27.07559	26.64083	26.21601	25.80088	25.39516
40	29.91585	29.37684	28.85172	28.34005	27.84144
45	32.55234	31.90411	31.27438	30.66254	30.06799
50	34.99969	34.23854	33.50121	32.78684	32.09457

n/r	2.0%	2.1%	2.2%	2.3%	2.4%
1	.98039	.97943	.97847	.97752	.97656
2	1.94156	1.93872	1.93588	1.93306	1.93024
3	2.88388	2.87828	2.87269	2.86711	2.86156
4	3.80773	3.79851	3.78932	3.78017	3.77105
5	4.71346	4.69981	4.68622	4.67270	4.65923
6	5.60143	5.58258	5.56382	5.54516	5.52659
7	6.47199	6.44719	6.42252	6.39800	6.37363
8	7.32548	7.29401	7.26274	7.23168	7.20081
9	8.16224	8.12342	8.08488	8.04660	8.00860
10	8.98259	8.93577	8.88931	8.84321	8.79746
11	9.78685	9.73141	9.67643	9.62191	9.56783
12	10.57534	10.51068	10.44660	10.38310	10.32015
13	11.34837	11.27393	11.20020	11.12717	11.05483
14	12.10625	12.02148	11.93757	11.85452	11.77230
15	12.84926	12.75365	12.65907	12.56551	12.47295
16	13.57771	13.47077	13.36504	13.26052	13.15718
17	14.29187	14.17313	14.05581	13.93990	13.82537
18	14.99203	14.86105	14.73172	14.60401	14.47790
19	15.67846	15.53482	15.39307	15.25318	15.11513
20	16.35143	16.19473	16.04019	15.88777	15.73744
21	17.01121	16.84107	16.67337	16.50808	16.34515
22	17.65805	17.47411	17.29293	17.11445	16.93863
23	18.29220	18.09413	17.89915	17.70718	17.51819
24	18.91393	18.70140	18.49231	18.28659	18.08417
25	19.52346	19.29618	19.07272	18.85297	18.63688
26	20.12104	19.87873	19.64062	19.40662	19.17664
27	20.70690	20.44930	20.19630	19.94782	19.70375
28	21.28127	21.00813	20.74002	20.47685	20.21851
29	21.84438	21.55546	21.27204	20.99399	20.72120
30	22.39646	22.09154	21.79260	21.49950	21.21211
31	22.93770	22.61659	22.30196	21.99365	21.69151
32	23.46833	23.13084	22.80035	22.47668	22.15968
33	23.98856	23.63452	23.28801	22.94886	22.61688
34	24.49859	24.12783	23.76518	23.41042	23.06336
35	24.99862	24.61100	24.23207	23.86160	23.49937
40	27.35548	26.88180	26.42004	25.96985	25.53087
45	29.49016	28.92849	28.38244	27.85151	27.33520
50	31.42361	30.77317	30.14252	29.53095	28.93777

n/r	2.5%	2.6%	2.7%	2.8%	2.9%
1	.97561	.97466	.97371	.97276	.97182
2	1.92742	1.92462	1.92182	1.91903	1.91625
3	2.85602	2.85051	2.84501	2.83952	2.83406
4	3.76197	3.75293	3.74392	3.73494	3.72600
5	4.64583	4.63248	4.61920	4.60598	4.59281
6	5.50813	5.48975	5.47147	5.45329	5.43519
7	6.34939	6.32529	6.30134	6.27751	6.25383
8	7.17014	7.13966	7.10938	7.07929	7.04940
9	7.97087	7.93339	7.89619	7.85924	7.82254
10	8.75206	8.70701	8.66230	8.61793	8.57390
11	9.51421	9.46103	9.40828	9.35597	9.30408
12	10.25776	10.19593	10.13464	10.07390	10.01369
13	10.98318	10.91221	10.84191	10.77227	10.70329
14	11.69091	11.61034	11.53059	11.45163	11.37346
15	12.38138	12.29078	12.20116	12.11248	12.02474
16	13.05500	12.95398	12.85409	12.75533	12.65767
17	13.71220	13.60037	13.48987	13.38067	13.27276
18	14.35336	14.23038	14.10893	13.98898	13.87052
19	14.97889	14.84443	14.71171	14.58072	14.45142
20	15.58916	15.44291	15.29865	15.15634	15.01596
21	16.18455	16.02623	15.87015	15.71629	15.56459
22	16.76541	16.59476	16.42663	16.26098	16.09775
23	17.33211	17.14889	16.96849	16.79084	16.61589
24	17.88499	17.68898	17.49609	17.30626	17.11943
25	18.42438	18.21538	18.00983	17.80765	17.60877
26	18.95061	18.72844	18.51005	18.29538	18.08433
27	19.46401	19.22850	18.99713	18.76982	18.54648
28	19.96489	19.71589	19.47140	19.23134	18.99561
29	20.45355	20.19092	19.93321	19.68029	19.43208
30	20.93029	20.65392	20.38287	20.11702	19.85625
31	21.39541	21.10519	20.82071	20.54185	20.26846
32	21.84918	21.54502	21.24704	20.95510	20.66906
33	22.29188	21.97370	21.66216	21.35710	21.05837
34	22.72379	22.39152	22.06637	21.74816	21.43670
35	23.14516	22.79875	22.45995	22.12856	21.80438
40	25.10278	24.68525	24.27798	23.88067	23.49303
45	26.83302	26.34453	25.86927	25.40682	24.95677
50	28.36231	27.80396	27.26210	26.73615	26.22555

Table B. Present Value of $1 Received per Period (cont'd)

n/r	3.0%	3.1%	3.2%	3.3%	3.4%
1	.97087	.96993	.96899	.96805	.96712
2	1.91347	1.91070	1.90794	1.90518	1.90244
3	2.82861	2.82318	2.81777	2.81237	2.80700
4	3.71710	3.70823	3.69939	3.69059	3.68182
5	4.57971	4.56666	4.55367	4.54074	4.52787
6	5.41719	5.39928	5.38146	5.36374	5.34610
7	6.23028	6.20687	6.18359	6.16044	6.13743
8	7.01969	6.99017	6.96084	6.93170	6.90274
9	7.78611	7.74993	7.71400	7.67831	7.64288
10	8.53020	8.48683	8.44379	8.40108	8.35868
11	9.25262	9.20159	9.15096	9.10075	9.05095
12	9.95400	9.89485	9.83620	9.77808	9.72045
13	10.63496	10.56726	10.50020	10.43376	10.36794
14	11.29607	11.21946	11.14360	11.06850	10.99414
15	11.93794	11.85204	11.76706	11.68296	11.59975
16	12.56110	12.46561	12.37118	12.27780	12.18545
17	13.16612	13.06073	12.95657	12.85363	12.75188
18	13.75351	13.63795	13.52381	13.41106	13.29969
19	14.32380	14.19782	14.07346	13.95069	13.82949
20	14.87747	14.74085	14.60606	14.47308	14.34187
21	15.41502	15.26756	15.12215	14.97878	14.83740
22	15.93692	15.77843	15.62224	15.46832	15.31663
23	16.44361	16.27393	16.10682	15.94223	15.78011
24	16.93554	16.75454	16.57638	16.40100	16.22834
25	17.41315	17.22070	17.03138	16.84511	16.66184
26	17.87684	17.67284	17.47226	17.27503	17.08108
27	18.32703	18.11139	17.89948	17.69122	17.48654
28	18.76411	18.53675	18.31345	18.09412	17.87867
29	19.18845	18.94932	18.71458	18.48414	18.25790
30	19.60044	19.34949	19.10328	18.86170	18.62466
31	20.00043	19.73762	19.47992	19.22721	18.97936
32	20.38877	20.11409	19.84488	19.58103	19.32240
33	20.76579	20.47923	20.19853	19.92355	19.65416
34	21.13184	20.83339	20.54121	20.25513	19.97501
35	21.48722	21.17691	20.87327	20.57612	20.28531
40	23.11477	22.74563	22.38534	22.03365	21.69030
45	24.51871	24.09227	23.67708	23.27277	22.87900
50	25.72976	25.24827	24.78058	24.32621	23.88471

Table B. Present Value of $1 Received per Period (cont'd)

n/r	3.5%	3.6%	3.7%	3.8%	3.9%
1	.96618	.96525	.96432	.96339	.96246
2	1.89969	1.89696	1.89423	1.89151	1.88880
3	2.80164	2.79629	2.79097	2.78566	2.78037
4	3.67308	3.66438	3.65571	3.64707	3.63847
5	4.51505	4.50229	4.48959	4.47695	4.46436
6	5.32855	5.31109	5.29372	5.27644	5.25925
7	6.11454	6.09179	6.06916	6.04667	6.02430
8	6.87396	6.84536	6.81694	6.78870	6.76063
9	7.60769	7.57274	7.53803	7.50356	7.46933
10	8.31661	8.27484	8.23340	8.19226	8.15142
11	9.00155	8.95255	8.90395	8.85574	8.80792
12	9.66333	9.60671	9.55058	9.49493	9.43976
13	10.30274	10.23814	10.17413	10.11072	10.04790
14	10.92052	10.84762	10.77544	10.70397	10.63320
15	11.51741	11.43593	11.35530	11.27550	11.19654
16	12.09412	12.00379	11.91446	11.82611	11.73873
17	12.65132	12.55192	12.45368	12.35656	12.26056
18	13.18968	13.08101	12.97365	12.86759	12.76281
19	13.70984	13.59171	13.47507	13.35992	13.24621
20	14.21240	14.08466	13.95861	13.83422	13.71147
21	14.69797	14.56048	14.42488	14.29115	14.15925
22	15.16712	15.01977	14.87453	14.73136	14.59024
23	15.62041	15.46310	15.30813	15.15545	15.00504
24	16.05837	15.89102	15.72625	15.56402	15.40427
25	16.48151	16.30407	16.12946	15.95763	15.78852
26	16.89035	16.70277	16.51829	16.33683	16.15834
27	17.28536	17.08762	16.89324	16.70215	16.51429
28	17.66702	17.45909	17.25481	17.05409	16.85687
29	18.03577	17.81766	17.60348	17.39315	17.18659
30	18.39205	18.16376	17.93971	17.71980	17.50394
31	18.73628	18.49784	18.26395	18.03449	17.80937
32	19.06887	18.82031	18.57661	18.33766	18.10334
33	19.39021	19.13157	18.87812	18.62973	18.38628
34	19.70068	19.43202	19.16887	18.91111	18.65859
35	20.00066	19.72203	19.44925	19.18218	18.92069
40	21.35507	21.02772	20.70803	20.39578	20.09076
45	22.49545	22.12179	21.75771	21.40292	21.05712
50	23.45562	23.03853	22.63302	22.23871	21.85522

Table B. Present Value of $1 Received per Period (cont'd)

n/r	4.0%	4.1%	4.2%	4.3%	4.4%
1	.96154	.96061	.95969	.95877	.95785
2	1.88609	1.88340	1.88070	1.87802	1.87534
3	2.77509	2.76983	2.76459	2.75937	2.75416
4	3.62990	3.62136	3.61285	3.60438	3.59594
5	4.45182	4.43934	4.42692	4.41455	4.40224
6	5.24214	5.22511	5.20818	5.19132	5.17456
7	6.00205	5.97994	5.95794	5.93607	5.91433
8	6.73274	6.70503	6.67749	6.65012	6.62292
9	7.43533	7.40157	7.36803	7.33473	7.30165
10	8.11090	8.07067	8.03074	7.99111	7.95177
11	8.76048	8.71342	8.66674	8.62043	8.57449
12	9.38507	9.33085	9.27710	9.22381	9.17097
13	9.98565	9.92397	9.86286	9.80231	9.74231
14	10.56312	10.49373	10.42501	10.35696	10.28957
15	11.11839	11.04105	10.96450	10.88874	10.81376
16	11.65230	11.56681	11.48225	11.39860	11.31586
17	12.16567	12.07186	11.97912	11.88744	11.79680
18	12.65930	12.55702	12.45597	12.35613	12.25747
19	13.13394	13.02308	12.91360	12.80549	12.69873
20	13.59033	13.47077	13.35278	13.23633	13.12139
21	14.02916	13.90084	13.77426	13.64941	13.52623
22	14.45112	14.31397	14.17876	14.04545	13.91402
23	14.85684	14.71082	14.56694	14.42517	14.28546
24	15.24696	15.09205	14.93949	14.78923	14.64124
25	15.62208	15.45826	15.29701	15.13829	14.98203
26	15.98277	15.81005	15.64013	15.47295	15.30846
27	16.32959	16.14798	15.96941	15.79381	15.62113
28	16.66306	16.47260	16.28542	16.10145	15.92062
29	16.98371	16.78444	16.58870	16.39641	16.20749
30	17.29203	17.08400	16.87975	16.67920	16.48227
31	17.58849	17.37176	17.15907	16.95034	16.74547
32	17.87355	17.64818	17.42713	17.21029	16.99758
33	18.14765	17.91372	17.68438	17.45953	17.23906
34	18.41120	18.16880	17.93127	17.69850	17.47036
35	18.66461	18.41383	18.16821	17.92761	17.69192
40	19.79277	19.50162	19.21710	18.93904	18.66726
45	20.72004	20.39141	20.07097	19.75848	19.45368
50	21.48218	21.11925	20.76608	20.42236	20.08777

Table B. Present Value of $1 Received per Period (cont'd)

n/r	4.5%	4.6%	4.7%	4.8%	4.9%
1	.95694	.95602	.95511	.95420	.95329
2	1.87267	1.87000	1.86734	1.86469	1.86205
3	2.74896	2.74379	2.73863	2.73349	2.72836
4	3.58753	3.57915	3.57080	3.56249	3.55420
5	4.38998	4.37777	4.36562	4.35352	4.34147
6	5.15787	5.14127	5.12475	5.10832	5.09196
7	5.89270	5.87120	5.84981	5.82855	5.80740
8	6.59589	6.56902	6.54232	6.51579	6.48942
9	7.26879	7.23616	7.20375	7.17156	7.13958
10	7.91272	7.87396	7.83548	7.79729	7.75937
11	8.52892	8.48371	8.43885	8.39436	8.35021
12	9.11858	9.06664	9.01514	8.96408	8.91345
13	9.68285	9.62394	9.56556	9.50771	9.45038
14	10.22283	10.15673	10.09127	10.02644	9.96223
15	10.73955	10.66609	10.59338	10.52141	10.45018
16	11.23402	11.15305	11.07295	10.99372	10.91532
17	11.70719	11.61859	11.53100	11.44438	11.35875
18	12.15999	12.06367	11.96848	11.87441	11.78145
19	12.59329	12.48916	12.38632	12.28475	12.18442
20	13.00794	12.89595	12.78541	12.67628	12.56856
21	13.40472	13.28485	13.16658	13.04989	12.93476
22	13.78442	13.65664	13.53064	13.40638	13.28385
23	14.14777	14.01209	13.87835	13.74655	13.61663
24	14.49548	14.35190	14.21046	14.07113	13.93387
25	14.82821	14.67677	14.52766	14.38085	14.23629
26	15.14661	14.98735	14.83062	14.67639	14.52459
27	15.45130	15.28427	15.11998	14.95838	14.79942
28	15.74287	15.56814	15.39636	15.22747.	15.06141
29	16.02189	15.83952	15.66032	15.48422	15.31116
30	16.28889	16.09897	15.91244	15.72922	15.54925
31	16.54439	16.34701	16.15323	15.96300	15.77621
32	16.78889	16.58414	16.38322	16.18607	15.99258
33	17.02286	16.81084	16.60289	16.39892	16.19883
34	17.24676	17.02757	16.81269	16.60202	16.39546
35	17.46101	17.23477	17.01308	16.79582	16.58290
40	18.40158	18.14185	17.88788	17.63954	17.39665
45	19.15635	18.86626	18.58319	18.30694	18.03730
50	19.76201	19.44479	19.13584	18.83488	18.54166

Table B. Present Value of $1 Received per Period (cont'd)

n/r	5.0%	5.1%	5.2%	5.3%	5.4%
1	.95238	.95147	.95057	.94967	.94877
2	1.85941	1.85678	1.85415	1.85154	1.84892
3	2.72325	2.71815	2.71307	2.70801	2.70296
4	3.54595	3.53773	3.52954	3.52138	3.51325
5	4.32948	4.31753	4.30564	4.29381	4.28202
6	5.07569	5.05950	5.04339	5.02736	5.01140
7	5.78637	5.76546	5.74467	5.72399	5.70342
8	6.46321	6.43717	6.41128	6.38555	6.35998
9	7.10782	7.07628	7.04494	7.01382	6.98290
10	7.72173	7.68437	7.64728	7.61046	7.57391
11	8.30641	8.26296	8.21985	8.17708	8.13464
12	8.86325	8.81347	8.76412	8.71517	8.66664
13	9.39357	9.33727	9.28148	9.22619	9.17139
14	9.89864	9.83566	9.77327	9.71148	9.65027
15	10.37966	10.30985	10.24075	10.17234	10.10462
16	10.83777	10.76104	10.68512	10.61001	10.53570
17	11.27407	11.19033	11.10753	11.02565	10.94468
18	11.68959	11.59879	11.50906	11.42037	11.33272
19	12.08532	11.98744	11.89074	11.79523	11.70087
20	12.46221	12.35722	12.25356	12.15121	12.05016
21	12.82115	12.70906	12.59844	12.48928	12.38156
22	13.16300	13.04382	12.92627	12.81033	12.69597
23	13.48857	13.36234	13.23790	13.11523	12.99428
24	13.79864	13.66541	13.53413	13.40477	13.27731
25	14.09394	13.95376	13.81571	13.67975	13.54583
26	14.37519	14.22813	14.08338	13.94088	13.80060
27	14.64303	14.48918	14.33781	14.18887	14.04232
28	14.89813	14.73756	14.57967	14.42438	14.27165
29	15.14107	14.97390	14.80957	14.64803	14.48923
30	15.37245	15.19876	15.02811	14.86043	14.69566
31	15.59281	15.41271	15.23584	15.06214	14.89152
32	15.80268	15.61628	15.43331	15.25369	15.07734
33	16.00255	15.80997	15.62102	15.43560	15.25365
34	16.19290	15.99426	15.79945	15.60836	15.42092
35	16.37419	16.16961	15.96906	15.77242	15.57962
40	17.15909	16.92669	16.69933	16.47687	16.25918
45	17.77407	17.51707	17.26610	17.02101	16.78160
50	18.25593	17.97744	17.70598	17.44131	17.18323

Table B. Present Value of $1 Received per Period (cont'd)

n/r	5.5%	5.6%	5.7%	5.8%	5.9%
1	.94787	.94697	.94607	.94518	.94429
2	1.84632	1.84372	1.84113	1.83854	1.83597
3	2.69793	2.69292	2.68792	2.68293	2.67797
4	3.50515	3.49708	3.48904	3.48103	3.47305
5	4.27028	4.25860	4.24697	4.23538	4.22385
6	4.99553	4.97973	4.96402	4.94838	4.93281
7	5.68297	5.66263	5.64240	5.62228	5.60228
8	6.33457	6.30931	6.28420	6.25925	6.23445
9	6.95220	6.92169	6.89139	6.86129	6.83139
10	7.53763	7.50160	7.46584	7.43033	7.39508
11	8.09254	8.05076	8.00931	7.96818	7.92737
12	8.61852	8.57079	8.52347	8.47654	8.43000
13	9.11708	9.06325	9.00991	8.95703	8.90463
14	9.58965	9.52960	9.47011	9.41118	9.35281
15	10.03758	9.97121	9.90550	9.84044	9.77602
16	10.46216	10.38940	10.31740	10.24616	10.17566
17	10.86461	10.78542	10.70710	10.62964	10.55303
18	11.24607	11.16043	11.07578	10.99210	10.90938
19	11.60765	11.51556	11.42458	11.33469	11.24587
20	11.95038	11.85186	11.75457	11.65849	11.56362
21	12.27524	12.17032	12.06676	11.96455	11.86366
22	12.58317	12.47189	12.36212	12.25383	12.14699
23	12.87504	12.75748	12.64155	12.52725	12.41453
24	13.15170	13.02791	12.90592	12.78568	12.66717
25	13.41393	13.28401	13.15602	13.02994	12.90573
26	13.66250	13.52652	13.39264	13.26081	13.13100
27	13.89810	13.75618	13.61650	13.47903	13.34372
28	14.12142	13.97365	13.82829	13.68528	13.54459
29	14.33310	14.17959	14.02866	13.88023	13.73427
30	14.53375	14.37462	14.21822	14.06449	13.91338
31	14.72393	14.55930	14.39756	14.23865	14.08251
32	14.90420	14.73418	14.56722	14.40326	14.24222
33	15.07507	14.89979	14.72774	14.55885	14.39303
34	15.23703	15.05662	14.87961	14.70590	14.53544
35	15.39055	15.20513	15.02328	14.84490	14.66992
40	16.04612	15.83759	15.63345	15.43360	15.23792
45	16.54773	16.31922	16.09592	15.87769	15.66437
50	16.93152	16.68598	16.44643	16.21268	15.98455

Table B. Present Value of $1 Received per Period (cont'd)

n/r	6%	7%	8%	9%	10%
1	0.9434	0.9346	0.9259	0.9174	0.9091
2	1.8334	1.8080	1.7833	1.7591	1.7355
3	2.6730	2.6243	2.5771	2.5313	2.4869
4	3.4651	3.3872	3.3121	3.2397	3.1699
5	4.2124	4.1002	3.9927	3.8897	3.7908
6	4.9173	4.7665	4.6229	4.4859	4.3553
7	5.5824	5.3893	5.2064	5.0330	4.8684
8	6.2098	5.9713	5.7466	5.5348	5.3349
9	6.8017	6.5152	6.2469	5.9952	5.7590
10	7.3601	7.0236	6.7101	6.4177	6.1446
11	7.8869	7.4987	7.1390	6.8051	6.4951
12	8.3838	7.9427	7.5361	7.1607	6.8137
13	8.8527	8.3577	7.9038	7.4869	7.1034
14	9.2950	8.7455	8.2442	7.7862	7.3667
15	9.7122	9.1079	8.5595	8.0607	7.6061
16	10.1059	9.4466	8.8514	8.3126	7.8237
17	10.4773	9.7632	9.1216	8.5436	8.0216
18	10.8276	10.0591	9.3719	8.7556	8.2014
19	11.1581	10.3356	9.6036	8.9501	8.3649
20	11.4699	10.5940	9.8181	9.1285	8.5136
21	11.7641	10.8355	10.0168	9.2922	8.6487
22	12.0416	11.0612	10.2007	9.4424	8.7715
23	12.3034	11.2722	10.3711	9.5802	8.8832
24	12.5504	11.4693	10.5288	9.7066	8.9847
25	12.7834	11.6536	10.6748	9.8226	9.0770
26	13.0032	11.8258	10.8100	9.9290	9.1609
27	13.2105	11.9867	10.9352	10.0266	9.2372
28	13.4062	12.1371	11.0511	10.1161	9.3066
29	13.5907	12.2777	11.1584	10.1983	9.3696
30	13.7648	12.4090	11.2578	10.2737	9.4269
31	13.9291	12.5318	11.3498	10.3428	9.4790
32	14.0840	12.6466	11.4350	10.4062	9.5264
33	14.2302	12.7538	11.5139	10.4644	9.5694
34	14.3681	12.8540	11.5869	10.5178	9.6086
35	14.4982	12.9477	11.6546	10.5668	9.6442
40	15.0463	13.3317	11.9246	10.7574	9.7791
45	15.4558	13.6055	12.1084	10.8812	9.8628
50	15.7619	13.8007	12.2335	10.9617	9.9148

n/r	11%	12%	13%	14%	15%
1	0.9009	0.8929	0.8850	0.8772	0.8696
2	1.7125	1.6901	1.6681	1.6467	1.6257
3	2.4437	2.4018	2.3612	2.3216	2.2832
4	3.1024	3.0373	2.9745	2.9137	2.8550
5	3.6959	3.6048	3.5172	3.4331	3.3522
6	4.2305	4.1114	3.9975	3.8887	3.7845
7	4.7122	4.5638	4.4226	4.2883	4.1604
8	5.1461	4.9676	4.7988	4.6389	4.4873
9	5.5370	5.3282	5.1317	4.9464	4.7716
10	5.8892	5.6502	5.4262	5.2161	5.0188
11	6.2065	5.9377	5.6869	5.4527	5.2337
12	6.4924	6.1944	5.9176	5.6603	5.4206
13	6.7499	6.4235	6.1218	5.8424	5.5831
14	6.9819	6.6282	6.3025	6.0021	5.7245
15	7.1909	6.8109	6.4624	6.1422	5.8474
16	7.3792	6.9740	6.6039	6.2651	5.9542
17	7.5488	7.1196	6.7291	6.3729	6.0472
18	7.7016	7.2497	6.8399	6.4674	6.1280
19	7.8393	7.3658	6.9380	6.5504	6.1982
20	7.9633	7.4694	7.0248	6.6231	6.2593
21	8.0751	7.5620	7.1015	6.6870	6.3125
22	8.1757	7.6446	7.1695	6.7429	6.3587
23	8.2664	7.7184	7.2297	6.7921	6.3988
24	8.3481	7.7843	7.2829	6.8351	6.4338
25	8.4217	7.8431	7.3300	6.8729	6.4641
26	8.4881	7.8957	7.3717	6.9061	6.4906
27	8.5478	7.9426	7.4086	6.9352	6.5135
28	8.6016	7.9844	7.4412	6.9607	6.5335
29	8.6501	8.0218	7.4701	6.9830	6.5509
30	8.6938	8.0552	7.4957	7.0027	6.5660
31	8.7331	8.0850	7.5183	7.0199	6.5791
32	8.7686	8.1116	7.5383	7.0350	6.5905
33	8.8005	8.1354	7.5560	7.0482	6.6005
34	8.8293	8.1566	7.5717	7.0599	6.6091
35	8.8552	8.1755	7.5856	7.0700	6.6166
40	8.9511	8.2438	7.6344	7.1050	6.6418
45	9.0079	8.2825	7.6609	7.1232	6.6543
50	9.0417	8.3045	7.6752	7.1327	6.6605

n/r	16%	17%	18%	19%	20%
1	0.8621	0.8547	0.8475	0.8403	0.8333
2	1.6052	1.5852	1.5656	1.5465	1.5278
3	2.2459	2.2096	2.1743	2.1399	2.1065
4	2.7982	2.7432	2.6901	2.6386	2.5887
5	3.2743	3.1993	3.1272	3.0576	2.9906
6	3.6847	3.5892	3.4976	3.4098	3.3255
7	4.0386	3.9224	3.8115	3.7057	3.6046
8	4.3436	4.2072	4.0776	3.9544	3.8372
9	4.6065	4.4506	4.3030	4.1633	4.0310
10	4.8332	4.6586	4.4941	4.3389	4.1925
11	5.0286	4.8364	4.6560	4.4865	4.3271
12	5.1971	4.9884	4.7932	4.6105	4.4392
13	5.3423	5.1183	4.9095	4.7147	4.5327
14	5.4675	5.2293	5.0081	4.8023	4.6106
15	5.5755	5.3242	5.0916	4.8759	4.6755
16	5.6685	5.4053	5.1624	4.9377	4.7296
17	5.7487	5.4746	5.2223	4.9879	4.7746
18	5.8178	5.5339	5.2732	5.0333	4.8122
19	5.8775	5.5845	5.3162	5.0700	4.8435
20	5.9288	5.6278	5.3527	5.1009	4.8696
21	5.9731	5.6648	5.3837	5.1268	4.8913
22	6.0113	5.6964	5.4099	5.1486	4.9094
23	6.0442	5.7234	5.4321	5.1668	4.9245
24	6.0726	5.7465	5.4509	5.1822	4.9371
25	6.0971	5.7662	5.4669	5.1951	4.9476
26	6.1182	5.7831	5.4804	5.2060	4.9563
27	6.1364	5.7975	5.4919	5.2151	4.9636
28	6.1520	5.8099	5.5016	5.2228	4.9697
29	6.1656	5.8204	5.5098	5.2292	4.9747
30	6.1772	5.8294	5.5168	5.2347	4.9789
31	6.1872	5.8371	5.5227	5.2392	4.9824
32	6.1959	5.8437	5.5277	5.2430	4.9854
33	6.2034	5.8493	5.5320	5.2462	4.9878
34	6.2098	5.8541	5.5356	5.2489	4.9898
35	6.2153	5.8582	5.5386	5.2512	4.9915
40	6.2335	5.8713	5.5482	5.2582	4.9966
45	6.2421	5.8773	5.5523	5.2611	4.9986
50	6.2463	5.8801	5.5541	5.2623	4.9995

n/r	21%	22%	23%	24%	25%
1	0.8264	0.8197	0.8130	0.8065	0.8000
2	1.5095	1.4915	1.4740	1.4568	1.4400
3	2.0739	2.0422	2.0114	1.9813	1.9520
4	2.5404	2.4936	2.4483	2.4043	2.3616
5	2.9260	2.8636	2.8035	2.7454	2.6893
6	3.2446	3.1669	3.0923	3.0205	2.9514
7	3.5079	3.4155	3.3270	3.2423	3.1611
8	3.7256	3.6193	3.5179	3.4212	3.3289
9	3.9054	3.7863	3.6731	3.5655	3.4631
10	4.0541	3.9232	3.7993	3.6819	3.5705
11	4.1769	4.0354	3.9018	3.7757	3.6564
12	4.2784	4.1274	3.9852	3.8514	3.7251
13	4.3624	4.2028	4.0530	3.9124	3.7801
14	4.4317	4.2646	4.1082	3.9616	3.8241
15	4.4890	4.3152	4.1530	4.0013	3.8593
16	4.5364	4.3567	4.1894	4.0333	3.8874
17	4.5755	4.3908	4.2190	4.0591	3.9099
18	4.6079	4.4187	4.2431	4.0799	3.9279
19	4.6346	4.4415	4.2627	4.0967	3.9424
20	4.6567	4.4603	4.2786	4.1103	3.9539
21	4.6750	4.4756	4.2916	4.1212	3.9631
22	4.6900	4.4882	4.3021	4.1300	3.9705
23	4.7025	4.4985	4.3106	4.1371	3.9764
24	4.7128	4.5070	4.3176	4.1428	3.9811
25	4.7213	4.5139	4.3232	4.1474	3.9849
26	4.7284	4.5196	4.3278	4.1511	3.9879
27	4.7342	4.5243	4.3316	4.1542	3.9903
28	4.7390	4.5281	4.3346	4.1566	3.9923
29	4.7430	4.5312	4.3371	4.1585	3.9938
30	4.7463	4.5338	4.3391	4.1601	3.9950
31	4.7490	4.5359	4.3407	4.1614	3.9960
32	4.7512	4.5376	4.3421	4.1624	3.9968
33	4.7531	4.5390	4.3431	4.1632	3.9975
34	4.7546	4.5402	4.3440	4.1639	3.9980
35	4.7559	4.5411	4.3447	4.1644	3.9984
40	4.7596	4.5439	4.3467	4.1659	3.9995
45	4.7610	4.5449	4.3474	4.1664	3.9998
50	4.7616	4.5452	4.3477	4.1666	3.9999

Table B.   Present Value of $1 Received per Period (cont'd)

n/r	26%	27%	28%	29%	30%	31%
1	0.7937	0.7874	0.7813	0.7752	0.7692	0.7634
2	1.4235	1.4074	1.3916	1.3761	1.3609	1.3461
3	1.9234	1.8956	1.8684	1.8420	1.8161	1.7909
4	2.3202	2.2800	2.2410	2.2031	2.1662	2.1305
5	2.6351	2.5827	2.5320	2.4830	2.4356	2.3897
6	2.8850	2.8210	2.7594	2.7000	2.6427	2.5875
7	3.0833	3.0087	2.9370	2.8682	2.8021	2.7386
8	3.2407	3.1564	3.0758	2.9986	2.9247	2.8539
9	3.3657	3.2728	3.1842	3.0997	3.0190	2.9419
10	3.4648	3.3644	3.2689	3.1781	3.0915	3.0091
11	3.5435	3.4365	3.3351	3.2388	3.1473	3.0604
12	3.6059	3.4933	3.3868	3.2859	3.1903	3.0995
13	3.6555	3.5381	3.4272	3.3224	3.2233	3.1294
14	3.6949	3.5733	3.4587	3.3507	3.2487	3.1522
15	3.7261	3.6010	3.4834	3.3726	3.2682	3.1696
16	3.7509	3.6228	3.5026	3.3896	3.2832	3.1829
17	3.7705	3.6400	3.5177	3.4028	3.2948	3.1931
18	3.7861	3.6536	3.5294	3.4130	3.3037	3.2008
19	3.7985	3.6642	3.5386	3.4210	3.3105	3.2067
20	3.8083	3.6726	3.5458	3.4271	3.3158	3.2112
21	3.8161	3.6792	3.5514	3.4319	3.3198	3.2147
22	3.8223	3.6844	3.5558	3.4356	3.3230	3.2173
23	3.8273	3.6885	3.5592	3.4384	3.3253	3.2193
24	3.8312	3.6918	3.5619	3.4406	3.3272	3.2209
25	3.8342	3.6943	3.5640	3.4423	3.3286	3.2220
26	3.8367	3.6963	3.5656	3.4437	3.3297	3.2229
27	3.8387	3.6979	3.5669	3.4447	3.3305	3.2236
28	3.8402	3.6991	3.5679	3.4455	3.3312	3.2241
29	3.8414	3.7001	3.5687	3.4461	3.3316	3.2245
30	3.8424	3.7009	3.5693	3.4466	3.3321	3.2248
31	3.8432	3.7015	3.5697	3.4470	3.3324	3.2251
32	3.8438	3.7019	3.5701	3.4473	3.3326	3.2252
33	3.8443	3.7023	3.5704	3.4475	3.3328	3.2254
34	3.8447	3.7026	3.5706	3.4477	3.3329	3.2255
35	3.8450	3.7028	3.5708	3.4478	3.3330	3.2256
40	3.8458	3.7034	3.5712	3.4481	3.3332	3.2257
45	3.8460	3.7036	3.5714	3.4482	3.3333	3.2258
50	3.8461	3.7037	3.5714	3.4483	3.3333	3.2258

Table B. Present Value of $1 Received per Period (cont'd)

n/r	32%	33%	34%	35%	36%	37%
1	0.7576	0.7519	0.7463	0.7407	0.7353	0.7299
2	1.3315	1.3172	1.3032	1.2894	1.2760	1.2627
3	1.7663	1.7423	1.7188	1.6959	1.6735	1.6516
4	2.0957	2.0618	2.0290	1.9969	1.9658	1.9355
5	2.3452	2.3021	2.2604	2.2200	2.1807	2.1427
6	2.5342	2.4828	2.4331	2.3852	2.3388	2.2939
7	2.6775	2.6187	2.5620	2.5075	2.4550	2.4043
8	2.7860	2.7208	2.6582	2.5982	2.5404	2.4849
9	2.8681	2.7976	2.7300	2.6653	2.6033	2.5437
10	2.9304	2.8553	2.7836	2.7150	2.6495	2.5867
11	2.9776	2.8987	2.8236	2.7519	2.6834	2.6180
12	3.0133	2.9314	2.8534	2.7792	2.7084	2.6409
13	3.0404	2.9559	2.8757	2.7994	2.7268	2.6576
14	3.0609	2.9744	2.8923	2.8144	2.7403	2.6698
15	3.0764	2.9883	2.9047	2.8255	2.7502	2.6787
16	3.0882	2.9987	2.9140	2.8337	2.7575	2.6852
17	3.0971	3.0065	2.9209	2.8398	2.7629	2.6899
18	3.1039	3.0124	2.9260	2.8443	2.7668	2.6934
19	3.1090	3.0169	2.9299	2.8476	2.7697	2.6959
20	3.1129	3.0202	2.9327	2.8501	2.7718	2.6977
21	3.1158	3.0227	2.9349	2.8520	2.7734	2.6991
22	3.1180	3.0246	2.9365	2.8533	2.7746	2.7000
23	3.1197	3.0260	2.9377	2.8543	2.7754	2.7008
24	3.1210	3.0271	2.9386	2.8550	2.7760	2.7013
25	3.1220	3.0279	2.9392	2.8556	2.7765	2.7017
26	3.1227	3.0285	2.9397	2.8560	2.7768	2.7019
27	3.1233	3.0289	2.9401	2.8563	2.7771	2.7022
28	3.1237	3.0293	2.9404	2.8565	2.7773	2.7023
29	3.1240	3.0295	2.9406	2.8567	2.7774	2.7024
30	3.1242	3.0297	2.9407	2.8568	2.7775	2.7025
31	3.1244	3.0299	2.9408	2.8569	2.7776	2.7025
32	3.1246	3.0300	2.9409	2.8569	2.7776	2.7026
33	3.1247	3.0301	2.9410	2.8570	2.7777	2.7026
34	3.1248	3.0301	2.9410	2.8570	2.7777	2.7026
35	3.1248	3.0302	2.9411	2.8571	2.7777	2.7027
40	3.1250	3.0303	2.9412	2.8571	2.7778	2.7027
45	3.1250	3.0303	2.9412	2.8571	2.7778	2.7027
50	3.1250	3.0303	2.9412	2.8571	2.7778	2.7027

n/r	38%	39%	40%	41%	42%	43%
1	0.7246	0.7194	0.7143	0.7092	0.7042	0.6993
2	1.2497	1.2370	1.2245	1.2122	1.2002	1.1883
3	1.6302	1.6093	1.5889	1.5689	1.5494	1.5303
4	1.9060	1.8772	1.8492	1.8219	1.7954	1.7694
5	2.1058	2.0699	2.0352	2.0014	1.9686	1.9367
6	2.2506	2.2086	2.1680	2.1286	2.0905	2.0536
7	2.3555	2.3083	2.2628	2.2189	2.1764	2.1354
8	2.4315	2.3801	2.3306	2.2829	2.2369	2.1926
9	2.4866	2.4317	2.3790	2.3283	2.2795	2.2326
10	2.5265	2.4689	2.4136	2.3605	2.3095	2.2605
11	2.5555	2.4956	2.4383	2.3833	2.3307	2.2801
12	2.5764	2.5148	2.4559	2.3995	2.3455	2.2938
13	2.5916	2.5286	2.4685	2.4110	2.3560	2.3033
14	2.6026	2.5386	2.4775	2.4192	2.3634	2.3100
15	2.6106	2.5457	2.4839	2.4249	2.3686	2.3147
16	2.6164	2.5509	2.4885	2.4290	2.3722	2.3180
17	2.6206	2.5546	2.4918	2.4319	2.3748	2.3203
18	2.6236	2.5573	2.4941	2.4340	2.3766	2.3219
19	2.6258	2.5592	2.4958	2.4355	2.3779	2.3230
20	2.6274	2.5606	2.4970	2.4365	2.3788	2.3238
21	2.6285	2.5616	2.4979	2.4372	2.3794	2.3243
22	2.6294	2.5623	2.4985	2.4378	2.3799	2.3247
23	2.6300	2.5628	2.4989	2.4381	2.3802	2.3250
24	2.6304	2.5632	2.4992	2.4384	2.3804	2.3251
25	2.6307	2.5634	2.4994	2.4386	2.3806	2.3253
26	2.6310	2.5636	2.4996	2.4387	2.3807	2.3254
27	2.6311	2.5637	2.4997	2.4388	2.3808	2.3254
28	2.6313	2.5638	2.4998	2.4389	2.3808	2.3255
29	2.6313	2.5639	2.4999	2.4389	2.3809	2.3255
30	2.6314	2.5640	2.4999	2.4389	2.3809	2.3255
31	2.6315	2.5640	2.4999	2.4390	2.3809	2.3255
32	2.6315	2.5640	2.4999	2.4390	2.3809	2.3256
33	2.6315	2.5641	2.5000	2.4390	2.3809	2.3256
34	2.6315	2.5641	2.5000	2.4390	2.3809	2.3256
35	2.6215	2.5641	2.5000	2.4390	2.3809	2.3256
40	2.6316	2.5641	2.5000	2.4390	2.3810	2.3256
45	2.6316	2.5641	2.5000	2.4390	2.3810	2.3256
50	2.6316	2.5641	2.5000	2.4390	2.3810	2.3256

n/r	44%	45%	46%	47%	48%	49%
1	0.6944	0.6897	0.6849	0.6803	0.6757	0.6711
2	1.1767	1.1653	1.1541	1.1430	1.1322	1.1216
3	1.5116	1.4933	1.4754	1.4579	1.4407	1.4239
4	1.7442	1.7195	1.6955	1.6720	1.6491	1.6268
5	1.9057	1.8755	1.8462	1.8177	1.7899	1.7629
6	2.0178	1.9831	1.9495	1.9168	1.8851	1.8543
7	2.0957	2.0573	2.0202	1.9842	1.9494	1.9156
8	2.1498	2.1085	2.0686	2.0301	1.9928	1.9568
9	2.1874	2.1438	2.1018	2.0613	2.0222	1.9844
10	2.2134	2.1681	2.1245	2.0825	2.0420	2.0030
11	2.2316	2.1849	2.1401	2.0969	2.0554	2.0154
12	2.2441	2.1965	2.1507	2.1068	2.0645	2.0238
13	2.2529	2.2045	2.1580	2.1134	2.0706	2.0294
14	2.2589	2.2100	2.1630	2.1180	2.0747	2.0331
15	2.2632	2.2138	2.1665	2.1211	2.0775	2.0357
16	2.2661	2.2164	2.1688	2.1232	2.0794	2.0374
17	2.2681	2.2182	2.1704	2.1246	2.0807	2.0385
18	2.2695	2.2195	2.1715	2.1256	2.0815	2.0393
19	2.2705	2.2203	2.1723	2.1263	2.0821	2.0398
20	2.2712	2.2209	2.1728	2.1267	2.0825	2.0401
21	2.2717	2.2213	2.1731	2.1270	2.0828	2.0403
22	2.2720	2.2216	2.1734	2.1272	2.0830	2.0405
23	2.2722	2.2218	2.1736	2.1274	2.0831	2.0406
24	2.2724	2.2219	2.1737	2.1275	2.0832	2.0407
25	2.2725	2.2220	2.1737	2.1275	2.0832	2.0407
26	2.2726	2.2221	2.1738	2.1276	2.0833	2.0408
27	2.2726	2.2221	2.1738	2.1276	2.0833	2.0408
28	2.2726	2.2222	2.1739	2.1276	2.0833	2.0408
29	2.2727	2.2222	2.1739	2.1276	2.0833	2.0408
30	2.2727	2.2222	2.1739	2.1276	2.0833	2.0408
31	2.2727	2.2222	2.1739	2.1276	2.0833	2.0408
32	2.2727	2.2222	2.1739	2.1277	2.0833	2.0408
33	2.2727	2.2222	2.1739	2.1277	2.0833	2.0408
34	2.2727	2.2222	2.1739	2.1277	2.0833	2.0408
35	2.2727	2.2222	2.1739	2.1277	2.0833	2.0408
40	2.2727	2.2222	2.1739	2.1277	2.0833	2.0408
45	2.2727	2.2222	2.1739	2.1277	2.0833	2.0408
50	2.2727	2.2222	2.1739	2.1277	2.0833	2.0408

Table C.   Present Value of Depreciation Charges from $1.00 of Assets Depreciated over *n* Years, Using the Sum-of-the-Years'-Digits Depreciation Method, Discounting at *r* Per Cent per Year, Assuming No Salvage Value *

n	1%	2%	3%	4%	5%
3	0.983580	0.967639	0.952159	0.937121	0.922507
4	0.980344	0.961356	0.943005	0.925262	0.908099
5	0.977125	0.955135	0.933984	0.913629	0.894031
6	0.973922	0.948974	0.925093	0.902218	0.880293
7	0.970734	0.942873	0.916330	0.891023	0.866876
8	0.967562	0.936831	0.907692	0.880038	0.853771
9	0.964405	0.930848	0.899179	0.869260	0.840968
10	0.961264	0.924923	0.890786	0.858684	0.828460
11	0.958139	0.919054	0.882513	0.848304	0.816238
12	0.955029	0.913243	0.874357	0.838117	0.804294
13	0.951934	0.907487	0.866317	0.828119	0.792621
14	0.948854	0.901786	0.858390	0.818304	0.781211
15	0.945790	0.896140	0.850574	0.808669	0.770057
16	0.942740	0.890548	0.842867	0.799210	0.759152
17	0.939705	0.885009	0.835268	0.789923	0.748488
18	0.936685	0.879523	0.827775	0.780805	0.738060
19	0.933680	0.874089	0.820386	0.771850	0.727861
20	0.930689	0.868706	0.813099	0.763056	0.717885
21	0.927713	0.863375	0.805913	0.754420	0.708125
22	0.924751	0.858093	0.798825	0.745937	0.698577
23	0.921804	0.852862	0.791835	0.737605	0.689234
24	0.918871	0.847679	0.784940	0.729420	0.680091
25	0.915952	0.842545	0.778139	0.721379	0.671142
26	0.913047	0.837459	0.771430	0.713478	0.662383
27	0.910157	0.832421	0.764812	0.705715	0.653808
28	0.907280	0.827430	0.758283	0.698087	0.645412
29	0.904417	0.822485	0.751843	0.690591	0.637192
30	0.901568	0.817586	0.745488	0.683224	0.629142
31	0.898733	0.812732	0.739219	0.675983	0.621258
32	0.895911	0.807923	0.733033	0.668866	0.613535
33	0.893102	0.803158	0.726929	0.661870	0.605970
34	0.890308	0.798438	0.720906	0.654992	0.598558
35	0.887527	0.793760	0.714962	0.648230	0.591295
36	0.884759	0.789126	0.709097	0.641581	0.584179
37	0.882004	0.784534	0.703308	0.635043	0.577204
38	0.879263	0.779984	0.697595	0.628615	0.570367
39	0.876534	0.775475	0.691957	0.622292	0.563666
40	0.873819	0.771007	0.686391	0.616074	0.557095
41	0.871116	0.766580	0.680898	0.609958	0.550653
42	0.868427	0.762193	0.675476	0.603942	0.544336
43	0.865750	0.757846	0.670123	0.598023	0.538141
44	0.863086	0.753537	0.664839	0.592201	0.532065
45	0.860434	0.749268	0.659623	0.586472	0.526105
46	0.857795	0.745036	0.654473	0.580836	0.520258
47	0.855169	0.740843	0.649388	0.575290	0.514521
48	0.852555	0.736687	0.644368	0.569831	0.508892
49	0.849953	0.732568	0.639411	0.564460	0.503368
50	0.847364	0.728486	0.634516	0.559173	0.497946

* Values tabled are

$$C(n,r) = \sum_{i=1}^{n} \frac{2(n-i+1)}{n(n+1)(1+r)^i}$$

Table C. Sum-of-the-Years'-Digits (cont'd)

n	6%	7%	8%	9%	10%
3	0.908300	0.894486	0.881048	0.867973	0.855247
4	0.891491	0.875412	0.859841	0.844756	0.830135
5	0.875151	0.856955	0.839408	0.822481	0.806142
6	0.859266	0.839089	0.819715	0.801101	0.783209
7	0.843821	0.821791	0.800728	0.780574	0.761279
8	0.828799	0.805040	0.782417	0.760858	0.740298
9	0.814188	0.788815	0.764753	0.741914	0.720217
10	0.799974	0.773096	0.747709	0.723706	0.700988
11	0.786143	0.757863	0.731257	0.706197	0.682566
12	0.772683	0.743098	0.715372	0.689355	0.664911
13	0.759582	0.728783	0.700031	0.673150	0.647983
14	0.746828	0.714902	0.685210	0.657550	0.631744
15	0.734410	0.701439	0.670888	0.642529	0.616160
16	0.722317	0.688377	0.657043	0.628059	0.601198
17	0.710538	0.675703	0.643657	0.614115	0.586827
18	0.699064	0.663401	0.630710	0.600674	0.573017
19	0.687885	0.651459	0.618184	0.587713	0.559741
20	0.676799	0.639863	0.606063	0.575209	0.546973
21	0.666373	0.628601	0.594329	0.563144	0.534688
22	0.656022	0.617660	0.582967	0.551496	0.522864
23	0.645931	0.607030	0.571963	0.540249	0.511478
24	0.636091	0.596698	0.561302	0.529385	0.500508
25	0.626495	0.586656	0.550970	0.518886	0.489937
26	0.617134	0.576891	0.540955	0.508738	0.479745
27	0.608001	0.567396	0.531244	0.498925	0.469915
28	0.599090	0.558159	0.521826	0.489433	0.460429
29	0.590394	0.549173	0.512689	0.480248	0.451273
30	0.581906	0.540429	0.503823	0.471358	0.442432
31	0.573619	0.531918	0.495217	0.462751	0.433891
32	0.565529	0.523632	0.486861	0.454414	0.425637
33	0.557628	0.515564	0.478746	0.446337	0.417657
34	0.549912	0.507707	0.470863	0.438509	0.409940
35	0.542374	0.500053	0.463203	0.430920	0.402474
36	0.535010	0.492595	0.455758	0.423561	0.395247
37	0.527815	0.485328	0.448521	0.416422	0.388251
38	0.520782	0.478244	0.441483	0.409494	0.381476
39	0.513909	0.471338	0.434638	0.402770	0.374911
40	0.507189	0.464604	0.427978	0.396242	0.368548
41	0.500619	0.458037	0.421498	0.389901	0.362379
42	0.494194	0.451630	0.415189	0.383741	0.356396
43	0.487911	0.445379	0.409048	0.377755	0.350592
44	0.481764	0.439280	0.403067	0.371936	0.344958
45	0.475751	0.433326	0.397241	0.366278	0.339490
46	0.469868	0.427514	0.391565	0.360775	0.334179
47	0.464110	0.421839	0.386034	0.355421	0.329019
48	0.458475	0.416296	0.380643	0.350212	0.324006
49	0.452958	0.410883	0.375386	0.345141	0.319132
50	0.447557	0.405594	0.370260	0.340203	0.314393

Table C.　Sum-of-the-Years'-Digits (cont'd)

n	11%	12%	13%	14%	15%
3	0.842856	0.830790	0.819035	0.807581	0.796417
4	0.815958	0.802209	0.788868	0.775920	0.763348
5	0.790365	0.775124	0.760394	0.746152	0.732375
6	0.766001	0.749442	0.733498	0.718140	0.703339
7	0.742793	0.725072	0.708074	0.691759	0.676091
8	0.720676	0.701935	0.684023	0.666892	0.650496
9	0.699586	0.679954	0.661256	0.643433	0.626432
10	0.679466	0.659057	0.639686	0.621284	0.603786
11	0.660260	0.639179	0.619238	0.600354	0.582453
12	0.641917	0.620259	0.599837	0.580559	0.562340
13	0.624389	0.602239	0.581419	0.561824	0.543359
14	0.607631	0.585066	0.563920	0.544077	0.525430
15	0.591601	0.568690	0.547283	0.527252	0.508479
16	0.576259	0.553065	0.531455	0.511289	0.492439
17	0.561569	0.538146	0.516385	0.496132	0.477248
18	0.547495	0.523895	0.502028	0.481728	0.462847
19	0.534005	0.510273	0.488341	0.468031	0.449185
20	0.521068	0.497244	0.475284	0.454995	0.436212
21	0.508655	0.484776	0.462819	0.442580	0.423883
22	0.496739	0.472838	0.450912	0.430747	0.412156
23	0.485295	0.461400	0.439530	0.419460	0.400994
24	0.474299	0.450436	0.428644	0.408687	0.390361
25	0.463727	0.439919	0.418225	0.398397	0.380222
26	0.453560	0.429828	0.408247	0.388562	0.370549
27	0.443776	0.420138	0.398686	0.379154	0.361313
28	0.434357	0.410829	0.389519	0.370150	0.352487
29	0.425285	0.401881	0.380723	0.361526	0.344043
30	0.416544	0.393276	0.372280	0.353262	0.335971
31	0.408117	0.384997	0.364171	0.345336	0.328238
32	0.399990	0.377026	0.356377	0.337730	0.320826
33	0.392148	0.369350	0.348882	0.330427	0.313720
34	0.384579	0.361953	0.341672	0.323411	0.306901
35	0.377269	0.354821	0.334730	0.316666	0.300353
36	0.370207	0.347943	0.328045	0.310178	0.294063
37	0.363382	0.341305	0.321603	0.303934	0.288015
38	0.356783	0.334897	0.315391	0.297921	0.282197
39	0.350400	0.328707	0.309400	0.292127	0.276598
40	0.344223	0.322726	0.303617	0.286541	0.271205
41	0.338244	0.316944	0.298034	0.281154	0.266008
42	0.332453	0.311351	0.292640	0.275955	0.260998
43	0.326844	0.305941	0.287427	0.270935	0.256164
44	0.321407	0.300703	0.282387	0.266086	0.251499
45	0.316136	0.295632	0.277511	0.261399	0.246993
46	0.311024	0.290719	0.272792	0.256868	0.242640
47	0.306064	0.285957	0.268223	0.252484	0.238432
48	0.301250	0.281341	0.263798	0.248241	0.234362
49	0.296577	0.276863	0.259510	0.244133	0.230424
50	0.292038	0.272519	0.255353	0.240153	0.226611

Table C.   Sum-of-the-Years'-Digits (cont'd)

n	16%	17%	18%	19%	20%
3	0.785532	0.774917	0.764562	0.754459	0.744599
4	0.751137	0.739274	0.727743	0.716534	0.705633
5	0.719044	0.706139	0.693640	0.681532	0.669796
6	0.689067	0.675298	0.662010	0.649179	0.636783
7	0.661035	0.646559	0.632633	0.619230	0.606323
8	0.634793	0.619745	0.605314	0.591467	0.578172
9	0.610202	0.594697	0.579874	0.565692	0.552115
10	0.587133	0.571272	0.556153	0.541729	0.527957
11	0.565469	0.549339	0.534006	0.519418	0.505526
12	0.545104	0.528779	0.513303	0.498616	0.484666
13	0.525939	0.509484	0.493925	0.479195	0.465237
14	0.507885	0.491356	0.475764	0.461039	0.447116
15	0.490862	0.474305	0.458723	0.444041	0.430189
16	0.474793	0.458249	0.442714	0.428108	0.414354
17	0.459612	0.443114	0.427657	0.413152	0.399522
18	0.445254	0.428832	0.413477	0.399097	0.385608
19	0.431663	0.415341	0.400110	0.385872	0.372540
20	0.418784	0.402583	0.387493	0.373412	0.360248
21	0.406571	0.390508	0.375573	0.361659	0.348673
22	0.394977	0.379066	0.364297	0.350561	0.337758
23	0.383962	0.368214	0.353621	0.340068	0.327454
24	0.373487	0.357912	0.343501	0.330136	0.317715
25	0.363517	0.348122	0.333899	0.320726	0.308499
26	0.354021	0.338812	0.324779	0.311801	0.299767
27	0.344967	0.329948	0.316110	0.303326	0.291487
28	0.336329	0.321503	0.307860	0.295271	0.283625
29	0.328081	0.313450	0.300002	0.287607	0.276152
30	0.320199	0.305763	0.292511	0.280309	0.269044
31	0.312661	0.298422	0.285364	0.273353	0.262274
32	0.305446	0.291403	0.278538	0.266716	0.255820
33	0.298536	0.284688	0.272014	0.260378	0.249663
34	0.291914	0.278259	0.265774	0.254321	0.243783
35	0.285562	0.272099	0.259800	0.248528	0.238162
36	0.279466	0.266192	0.254077	0.242981	0.232786
37	0.273611	0.260524	0.248590	0.237668	0.227638
38	0.267984	0.255082	0.243325	0.232573	0.222705
39	0.262573	0.249853	0.238270	0.227684	0.217975
40	0.257366	0.244825	0.233413	0.222990	0.213435
41	0.252353	0.239988	0.228744	0.218479	0.209076
42	0.247524	0.235331	0.224251	0.214142	0.204886
43	0.242868	0.230845	0.219926	0.209969	0.200856
44	0.238378	0.226521	0.215759	0.205951	0.196978
45	0.234045	0.222351	0.211743	0.202079	0.193243
46	0.229861	0.218327	0.207869	0.198347	0.189644
47	0.225819	0.214441	0.204131	0.194747	0.186174
48	0.221912	0.210688	0.200521	0.191273	0.182826
49	0.218134	0.207060	0.197034	0.187918	0.179594
50	0.214479	0.203552	0.193664	0.184676	0.176473

Table D. Present Value of Depreciation Charges from $1.00 of Assets Depreciated over n Years, Using the Twice Straight-Line Declining Balance Depreciation Method, Discounting at r Per cent per Year, Assuming No Salvage Value *

n	1%	2%	3%	4%	5%
3	.985753	.971890	.958397	.945260	.932465
4	.981570	.963759	.946539	.929883	.913765
5	.977620	.956126	.935471	.915611	.896505
6	.973593	.948394	.924329	.901332	.879339
7	.969722	.941004	.913741	.887838	.863203
8	.965781	.933528	.903095	.874349	.847170
9	.961962	.926325	.892896	.861498	.831973
10	.958088	.919063	.882674	.848693	.816918
11	.954316	.912033	.872833	.836432	.802576
12	.950500	.904965	.862998	.824248	.788403
13	.946772	.898100	.853497	.812540	.774853
14	.943010	.891213	.844023	.800930	.761488
15	.939326	.884508	.834848	.789745	.748676
16	.935615	.877793	.825713	.778670	.736058
17	.931974	.871243	.816850	.767980	.723936
18	.928312	.864693	.808038	.757408	.712010
19	.924714	.858295	.799475	.747187	.700533
20	.921098	.851904	.790970	.737088	.689251
21	.917543	.845654	.782695	.727311	.678378
22	.913973	.839416	.774483	.717659	.667697
23	.910459	.833309	.766484	.708302	.657388
24	.906935	.827220	.758552	.699071	.647267
25	.903462	.821253	.750819	.690114	.637488
26	.899982	.815306	.743155	.681281	.627890
27	.896550	.809476	.735677	.672703	.618607
28	.893112	.803668	.728269	.664247	.609498
29	.889721	.797971	.721036	.656027	.600680
30	.886326	.792298	.713874	.647927	.592029
31	.882974	.786729	.706876	.640049	.583647
32	.879620	.781187	.699949	.632287	.575425
33	.876309	.775744	.693178	.624731	.567452
34	.872995	.770330	.686477	.617289	.559631
35	.869722	.765009	.679923	.610041	.552042
36	.866449	.759718	.673438	.602902	.544599
37	.863214	.754516	.667093	.595945	.537370
38	.859981	.749344	.660816	.589004	.530281
39	.856784	.744259	.654672	.582414	.523391
40	.853589	.739204	.648595	.575837	.516633
41	.850430	.734231	.642643	.569420	.510063
42	.847273	.729289	.636757	.563101	.503617
43	.844150	.724426	.630991	.556934	.497346
44	.841031	.719594	.625289	.550862	.491193
45	.837945	.714838	.619701	.544933	.485204
46	.834863	.710113	.614176	.539095	.479328
47	.831813	.705461	.608760	.533391	.473604
48	.828767	.700840	.603405	.527776	.467988
49	.825752	.696289	.598153	.522287	.462514
50	.822742	.691769	.592961	.516883	.457143

* Values tabled are

$$D(n,r) = \sum_{i=1}^{n} \frac{d_i}{(1+r)^i}$$

where $d_i = \begin{cases} (2/n)(1-2/n)^{i-1} & \text{for } i < k \\ \dfrac{(1-2/n)^{k-1}}{n+1-k} & \text{for } i > k \end{cases}$ and k is the smallest integer greater than or equal to $(n/2 + 1)$

Table D. Twice Straight-Line Declining Balance (cont'd)

n	6%	7%	8%	9%	10%
3	.919999	.907850	.896007	.884459	.873195
4	.898161	.883049	.868405	.854212	.840448
5	.878113	.860399	.843330	.826873	.810998
6	.858291	.838135	.818819	.800297	.782525
7	.839757	.817424	.796132	.775819	.756424
8	.821445	.797073	.773962	.752024	.731181
9	.804178	.777979	.753259	.729907	.707825
10	.787165	.759267	.733076	.708455	.685282
11	.771038	.741615	.714123	.688399	.664295
12	.755187	.724354	.695683	.668981	.644070
13	.740105	.708006	.678296	.650747	.625155
14	.725308	.692046	.661403	.633114	.606944
15	.711188	.676885	.645423	.616490	.589849
16	.697352	.662101	.629912	.600443	.573398
17	.684121	.648022	.615200	.585272	.557908
18	.671167	.634304	.600928	.570615	.543003
19	.658756	.621213	.587360	.556731	.528930
20	.646613	.608464	.574202	.543320	.515386
21	.634960	.596275	.561668	.530587	.502568
22	.623565	.584409	.549515	.518288	.490228
23	.612613	.573046	.537917	.506587	.478522
24	.601907	.561985	.526671	.495281	.467249
25	.591605	.551378	.515921	.484505	.456532
26	.581536	.541054	.505496	.474090	.446205
27	.571835	.531140	.495515	.464146	.436369
28	.562355	.521489	.485834	.454531	.426886
29	.553212	.512211	.476552	.445336	.417837
30	.544278	.503178	.467546	.436441	.409106
31	.535651	.494483	.458901	.427921	.400760
32	.527222	.486017	.450509	.419674	.392703
33	.519076	.477859	.442442	.411764	.384988
34	.511116	.469914	.434610	.404104	.377534
35	.503416	.462249	.427071	.396746	.370386
36	.495891	.454783	.419749	.389616	.363474
37	.488606	.447573	.412693	.382758	.356836
38	.481485	.440547	.405836	.376109	.350413
39	.474586	.433757	.399221	.369706	.344236
40	.467841	.427138	.392791	.363494	.338254
41	.461301	.420735	.386580	.357504	.332493
42	.454907	.414491	.380540	.351689	.326910
43	.448702	.408445	.374701	.346076	.321527
44	.442633	.402549	.369018	.340624	.316306
45	.436740	.396834	.363520	.335354	.311265
46	.430976	.391258	.358166	.330233	.306373
47	.425374	.385850	.352981	.325279	.301644
48	.419894	.380571	.347930	.320460	.297051
49	.414565	.375446	.343034	.315794	.292607
50	.409349	.370443	.338262	.311254	.288288

Table D. Twice Straight-Line Declining Balance (cont'd)

n	11%	12%	13%	14%	15%
3	.862205	.851479	.841009	.830785	.820799
4	.827096	.814139	.801561	.789345	.777477
5	.795677	.780884	.766593	.752782	.739427
6	.765462	.749069	.733311	.718155	.703569
7	.737891	.720170	.703213	.686975	.671415
8	.711362	.692499	.674530	.657399	.641054
9	.686922	.667114	.648326	.630487	.613533
10	.663444	.642841	.623381	.604978	.587558
11	.641678	.620426	.600432	.581597	.563831
12	.620795	.599014	.578601	.559443	.541436
13	.601339	.579138	.558408	.539018	.520855
14	.582687	.560159	.539199	.519662	.501419
15	.565240	.542468	.521351	.501731	.483465
16	.548517	.525574	.504369	.484727	.466494
17	.532823	.509768	.488526	.468906	.450743
18	.517778	.494669	.473441	.453890	.435837
19	.503615	.480496	.459318	.439865	.421946
20	.490034	.466948	.445860	.426537	.408781
21	.477215	.454194	.433219	.414046	.396465
22	.464915	.441993	.421160	.402160	.384774
23	.453276	.430474	.409799	.390984	.373799
24	.442102	.419446	.398950	.380335	.363365
25	.431503	.409008	.388700	.370291	.353538
26	.421320	.399004	.378899	.360707	.344178
27	.411640	.389513	.369616	.351643	.335337
28	.402333	.380407	.360728	.342981	.326903
29	.393467	.371749	.352289	.334766	.318913
30	.384935	.363433	.344200	.326906	.311278
31	.376792	.355509	.336501	.319432	.304026
32	.368948	.347891	.329112	.312271	.297087
33	.361449	.340617	.322065	.305446	.290478
34	.354219	.333617	.315293	.298897	.284144
35	.347294	.326919	.308820	.292643	.278100
36	.340612	.320467	.302593	.286633	.272297
37	.334201	.314283	.296630	.280882	.266747
38	.328010	.308319	.290887	.275348	.261413
39	.322061	.302594	.285377	.270043	.256300
40	.316309	.297067	.280063	.264932	.251379
41	.310775	.291752	.274957	.260023	.246655
42	.305420	.286616	.270028	.255288	.242101
43	.300261	.281670	.265284	.250732	.237722
44	.295264	.276886	260699	.246333	.233496
45	.290443	.272273	.256280	.242095	.229425
46	.285770	.267806	.252005	.237998	.225492
47	.281255	.263492	.247879	.234044	.221698
48	.276876	.259312	.243882	.230218	.218029
49	.272641	.255271	.240021	.226521	.214484
50	.268529	.251351	.236277	.222940	.211052

Table D. Twice Straight-Line Declining Balance (cont'd)

n	16%	17%	18%	19%	20%
3	.811044	.801511	.792194	.783085	.774177
4	.765944	.754731	.743827	.733220	.722897
5	.726509	.714007	.701903	.690179	.678819
6	.689524	.675993	.662949	.650369	.638231
7	.656495	.642180	.628435	.615231	.602537
8	.625447	.610531	.596266	.582613	.569537
9	.597406	.582052	.567419	.553463	.540141
10	.571048	.555386	.540513	.526374	.512921
11	.547053	.531189	.516172	.501941	.488440
12	.524488	.508516	.493443	.479202	.465728
13	.503814	.487801	.472734	.458535	.445137
14	.484356	.468368	.453365	.439263	.425989
15	.466428	.450508	.435606	.421633	.408508
16	.449534	.433726	.418965	.405154	.392209
17	.433891	.418222	.403621	.389989	.377236
18	.419128	.403626	.389212	.375779	.363236
19	.405398	.390077	.375859	.362632	.350301
20	.392417	.377297	.363290	.350281	.338171
21	.380295	.365382	.351588	.338798	.326907
22	.368814	.354118	.340548	.327981	.316315
23	.358052	.343575	.330225	.317880	.306431
24	.347840	.333588	.320464	.308341	.297111
25	.338234	.324205	.311301	.299395	.288377
26	.329101	.315298	.302616	.290926	.280118
27	.320483	.306900	.294434	.282955	.272349
28	.312275	.298913	.286662	.275390	.264984
29	.304506	.291359	.279316	.268244	.258031
30	.297092	.284160	.272323	.261448	.251423
31	.290056	.277331	.265693	.255008	.245164
32	.283330	.270810	.259368	.248870	.239203
33	.276930	.264609	.253355	.243037	.233540
34	.270802	.258676	.247608	.237465	.228135
35	.264956	.253020	.242131	.232157	.222986
36	.259350	.247600	.236887	.227078	.218062
37	.253991	.242420	.231876	.222226	.213360
38	.248844	.237449	.227070	.217576	.208855
39	.243913	.232689	.222469	.213124	.204544
40	.239170	.228112	.218049	.208850	.200407
41	.234618	.223722	.213809	.204750	.196439
42	.230234	.219495	.209729	.200808	.192625
43	.226018	.215432	.205808	.197019	.188960
44	.221953	.211515	.202030	.193371	.185432
45	.218038	.207745	.198394	.189859	.182037
46	.214257	.204105	.194885	.186473	.178764
47	.210611	.200596	.191503	.183208	.175610
48	.207086	.197205	.188235	.180056	.172565
49	.203682	.193930	.185081	.177013	.169625
50	.200387	.190762	.182030	.174071	.166785

Table E. e^{-x}

x	0	.01	.02	.03	.04
0	1.000000	.990050	.980199	.970446	.960789
.10	.904837	.895834	.886920	.878095	.869358
.20	.818731	.810584	.802519	.794534	.786628
.30	.740818	.733447	.726149	.718924	.711770
.40	.670320	.663650	.657047	.650509	.644036
.50	.606531	.600496	.594521	.588605	.582748
.60	.548812	.543351	.537944	.532592	.527292
.70	.496585	.491644	.486752	.481909	.477114
.80	.449329	.444858	.440432	.436049	.431711
.90	.406570	.402524	.398519	.394554	.390628
1.00	.367879	.364219	.360595	.357007	.353455
1.10	.332871	.329559	.326280	.323033	.319819
1.20	.301194	.298197	.295230	.292293	.289384
1.30	.272532	.269820	.267135	.264477	.261846
1.40	.246597	.244143	.241714	.239309	.236928
1.50	.223130	.220910	.218712	.216536	.214381
1.60	.201897	.199888	.197899	.195930	.193980
1.70	.182684	.180866	.179066	.177284	.175520
1.80	.165299	.163654	.162026	.160414	.158817
1.90	.149569	.148080	.146607	.145148	.143704
2.00	.135335	.133989	.132655	.131336	.130029
2.10	.122456	.121238	.120032	.118837	.117655
2.20	.110803	.109701	.108609	.107528	.106459
2.30	.100259	.099261	.098274	.097296	.096328
2.40	.090718	.089815	.088922	.088037	.087161
2.50	.082085	.081268	.080460	.079659	.078866
2.60	.074274	.073535	.072803	.072078	.071361
2.70	.067206	.066537	.065875	.065219	.064570
2.80	.060810	.060205	.059606	.059013	.058426
2.90	.055023	.054476	.053934	.053397	.052866
3.00	.049787	.049292	.048801	.048316	.047835
3.10	.045049	.044601	.044157	.043718	.043283
3.20	.040762	.040357	.039955	.039557	.039164
3.30	.036883	.036516	.036153	.035793	.035437
3.40	.033373	.033041	.032712	.032387	.032065
3.50	.030197	.029897	.029599	.029305	.029013
3.60	.027324	.027052	.026783	.026516	.026252
3.70	.024724	.024478	.024234	.023993	.023754
3.80	.022371	.022148	.021928	.021710	.021494
3.90	.020242	.020041	.019841	.019644	.019448
4.00	.018316	.018133	.017953	.017774	.017597
4.10	.016573	.016408	.016245	.016083	.015923
4.20	.014996	.014846	.014699	.014552	.014408
4.30	.013569	.013434	.013300	.013168	.013037
4.40	.012277	.012155	.012034	.011914	.011796
4.50	.011109	.010998	.010889	.010781	.010673
4.60	.010052	.009952	.009853	.009755	.009658
4.70	.009095	.009005	.008915	.008826	.008739
4.80	.008230	.008148	.008067	.007987	.007907
4.90	.007447	.007372	.007299	.007227	.007155

Table E. e^{-x} (cont'd)

x	.05	.06	.07	.08	.09
0	.951229	.941765	.932394	.923116	.913931
.10	.860708	.852144	.843665	.835270	.826959
.20	.778801	.771052	.763379	.755784	.748264
.30	.704688	.697676	.690734	.683861	.677057
.40	.637628	.631284	.625002	.618783	.612626
.50	.576950	.571209	.565525	.559898	.554327
.60	.522046	.516851	.511709	.506617	.501576
.70	.472367	.467666	.463013	.458406	.453845
.80	.427415	.423162	.418952	.414783	.410656
.90	.386741	.382893	.379083	.375311	.371577
1.00	.349938	.346456	.343009	.339596	.336216
1.10	.316637	.313486	.310367	.307279	.304221
1.20	.286505	.283654	.280832	.278037	.275271
1.30	.259240	.256661	.254107	.251579	.249075
1.40	.234570	.232236	.229925	.227638	.225373
1.50	.212248	.210136	.208045	.205975	.203926
1.60	.192050	.190139	.188247	.186374	.184520
1.70	.173774	.172045	.170333	.168638	.166960
1.80	.157237	.155673	.154124	.152590	.151072
1.90	.142274	.140858	.139457	.138069	.136695
2.00	.128735	.127454	.126186	.124930	.123687
2.10	.116484	.115325	.114178	.113042	.111917
2.20	.105399	.104350	.103312	.102284	.101266
2.30	.095369	.094420	.093481	.092551	.091630
2.40	.086294	.085435	.084585	.083743	.082910
2.50	.078082	.077305	.076536	.075774	.075020
2.60	.070651	.069948	.069252	.068563	.067881
2.70	.063928	.063292	.062662	.062039	.061421
2.80	.057844	.057269	.056699	.056135	.055576
2.90	.052340	.051819	.051303	.050793	.050287
3.00	.047359	.046888	.046421	.045959	.045502
3.10	.042852	.042426	.042004	.041586	.041172
3.20	.038774	.038388	.038006	.037628	.037254
3.30	.035084	.034735	.034390	.034047	.033709
3.40	.031746	.031430	.031117	.030807	.030501
3.50	.028725	.028439	.028156	.027876	.027598
3.60	.025991	.025733	.025476	.025223	.024972
3.70	.023518	.023284	.023052	.022823	.022596
3.80	.021280	.021068	.020858	.020651	.020445
3.90	.019255	.019063	.018873	.018686	.018500
4.00	.017422	.017249	.017077	.016907	.016739
4.10	.015764	.015608	.015452	.015299	.015146
4.20	.014264	.014122	.013982	.013843	.013705
4.30	.012907	.012778	.012651	.012525	.012401
4.40	.011679	.011562	.011447	.011333	.011221
4.50	.010567	.010462	.010358	.010255	.010153
4.60	.009562	.009466	.009372	.009279	.009187
4.70	.008652	.008566	.008480	.008396	.008312
4.80	.007828	.007750	.007673	.007597	.007521
4.90	.007083	.007013	.006943	.006874	.006806

index

462

Refunding of debt, 9
Relative cash flows, 115–17
Removal costs, 121
Replacement of equipment, 8, 95–96, 327–28
Return on investment analysis, 27*n*.
Return on investments, *see* Yield
Risk, 23
    attitudes toward, 241–44
        utility function, 242–47
        whose attitudes are relevant, 247–49
    in buy or lease option, 276–77
    cost of capital and, 175–78
    means of decreasing, 214
        application of stock prices theory, 220–25, 230–35
        in market portfolio, 215–18
        portfolio problem and, 193–206
    preference, *see* Utility function
    present-value method and, 11
    probability of ruin and, 370–78
    reasonable measure of, 214
    of stocks and bonds, 316–17
    systematic and unsystematic, 214
    see also Uncertainty
Risk-discount approach to cost of capital, 175–78
"Risk-free" investments, 215–17, 366–67
    interest rates, 179–80
Ruin, probability of, 370–78

S

St. Petersburg paradox, 249, 250
Salvage costs in cash flow computations, 121–22
Salvage value
    depreciation and, 135, 136
    taxes and, 138
Samuelson, P. A., 361*n*.
Savings account, risk factor of, 241*n*.
Savings vs. consumption in national evaluation of investments, 333
Schumpeter, Joseph A., quoted, 41, 329
Seasonable fluctuations in demand, output, etc., 346–51
Security market line, 217–18
Segall, Joel, quoted, 292

Sequence-by-sequence summaries of possible cash-flow outcomes, 174–75
Shankly, Bill, quoted, 320
Sharpe, W. F., 361*n*., 388
Sharpe's single index model, 388–93
Sloan, Alfred P., 3
Solow, Robert M., quoted, 239
Sorenson, Theodore C., quoted, 267
Standard deviation between present and expected values, 169–71
Statistically dependent investments, 87, 250
Statistically independent investments, 198–201, 250
    defined, 199
    probability of ruin and, 370–78
Stigler, George J., quoted, 230
Stock dividends
    inflation and, 316–17
    internal capital rationing and, 152–53
Stock prices, theory of, 213–26
    application of
        to multiperiod investments, 230–35
        to one-period investments, 220–25
Subjective probabilities, 164–65
Subjective time preference, 71–72
Substitute investments, 42, 86, *see also* Mutually exclusive investments
Systematic risk, 214

T

Taxes
    capital gains, 302
    income, *see* Income taxes
    in national evaluation of investments, 333–34
Terminal value
    cash flows and, 122
    taxes and, 137–39
Time discounting, 16–18
Time value of money, 12–15
Timing
    of cash flows, 11–13, 27, 113–14
    of income tax payments, 140–41
    of investment decisions, 320–28
    subjective preferences, 71–72
Transaction costs, 193
Tree farm example, 325–27